Alan F. Crouchman

FLAK·BAIT

The Only American Aircraft to Survive 200 Bombing
Missions during the Second World War

SCHIFFER MILITARY

4880 Lower Valley Road   Atglen, PA 19310

Designed by Justin Watkinson
Cover design by Ashley Millhouse
Type set in CCBiffBamBoomOutline/Industry/Minion Pro/Univers LT Std

ISBN: 978-0-7643-6343-6
Printed in India

Published by Schiffer Publishing, Ltd.
4880 Lower Valley Road
Atglen, PA 19310
Phone: (610) 593-1777; Fax: (610) 593-2002
Email: Info@schifferbooks.com
Web: www.schifferbooks.com

For our complete selection of fine books on this and related subjects, please visit our website at www.schifferbooks.com. You may also write for a free catalog.

Schiffer Publishing's titles are available at special discounts for bulk purchases for sales promotions or premiums. Special editions, including personalized covers, corporate imprints, and excerpts, can be created in large quantities for special needs. For more information, contact the publisher.

We are always looking for people to write books on new and related subjects. If you have an idea for a book, please contact us at proposals@schifferbooks.com.

US Army Air Force insignia

8th Air Force insignia

9th Air Force insignia

322nd Bomb Group
insignia

CONTENTS

449th Bomb Squadron (M)
insignia

FOREWORD

The combat record of the Martin B-26 Marauder operating under control of the 9th Army Air Force Bomber Command was second to none. Serving with eight bomb groups and one Pathfinder squadron, they carried the air war to German targets in occupied Europe and into Germany itself. Bombing from medium altitude between 8,000 to 10,000 feet without the luxury of oxygen, they bombed airfields, V weapon sites, marshaling yards, troop concentrations, and many other military targets. All those targets were protected by hundreds of antiaircraft guns manned by experienced crews using radar-finding devices. They quickly learned how lethal flak was, and they treated it with great respect. As the German army retreated eastward after the military battles in France after D-day, on June 6, 1944, and the targets the bombers were flying against were retreating to Germany itself, they encountered even more flak defenses with ever-increasing target defenses. Now the risks were steadily more dangerous; the "Bait" was there. While losses were small per number of missions flown, flak was the major cause of Marauder losses.

It was the custom among many Marauder crews and their ground crews to apply a name or picture to their charges, and one Marauder was destined to be named "Flak-Bait"; it served with the 449th Bomb Squadron (BS) of the 322nd Bomb Group (BG). The name was aptly chosen, since it frequently returned to base with flak damage, but its luck continued to fly with it, and it flew its 200th combat mission on the April 17, 1945, when that target was Magdeburg in Germany. The name it carried was justly deserved. Postwar it was the only Martin B-26 Marauder to be dismantled for return to the United States of America, being stored for many years in the Smithsonian Institute.

Trevor J. Allen
B-26 historian

AUTHOR'S NOTE

The facts and details presented in this operational diary of the missions that "Flak-Bait" took part in have been taken directly from the 322nd Bomb Group (M) and the individual squadron records that were compiled at the time. However, the reader is urged to consider the following notes when reviewing this record.

First, a word about the spelling of individuals' names. In the records themselves, some names are spelled differently, even on the same page! Where possible, reference has been made with medal award references on the assumption that these would be correct; however, since these award notifications are not complete, some cannot be verified, and in these instances the most commonly used spelling is used, but if there is only a single entry, then this has had to be accepted as the correct spelling. On the day-to-day mission summaries, only the crew's first-name initials are used, but in the roster of crew members who flew on "Flak-Bait," full names are used where they are known. The rank shown is that at the time of the first mission flown by that person on "Flak-Bait"; if further promotions are known, then this is recorded after the crew position in parentheses as part of the main roster in Appendix 2.

Among the crew rosters, reference is drawn to the crew position of "togglier"; this was an unofficial but widely used title for an enlisted man who acted as a bombardier. Because bombing was done by flights or boxes, only the lead and deputy lead aircraft of each flight or box needed to carry out a sighting operation. The wingmen in each formation would need to release only upon the leader's drop. Therefore, due to a shortage of trained navigator/bombardiers, enlisted men were sometimes utilized in this role. The practice began as early as September 5, 1943, but became more prevalent during 1944. On "Flak-Bait" the first use of a "togglier" was on the March 15, 1944, mission to Aulnoye.

The mission timings shown also need some clarification; the takeoff time and attack times are those of the formation or box leader's aircraft. However, the time of return is rather more ambiguous; generally they would show the time for the last aircraft down, but it is known that on some occasions the time recorded is for the first aircraft down. Therefore the return times should be taken as an indication of when the bomb group returned. If more than one time is recorded, this represents each box or formation in numerical order. On a few occasions the actual timings for "Flak-Bait" are recorded, and these are included in the notes.

With regard to the briefed routings, these are presented as shown on the teletype orders, and if a route deviation is known, then this is included in the summary; however, if no deviations have been discovered in the records, it must be assumed that the route was flown as briefed. In a lot of the briefings, a turning point or location is indicated by the latitude/longitude coordinates; these are as shown on the teletype order. However, as an aid to the reader, I have included in parentheses the nearest town or village as a reference, although it must be borne in mind that this position may have been for a prominent landmark, river bend, or conspicuous junction in the immediate area. Later in the war, locations—mainly in Holland and Germany—were identified by a letter followed by a four-figure number; no index of these locations has been found by the author, but these are included for completeness.

Under the "Flak-Bait" debriefing notes, every comment recorded on the debrief forms (where actually readable) has been presented, although who actually made the comment is not shown on the form.

With the "Other Crew Comments," any recorded comments have been included at the discretion of the author. Nearly every crew made some sort of comment after a mission, so only a selection of those made that the author felt added a little to the overall picture of events has been included.

Details of aircraft declared missing in action (MIA) while taking part in the missions that "Flak-Bait" flew have been taken from the Missing Air Crew Reports (MACR) filed for each loss. An index of all the MACR reports for the 322nd Bomb Group is included in appendix 9. Additional details and aircraft nicknames have been kindly supplied by Trevor J. Allen from his extensive archive.

Details of aircraft that were declared Category E have also been taken from the records, if any such details are recorded therein. Again, additional information has come from the archives of Trevor Allen. However, it must be stressed that other aircraft may have been re-categorized as Category E at a later date, after a more detailed inspection of any damage received, and, as such, are not recorded. On one or two occasions, details of these are known and are mentioned in the text.

In addition to the day-to-day operational record, a number of "Events" have also been included; again, these are at the discretion of the author and show any significant command changes or facts that are considered of interest.

As a final note, while every care has been taken to check the many facts included herein, any errors, mistakes, or typos that may come to light are purely unintentional and are the responsibility of the author and him alone.

ACKNOWLEDGMENTS

While the bulk of the information contained within comes from the official records, a work such as this could not be complete without the help and support of others.

Chief among these has been noted B-26 historian Trevor J. Allen, who provided the foreword for this book and willingly opened up his extensive photo archive for the author. Trevor also helped with many facts pertaining to the aircraft of the 322nd Bomb Group. Without his support the finished product could not have been achieved.

A special thanks to Trevor Jago, who produced the aircraft profiles especially for this publication and went to extreme lengths to make them as accurate as possible.

Mike Smith, who maintains the B26.com website, has also been a stalwart friend and supporter of the project from its early stages right through till the finish.

Also thanks to Thomas Farrell, son of James Farrell, "Flak-Bait's" original pilot, for providing information from his own records and for photographs of his father.

A big thank-you to the staff at the NASM Udvar-Hazy Center for allowing me access to "Flak-Bait" during her restoration, with particular thanks to Jeremy Kinney and Pat Robinson, who gave up their time to escort me and answer questions about the restoration processes involved. In the Archives Division of the NASM, Kate Igoe and Heidi Stover helped with photographic requests.

At the AFSHRA facility at Maxwell Air Force Base (AFB), Archie Di Fante has helped the author on many projects over the years, spending time searching for various documentation and records, including specific requests for information on "Flak-Bait."

Andrew Boehly at the Pima Air & Space Museum kindly scanned photographs of "Flak-Bait" in their collection, and Maddie Beeson at the Imperial War Museum Images Division assisted with requests for images from the Roger Freeman Collection, now held within their archive.

Thanks to Randy Wells for sharing his information and photographs of Lt. Terrance J. O'Neill, and to Douglas Robin Barker for allowing me to use some images from his records of his father's service with the 449th BS. At the B-26 Marauder Historical Society, Melinda Stomel helped with my inquiries and provided permissions for the Svenn Norstrom write-up about the February 22, 1945, mission.

Paul Clouting provided evadee reports for downed B-26 airmen, which proved to be a useful resource, and the staff at the Glenn L. Martin Maryland Aviation Museum provided production line photographs. Thanks to Mark Copeland for supplying the photo of the Langer crew, and to Ronald Strawser of M C Graphic Decals Inc. for allowing me to use his images of the unit insignia.

Mention should be made of the late Roger A. Freeman, noted author of all matters relating to the USAAF, who helped mentor the author in his early days of research and allowed access to his extensive records over the years, and last to my late father, Peter Crouchman, who supported me in my projects over the years with words of encouragement and advice, and whose interest in the B-26 Marauder and the 387th BG was the catalyst for my own interest.

Alan F. Crouchman
July 2020

Ordered as part of a follow-on batch of 500 Martin B-26 aircraft under contract number AC-46DA, the aircraft that was to become "Flak-Bait" rolled off the Martin production line in late April 1943, the 1,332nd B-26 to be built at the Baltimore, Maryland, plant. Her record card shows a cost of $191,131.00 to the US taxpayer.

Bearing the manufacturer's production number 3487, she was given the USAAF serial number 41-31773 and was the first of a batch of 100 aircraft built as the subseries known as the B-26B-25-MA.

Changes from the previous B-26B-20-MA model included the installation of the Martin 250CE Spec 212 top turret, as opposed to the Spec 165 version as on previous models. This later version included additional armor plating to help protect the gunner. The B-26B-25-MA model also saw the deletion of the aft bomb-bay operating mechanism. The rear bomb bay did see use in the Pacific theater but was hardly, if ever, used operationally in the MTO and ETO.

By studying her AFLC card, we can see that she was accepted by the US Army Air Force (USAAF) on

B-26s on the Baltimore production line; this photo, dated August 12, 1943, shows either B-26B-45 or B-26B-50 models being produced. Many of these served with the 344th or 391st Bomb Groups. *Glenn L. Martin Maryland Aviation Museum*

The Glenn L. Martin Plant II at Baltimore, Maryland. There were 3,681 out of a total of 5,266 B-26 models built that were assembled there, with the remainder built at Omaha, Nebraska. *Glenn L. Martin Maryland Aviation Museum*

Monday, April 26, 1943, and was flown to the Martin Modification Center, at Fort Crook, Nebraska, some three days later. Fort Crook was also the home to the Martin-Omaha production line that produced the B-26C models, prior to switching to production of the Boeing B-29.

It was usual for newly produced aircraft to be flown to modification centers where the latest changes could be incorporated, in the light of operational use and experience, and while the production line was geared up to bring these changes into the production sequence.

The most obvious change incorporated on the B-26B-25-MA was the addition of armor plating to the outside of the fuselage, on the pilot's side. This modification became a production line change at Baltimore with the following B-26B-30-MA model.

Stenciled onto the nose there also appears a project number, and on 41-31773 this was originally painted on as 92——R (possibly 92113R), but this has been painted out and replaced by the number 92096R. The precise meaning of these numbers is not clear but is believed to indicate changes that were specific to the theater of operations to which the aircraft was destined to serve. With all such modifications complete, the model number was changed to that of a B-26B-26-MA, to reflect the changes made to the airframe.

Previously published sources state that the original combat crew of "Flak-Bait," led by 1Lt. James J. Farrell, picked up 41-31773 from Hunter Field and ferried her to England via the southern ferry route. We now know that this is incorrect; information from James Farrell's personnel records shows that he departed the US on May 2, 1943, arriving in England on May 27, 1943. At this time, 41-31773 was still at Omaha undergoing modifications. As to the aircraft this crew flew across the Atlantic, the 449th Bomb Squadron records show that they received one B-26B-2 and five B-26B-3 models on May 28 or 29, so it is possible that the crew was flying one of these aircraft.

The next entry on the record card shows her at New Castle Army Air Base (AAB), at Wilmington, Delaware, on May 13, 1943. New Castle AAB had only recently been opened and was the home to the 2nd Ferrying Group, Air Transport Command, the parent unit responsible for overseeing the ferrying of aircraft overseas via the northern ferry route.

Two days later, on May 15, 1943, she is reported at Savannah, Georgia, which was the location of Hunter Field AAB, where crews picked up combat-ready B-26 aircraft to take overseas.

Her next stop, on May 21, 1943, was at Memphis, Tennessee, home to the 4th Ferrying Group, and then returning to New Castle AAB on May 24, 1943. While the exact nature of these flights is not known, they may well have been calibration flights, which were usually carried out to check such things such as fuel consumption and the navigational equipment prior to the long overseas flights.

The record card for 41-31773 shows that she arrived at Presque Isle, Maine, on May 25. Presque Isle was home to the North Atlantic Wing of Air Transport Command, the parent unit for overseeing those aircraft that flew via the northern ferry route across the Atlantic. Those aircraft that went via the southern ferry route would stage through Morrison Field, West Palm Beach, Florida.

The final entry on the record card for 41-31773 shows that she was to be delivered to "Ugly" (one of the code words used for the VIII Air Force in England), being assigned on May 26, 1943, and received on June 13, 1943. Despite searches of the archives, it is unfortunate that the names of the crew who actually flew the aircraft to England remains unknown.

Upon arrival, 41-31773 would be allocated to the 449th Bomb Squadron (M) of the 322nd Bomb Group (M).*

As to when the aircraft actually joined the squadron, the weekly status reports (Form 34s) record that the 449th Bomb Squadron received three B-26B-26-MA aircraft in the week starting July 4, 1943. It is believed that these were 41-31773, which became PN-O "Flak-Bait," 41-31779, which would become PN-C "Idiots Delight" (formerly "Warm Front"), and 41-31788, which became PN-A "Truman Committee."

Once received by the 449th Bomb Squadron, 41-31773 came under the care of crew chief TSgt. Charles F. Thompson, along with his assistant, SSgt. Clare Goodrich, and mechanic PFC George Sangregorio. It was the duty of these men to service and repair the aircraft in all weather conditions. At some point later, TSgt. Thompson was rotated and SSgt. Clare Goodrich took over as the crew chief, and Cpl. Dave Rich was assigned as his assistant.

The original combat crew of "Flak-Bait" was made up as follows:

1Lt. James J. Farrell	pilot
F/O Thomas F. Moore	copilot
2Lt. Owen J. Redmond Jr.	navigator/bombardier
TSgt. Donald L. Tyler	engineer/gunner, who usually manned the tail turret
SSgt. Joseph B. Manuel	radio/gunner, who usually manned the waist guns
SSgt. Norman E. Thielan	gunner, who usually manned the top turret

On most B-26 Marauder crews the engineer/gunner would normally man the top turret, and the dedicated gunner would man the tail turret, but the placing of the crew member's names painted on the airframe and the combat reports of e/a (enemy aircraft) encounters show the above locations as being used by this crew.

After arrival at Andrews Field, "Flak-Bait," like all newly arrived aircraft, required further in-theater modifications to make her combat ready; this included the installation of a VHF SCR-522 command radio, and crystal changes to other radio equipment. Also at this time, the deicer boots were removed, since these were considered unnecessary and could cause additional damage to the airframe if they became dislodged due to battle damage. With these modifications complete, "Flak-Bait" was ready to begin her combat career.

* *Author's Note*: The official designation for the group was the 322nd Bomb Group (M), to signify a medium bomber unit. From this point forward in the text, the (M) will not be included in the squadron or group designations of the units mentioned.

The 322nd BG was activated at MacDill Field, Florida, on July 17, 1942, together with its four component squadrons: the 449th, 450th, 451st, and 452nd Bomb Squadrons. The initial cadre of officers and enlisted men came from the resident 21st BG and its assigned units, and over the next couple of months the numbers swelled with personnel transferred from other locations or direct from training units.

On August 8, 1942, Maj. Jacob J. Brogger assumed command of the group, and two days later operational training began.

The group moved to Drane Field, Lakeland, Florida, on September 22, 1942, with the ground personnel moving by road convoy while the air echelon flew aircraft in on the same day. Here the group would train under field conditions, operating without hangars or permanent facilities. Simulated combat missions were conducted, including practice low-level attacks against a supposed invading army on the Florida coast.

Temporary command of the group was passed to Lt. Col. John F. Batjer after Lt. Col. Joseph J. Brogger had been called away due to a family illness, until the appointment of Col. Robert R. Selway Jr., who took over on October 21, 1942, whereupon Lt. Col. Batjer took up the position of group executive officer.

During this training period the group lost four aircraft in accidents, one while flying out of MacDill and three while flying from Drane Field, resulting in the loss of twenty-one lives, with only one crewman, Pvt. Charles E. Stuart, surviving.

Movement overseas began on November 21, 1942, when the ground echelon of the group left by troop train and arrived at Camp Kilmer, New Brunswick, at 2145 hours (hrs.) the following day.

The personnel soon learned that they would be traveling across the Atlantic on board RMS *Queen Elizabeth*, with the ship slipping its moorings at 0645 hrs. on Tuesday, November 24, 1942, to begin her solo crossing; using her speed and a zigzag pattern to avoid the German U-boat threat, she arrived at Greenock, Scotland, on the evening of November 29, 1942.

After spending the night on board ship, the personnel disembarked the following day and traveled by rail to Bury St. Edmunds, Suffolk, where they arrived on the morning of December 1 and were transported to AAF Station No. 468 at Rougham Airfield by truck.

Upon arrival, the personnel of the 451st and 452nd Squadrons were dispatched to the satellite airfield at Rattlesden, near the town of Stowmarket, about 18 miles from Rougham. After settling in, a program of in-theater training courses, hosted by RAF personnel, was conducted as an introduction to the procedures then in use in England, while they awaited the arrival of the air echelons.

With the departure of the ground echelon, the air echelon initially remained at Drane Field, but with the arrival of new aircraft, the basic facilities at Drane Field were deemed unsuitable for the purposes of calibrating the new equipment, so on November 22, 1942, the 450th BS moved back to MacDill Field, with the remaining three squadrons joining them on December 4, 1942. Here, better facilities and hangars were available to help make any adjustments after performing the necessary shakedown flights prior to the long overseas flights. During this period the group lost two further aircraft in accidents, with the loss of both crews.

The air echelon of the 450th BS was the first of the squadrons of the group to begin their journey overseas, departing MacDill, via the southern ferry route, on February 6, 1943, the first eight aircraft arriving at Rougham on March 8, 1943.

On February 22, 1943, Col. Selway was transferred to take overall command of Sarasota Airfield, Florida, and once again Lt. Col. Batjer took over temporary command, until the appointment Lt. Col. Robert M. Stillman on March 17, 1943. Lt. Col. Stillman had been the group executive officer of the 387th BG, then working up at MacDill.

Later in the month of March 1943, the first elements of the 452nd BS began arriving at Rougham, and the ground personnel that had been dispersed at Rattlesden rejoined the rest of the group at Rougham.

Briefing for the May 14 mission to Ijmuiden. Lt. Col. Robert M. Stillman (wearing a "Mae West" survival vest), who led the mission, is standing behind the officer reading from his notes. *IWM / Roger A. Freeman collection, FRE9255*

The air echelon of the 451st BS arrived at Rougham in the middle of May, with the 449th BS following, the final elements of which did not arrive until May 28, 1943, ending a rather long and drawn-out overseas deployment for the group.

During the course of these ferry flights, one aircraft from the 452nd BS was lost off the coast of Portugal, with the loss of one crew member and injuries to three others, while another, from the 449th BS, had to put down in the African desert, north of Tindouf, with the aircraft having to be destroyed but the crew being rescued.

In addition, the commanding officer of the 449th BS, Maj. Ervin H. Berry, fell off the wing of a B-26 at Ascension Island, injuring his back, and had to be repatriated to the US, whereupon Capt. B. G. Willis took over as CO of the 449th BS.

Upon arrival in the UK, the 322nd BG was assigned to the 3rd Bomb Wing of the VIII Bomber Command.

As early as April 28, 1943, the group received its first five replacement crews, these having been transferred direct from the 335th BG at Barksdale Field, Louisiana, a B-26 Marauder replacement training unit. On the same day, two other notable events occurred: the formal handing over of Rougham airfield to US control and, sadly, the loss of a B-26 in a crash near Cambridge, with the loss of its crew of five.

Once the first of the air echelons had arrived in England, an intensive training program was instigated under the supervision of Lt. Col. Glenn C. Nye and Maj. Grover C. Brown from the 3rd Bomb Wing, with simulated low-level missions being flown over the East Anglian countryside.

Finally, on the evening of May 13, 1943, confirmation came through of the group's first combat mission: to attack the power station at Ijmuiden, Holland, on the following day.

Briefing was held at 0800 hrs., and the first of twelve aircraft took off at 0950 hrs., led by the group CO, Lt. Col. Robert M. Stillman. Upon entering the enemy coast, one aircraft suffered flak damage, which shot out one engine and forced it to turn back for base. The remaining eleven aircraft reached the target and released their bombs from an altitude of 200 to 300 ft. at 1100 hrs. Results were not observed due to the use of British 300 lb. bombs with delayed-action fuses, which allowed the Dutch employees a chance to make an escape, although returning bombardiers thought that some hits had been achieved.

Intense flak was encountered and two aircraft returned with hydraulic problems. The aircraft piloted by Maj. Gove C. Celio could lower only one main wheel and the nosewheel; the engineer, SSgt. C. T. Cook, managed to stem most of the leaks while the copilot, Capt. Robert A. Porter, pumped down the left main gear to allow for a forced landing to be made at RAF Honington.

The lead ship for the May 14 mission, 41-17995 "Tondelayo," was flown by Lt. Col. Robert M. Stillman and crew. *Trevor J. Allen collection*

Maj. Celio's B-26, 41-17996, force-landed at RAF Honington, having received major flak damage. *USAAF*

The aircraft piloted by 1Lt. John J. Howell had more-severe damage, and upon arriving overhead Rougham, he ordered his crew to bail out, but while trying to make a crash landing he lost control and crashed, killing the pilot. In addition, eight other crew members received flak wounds on the mission.

While the crews were confident that they had hit the target, photoreconnaissance failed to show any damage. It was later ascertained that the Germans, who were familiar with the British delayed-action fuses, had ordered that the bombs that had hit the power station be removed to an adjacent field, where they exploded harmlessly.

Much to everyone's surprise, a second mission was ordered for Monday, May 17, 1943, to the same target area, with one flight to attack Ijmuiden again and another to attack the power station at nearby Haarlem. Lt. Col. Stillman protested about the stupidity of going after the same target so soon after the previous attack with an alerted enemy; however, his concerns were brushed aside and he was told that if he didn't order the mission, then someone else would be appointed in his place to do so.

With misgivings, the mission was ordered; Lt. Col. Stillman would lead the mission himself, and his flight

of six would attack Ijmuiden, while the second flight, led by Lt. Col. William R. Purinton, would lead a flight of five aircraft to attack Haarlem.

The eleven aircraft, drawn from the 450th and 452nd Bomb Squadrons (the other two squadrons were still in the process of arriving in England), took off at 1050 hrs. and set course. Over the North Sea, the aircraft of Capt. R. D. Stephens, in the second flight, developed an electrical failure and aborted the mission; in doing so and by following standard operating procedures, he climbed to 1,000 ft. to allow enough height for the crew to bail out if necessary, and returned to base. Some thought that this may have alerted the Germans of the incoming raid, since it would probably have appeared on their radar. Upon return to base it was found that the generators had been switched off by the ground crews after they had checked their operation, a habit that they had gotten into, and the crew did not realize that this had happened, since they would normally be left in the on position.

As the expected time of the return approached, tensions began to mount, but with no sign of the returning aircraft, a sense of foreboding began to

The burning wreckage of 1Lt. John Howell's B-26, 41-17988; he ordered his crew to bail out over the field he crashed on while trying to perform a forced landing. *IWM / Roger A. Freeman collection, FRE4535*

spread among the waiting personnel. Phone calls were made to neighboring bases in case they had diverted, and more worrying was the fact that there were no reports of the aircraft having crossed the English coast.

Finally, as the time that the aircraft would have run out of fuel arrived, concern turned to despair, as the extent of the tragedy hit home. Ten aircraft missing, along with the sixty men on board!

For others, May 17, 1943, was a day of celebration. On the previous night, May 16–17, the RAF had mounted the daring Dambusters Raid, flown by No. 617 Squadron, under the command of Wing Commander Guy Gibson, which was lauded in the press, and, at Bassingbourne, in Cambridgeshire, the B-17F "Memphis Belle," of the 91st BG, completed her twenty-fifth combat mission and entered into the history books.

At Rougham the moral of the men in the 322nd BG took a plunge as a desperate search for answers was begun. With the CO missing, Lt. Col. Cecil C. McFarland took over as acting CO until the appointment of Lt. Col. Glenn C. Nye two days later.

Shortly thereafter the group adopted the sobriquet "Nye's Annihilators," and later, after his departure from the group, just the "Annihilators."

Photoreconnaissance again showed no damage to either target, and, for the time being the loss of the ten aircraft remained something of a mystery.

Suspicions fell upon some local people and RAF service personnel who, allegedly, had prior information about the mission, but nothing was finally proven. In addition, for a period of five days after the mission, all phone calls in and out of Rougham Airfield were monitored, but again nothing untoward was discovered.

Then, some five days after the mission, two exhausted gunners were picked up in a dinghy by the British warship HMS *Southdown*. These two gunners, SSgt. Jesse Lewis and SSgt. George Williams, had been part of Capt. Jack Crane's crew. Having been brought to shore at Harwich, they underwent a debriefing while recovering in the hospital, and the full story of the tragedy became clear.

Shortly after Capt. Stephens's aircraft had aborted, the formation encountered a small coastal convoy, which, in avoiding, put the formation off course to the south. Upon crossing the enemy coast, Lt. Col. Stillman's aircraft was hit by 20 mm flak and was seen to crash inverted into the sand dunes, followed shortly thereafter by the aircraft of Lt. Vincent Garrambone, who crashed into the Maas River. A few minutes later, the aircraft of Capt. William Converse and 1Lt. Richard

Col. Glenn C. Nye, who took over command of the 322nd Bomb Group on May 19, 1943. *Author's collection*

O. Wolfe collided while performing evasive action, and debris hit the aircraft flown by 1Lt. David V. Wurst, forcing it to make a crash landing as well.

The remaining five aircraft continued under the leadership of Lt. Col. Purinton, but they were not sure of their position so they decided to head west and return. Upon making the turn, the lead bombardier spotted what looked like the target and the aircraft attacked, although in reality this was a gas holder on the outskirts of Amsterdam.

Heading for the coast, they ironically exited over Ijmuiden, where intense flak brought down the three aircraft flown by Lt. Col. William R Purinton, 1Lt. Joseph H. Jones, and 2Lt. Edward R. Norton, all of which came down in the sea, with Lt. Col. Purinton managing to ditch near a fishing boat.

The surviving two Marauders, flown by Capt. Jack Crane and 1Lt. Frederick H. Matthew, continued out to sea, only to become victims to Fw 190s of JG 1, from which only the two gunners from Capt. Crane's aircraft managed to escape, to begin their five-day ordeal in the dinghy. They managed to paddle some 70 miles toward the English coast before they were finally rescued by the Royal Navy.

Of the sixty men on these ten aircraft, it was later learned that thirty-four had been killed or remained

MIA, while twenty-four became POWs. Sadly, one man, Sgt. Kleber L. Jones, the engineer on Lt. Wolfe's aircraft, committed suicide five months later. He had a leg amputated and suffered from bad head injuries; it was felt that this proved too much for him to accept, and he leaped out of a window to his death. Toward the end of October 1943, the tail gunner on Lt. Col. Purinton's aircraft, Sgt. Lester F. Miller, was repatriated after he had lost a foot due to the injuries received.

The disaster of the Ijmuiden mission spelled the end of low-level bombing for the B-26; it may have worked in the Pacific theater, where the flak, while just as accurate, was not as concentrated as in the European theater of operations (ETO). The B-26, while fast for a medium bomber, was simply too vulnerable to the in-depth German defenses.

In the interim, training flights continued, but a further blow was felt by the 322nd when 2Lt. Robert F. MacDonald and crew, from the 452nd BS, were lost when they crashed while practicing violent evasive action over Rougham airfield on May 29, 1943.

The dilemma for VIII Bomber Command was what to do with the B-26 Marauder groups; the 322nd and 323rd were already in England and were shortly to be joined by the 386th and 387th Bomb Groups, making an available force of 256 B-26s.

It was decided that concurrent with the exchange of bases between the 3rd and 4th Bomb Wings, the B-26 groups would transfer to VIII ASC at noon on July 12, since it was felt that this better reflected the role that the B-26 was designed for: the support of the ground forces.

Initial thoughts as to the continued use of the B-26 in the ETO considered the use of the type in antishipping strikes or in medium-altitude bombing.

The RAF expressed serious misgivings about the antishipping role for the B-26, for the same reason that low-level bombing had failed—the effectiveness of the German antiaircraft defenses. The 322nd BG was selected to fly a series of three practices against shipping in the Felixstowe and Harwich area during the first twelve days of July 1943. However, just like the vulnerability demonstrated in the low-level bombing role, the speed and maneuverability of the B-26 were deemed not sufficient in this difficult task.

The other option was to use the B-26 in medium-altitude bombing missions, attacking from heights between 10,000 and 14,000 ft., which would be out of the range of most of the deadly light flak, with an escort provided by RAF 11 Group to help ward off the Luftwaffe.

The 323rd BG was chosen to develop this concept, which had already been tried with success in the Mediterranean theater of operations (MTO) by the medium bomber units there. Formations would fly in a box formation with three flights of six aircraft—lead, high, and low flights—offering mutual protection. Initially the RAF thought that they would be able to support only one box of eighteen aircraft, and this was what was first tried. However, it soon became apparent that two boxes could be supported adequately, and eventually it was usual for two groups to be sent to the same target as four boxes of eighteen aircraft, in trail.

One logistics problem was the need for the acquisition of Norden bombsights to replace the D-8 low-level sights then fitted to the B-26. Because of supply shortages, only the lead and deputy lead aircraft in each flight would be equipped with a bombsight, with the wingmen dropping on the lead aircraft's release.

Even as late as August 1943, the group was still conducting low-level training. *Trevor J. Allen collection*

B-26 Marauders of the 322nd Bomb Group taxi out for what was thought to be the evening diversionary mission on July 28, 1943; 41-34959 SS-Q, "Clark's Little Pill," in the foreground, followed by 41-34847 SS-K, "Idiots Delight." *USAAF*

On July 16, 1943, the 323rd BG conducted the first medium-altitude mission when sixteen aircraft were dispatched against the marshaling yards at Abbeville, with fourteen dropping their bombs and, more importantly, no losses, although ten aircraft did receive flak damage and two crewmen were injured.

Between then and July 29, the 323rd carried out a total of eight missions, one of which was recalled because of a lack of fighter escort, all without loss; it was an encouraging start.

The dubious distinction for the first B-26 to be lost on medium-altitude missions fell to the 386th BG while on their first combat mission, to Woensdrecht Airdrome on July 30, 1943, with another aircraft written off due to battle damage.

During this period the 322nd BG conducted four diversionary sweeps—one each on July 17 and 27, and two on the 28th, to help confuse the enemy. Their return to combat missions occurred on July 31, with an attack on Tricqueville Airfield, where five aircraft received battle damage.

The scene was now set for the role that the B-26 would adopt with mounting success in bombing accuracy, and for "Flak-Bait," having already taken part in the diversionary sweep of July 27, the time had come for her to begin her illustrious bombing career.

OPERATIONAL RECORD

Part 1:
July 27, 1943–June 5, 1944, Air Offensive Europe Campaign

Date: July 27, 1943
Target: Diversion Le Treport / Dieppe Area
Field Order: VIII ASC 3rd BW F/O 13

"Flak-Bait" Crew

1Lt. J. J. Farrell, pilot
2Lt. R. W. Bradley, copilot
2Lt. O. J. Redmond, navigator/bombardier

TSgt. D. L. Tyler, engineer/gunner
SSgt. J. B. Manuel, radio/gunner
SSgt. N. E. Thielan, gunner

Briefing started at 1440 hrs. and ended 1537 hrs.
T/off: 1652 hrs.   Target: not recorded   Return: 1902 hrs.

Mission Narrative

The group's second of four diversionary missions flown.

The 322nd Bomb Group dispatched thirty-six aircraft, led by Lt. Col. G. C. Nye, the group CO; the 2nd Box was led by 1Lt. L. J. Sebille, on a diversion off the French coast, in the Le Treport / Dieppe area, in support of a formation of eighteen B-26s of the 323rd Bomb Group attacking Tricqueville Airfield. No bombs were carried. Escort was provided by three squadrons of VIII FC P-47s.

Briefed route was from Base to Bradwell Bay to Dungeness to the turnaround point in the English Channel, to Beachy Head and then to Base.

The mission was completed without incident; one aircraft returned early due to mechanical difficulties. Interrogation of crews finished at 1925 hrs.

Mission Notes and "Flak-Bait" Crew Debrief Comments

"Flak-Bait" flew in the no. 5 position, low flight, 1st Box; her actual takeoff time was 1701 hrs., and landing was at 1902 hrs.

The crew thought that the ammunition was in the way if crew members had to bail out in an emergency.

Date: August 4, 1943
Target: Le Trait Shipyards
Field Order: VIII ASC 3rd BW F/O 25

"Flak-Bait" Crew

1Lt. H. V. Smythe, pilot
2Lt. R. W. Bradley, copilot
1Lt. W. L. Juneau, navigator/bombardier

SSgt. S. R. Holliday, engineer/gunner
SSgt. D. F. Milligan, radio/gunner
SSgt. E. W. Lowery, gunner

Briefing started at 1500 hrs.; no end time recorded.
T/off: 1749 hrs.   Rendezvous: 1900 hrs.   Landfall: 1917 hrs.
Target: 1926 hrs.   Coast Out: not recorded   Return: 2047 hrs.

B-26s of the 322nd BG depart on a mission; normally a twenty-second-interval delay would be between each aircraft's takeoff run. *Peter Dole*

Mission Narrative

Thirty-six aircraft dispatched; the 1st Box was led by Lt. Col. G. C. Nye and the 2nd Box by Capt. L. J. Sebille, to attack the shipyards at Le Trait.

Briefed route was from Base to Hastings, where rendezvous with the escort of ten squadrons of RAF Spitfires was made at 12,000 ft., to Veules, and then to the target.

Thirty-three aircraft released 160 × 500 GP [general purpose] bombs on the target at 1926 hrs., from 11,000 ft. through a gap in the 5/10th cloud cover, for good results; one aircraft jettisoned 2 × 500 GP bombs in vicinity of the target through a rack malfunction. One aircraft returned early, through lack of power. A total of 20 × 500 GPs were jettisoned by five aircraft, mainly through release mechanism malfunctions. "Flak-Bait" was one of these, jettisoning 5 × 500 GP bombs.

A few inaccurate bursts of flak were encountered at Veules, at 1917 hrs., and meager inaccurate flak was met just before and over the target. Moderate inaccurate gunfire to port and below from Cany-Barville area was encountered at 1932 hrs. One aircraft received damage to a propeller by a 0.50 shell dropped from a preceding aircraft.

After the target the routing was a right turn to 6 miles east of Fecamp, then to Hastings, although the actual briefed route should have been via Beachy Head, and on to Base.

One aircraft landed at Gravesend, involving a fuel shortage due to a fuel transfer malfunction; returned to Base at 2130 hrs.

Interrogation of crews began at 2030 hrs. and finished at 2148 hrs.

Mission Notes and "Flak-Bait" Crew Debrief Comments

"Flak-Bait" flew in the No. 2 position in the low flight, 2nd Box; her takeoff time was 1800 hrs.

5 × 500 GPs jettisoned.

"Flak-Bait" reported that the prop pitch and hydraulic pressure dropped to zero after leaving the English coast, and aircraft dropped out of formation and then trailed the formation over the target covered by RAF Spitfires.

The crew also stated that they thought that the copilot should not be used as a waist gunner; too much else to do, especially during emergency such as engine failure (two other crews also reported that this was a bad practice).

Other Crew Comments
Keep out of the prop wash. Spread out flights when going through clouds.

```
Date: August 16, 1943
Target: Beaumont-le-Roger A/D
Field Order: VIII ASC 3rd BW F/O 40
```

"Flak-Bait" Crew

1Lt. J. J. Farrell, pilot
F/O T. F. Moore, copilot
2Lt. O. J. Redmond, navigator/bombardier

TSgt. D. L. Tyler, engineer/gunner
SSgt. J. B. Manuel, radio/gunner
SSgt. N. E. Thielan, gunner

Briefing started at 1330 hrs. and ended 1425 hrs.

T/off: 1520 hrs.	Rendezvous: 1630 hrs.	Landfall: 1647 hrs.
Target: 1700 hrs.	Coast Out: 1716 hrs.	Return: 1830 hrs.

Taxiing for the main runway 27 at Andrews Field in the summer of 1943; aircraft in the foreground is 41-18054 DR-H, "Jezabell." *Trevor J. Allen collection*

Aircraft of the 452nd BS taxi past the 451st BS area; aircraft to the right is 41-34950 SS-O, "Rack Em Back Jr.," and the B-17 behind is from the 338th BS, 96th BG, the unit previously based at Andrews Field, and may be a straggler of the move. *Trevor J. Allen collection*

Mission Narrative

Thirty-six aircraft dispatched to attack Beaumont-le-Roger A/D. The formation was led by Maj. F. E. Fair; the 2nd Box was led by Capt. B. G. Willis. The 323rd BG flew a diversionary sweep in support.

Briefed route was Base to Beachy Head, where the RAF Spitfire escort was met, to 5 miles northeast of Fecamp to the Brionne (the IP) to the target.

Twenty-nine aircraft attacked the primary with fair results, dropping 226 × 300 GP bombs at 1700 hrs. from 10,000 ft. in CAVU [ceiling and visibility unlimited] conditions. Three aircraft failed to locate the primary and released 24 × 300 GPs on an airfield, thought to be Conches, at 1702 hrs.; two other aircraft failed to locate the target. Two aircraft returned early, and a total of 38 × 300 GP were returned.

Meager inaccurate gunfire encountered 3 miles north of Brionne at 1655 hrs. and again at the target, which burst behind and below the formation. Meager inaccurate flak was also reported at 1711 hrs. near Liseaux on the route back.

Six to eleven enemy aircraft (e/a), reported as Me 109s and Fw 190s, encountered during the bomb run at 1658 hrs., just north of Brionne; these were driven off by the RAF escort, and eleven of the B-26s engaged the e/a.

Three aircraft received Category A damage, one had a tire blow out on landing, and two others were slightly damaged, not through battle damage, one of which was hit by a metal fragment from preceding aircraft.

Route back was a right turn to Broglie to 3 miles northeast of Dives to Selsey Bill to Base.

Interrogation of crews began at 1830 hrs. and finished at 2030 hrs.

Mission Notes and "Flak-Bait" Crew Debrief Comments

"Flak-Bait" flying No. 5 position in the lead flight of the 2nd Box; takeoff time was 1535 hrs.

8 × 300 GPs dropped on the lead aircraft.

Aircraft 773 too slow; couldn't keep up on outside turn.

Fuel consumption bad.

Tail turret booster motor went out, and the light was loose.

Crew reported seeing three dogfights.

"Flak-Bait" Encounter Report

Sgt. Thielan, tail gunner on "Flak-Bait," fired 150 rounds at one of the Fw 190s (reported as having a yellow nose) that attacked from head on and below, toward the No. 6 aircraft in the flight, making only the one pass. It was thought that the Spitfire escort finally shot him down.

Event: Field Maneuvers

On August 17, 1943, the 449th BS held field maneuvers; the object was to set up a camp in a short period of time, camouflaging the installations, and to set up communications. The weather conditions were perfect. Lt. Col. Nye, the group CO, flew over the camp in a Piper Cub and declared the results as "well done."

Date: August 19, 1943
Target: Bryas/Sud A/D
Field Order: VIII ASC 3rd BW F/O 46

"Flak-Bait" Crew

1Lt. J. J. Farrell, pilot
F/O T. F. Moore, copilot
2Lt. O. J. Redmond, navigator/bombardier

TSgt. D. L. Tyler, engineer/gunner
SSgt. J. B. Manuel, radio/gunner
SSgt. N. E. Thielan, gunner

Briefing started at 1315 hrs. and ended 1422 hrs.

T/off: 1552 hrs.	Rendezvous: 1655 hrs.	Landfall: 1706 hrs.
Target: 1719 hrs.	Coast Out: 1730 hrs.	Return: 1827 hrs.

Mission Narrative

Thirty-six aircraft dispatched to attack Bryas/Sud A/D, led by Lt. Col. G. C. Nye; the 2nd Box was led by Maj. F. E. Fair.

Route out was Base to Hastings, where rendezvous with RAF Spitfire escort was made, to 1 mile northeast of Le Touquet to target.

9/10th cloud was encountered at the target so no attack was made, although one aircraft had an accidental release, dropping 10 × 300 GP bombs. The remainder returned 350 × 300 GPs.

Weak inaccurate flak was encountered at landfall north of Le Touquet; none encountered at the target, but moderate accurate heavy flak fire was encountered at the coast out from Hardelot and possibly Boulogne areas at 1728–1729 hrs.; this was because the formation was 3 miles north of the briefed course. Nine aircraft received Cat. A damage.

Some crews reported seeing dogfights between Spitfires and e/a when formation was two minutes from the enemy coast.

Briefed return route was a right turn to Le Touquet (see note above; actual route was 3 miles to the north) to Hastings to Base.

Interrogation of crews began at 1825 hrs. and finished at 1955 hrs.

Mission Notes and "Flak-Bait" Crew Debrief Comments

"Flak-Bait" flew in the No. 2 position of the high flight, 1st Box; her takeoff time was 1554 hrs.

10 × 300 GPs returned—10/10th cloud cover.

Cat. A flak damage—received a ½" hole in left nacelle and a 2½" gash in bottom of left bomb bay.

Crew observed six gun emplacements approx. 1–2 miles south of Le Touquet firing.

Crew also request sandwiches be available prior to takeoff.

Other Crew Comments

A Spitfire seen in the water at 1703 hrs., 25 miles from Hastings; dinghy inflated.

A Spitfire seen in the water 3 miles north of Le Touquet at 1727 hrs.

At 1731 hrs., a Spitfire was seen to be hit by flak and go down three minutes off the enemy coast; pilot bailed out and other Spitfires were seen to circle the dinghy.

At 1732 hrs. a possible B-17 seen in the water off the English coast, with four dinghies tied together.

Group CO Receives Promotion

On August 24, 1943, news came through that Lt. Col. Glenn C. Nye had been promoted to full colonel.

> **Date: September 2, 1943**
> **Target: Hesdin C/W**
> **Field Order: VIII ASC 3rd BW F/O 66**

"Flak-Bait" Crew

1Lt. J. J. Farrell, pilot	TSgt. D. L. Tyler, engineer/gunner
F/O T. F. Moore, copilot	SSgt. J. B. Manuel, radio/gunner
2Lt. O. J. Redmond, navigator/bombardier	SSgt. N. E. Thielan, gunner

Briefing started at 1445 hrs. and ended 1545 hrs.

T/off: 1700 hrs.	Rendezvous: 1821 hrs.	Landfall: 1840 hrs.
Target: 1846 hrs.	Coast Out: 1852 hrs.	Return: 1926 hrs.

Mission Narrative

Thirty-six aircraft dispatched led by Lt. Col. G. C. Nye; the 2nd Box was led by Capt. L. J. Sebille.

The group to join a formation from the 323rd BG.

Route out was Base to Splasher Beacon No. 9, to Tunbridge Wells, to Hastings to Berck-sur-Mer to the target. RAF Spitfire escort was to be shared by the 322nd and 323rd Groups.

Target attacked at 1846 hrs. from 10,800 ft., dropping 284 × 100 IBs and 177 × 300 GPs; eight aircraft had some sort of rack failures. Thirteen × 100 IBs were jettisoned and 27 × 100 IB and 3 × 300 GP bombs were returned. Good results were observed; some bursts just right of the target and woods surrounding the target seen to be burning.

Weak inaccurate light and heavy flak was encountered at landfall. Weak inaccurate flak, which was well below the formation over the target, and upon exit near Le Touquet, weak inaccurate flak was encountered, which was to the right of the formation. No aircraft were damaged.

Briefed return route was a left turn to Le Touquet to Hastings to Base; actual landfall was made at Rye instead of Hastings.

Interrogation of crews began at 2005 hrs. and finished at 2120 hrs.

Mission Notes and "Flak-Bait" Crew Debrief Comments

"Flak-Bait" flying No. 5 position of the lead flight, 1st Box, taking off at 1702 hrs. and landed at 1926 hrs.

18 × 100 IBs released, observing good results. The gunners request green lenses for glasses, since they couldn't see a thing in the glare.

```
Date: September 4, 1943
Target: St.-Pol M/Y
Field Order: VIII ASC 3rd BW F/O 69
```

"Flak-Bait" Crew

1Lt. J. J. Farrell, pilot
F/O T. F. Moore, copilot
2Lt. O. J. Redmond, navigator/bombardier

TSgt. D. L. Tyler, engineer/gunner
SSgt. J. B. Manuel, radio/gunner
SSgt. N. E. Thielan, gunner

Briefing started at 1445 hrs. and ended 1550 hrs.

T/off: 1708 hrs.
Target: 1833 hrs.

Rendezvous: 1815 hrs.
Coast Out: 1848 hrs.

Landfall: 1825½ hrs.
Return: 1928 hrs.

Mission Narrative

Thirty-six aircraft dispatched, led by Maj. F. E. Fair and Maj. O. D. Turner; the 2nd Box was led by Capt. N. L. Harvey.

Route out was Base to Dungeness, where rendezvous with RAF Spitfire escort was made, to Berck-sur-Mer to Hesdin to target.

Twenty-four aircraft attacked at 1833 hrs., in CAVU conditions from heights 9,500 ft. and 11,000 ft.; 70 × 1,000 GPs dropped for fair results; twelve aircraft failed to attack, six because the leader failed to drop due to a rack failure, and six others because of further rack failures. One aircraft returned early since it could not catch the formation. A total of 38 × 1,000 GP bombs returned.

Slight inaccurate light and heavy flak encountered at target, Hesdin and Berck-sur-Mer, while slight inaccurate flak was encountered from Bruay, Fruges, and 4 miles southeast of Montreuil. Two aircraft received Cat. A damage.

Between St.-Pol and Hesdin, at 1836 to 1840 hrs., two to six Me 109s engaged the 2nd Box; in three instances they attacked in pairs. They flew alongside formation, acting like the escort and waggling their wings for approx. two minutes; e/a peeled off suddenly and attacked from the one to two o'clock position. They generally closed to 200 yds. before opening fire and then closed to 75 yds., concentrating on lead and low flights of the 2nd Box. Fourteen encounters were recorded, but no claims against the e/a were made.

Route back was a left turn off the target to Berck-sur-Mer to Dungeness to Base.

Interrogation of crews began at 1945 hrs. and finished at 2140 hrs.

Mission Notes and "Flak-Bait" Crew Debrief Comments

"Flak-Bait" flew No. 2 position, high flight, 2nd Box; took off at 1721 hrs. and landed 1947 hrs.

3 × 1,000 GP bombs returned (only three loaded on aircraft) since leader did not drop. Observed bombing of the other aircraft, reporting good results. Formation was north of course on leaving target.

Someone in low flight, 2nd Box, fired at Spitfire escort. Gunners request green goggles.

Aerial view of Andrews Field, in a photo taken on September 4, 1943, the day that the 322nd BG attacked St. Pol Marshaling Yards. *Crown copyright*

Other Crew Comments

Spitfire seen to go down at 1853 hrs., off Berck-sur-Mer; pilot seen to bail out; others were seen to be circling the spot.

Event: Combat Crews in Meeting with Gen. Hap Arnold

On the morning on September 4, 1943, the combat crews of all four groups of VIII ASC were transported to 3rd Bomb Wing Headquarters at Marks Hall, where they heard Four-Star General H. H. Arnold, chief of the USAAF, give a speech in which he declared that "the Marauder has found its place in the sun."

```
Date: September 5, 1943
Target: Ghent M/Y
Field Order: VIII ASC 3rd BW F/O 70
```

"Flak-Bait" Crew

F/O W. E. Mildren, pilot
F/O E. O. Grubb, copilot
2Lt. S. S. Bolesta, navigator/bombardier

SSgt. K. M. Rimer, engineer/gunner
SSgt. W. K. Lahm, radio/gunner
SSgt. H. T. Cunningham, gunner

Briefing started at 0415 hrs. and ended 0520 hrs.

T/off: 0640 hrs.	Rendezvous: 0800 hrs.	Landfall: 0819 hrs.
Target: 0831 hrs.	Coast Out: 0846 hrs.	Return: 0914 hrs.

Mission Narrative

Thirty-six aircraft dispatched, led by Lt. Col. G. C. Nye and Capt. R. A. Porter, the 2nd Box by Capt. C. Cordill.

Route out was Base to Splasher Beacon No. 6, where rendezvous was made with the 323rd BG, the 322nd to lead, to Orfordness to Clacton to Nth [North] Foreland, where rendezvous was made with RAF Spitfire escort, then to 3 miles northeast of Blankenberge to 5 miles northeast of Ghent to target.

Thirty-two aircraft attacked at 0831 hrs., dropping 189 × 500 GPs; one aircraft dropped 6 × 500 GPs in Channel due to engine failure, and three others returned 21 × 500 GPs due to rack malfunction and the leader not dropping. Most hits were over the target, some in target area among buildings and tracks.

At landfall near Heyst, weak flak was encountered, accurate for height but not course; none at the target but weak in the area of the secondary and route out. Slight inaccurate flak was encountered upon exit at Nieuport at 0845 hrs. One aircraft received Cat. A damage.

Route back was a right turn off the target to 2 miles southwest of Nieuport to Nth Foreland to Base.

Interrogation of crews began at 0955 hrs. and finished at 1050 hrs.

Mission Notes and "Flak-Bait" Crew Debrief Comments

"Flak-Bait" flying No. 6 position, high flight, 1st Box; takeoff was at 0645 hrs. and landed at 0932 hrs.

6 × 500 GP dropped; saw bombs on each end of shed with some over; also bombs observed on tracks.

Pilots interphone out, bad mike.

Tail guns fired a few rounds and then jammed.

Typical view of a crew being debriefed after a mission at Andrews Field. *Trevor J. Allen collection*

"Flak-Bait" Crew

1Lt. J. J. Farrell, pilot

F/O T. F. Moore, copilot

2Lt. O. J. Redmond, navigator/bombardier

TSgt. D. L. Tyler, engineer/gunner

SSgt. J. B. Manuel, radio/gunner

SSgt. N. E. Thielan, gunner

Briefing started at 1345 hrs. and ended 1405 hrs.

T/off: 1615 hrs.

Target: 1756 hrs.

Rendezvous: 1730 hrs.

Coast Out: 1811 hrs.

Landfall: 1745½ hrs.

Return: 1915 hrs.

Mission Narrative

Thirty-six aircraft dispatched, led by Capt. L. J. Sebille with Maj. O. D. Turner; the 2nd Box was led by 1Lt. H. V. Smythe.

Routing was Base to Splasher Beacon No. 8, where rendezvous was made with the 323rd BG, who were to lead, to Dungeness, where fighter rendezvous was made with RAF Spitfires, to Cayeux to 3 miles north of Poix to target.

Thirty-two aircraft attacked, dropping 186 × 500 GPs, from 10,000 to 10,500 ft. in clear conditions, for good results. Four aircraft were abortive, three due to engine trouble and one because of a fuel pump failure. One aircraft jettisoned 5 × 500 GPs, while five other aircraft brought back a total of 25 × 500 GP bombs. The 1st Box obtained a good concentration in target area, whereas those of the 2nd Box were mainly to the left of the target.

Light inaccurate light flak near Amiens at 1800 hrs. after leaving the target and southwest of Abbeville at 1804 hrs.; slight inaccurate light and heavy flak, mostly low, 5 miles south of Cayeux on the coast out at 1811 hrs.

In the vicinity of Abbeville, at 1804 hrs., 4–10 Me 109s and four Fw 190s were reported approaching from out of the sun. Fourteen engagements took place; on at least three occasions these attacks were by four aircraft in line astern; breakaway was low and to the left. Two aircraft were damaged Cat. A in the high flight, 2nd Box, including "Flak-Bait."

Return routing was a left turn off the target to 8 miles south of Abbeville to Cayeux to Dungeness to Base. Interrogation of crews began at 1915 hrs. and finished at 2030 hrs.

Mission Notes and "Flak-Bait" Crew Debrief Comments

"Flak-Bait" flew as the No. 6 ship in the high flight, 2nd Box.

6 × 500 GPs dropped for good results.

Electrical instruments out.

Crew observed a fire in a long shed at the target, and a large fire to the west side of the target.

"Flak-Bait" Encounter Report

A Me 109 attacked "Flak-Bait" from one o'clock high, and out of the sun while the formation was about 8 miles WNW of Amiens; breakaway was to the seven o'clock direction in a dive. E/a fire entered the nose behind the Plexiglas; explosion went right in and knocked out the electrical instruments. Top turret gunner Sgt. Tyler fired thirty rounds from 300 down to 100 yards, and Sgt. Thielan, the tail gunner, fired twenty rounds from 100 yards; no hits were observed. Spitfires were too close for gunners to engage properly. Pilot 1Lt. J. J. Farrell received a slight wound in the left leg below the knee, Aircraft radioed back news of the injury. Aircraft damaged Cat. A.

Recorded on the debrief chart was the comment that "the Boss made the best landing he ever made, even though he had a 20 mm fragment in his leg." (*Author*: In the Devon Francis book *Flak-Bait*, this is attributed to TSgt. D. L. Tyler, although there is no reference to who actually said this on the chart).

"Flak-Bait" Crew

1Lt. J. J. Farrell, pilot

F/O T. F. Moore, copilot

2Lt. O. J. Redmond, navigator/bombardier

TSgt. D. L. Tyler, engineer/gunner

SSgt. J. B. Manuel, radio/gunner

SSgt. N. E. Thielan, gunner

Briefing started at 0330 hrs. and ended 0430 hrs.

T/off: 0619 hrs.   Rendezvous: Landfall: 0736, 0742 & 0758½ hrs.

Target: 0745, 0747 & 0800½ hrs.   Coast Out: 0745½, 0747½ & 0801½ hrs.   Return: 0820 hrs.

Mission Narrative

Fifty-four aircraft dispatched in three boxes of eighteen to attack three Coastal Defense positions on the coast, in support of military exercises in the Channel. The 1st Box was led by Capt. L. J. Sebille with Maj. O. D. Turner, the 2nd Box was led by Capt. H. M. Posson, and the 3rd by Capt. G. B. Simler with Maj. F. E. Fair.

Routing was Base to Dover to Cap Gris-Nez to the targets; six squadrons of RAF Spitfires to provide umbrella cover for all groups in the target area. Crews were briefed that any shipping encountered en route was to be considered friendly and to exercise caution if jettisoning any bombs.

A total of fifty-two aircraft attacked, all eighteen in the 1st Box, dropping 108 × 500 GPs from 10,000 ft., seventeen from the 2nd Box dropping 90 × 500 GPs from 10,500 ft., and seventeen from the 3rd Box dropping 78 × 600 GPs and 24 × 500 GP bombs, from 12,000 ft. Two aircraft jettisoned 6 × 500 GPs and 6 × 600 GPs in the Channel through rack failures. Results were assessed as fair.

The 1st and 3rd Boxes encountered both heavy and light flak from landfall to exit, the first two Boxes reporting intense barrage fire. The 2nd Box encountered weak inaccurate heavy flak for entire period they were overland. Nineteen aircraft were damaged Cat. A; one aircraft shot down by flak; seven MIA.

Four Me 109s passed below the high flight of the 1st Box at 0748 hrs.; while over the Channel on return trip, fired at by one aircraft but no claim was made.

Route back was a right turn off the targets to Folkstone to Base.

Interrogation of crews began at 0900 hrs. and finished at 1030 hrs.

Mission Notes and "Flak-Bait" Crew Debrief Comments

"Flak-Bait" flew No. 3 position, low flight in the 1st Box, taking off at 0624 hrs.

6 × 500 GPs released; bombs fell toward back of the target, for good results.

No damage received.

MIA Information

41-18058 ER-S

Flying in the No. 4 position of the lead flight, 2nd Box. Aircraft was hit by flak and seen with the left engine on fire. Observed to go into a flat spin and briefly recovered at about 8,000 ft. and then spun into the water. Two or possibly three chutes were reported.

1Lt. J. B. Reynolds, pilot	KIA
F/O L. W. Colby, copilot	KIA
2Lt. R. W. Handsel, navigator/bombardier	KIA
TSgt. J. L. Guiliano, radio/gunner	KIA
SSgt. Q. E. Lecker, engineer/gunner	KIA
SSgt. P. L. Brinson, gunner	KIA
2Lt. R. H. Edwards, combat camera unit	KIA

"Flak-Bait" Crew

1Lt. J. J. Farrell, pilot
F/O T. F. Moore, copilot
2Lt. O. J. Redmond, navigator/bombardier

TSgt. D. L. Tyler, engineer/gunner
SSgt. J. B. Manuel, radio/gunner
SSgt. N. E. Thielan, gunner

Briefing started at 1312 hrs. and ended 1400 hrs.

T/off: 1447 hrs.	Rendezvous: 1630 hrs.	Landfall: 1649 hrs.
Target: 1704 hrs. (S)	Coast Out: 1711 hrs.	Return: 1755 hrs.

Mission Narrative

Twenty-one aircraft dispatched to attack Rouen Power Station, led by Capt. F. F. Rezabek with Capt. R. A. Porter.

Routing was Base to Hastings, where rendezvous was made with RAF Spitfires, to 3 miles east of St.-Valery-en-Caux, to Bourg-Achard to target.

The primary target was obscured by 6/10th heavy cumulus cloud, so formation attacked secondary target, Le Trait Shipyards, through 4/10th cumulus, from 11,000 to 11,400 ft., dropping 111 × 500 GP bombs for good results. One aircraft was abortive, returning 6 × 500 GPs, and another two had bombs hang up, returning 3 × 500 GPs.

Weak to moderate flak encountered at landfall, and slight inaccurate flak was encountered on the bomb run for the secondary; moderate accurate heavy flak was encountered at the coast near St.-Valery on route out. Fourteen aircraft received Cat. A damage.

Fifteen e/a were observed, with two encounters reported; these came from nine and eleven o'clock level, just before reaching the secondary target. Crews reported seeing two e/a destroyed by the RAF Spitfire escort.

Return was a left turn to 5 miles east of St.-Valery to Beachy Head to Base.

Interrogation of crews began at 1800 hrs. and finished at 1910 hrs.

Mission Notes and "Flak-Bait" Crew Debrief Comments

"Flak-Bait" flew as No. 5 aircraft in the low flight; takeoff was at 1502 hrs. and landing at 1813 hrs.

6 × 500 GPs dropped on secondary due to clouds over primary.

Cat. A damage—a small hole in the horizontal stabilizer. Crew reported that formation went in to the right of course and came out to the left of briefed course. Crew reported seeing five e/a, but no attacks made on this aircraft. Results observed as fair, with bombs in the right of the target area.

"Flak-Bait" Crew

1Lt. J. J. Farrell, pilot
F/O T. F. Moore, copilot
2Lt. O. J. Redmond, navigator/bombardier

TSgt. D. L. Tyler, engineer/gunner
SSgt. J. B. Manuel, radio/gunner
SSgt. N. E. Thielan, gunner

Briefing started at 1320 hrs. and ended 1445 hrs.

T/off: 1541 hrs.	Rendezvous: 1715 hrs.	Landfall: 1721 hrs.
Target: 1735 hrs.	Coast Out: 1746 hrs.	Return: 1841 hrs.

Mission Narrative

Thirty-six aircraft dispatched, led by Lt. Col. G. C. Nye; the 2nd Box was led by Maj. F. E. Fair.

Route was Base to 50.10'N, 00.40'E (over the English Channel off St.-Valery-en-Caux), to target. Rendezvous was made with RAF Spitfire escort over the Channel as briefed.

Thirty-six aircraft attacked, dropping 348 × 300 GPs on primary from 11,000 ft., in clear conditions, for Good results. Five aircraft suffered rack malfunctions and brought at total of 12 × 300 GP bombs back.

Weak inaccurate flak encountered from 2 miles to 6 miles southeast of St.-Valery-en-Caux at 1723 hrs., accurate for height only, bursting in salvoes of four, to the right and behind the formation. When 12 miles north of the target at 1732 hrs., weak but accurate heavy flak was encountered; crews reported hearing the bursts and felt the concussions. Very inaccurate flak from the Le Havre area, far to the right of the formation at exit near Trouville. Two aircraft received Cat. A damage.

E/a opposition was generally weak; 4–10 e/a, mostly Me 109s, made passes at the formation between 1035 hrs. and 1040 hrs., from the 10:30 to 11:00 direction, predominantly in pairs. Passes made at 1st Box mainly against the lead flight. Eight to eleven encounters reported. One e/a was claimed as probably destroyed.

Return route was a right turn to 3 miles southwest of Trouville, to Selsey Bill to Base.

Interrogation of crews began at 1855 hrs. and finished at 2025 hrs.

Mission Notes and "Flak-Bait" Crew Debrief Comments

"Flak-Bait" flew No. 2 position in high flight, 1st Box. Takeoff was at 1541 hrs. and landing was at 1847 hrs.

10 × 300 GPs released—crew reported that bombs were seen to drop in dispersal area.

```
Date: September 22, 1943
Target: Beauvais-Tille A/D
Field Order: VIII ASC 3rd BW F/O 99
```

"Flak-Bait" Crew

2Lt. E. W. Goodwin, pilot
2Lt. L. U. Yount, copilot
2Lt. R. G. Caldwell, navigator/bombardier

SSgt. R. P. Bender, engineer/gunner
SSgt. V. J. Christian, radio/gunner
Sgt. A. J. Sosenko, gunner

Briefing started at 1140 hrs. and ended 1230 hrs.

T/off: 1343 hrs.   Target: no attack   Return: 1558 hrs.

Mission Narrative

Thirty-six aircraft dispatched, led by Lt. Col. G. C. Nye with Capt. H. V. Smythe; the 2nd Box was led by Capt. C. Cordill.

Routing was Base to rendezvous with 387th BG at Splasher Beacon No. 8, the 387th BG to lead, to Hastings to fighter rendezvous at 50.20'N, 01.00'E (over the Channel off Dieppe). Rendezvous made as scheduled but the formation was recalled by the fighters just before the enemy coast, 8–9/10th cumulus and stratocumulus along the enemy coast. Thirty-six aircraft returned 360 × 300 GP bombs.

Interrogation of crews began at 1600 hrs. and finished at 1700 hrs.

Mission Notes and "Flak-Bait" Crew Debrief Comments

"Flak-Bait" flew as No. 6 aircraft, high flight, 2nd Box.

10 × 300 GP bombs returned.

Col. G. C. Nye, Group CO, Comments

Would suggest that the lead group (387th) start from Base at such a time as not to have to make a 360-degree turn en route. 322nd assembled on them en route to Splasher Beacon No. 8. At this point the 387th made a 360-degree turn. English coast was left five minutes too early, and when they reached the r/v point in the Channel they made another 360-degree turn, which gave the enemy a chance well in advance their fighters up to intercept our formation at the enemy coast.

"Flak-Bait" Crew

2Lt. E. W. Goodwin, pilot
2Lt. L. U. Yount, copilot
2Lt. R. G. Caldwell, navigator/bombardier

SSgt. V. J. Christian, engineer/gunner
SSgt. R. P. Bender, radio/gunner
Sgt. A. J. Sosenko, gunner

Briefing started at 0445 hrs. and ended 0530 hrs.

T/off: 0714 hrs.
Target: 0906½ hrs.

Rendezvous: 0840 hrs.
Coast Out: 0925 hrs.

Landfall: 0849½ hrs.
Return: 1012 hrs.

Mission Narrative

Thirty-six aircraft dispatched, led by Lt. Col. G. C. Nye with Capt. H. V. Smythe; the 2nd Box was led by Capt. C. Cordill.

Routing was Base to rendezvous with 387th BG at Splasher Beacon No. 8, the 322nd to lead, to Lewes, to rendezvous with RAF Spitfires at 50.10'N, 00.10'E (English Channel off Fecamp), to 5 miles northeast of Fecamp to Quittebeuf to target.

Thirty-five aircraft released 344 × 300 GPs in CAVU conditions from 10,700 to 11,200 ft., for good results. One aircraft jettisoned 2 × 300 GPs in the Channel; another aircraft returned 4 × 300 GPs through rack failures. One aircraft had a loss of power and aborted, returning 10 × 300 GP bombs.

A few bursts of HFF at landfall near Eletot, low and inaccurate. Also weak and inaccurate LFF at landfall and the target. Weak inaccurate LFF and HFF encountered from Fecamp, the majority if not all from flak ships. No damage received.

Route back was a right turn to Serquigny to 8 miles northeast of Fecamp, to Beachy Head to Base.

Interrogation of crews began at 1015 hrs. and finished at 1135 hrs.

Mission Notes and "Flak-Bait" Crew Debrief Comments

"Flak-Bait" flew in the No. 6 position, high flight, 2nd Box. Takeoff was at 0727 hrs. and landing at 1030 hrs.

10 × 300 GPs dropped; crew reported all bombs on target for fair results.

Suggest that ground crew get on time—crew had to preflight the ship.

"Flak-Bait" Crew

1Lt. J. J. Farrell, pilot
2Lt. R. E. Moninger, copilot
2Lt. O. J. Redmond, navigator/bombardier

TSgt. D. L. Tyler, engineer/gunner
SSgt. J. B. Manuel, radio/gunner
SSgt. N. E. Thielan, gunner

Briefing started at 1215 hrs. and ended 1340 hrs.

T/off: 1413 hrs.
Target: 1603 hrs.

Rendezvous: 1540 hrs.
Coast Out: 1618 hrs.

Landfall: 1547 hrs.
Return: 1717 hrs.

Mission Narrative

Thirty-six aircraft dispatched, led by Capt. R. A. Porter; the 2nd Box was led by Capt. H. V. Smythe.

Route was Base to Splasher Beacon No. 9, for rendezvous with the 323rd BG, who were to lead, to Hastings to 50.10'N, 01.00'E (off Dieppe), for rendezvous with RAF Spitfire escort, to 3 miles northeast of Creil to Onsembray to target. However, a route deviation increased to 7 miles before reaching the IP, necessitating a sharp left turn to make the bomb run.

Thirty-six aircraft released 179 × 300 GPs and 310 × 100 GPs through 4/10th cloud cover from 10,500 ft.; results unobserved but believed to be rated as fair. One aircraft jettisoned 5 × 100 GPs in Channel, and two aircraft returned 1 × 300 GP and 9 × 100 GP bombs through rack failures.

Moderate accurate HFF encountered in target area, starting at Beauvais and continuing till 4 miles beyond the target; some appeared to come from railway tracks southeast of Beauvais.

Ten to fifteen e/a sighted south of the target, between 1602 hrs. and 1604 hrs., while on the bomb run and beyond the target, mostly Fw 190s. Eleven encounters reported most from the 5–8 o'clock position both low and level. One e/a confirmed as shot down by SSgt. L. B. Warren of the 452nd BS. One man slightly wounded in hand by flak (2Lt. J. L. Littwin, 449th BS).

Seven aircraft received Cat. A damage from flak, while one aircraft was Cat. AC from flak and e/a damage. One aircraft had nose Plexiglas smashed by a 0.50 shell dropped by a preceding aircraft.

Return route was a left turn off the target to Creil to Beachy Head to Base.

Interrogation of crews began at 1720 hrs. and finished at 1850 hrs.

Mission Notes and "Flak-Bait" Crew Debrief Comments

"Flak-Bait" flying No. 5 position, lead flight, 2nd Box; takeoff was at 1424 hrs. and landing at 1917 hrs.

18 × 100 GP dropped; results unobserved.

Cat. A damage, small hole in radio compartment due to flak. Crew requesting green lenses in goggles.

Observed one aircraft from the 323rd BG with engine smoking over the target.

Saw 3–4 e/a, but they made no attacks on this aircraft.

Heard Ground Sector Control asking for a reception check on VHF radio.

Other Crew Comments

A number of crews reported a 323rd BG B-26 fall out of formation, with its right engine smoking at 1602 hrs., seemingly under control (no aircraft were reported MIA this day).

One crew reported seeing three Spitfires chasing a Me 109 that was descending with its engine smoking, but did not observe it to crash.

E/a observed to follow formation back to the coast, sometimes flying alongside some 1,000 yds. out.

Crews reported outstanding support from RAF Spitfires, prevented the e/a pressing home attacks on our aircraft on virtually every encounter.

Date: September 25, 1943
Target: St.-Omer-Longuenesse A/D
Field Order: VIII ASC 3rd BW F/O 105

"Flak-Bait" Crew

2Lt. V. N. Liniger, pilot
2Lt. C. A. Forrester, copilot
2Lt. R. W. Fletcher, navigator/bombardier

SSgt. J. O. Mullen, engineer/gunner
SSgt. R. F. Stickney, radio/gunner
SSgt. J. B. Mitchell, gunner

Briefing started at 1330 hrs.; no end time recorded.

T/off: 1528 hrs.	Rendezvous: 1659 hrs.	Landfall: 1710 hrs.
Target: 1717 hrs.	Coast Out: 1725 hrs.	Return: 1825 hrs.

Mission Narrative

Thirty-six aircraft dispatched, led by Capt. L. J. Sebille; the 2nd Box was led by Capt. G. B. Simler.

Routing was Base to Splasher Beacon No. 9 for rendezvous with the 387th BG, the 322nd to lead, to rendezvous with RAF Spitfires at Hastings to 4 miles south of Hardelot to target.

Route was virtually obscured with 6–8/10th cloud; mission conducted on Dead Reckoning.

Thirty-five aircraft dropped 203 × 500 GPs on the target for fair results at 1717 hrs., from 11,500 ft. One aircraft failed to release because of an aircraft below, returning 6 × 500 GP bombs. Two aircraft returned 5 × 500 GPs, and another jettisoned 2 × 500 GPs in the Channel through rack failures.

Slight inaccurate flak encountered at Hardelot at 1710 hrs. on coast in, fired through the clouds, bursting to the left of the formation. At 1712 hrs., slight inaccurate and automatic fire came from the Samur area. At 1717 hrs., moderate inaccurate gunfire, accurate for height only, and box barrage from the St. Omer / Ft Rouge area was encountered. Further slight inaccurate fire from Cassel area at 1720 hrs., and on exit from the coast slight, very inaccurate fire, from the Dunkirk area. Two aircraft received Cat. A damage.

Route back was a left turn off the target to 3 miles northwest of Furnes to Nth Foreland to Base.

Interrogation of crews began at 1817 hrs. and finished at 1915 hrs.

Mission Notes and "Flak-Bait" Crew Debrief Comments

"Flak-Bait" flying No. 6 position, high flight, 1st Box. Takeoff was at 1633 hrs. and landing at 1810½ hrs.

6 × 500 GPs released; results unobserved.

Crew reported that the flak appeared to be aimed at the fighter escort; bursts seen among the escort.

They also reported that the navigation by the lead ship was excellent.

Date: September 27, 1943
Target: Beauvais-Tille A/D
Field Order: VIII ASC 3rd BW F/O 107

"Flak-Bait" Crew

2Lt. V. N. Liniger, pilot
2Lt. C. A. Forrester, copilot
2Lt. R. W. Fletcher, navigator/bombardier

SSgt. R. F. Stickney, engineer/gunner
SSgt. J. O. Mullen, radio/gunner
SSgt. J. B. Mitchell, gunner

Briefing started at 0620 hrs. and ended 0706 hrs.

T/off: 0849 hrs.	Rendezvous: 1025 hrs.	Landfall: 1030 hrs.
Target: 1044 hrs.	Coast Out: 1059 hrs.	Return: 1150 hrs.

Mission Narrative

Thirty-six aircraft dispatched, led by Capt. B. G. Willis with Maj. F. P. Taylor; the 2nd Box was led by Capt. F. F. Rezabek.

Routing was Base to Splasher Beacon No. 9, for rendezvous with the 387th BG, the 322nd to lead. To Hastings and rendezvous with RAF Spitfire escort, to 50.10'N, 01.10'E (off Criel-sur-Mer), to Ault. Formation continued 5 miles to right of briefed course to the IP (Crevecoeur), resulting in a shorter bomb run.

Heavy swelling cumulus at enemy coast, tops 11,000 ft., and 6–8/10th altostratus over target area at 8,000–10,000 ft.

Twenty-nine aircraft released 276 × 300 GPs from 11,500 ft. at 1044 hrs.; one aircraft failed to release because of an aircraft below, two because of mechanical problems, two because of rack malfunctions, and one because of personnel failure, another having returned early. A total of 44 × 300 GPs were jettisoned and 40 × 300 GPs returned.

Moderate fairly accurate flak encountered just past the IP, increasing in intensity and accuracy at the target and continuing for one minute past the target. Moderate accurate heavy and weak inaccurate light flak to the west of the target after formation had turned off the target. Intermittent heavy and light flak, mostly inaccurate, encountered along remainder of route until 10 miles south of Tocqueville.

Ten to fifteen e/a, both Me 109s and Fw 190s, attacked the formation in the target area, and beyond, from 1041 hrs., when just south of Crevecoeur, continuing until 1059 hrs., when the formation was northwest of Serqueux. E/a used clouds below formation to good advantage, making a quick pass at the formation and then taking cover in the clouds. At least nineteen encounters reported, mostly from the 5–7 o'clock direction and low. Gunners awarded two e/a destroyed, by Sgt. F. J. Driscoll of the 452nd BS and Sgt. W. G. Perry of the 450th BS, and two probably destroyed, by Sgt. F. J. Driscoll, 452nd BS and TSgt. A. J. Pramuk, 450th BS. Attacks were aimed at the 2nd Box and the 387th BG, who also claimed two e/a destroyed.

Twelve aircraft received Cat. A damage.

Return was a right turn to Tocqueville to Hastings to Base.

Interrogation of crews began at 1235 hrs. and finished at 1350 hrs.

Mission Notes and "Flak-Bait" Crew Debrief Comments

"Flak-Bait" flew No. 3 position, high flight, 1st Box. Takeoff was at 0854 hrs. and landing at 1153 hrs.

10 × 300 GP dropped, observing good results.

Crew complained that boxes not forming, and not in formation and on course when leaving the field.

Had difficulty in regulating the oil temperature.

Could hear and feel concussions from the flak.

Several e/a observed, first over the target and continued for up to 5–10 minutes; crew unable to identify types; no encounters made.

Other Crew Comments

Several crews complained that the formation was not assembled properly and that the lead left Base on route too soon.

387th BG almost under 322nd formation at time of bomb release.

Spitfires reported as providing excellent cover in the face of determined attacks by e/a; excellent cover was provided for stragglers and damaged bombers.

Several crews reported a B-26 (from the 387th BG) to be hit by the e/a and catch fire at 1046 hrs.; the aircraft dropped out of formation with two chutes observed. Aircraft was seen on the way back, escorted by Spitfires, the three gunners having bailed out. A total of four gunners bailed out of two battle-damaged aircraft from the 387th BG on this day, two of whom evaded capture.

```
Date: October 2, 1943
Target: St.-Omer-Longuenesse A/D
Field Order: VIII ASC 3rd BW F/O 110
```

"Flak-Bait" Crew

1Lt. J. J. Farrell, pilot
2Lt. D. A. Palmer, copilot
2Lt. O. J. Redmond, navigator/bombardier

TSgt. D. L. Tyler, engineer/gunner
SSgt. J. B. Manuel, radio/gunner
SSgt. N. E. Thielan, gunner

Briefing started at 1400 hrs. and ended 1440 hrs.

T/off: 1542 hrs.	Rendezvous: 1700 hrs.	Landfall: 1708 hrs.
Target: 1715 hrs.	Coast Out: 1729 hrs.	Return: 1815 hrs.

Mission Narrative

Thirty-six aircraft dispatched, led by Maj. O. D. Turner with Capt. H. M. Posson. The 2nd Box was led by Capt. B. F. McCuistion.

Briefed route was Base to Splasher Beacon No 8, for rendezvous with the 387th BG, the 322nd to lead, to Ashford, to Dungeness for rendezvous with RAF Spitfires, to 4 miles south of Hardelot to target.

Actual routing was a landfall at Boulogne; formation then turned right parallel to the coast, 2 miles offshore, to briefed point of entry, to a point near Furnes, then made a right turn and left enemy coast between Ostend and Knocke, near Blankenberge.

Only six aircraft, of the high flight of the 2nd Box, attacked, dropping 36 × 500 GPs on the target from 11,500 ft. Thirty aircraft were abortive, twenty-eight due to weather because of the 8–10/10th cloud cover; two others were abortive due to engine failure and a loss of power. A total of 180 × 500 GPs returned.

Moderate accurate HFF from Boulogne and following along the coast beyond Hardelot and observed as far south as Le Touquet. In target area, weak inaccurate HFF observed, seemingly directed at the fighter escort. Between Ostend and Knocke, where exit was made, very accurate intense tracer fire encountered along with moderate to intense, fairly accurate HFF, from both Ostend and Bruges areas.

Ten aircraft Cat. A and one aircraft Cat. AC damage. SSgt. W. L. Dumas, 450th BS, was killed by flak at landfall; three others wounded, 1Lt. J. J. Tyson, 2Lt. H. R. Fletcher, and SSgt. E. J. Pogodzinski, all from the 452nd BS, but in different crews.

The briefed return route was a left turn off the target to Furnes to Nth Foreland to Base, although actual exit was made at Knocke as related above.

Interrogation of crews began at 1830 hrs. and finished at 1940 hrs.

Mission Notes and "Flak-Bait" Crew Debrief Comments
"Flak-Bait" flew as the No. 5 aircraft, low flight, 2nd Box.

6 × 500 GPs returned.

Formation to left of course at landfall, too close to Boulogne; came out over Ostend.

Gunners want sunglasses.

Saw 387th BG aircraft peel off to right, two minutes past coast at 1711 hrs., with both engines running and not smoking, losing altitude fast, and disappeared in cloud toward the coast in a descent. (No aircraft were MIA this day).

Other Crew Comments
It was reported by the lead aircraft that the 387th got ahead of the formation to the left, after turning away from the target; this scattered our formation all over the sky, and the Spitfire escort had a hell of a time covering.

Many crews criticized poor navigation and the fact that formation tracked the coast close to Boulogne in poor weather while encountering flak fire.

```
Date: October 3, 1943
Target: Amsterdam-Schipol A/D
Field Order: VIII ASC 3rd BW F/O 111
```

"Flak-Bait" Crew
1Lt. J. J. Farrell, pilot
2Lt. W. F. Dreyer, copilot
2Lt. O. J. Redmond, navigator/bombardier

TSgt. D. L. Tyler, engineer/gunner
SSgt. J. B. Manuel, radio/gunner
SSgt. N. E. Thielan, gunner

Briefing started at 0730 hrs. and ended 0835 hrs.

T/off: 0930 hrs.	Rendezvous: 1105 hrs.	Landfall: 1113½ hrs.
Target: 1121 hrs.	Coast Out: 1126 hrs.	Return: 1228 hrs.

Mission Narrative
Thirty-six aircraft off, led by Capt. F. F. Rezabek with Capt. R. A. Porter. The 2nd Box was led by Capt. C. Cordill.

Route was Base to Splasher Beacon No. 5, for rendezvous with the 323rd BG, who were to lead, to Lowestoft to 52.15'N, 03.40'E (Nth Sea off The Hague), for the rendezvous with the RAF Spitfire escort, to 5 miles southwest of Katwijk to 5 miles northwest of Woerden to target.

Thirty-five aircraft dropped 211 × 500 GPs from 10,500 ft. at 1121 hrs., through 3–4/10th cloud, for good to fair results. One aircraft jettisoned 5 × 500 GPs in the sea.

Weak inaccurate flak at Katwijk and Leiden upon landfall. Intense HFF, in box barrage, at target lasting for two minutes. From target to exit at Zandvoort, formation encountered intermittent gunfire, varying from weak to moderate, accurate for height but not course.

Four encounters with four e/a, the first at 1121 hrs. over the target directed at the lead ship, two others at 1123 hrs. 5 miles northwest of the target, and the final attack was one minute before exit at the coast; no claims made.

Nine aircraft received Cat. A damage, and one person seriously wounded: SSgt. L. K. Nichols, 451st BS.

Return route was a left turn off the target to Zandvoort to Lowestoft to Base.

Interrogation of crews began at 1237 hrs. and finished at 1355 hrs.

Mission Notes and "Flak-Bait" Crew Debrief Comments
"Flak-Bait" flew as No. 6 aircraft in the low flight, 2nd Box. Takeoff was at 0946 hrs. and landing at 1245 hrs.

Crew observed good results, releasing 6 × 500 GPs on the lead ship.

On the way back, heard someone give directions as to course on the command channel.

At 1143 hrs., while at 7,000 ft., observed a B-26 losing altitude, with the right engine giving off black and white smoke; aircraft was under control, followed by another unidentified aircraft.

Other Crew Comments
One crew reported as seeing one tail gunner firing at a Spitfire over the target.

Event: 449th BS CO Receives Promotion
On October 6, 1943, it was learned that the 449th BS CO, Capt. Benjamin G. Willis, had been promoted to the rank of major.

> Date: October 8, 1943
> Target: Chievres A/D
> Field Order: VIII ASC 3rd BW F/O 115

"Flak-Bait" Crew
2Lt. V. N. Liniger, pilot
2Lt. C. A. Forrester, copilot
2Lt. R. W. Fletcher, navigator/bombardier

SSgt. J. O. Mullen, engineer/gunner
SSgt. R. F. Stickney, radio/gunner
SSgt. J. B. Mitchell, gunner

Briefing started at 1300 hrs. and ended 1430 hrs.

T/off: 1457 hrs.	Rendezvous: 1620 hrs.	Landfall: 1633 hrs.
Target: 1651 hrs.	Coast Out: 1712 hrs.	Return: 1756 hrs.

Mission Narrative
Thirty-six aircraft dispatched, led by Capt. G. B. Simler, with Maj. F. E. Fair; the 2nd Box was led by Capt. H. V. Smythe.

Routing was Base to rendezvous with the 387th BG at Splasher Beacon No. 8, to Nth Foreland, where fighter rendezvous was made, to 3 miles northwest of Furnes to 4 miles west of Renaix to 4 miles west of Lenze to target.

All aircraft abortive, one through engine trouble, the rest because of weather, 4/10th cloud, base at 3,500 ft. and tops 7,000 ft.; visibility less than 1 mile. Thirty-three aircraft returned 199 × 500 GPs; three aircraft jettisoned 17 × 500 GPs in the sea.

No flak at landfall, HFF continuous in target area, weak inaccurate LFF from Nieuport at exit, mostly about 2,000 ft. below formation. One aircraft received Cat. A damage.

Route back was a left turn off the target to 3 miles northwest of Furnes to Nth Foreland to Base.

Interrogation of crews began at 1815 hrs. and finished at 1850 hrs.

Mission Notes and "Flak-Bait" Crew Debrief Comments
"Flak-Bait" flew as No. 3 aircraft in the lead flight, 2nd Box.

Returned 6 × 500 GPs; couldn't see target.

Other Crew Comments
Formation should land according to proper procedure and not downwind.

Some crews thought that the secondary target, Moorseele A/D, could have been attacked.

Event: Transfer to the 9th Air Force
On October 16, 1943, the VIII ASC became the nucleus of the newly reformed 9th Air Force in the UK, and the 3rd Bomb Wing became 9th Bomber Command.

The Ninth Air Force would be used in direct support of the ground forces once the invasion had taken place.

Shortly thereafter, two combat bomb wings was formed, and the four groups then in the UK would be divided among them for administrative and, later, from April 1944, operational control.

The 323rd and 387th BGs were assigned to the 98th CBW, and the 322nd, and 386th BGs to the 99th CBW. Later the remaining four B-26 groups to be assigned to the 9th Air Force would join them so that each CBW controlled four groups each. The 344th and 391st BGs joined the 99th CBW, while the 394th and 397th were assigned to the 98th CBW.

In addition, the 97th CBW was later formed to control the three A-20 groups assigned to the 9th Air Force.

Date: October 18, 1943
Target: Evreux-Fauville A/D
Field Order: 9th BC F/O 119

"Flak-Bait" Crew

2Lt. V. N. Liniger, pilot	SSgt. J. O. Mullen, engineer/gunner
2Lt. C. A. Forrester, copilot	SSgt. R. F. Stickney, radio/gunner
2Lt. R. W. Fletcher, navigator/bombardier	SSgt. J. B. Mitchell, gunner

Briefing started at 0515 hrs. and ended 0615 hrs.

T/off: 0720 hrs.	Rendezvous: 0900 hrs.	Landfall: 0908 & 0907 hrs.
Target: 0926 hrs.	Coast Out: 0947 hrs.	Return: 1008 hrs.

Mission Narrative

Thirty-six aircraft dispatched, led by Maj. G. C. Celio with Capt. F. F. Rezabek; the 2nd Box was led by Capt. B. G. Willis.

Routing was Base to Splasher Beacon No. 9 and rendezvous with the 387th BG, the 322nd to lead. To 50.10'N, 00.10'E (off Fecamp), where fighter rendezvous was made, to Eletot to Autheuil to target.

10/10th cloud at target prevented bombing; all aircraft returned 216 × 500 GP bombs.

Slight inaccurate gunfire at landfall over Eletot area and over the Rouen area, bursting behind the formation. One aircraft Cat. A damage; cause unknown.

Return was a right turn off the target, to the secondary at Beaumont-le-Roger A/D, to Eletot to Beachy Head to Base.

Interrogation of crews began at 1040 hrs. and finished at 1140 hrs.

Mission Notes and "Flak-Bait" Crew Debrief Comments

"Flak-Bait" flew as No. 3 in lead flight of 2nd Box.

Too cloudy to see target; 6 × 500 GPs returned.

Date: October 18, 1943
Target: St.-Omer-Longuenesse A/D
Field Order: 9th BC F/O 120

"Flak-Bait" Crew

No crew manifest in the records

No briefing or interrogation timings recorded.

T/off: 1511 hrs.	Target: no attack:	Return: 1727 hrs.

Mission Narrative

Thirty-six aircraft dispatched. Mission abortive due to weather.

Route was Base to Splasher Beacon No. 8 to Rye to Dungeness to Folkestone and return to Base.

The leading 387th BG were four minutes late at the fighter rendezvous; fighters turned the formation back three minutes before reaching landfall. Turned back because of 10/10th altocumulus at 14,000 ft.

Mission Notes and "Flak-Bait" Crew Debrief Comments
"Flak-Bait" is listed on the radio form as having used Splasher Beacon Nos. 7 and 8, but no other details about this abortive mission are known.

```
Date: October 21, 1943
Target: Evreux-Fauville A/D
Field Order: 9th BC F/O 122
```

"Flak-Bait" Crew
No crew manifest in the records

No briefing or interrogation timings recorded.

| T/off: 0757 hrs. | Target: no attack | Return: 0922 hrs. |

Mission Narrative
Due to attack Evreux-Fauville A/D with the 387th BG; thirty-six aircraft dispatched but recalled by 9th Bomber Command at 0851 hrs., while over the north Kent coast, when the formation was heading toward Splasher Beacon No. 8, and prior to the fighter rendezvous.

Mission Notes and "Flak-Bait" Crew Debrief Comments
"Flak-Bait" is one of thirty-six aircraft on the radio call sheet, all aircraft listed as having used Splasher Beacon No. 8; no further details known.

```
Date: October 22, 1943
Target: Evreux-Fauville A/D
Field Order: 9th BC F/O 124
```

"Flak-Bait" Crew
1Lt. J. J. Farrell, pilot
F/O T. F. Moore, copilot
2Lt. O. J. Redmond, navigator/bombardier

TSgt. D. L. Tyler, engineer/gunner
SSgt. J. B. Manuel, radio/gunner
SSgt. N. E. Thielan, gunner

Briefing started at 0758 hrs. and ended 0805 hrs.

| T/off: 0845 hrs. | Rendezvous: 0956 hrs. | Landfall: 1009 hrs. |
| Target: 1030½ hrs. | Coast Out: 1046 hrs. | Return: 1126 hrs. |

Mission Narrative
Thirty-five aircraft dispatched, led by Lt. Col. G. C. Nye, with Maj. G. C. Celio. The 2nd Box was led by Maj. O. D. Turner.

Briefed route was Base to Splasher Beacon No. 8, and rendezvous with 387th BG, the 322nd to lead. To Beachy Head to 50.10'N, 00.20'E (off Fecamp), and rendezvous with the RAF Spitfire escort to 5 miles southwest of St.-Valery-en-Caux to Autheuil to target. Formation left English coast between Newhaven and Beachy Head, and evasive action took formation to the left of Rouen and then remained to left of the briefed course all the way to the IP.

Thirty-two aircraft attacked primary, dropping 189 × 500 GP bombs for fair results. Four aircraft aborted; one couldn't catch the formation and three because of mechanical problems. A total of 27 × 500 GP bombs returned, three of which were from rack failures.

Slight inaccurate gunfire from Rouen area on route in at 1024 hrs. and on route out at 1038 hrs.

From the target to the coast formation, flew to right of briefed course and made exit 3 miles to east of briefed exit point and entered English coast at Bexhill instead of Beachy Head; these deviations were due to a wind shift.

Interrogation of crews began at 1115 hrs. and finished at 1230 hrs.

Mission Notes and "Flak-Bait" Crew Debrief Comments

"Flak-Bait" flew as No. 5 aircraft, low flight, 1st Box.

Abortive: turned back over French coast at 1005 hrs., due to left engine trouble; the oil pressure was down and temperature up. Upon return, this was put down to pilot error, since the oil shutters had not been checked properly. 6 × 500 GP bombs jettisoned in the Channel. Requested a QDM from West Malling. Crew thought they had made landfall, but mission denied and declared abortive.

Crew also recommends that all pilots should have a cold-weather briefing and a procedure set up teaching them exactly what to do in poor weather conditions. The navigator didn't get a weather brief and should have.

> **Date: October 24, 1943**
> **Target: Montdidier A/D**
> **Field Order: 9th BC F/O 126**

"Flak-Bait" Crew

1Lt. J. J. Farrell, pilot
F/O T. F. Moore, copilot
1Lt. C. H. Richardson, navigator/bombardier

TSgt. D. L. Tyler, engineer/gunner
SSgt. J. B. Manuel, radio/gunner
SSgt. N. E. Thielan, gunner

No briefing or interrogation timings recorded.

T/off: 1018 hrs.	Rendezvous: 1153 hrs.	Landfall: 1210 hrs.
Target: 1229 hrs.	Coast Out: 1245 hrs.	Return: 1320 hrs.

Mission Narrative

Thirty-six aircraft dispatched; the 1st Box was led by Maj. B. G. Willis with Maj. O. D. Turner, and the 2nd Box was led by Capt. G. B. Simler.

Route was Base to Nth Foreland, for rendezvous with the 323rd BG, to Rye for rendezvous with the RAF Spitfire escort, to Cayeux to Breteuil to target.

Thirty-one aircraft attacked at 1229 hrs. from 11,300 ft., in CAVU conditions, releasing 120 × 1,000 GP bombs. One aircraft jettisoned 4 × 1,000 GPs one minute before the IP due to e/a attacks, while in distress, and another three jettisoned over the sea, two through rack failures and one because of personnel failure; a total of 8 × 1,000 GPs jettisoned. Another aircraft returned early with 4 × 1000 GPs because the navigator was sick.

Inaccurate flak encountered in Cayeux area at 1210 hrs., and moderate inaccurate HFF and intense inaccurate LFF at 1213 hrs. encountered when 10 miles northwest of Abbeville. At 1227, intense accurate HFF fire was encountered at Breteuil and intense accurate HFF over the target. On return route, moderate inaccurate LFF encountered near Ault at 1245 hrs.

E/a attacked formation in Breteuil area from 1220 to 1230 hrs., when in the Montdidier area; the RAF Spitfire escort estimated seeing approximately 70 e/a. The e/a took advantage of the cloud cover and made approximately fifty passes at the formation, resulting in seventy-one encounter reports. Of the thirty-five B-26s in the formation, twenty-eight were engaged by approximately forty e/a, at least fifty-four times; in several instances the e/a attacked in pairs, threes, and fours. Determined and repeated attacks were made down to approximately 30 yards. Head-on attacks from eleven o'clock, high, predominated, although some tail approaches were made from below. Gunners claimed three e/a destroyed; claims were awarded to TSgt. D. L. Tyler on "Flak-Bait," Sgt. G. Gans, 450th BS, and to Sgt. D. L. Nimblett, 452nd BS; two e/a were claimed as probably destroyed and two damaged, shared by several gunners.

Thirteen aircraft damaged Cat. A, four Cat. AC, and one Cat. B mostly by flak; two aircraft by flak and e/a damage, and one by e/a alone. One person KIA: SSgt. A. D. Moser, 451st BS, and six were wounded: SSgt. W. F.

Stark, 449th BS; SSgt. A. D. Moser, 451st BS; and SSgt. B. W. Allenbaugh, SSgt. N. J. Huschka, and Sgt. E. C. Peterson of the 450th BS—the last three men all in the aircraft 41-31746 ER-K "Lorraine II," which was damaged Cat. B by the e/a and was subsequently written off.

Return route was a left turn off the target to Ault to Hastings to Base.

Mission Notes and "Flak-Bait" Crew Debrief Comments

"Flak-Bait" flew as No. 6 in the high flight, 1st Box.

Aircraft received Cat. AC damage. 20 mm shell hole through nacelle of left engine and to bomb bay doors, making a 6" hole. Small flak hole to aileron.

4 × 1,000 GPs released; crew reported one bomb on the runway and balance in the target area, for good results. Saw fires start in a building.

"Flak-Bait" Encounter Report

Attack came at 1228 hrs. in the target area while at 11,500 ft. Four e/a made pass, but only one attacked. E/a (a Fw 190) had a yellow nose. Came in at eleven o'clock high out of the clouds and went away at 5–6 o'clock. The bombardier (1Lt. Richardson) fired twenty rounds from 150 to 50 yards, the turret gunner (Sgt. Thielan) fired sixty rounds from 150 yards, the waist gunner (Sgt. Manuel) fired forty rounds from 150 yards, and the tail gunner (Sgt. Tyler) fired 175 rounds from 150 yards, all saying that they saw hits to the e/a. Crew reported that the e/a started smoking after the turret gunner fired; tail gunner saw e/a crash after watching uncontrolled dive.

After reinterrogation the gunners agreed that TSgt. D. L. Tyler, the tail gunner, should be given the credit.

Other Crew Comments

Spitfire, hit by flak, seen to spiral down in the target area.

Several crews complained that the formation was flown too loose and too fast.

Gunners need more air-to-air practice.

One crew reported seeing four gunners crawl out of turrets immediately on leaving enemy coast; also some waist gunners seen to close windows at this time.

Category E Information
41-31746 ER-K, "Lorraine II"

Pilot was Capt. M. E. McNulty, flying in the No. 6

While flak was an ever-present danger, as is evident with a shell bursting close to 41-18277 SS-D, "Satan's Sister," this photo also seems to show the smoke trail of an aircraft, possibly an enemy fighter, spinning down; despite research, the actual date of the photo has not been identified. *Trevor J. Allen collection*

41-18289 PN-R, "Colonel Rebel," was flying alongside "Flak-Bait" on her last mission to Montdidier on October 24, 1943, piloted by 2Lt. E. R. Bruner and crew. Suffering Cat. AC damage, with numerous dents to the fuselage, flak damage to the rudder and top turret, and a 20 mm shell in the right engine. The aircraft was repaired at a depot and reassigned to the 323rd BG. *IWM / Roger A. Freeman collection, FRE4556*

position in the low flight, 1st Box. Damaged in the e/a attacks, all three gunners were wounded and were in distress before reaching the IP; jettisoned 4 × 1,000 GPs in the Channel. Landed with both main tires flat; aircraft declared Cat. B damage but was subsequently written off.

41-31746 ER-K, "Lorraine II." *Mike Smith, B26.com*

"Lorraine II" after her return from the Montdidier mission; all three gunners were wounded in the enemy aircraft (e/a) attacks. *USAAF*

Date: November 3, 1943
Target: St.-Andre-de-l'Eure A/D
Field Order: 9th BC F/O 129

"Flak-Bait" Crew

1Lt. J. J. Farrell, pilot
F/O T. F. Moore, copilot
2Lt. R. G. Caldwell, navigator/bombardier

TSgt. D. L. Tyler, engineer/gunner
SSgt. J. B. Manuel, radio/gunner
SSgt. N. E. Thielan, gunner

Briefing started at 0715 hrs. and ended 0800 hrs.

T/off: 0914 hrs.	Rendezvous: 1043 hrs.	Landfall: 1041 hrs.
Target: 1102 hrs.	Coast Out: 1122 hrs.	Return: 1230 hrs.

Mission Narrative

Thirty-six aircraft dispatched, led by Capt. R. A. Porter; the 2nd Box was led by Maj. O. D. Turner.

Briefed route was Base to Splasher Beacon No. 8, for rendezvous with the 387th BG, who were to lead, to Pevensey Bay to 50.10'N, 00.40'E (off St.-Valery-en-Caux), for fighter rendezvous, to 3 miles northeast of St.-Valery-en-Caux to Arnieres to target. Landfall was actually made south of Fecamp, to catch up with the 387th BG, who were off course; rest of route was flown continually to the right of briefed course up to the IP. Rendezvous with the RAF Spitfires was made inside the French coast, at 1043 hrs.; formation made "S" turns while waiting.

Six aircraft attacked at 1102 hrs., from 10,000 ft., releasing 143 × 1,000 GP for good results. One aircraft jettisoned 1 × 1,000 GP. Weather in target area was 3–4/10th stratocumulus.

Weak inaccurate LFF encountered 5 miles northeast of St.-Valery; no flak in immediate target area. Weak inaccurate LFF and HFF from Evreux and Conches and weak to moderate HFF in the Cany-Barville area and from southwest of St.-Valery upon exit.

"Lil Po'k Chop," 41-18250 SS-B, turning off the target at St.-Andre-de l'Eure on November 3, 1943, just prior to the e/a attacks. *Author's collection*

A large number of e/a were seen in the vicinity of the formation; 12–15 Fw 190s and Me 109s approached at 1108 hrs. when the formation was at 10,000 ft. in the Elbeuf area. Attacking from out of the sun, 4–7 e/a got through to the formation, resulting in eleven encounters with the bombers. Attacks predominantly from six o'clock low; apart from the aircraft MIA, no other damage was received. Last encounter was reported at 1120 hrs., when in vicinity of Verville.

One aircraft MIA due to e/a action, six MIA. E/a claims made were 1-0-1, but allowed claims were 0-0-2. Return was a right turn to 5 miles southwest of St.-Valery-en-Caux to Beachy Head to Base. Interrogation of crews began at 1225 hrs. and finished at 1410 hrs.

Mission Notes and "Flak-Bait" Crew Debrief Comments
"Flak-Bait" flew as No. 2 low flight, 2nd Box; takeoff was at 0928 hrs. and landed at 1227 hrs.

4 × 1,000 GPs dropped; crew reported good results. Observed e/a taking off from St.-Andre-de-l'Eure after it had been bombed.

"Flak-Bait" Encounter Report
Approximately ten minutes after the target, a Fw 190 came in level from six o'clock position and fired at this B-26. SSgt. D. L. Tyler fired from 175 to 200 yards and observed hits in cowling and wings; didn't see anything fall off but was sure he hit him. E/a departed to nine o'clock under control but smoking. E/a described as being silver with a yellow nose and had a black number on the side—probably "57." When last seen, Spitfires were seen closing in on e/a. SSgt. D. L. Tyler, tail gunner, credited with one e/a damaged.

MIA Information
41-34763 PN-J, "Duchess of Barksdale"
Flying as No. 5 aircraft in low flight, 2nd Box (same flight as "Flak-Bait"), dropped behind and below the formation after the target was bombed. Two Fw 190s attacked twice simultaneously from nine and three o'clock above. Aircraft started to fall to about 500 ft.,

41-34763 PN-J, "Duchess of Barksdale," seen in the background behind 41-31788 PN-A, which would be named "Truman Committee"; a photo taken during the summer of 1943 while flying over England. *USAAF*

then nosed down and crashed and exploded in Quittebeuf / Le Neubourg area. Three returning crews reported seeing from 1 to 4 and possibly five chutes.

F/O W. E. Mildren, pilot	POW
F/O E. O. Grubb, copilot	Evaded, returned to the UK on March 2, 1944
2Lt. S. S. Bolesta, navigator/bombardier	initially evaded, captured February 26, 1944
TSgt. K. M. Rimer, engineer/gunner	POW
SSgt. W. K. Lahm, radio/gunner	POW
SSgt. H. T. Cunningham, gunner	POW

Date: November 5, 1943
Target: Mimoyecques C/W
Field Order: 9th BC F/O 132

"Flak-Bait" Crew

1Lt. J. J. Farrell, pilot	TSgt. D. L. Tyler, engineer/gunner
F/O T. F. Moore, copilot	SSgt. J. B. Manuel, radio/gunner
2Lt. O. J. Redmond, navigator/bombardier	SSgt. N. E. Thielan, gunner

Briefing started at 0940 hrs. and ended 1000 hrs.

T/off: 1147, 1156 & 1206 hrs.   Rendezvous: 1310 & 1320 hrs.   Landfall: 1313 & 1323 hrs.

Target: 1320 & 1329 hrs.   Coast Out: 1322 & 1331 hrs.   Return: 1438 hrs.

Mission Narrative

Fifty-four aircraft dispatched; the 1st Box was led by Capt. G. B. Simler, the 2nd Box by Capt. H. M. Posson, and the 3rd Box by Capt. F. F. Rezabek.

Route was Base to Dungeness to 50.40'N, 01.25'E (off Berck-sur-Mer), rendezvous with RAF Spitfires was made 8 miles from the French coast, to 4 miles south of Hardelot to Samer to Haute Foret to target.

Fifty-two aircraft attacked, dropping 97 × 2,000 GP bombs from 10,000 ft. through 5/10th cloud cover, for fair results; the remainder of the route was 10/10th cloud covered. Three aircraft jettisoned 3 × 2,000 GPs in Channel, and five aircraft returned a total of 6 × 2,000 GP bombs through rack failures. One aircraft was shot down by flak prior to the target.

Moderate inaccurate HFF at landfall, slight inaccurate from Samer. Intense very accurate HFF from beginning of the turn into the bombing run and followed beyond the coast on exit. Thirty-three aircraft received Cat. A damage, and one aircraft MIA, seven MIA, and one man wounded: 1Lt. G. T. Fleming, 451st BS.

Return route was a left turn off the target to Hythe to Base.

Some crews reported that P-38s and P-47s were flying around the field and disrupted the entire landing procedure for the formation.

Interrogation of crews began at 1350 hrs. and finished at 1605 hrs.

Mission Notes and "Flak-Bait" Crew Debrief Comments

"Flak-Bait" flew in the No. 6 position, low flight, 1st Box.

2 × 2,000 GP bombs dropped; results unobserved.

Bomb run was too long.

A six-gun battery observed 1 mile northwest of the target.

Crew reported that transportation was lousy; waited forty-five minutes and no sandwiches left for this crew.

Also request a decent latrine at the crew room and issue extra cigarettes to crews; seven packs a week is not enough.

Reported as Cat. A damage on one report, but none reported on the debrief form.

MIA Information
41-18075 DR-J, "Mr. Five by Five"

Flying as No. 4 aircraft in lead flight; 1st Box received a direct hit about ten seconds before the bomb release point, at 1319 hrs. Flak exploded in the radio compartment, and the aircraft burst into flames. Aircraft slid to the left under control and was seen to disintegrate, with both wings to come off, when about 500 ft. below the formation. Three possibly four chutes were reported.

1Lt. H. M. Price, pilot	KIA
2Lt. W. R. Rawlings, copilot	KIA
2Lt. J. W. Bunker, bombardier	KIA
2Lt. A. W. Joyner, navigator	KIA
SSgt. J. E. Gust, engineer/gunner	KIA
TSgt. J. V. May, radio/gunner	KIA
SSgt. W. P. Creekmore, gunner	POW

"Flak-Bait" Crew

1Lt. K. L. Bayles, pilot
2Lt. S. M. Chase, copilot
1Lt. J. Papastergiou, navigator/bombardier

TSgt. C. M. Smajenski, engineer/gunner
SSgt. P. Saffron, radio/gunner
SSgt. I. C. Wynn, gunner

No briefing or interrogation timings recorded.

T/off: 0820 hrs.
Target: 1001 hrs.

Rendezvous: 0938 hrs.
Coast Out: 1023 hrs.

Landfall: 0943 hrs.
Return: 1115 hrs.

Mission Narrative

Combined formation consisting of a box of eighteen aircraft each from the 322nd, 323rd, 386th, and 387th BGs.

Maj. B. G. Willis led the 322nd BG Box.

Route was Base to West Malling, for rendezvous with the 323rd BG, to Splasher Beacon No. 9 for rendezvous with the 386th and 387th formation, to Beachy Head to 50.10'N, 00.40'E (off St.-Valery-en-Caux), for fighter rendezvous; escort provided by P-38s and P-47s from VIII FC, to 6 miles west of Pointe d'Ailly to Limay to IP. Since the target was obscured, formation headed for secondary (Beauvais-Tille A/D) and turned when it was seen that this and last-resort target (Poix/Nord A/D) were both cloud covered.

One aircraft ("Flak-Bait") returned early through loss of power, and seventeen aborted because of weather; 108 × 500 GPs returned.

Intermittent slight inaccurate HFF en route to target from west of Pointe d'Ailly, Yvetot, Rouen area, Les Andelys area, Vernon, Mantes-Gassicourt, and primary target area. None encountered on the route back.

Six e/a tried to attack the formation four times, from 1052 hrs. while near Guyon, predominantly from the clouds below, but the P-38s did not allow them to break through closer than 800 yards. Three encounters took place, but the closeness of the P-38s to the e/a prevented the gunners from firing.

Exit of the enemy coast was made at Pointe d'Ailly to Hastings to Base.

Mission Notes and "Flak-Bait" Crew Debrief Comments

"Flak-Bait" to fly as No. 2 in the high flight but aborted due to a loss of power.

Abortive: 6 × 500 GPs returned—early return due to loss of power—oil congealed and oil temperature went up to 120 degrees and the pressure dropped. Left engine dropped 300 rpm but returned to normal at 5,000 ft.

"Flak-Bait" Crew

1Lt. J. J. Farrell, pilot
F/O T. F. Moore, copilot
2Lt. G. L. McMillan, navigator/bombardier

TSgt. D. L. Tyler, engineer/gunner
SSgt. J. B. Manuel, radio/gunner
SSgt. N. E. Thielan, gunner

Briefing started at 1115 hrs. and ended 1200 hrs.

T/off: 1314 hrs.
Target: 1452 hrs.

Rendezvous: 1430 hrs.
Coast Out: 1517 hrs.

Landfall: 1434 hrs.
Return: 1605 hrs.

Mission Narrative

All four groups to provide a box of eighteen aircraft to form composite formations.

Eighteen aircraft dispatched, led by Maj. F. F. Rezabek.

Route was Base to Splasher Beacon No. 9 for rendezvous with the 323rd BG, who were to lead, to Beachy Head, where a formation made up of boxes from the 386th and 387th BGs was met, to 50.10'N, 01.00'E (off Dieppe), where rendezvous with VIII FC P-38s and P-47s was made, to 10 miles northeast of Dieppe to 5 miles south of Poix to Breteuil to target.

No attack due to weather, 6–8/10th cloud at target; sixteen aircraft returned 96 × 500 GPs; two aircraft jettisoned 12 × 500 GPs in Channel, one due to engine trouble.

Slight inaccurate LFF and HFF in Breteuil area, and slight inaccurate HFF just north of Montdidier and near Arras, Guines, St. Inglevert, and east of Sangatte within 5 miles of Calais. Intense accurate LFF and HFF from the Calais defenses. Eleven aircraft received Cat. A damage. One man wounded: 2Lt. W. E. Schuele, 452nd BS.

Briefed return was to exit coast at Pointe Haute, but route back flown was to Albert, to the left of St.-Omer, then to Sangatte to Nth Foreland to Base.

Interrogation of crews began at 1620 hrs. and finished at 1700 hrs.

Mission Notes and "Flak-Bait" Crew Debrief Comments

"Flak-Bait" flew as the No. 6 ship in the low flight.

Takeoff and route to target as briefed; slight inaccurate flak before target.

Did not bomb primary due to clouds obscuring target. Secondary seen but not bombed. 6 × 500 GPs returned.

Exit from coast made to right of Calais instead of following 323rd.

Heavy intense accurate flak over exit; no damage received.

P-47 and P-38 escort excellent.

Crew requests cigarettes be issued instead of candy, and more fuel for the Huts.

Other Crew Comments

Formation felt prop wash from the P-38s throughout entire mission.

Poor navigation by the lead box from the 323rd Bomb Group.

> **Date: November 11, 1943**
> **Target: Martinvast C/W**
> **Field Order: 9th BC F/O 138**

"Flak-Bait" Crew

1Lt. J. J. Farrell, pilot
F/O T. F. Moore, copilot
2Lt. G. S. Goldstein, navigator/bombardier

TSgt. D. L. Tyler, engineer/gunner
SSgt. J. B. Manuel, radio/gunner
SSgt. N. E. Thielan, gunner

Briefing started at 0830 hrs. and ended 1000 hrs.

T/off: 1035 & 1038 hrs.	Rendezvous: 1205 & 1208 hrs.	Landfall: 1218 & 1225 hrs.
Target: 1225 & 1231 hrs.	Coast Out: 1229 & 1235 hrs.	Return: 1409 & 1405 hrs.

Mission Narrative

All four groups detailed to send three boxes, a thirty-six-ship formation, and a further box of eighteen to make up composite formations, a few minutes later.

Thirty-six-ship formation led by Capt. H. M. Posson, with the 2nd Box led by Capt. R. A. Porter, and an eighteen-ship formation led by Capt. H. V. Smythe, which was to lead a box from the 323rd BG.

A total of fifty-two aircraft dispatched; route was Base to Gravesend to Selsey Bill to 50.20'N, 01.00'E (off Criel-sur-Mer), for fighter rendezvous, to Isle-de-St.-Marcouf to Quineville to target.

Forty-nine aircraft released 96 × 2,000 GPs, from 11,500 ft., through 5–7/10th cloud with tops at 6,000 ft., for good results. One aircraft jettisoned 1 × 2,000 GP. Three aircraft were early returns, two through engine trouble and another that couldn't catch the formation due to a late takeoff. A total of 7 × 2,000 GPs returned.

Formation of thirty-six encountered moderate fairly accurate HFF over the target, which seemed to be set up in barrage form by guns in Cherbourg area. Between Cap Hague and Alderney Island, moderate fairly accurate HFF was encountered, most of which came from Alderney.

Second group of eighteen, following six minutes later, met intense accurate HFF in both target area and also between Cap Hague and Alderney.

Thirteen aircraft received Cat. A damage; two gunners were injured by flak: TSgt. C. M. Smajenski and SSgt. C. T. Duke, both from the 449th BS.

Return was target to 49.35'N, 02.00'W (north of Jersey), to 5 miles east of Alderney to Selsey Bill to Base. Interrogation of crews began at 1345 hrs. and finished at 1510 hrs.

Mission Notes and "Flak-Bait" Crew Debrief Comments

"Flak-Bait" flew as No. 2 in the high flight of the eighteen-ship formation. Took off at 1101 hrs. and landed at 1415 hrs.

2 × 2,000 GPs released for good results.

Intense accurate HFF from Alderney Island; at least fifteen guns seen firing from center of island.

Aircraft 773 had radio wiring shot up—wiring now being checked. Two holes in left nacelle.

Comment on debrief form: "Get something to eat over here." (*Author*: presumably meaning at the debriefing session).

Other Crew Comments

Spitfire observed to go down in water at 1257 hrs., 10 miles off enemy coast; saw chute open.

> **Date: November 19, 1943**
> **Target: St.-Andre-de-l'Eure A/D**
> **Field Order: 9th BC F/O 141**

"Flak-Bait" Crew

2Lt. E. R. Bruner, pilot	TSgt. W. H. Evans, engineer/gunner
2Lt. R. R. Crusey, copilot	SSgt. B. O. Benoit, radio/gunner
2Lt. R. P. Gilmore, navigator/bombardier	SSgt. E. W. Gibson, gunner

Briefing started at 0900 hrs. and ended 1015 hrs.

T/off: 1242 hrs.	Rendezvous: 1359 hrs.	Landfall: 1403 hrs.
Target: no attack	Coast Out: 1403½ hrs.	Return: 1502 hrs.

Mission Narrative

Thirty-six aircraft dispatched, led by Capt. G. B. Simler; the 2nd Box led by Capt. G. H. Watson.

Route was to be Base to Splasher Beacon No. 8 for rendezvous with the 323rd BG, to Brighton to 50.00'N, 00.00'E (off Etretat), for rendezvous with RAF Spitfires, to 5 miles southwest of Fecamp. Route back was to be via Beachy Head to Base.

Bad weather and icing conditions prevented formation from assembling properly. One had mechanical failure, seven returned due to icing, and twelve were unable to form up; sixteen further aircraft were recalled due to 8/10th cloud over the Channel. 108 × 500 GP and 180 × 300 GP bombs returned.

Three flights managed to rendezvous with the 323rd and followed four minutes behind them to the fighter rendezvous point, arriving one minute early. Course set for enemy coast and caught up with 323rd at Etretat, on the enemy coast. Made a 360-degree turn with them and exited 2 miles southwest of Fecamp, and returned via Beachy Head. Fighters were not seen until formation was turning back over the French coast.

Two crews reported slight inaccurate HFF over Fecamp at 1403 hrs.

High flight of the 2nd Box, consisting of five aircraft (including "Flak-Bait") tacked onto the 387th BG formation over the Channel, who were scheduled to bomb Evreux-Fauville A/D, but formation turned back 10 miles from the enemy coast. Did not hear any recall signal.

Interrogation of crews began at 1500 hrs. and finished at 1605 hrs.

Mission Notes and "Flak-Bait" Crew Debrief Comments
"Flak-Bait" No. 6 ship in the high flight of the 2nd Box; this flight attached itself to the 387th BG formation but turned back with them when 10 miles from enemy coast.

Flight leader seemed to be having trouble over England; made a sharp turn and stalled the other aircraft out. They made an "S" turn and got back in formation, but flight never got into box formation (flight leader was an early return—could not maintain airspeed). Saw two possible Me 109s at French coast; they did not try to engage. 10 × 300 GPs returned.

No sandwiches left when this crew got back.

Date: November 23, 1943
Target: St.-Omer-Longuenesse A/D
Field Order: 9th BC F/O 143

"Flak-Bait" Crew

1Lt. J. J. Farrell, pilot
F/O T. F. Moore, copilot
2Lt. O. J. Redmond, navigator/bombardier

TSgt. D. L. Tyler, engineer/gunner
SSgt. J. B. Manuel, radio/gunner
SSgt. N. E. Thielan, gunner

Briefing started at 0830 hrs. and ended 0930 hrs.

T/off: 1132 hrs.	Rendezvous: 1245 hrs.	Landfall: 1256 hrs.
Target: 1304 hrs.	Coast Out: 1319 hrs.	Return: Various (formation diverted)

Mission Narrative
Thirty-six aircraft dispatched; the 1st Box was led by Capt. G. B. Simler, and the 2nd Box by Capt. G. H. Watson.

Routing was Base to Splasher Beacon No. 9, for rendezvous with the 323rd BG, the 322nd to lead, to Hastings, and rendezvous with RAF Spitfire escort, to 5 miles south of Hardelot to Desvres to target.

Formation made two runs at the target; the lead bombardier of the 1st Box failed to pick out the target until he was right over it so could not make a sighting. The lead aircraft of the high flight, 1st Box, did release, as did three others in that flight. The 2nd Box attacked. A total of twenty-two aircraft dropped 169 × 300 GP and 24 × 500 GP bombs for poor results, two aircraft jettisoned 6 × 500 GPs and 1 × 300 GP in the Channel, and thirteen aircraft returned 78 × 500 GP bombs. One aircraft was a mechanical abort and returned early.

"Clarks Little Pill," in the foreground, taxies out, leading other Marauders from the 322nd BG for another mission. *USAAF*

Weak scattered HFF at landfall; intense accurate HFF from the IP through the bombing run and in the target area. Considerable tracer fire was also experienced here. In making turn past target, HFF was experienced from Hazebrouck and Aire, which was moderate and accurate. Moderate accurate HFF between Fruges and Hucqueliers. Weak to moderate HFF from Sames/Desvres area, and both LFF and HFF, mostly weak and inaccurate, from coast south of Hardelot to Le Touquet.

Twenty-nine aircraft damaged by flak, all Cat. A; one aircraft was shot down by flak over the target, six MIA. Two men were slightly wounded. Wounded were treated at Mildenhall (2Lt. R. G. Caldwell, 449th BS) and Molesworth (2Lt. H. R. Fletcher, 452nd BS).

Return route was a right turn off the target to 5 miles south of Hardelot to Hastings to Base. Formation flew over home field at 1354 hrs. but then proceeded to diversion fields, because of poor visibility. Fifteen landed at Molesworth, ten at Lakenheath, seven at Mildenhall, one at Feltwell, and one at Chelveston, and "Flak-Bait," which was reported as landing at Haywards Heath.

Interrogation of crews began at 2130 hrs. and finished at 2210 hrs., for some crews—remainder interrogated the following morning starting at 0930 hrs. and finished at 1145 hrs.

Mission Notes and "Flak-Bait" Crew Debrief Comments

"Flak-Bait" flew as No. 6 in the low flight, 1st Box. Takeoff was at 1118 hrs. and landed at Haywards Heath at 1420 hrs.

Cat. A flak damage—air scoop on right engine, leading edge to wing, top turret glass, rudder, and elevator.

Flak bursting below the formation. *Author's collection*

Returned 6 × 500 GPs since leader did not drop; reason unknown.

Command set intermittent—checked out OK on ground.

Gunners reported seeing only a few Spitfires.

Other Crew Comments

All squadron ops officers should be given same hour of briefing; all squadrons given different times.

Why do engineer/gunners have to work on the line when not flying?

Got to landfall late; there was too much evasive action on the run in, when there was no flak or very little; formation lost 2½ minutes. Target reached at 1307 hrs., but formation was to right of the target and didn't drop. Did evasive action to the left and went over St.-Omer town, then turned right and made another run.

Suggest no second runs on targets; antiaircraft have been getting altitude too accurate; suggest changes in altitude during evasive action.

Saw Spitfires dogfighting at about 6,000 ft. northwest of the target.

Two B-26s seen to go down in flames at 1306 and 1307 hrs.

Spitfire seen to go down in target area; pilot bailed out.

MIA Information
41-31817 DR-W, "No Regrets"
Flying the No. 4 position in the lead flight, 2nd Box, hit by flak just after bomb release. Right wing caught fire and came off; seven crews reported seeing one chute.

Maj. F. F. Rezabek, pilot	KIA
2Lt. J. G. Siroki, copilot	KIA
1Lt. F. M. Matthews, navigator/bombardier	KIA
TSgt. C. T. Cook, engineer/gunner	KIA

SSgt. W. A. Terhune, radio/gunner   KIA
SSgt. R. H. Lussier, gunner   KIA

Maj. Rezabek was on his twenty-fifth and last mission with the 322nd BG prior to joining the newly formed 99th CBW as a member of staff.

Crews report that about fifteen seconds later, a 323rd BG ship was seen to be hit and go into a spin; no chutes observed (this aircraft, 41-34713 RJ-D "Stinkin Clinkin," was actually hit by a bomb from another aircraft that had hung up and then fallen, striking the left wing, which crumpled).

Date: November 29, 1943
Target: Chievres A/D
Field Order: 9th BC F/O 147

"Flak-Bait" Crew

1Lt. J. J. Farrell, pilot   TSgt. D. L. Tyler, engineer/gunner
F/O T. F. Moore, copilot   SSgt. J. B. Manuel, radio/gunner
2Lt. O. J. Redmond, navigator/bombardier   SSgt. N. E. Thielan, gunner

Briefing started at 0530 hrs. and ended 0630 hrs.

T/off: 0810 hrs.   Rendezvous: 0920 hrs.   Landfall: 0926 hrs.
Target: 0942 hrs.   Coast Out: 1003 hrs.   Return: 1041 hrs.

Mission Narrative

Thirty-six aircraft dispatched; the 1st Box was led by Capt. N. L. Harvey with Capt. L. J. Sebille. The 2nd Box was led by Capt. D. E. Harnly with Maj. B. G. Willis.

Route was Base to Bradwell Bay, where rendezvous was made with the 386th BG, the 322nd to lead, to Nth Foreland, to 51.20'N, 02.00'E (off Dunkirk), for rendezvous with RAF Spitfires, to 4 miles northwest Furnes to 4 miles northeast of Courtrai to Leuze to target.

Thirty-one aircraft attacked the target, in clear conditions, releasing 184 × 500 GPs from 12,000 ft. for good results. One aircraft jettisoned 6 × 500 GPs in the Channel, and four others returned 20 × 500 GPs. Ice forming on the Plexiglas nose cones made identification of the target difficult; one bombardier could not see at all so did not release.

Weak flak, accurate for height but not course, from just beyond the IP to past the target. Inaccurate LFF from the target, Dixmunde and Furnes areas. A few bursts of inaccurate HFF believed to have been fired from Nieuport area at exit. Six aircraft received Cat. A damage.

Return route was a left turn off the target to 4 miles northeast of Courtrai to 4 miles northwest of Furnes, to Nth Foreland to Base.

Interrogation of crews began at 1045 hrs. and finished at 1235 hrs.

Mission Notes and "Flak-Bait" Crew Debrief Comments

"Flak-Bait" flew as No. 6 aircraft, high flight, 2nd Box.

6 × 500 GP on target.

Route flown as briefed; no flak at landfall; slight heavy, fairly accurate at target. Bombing results observed as good; no flak at exit.

Tail gunner fired thirty rounds at a Fw 190 at 800 yards' range when just past target; no claim made.

Tail guns had an electrical fault after leaving French coast.

Combat crews waited 1½ to 2 hours for parachute department to open. Chute for Sgt. Thielan had been there for four days for repacking and had not been touched.

Fifty missions too much!

Other Crew Comments

Two crews reported hearing on VHF that an aircraft K for King (from another group) was bailing crew out at 1020 hrs., position 50.14'N, 00.40'E (in the Channel between St.-Valery-en-Caux and Eastbourne). It was also reported that this aircraft was now returning to base and that two crewmen had bailed out.

```
Date: December 1, 1943
Target: Lille-Vendeville A/D
Field Order: 9th BC F/O 149
```

"Flak-Bait" Crew

1Lt. D. Isgrig, pilot
2Lt. C. J. Gemmell, copilot
1Lt. C. H. Richardson, navigator/bombardier

SSgt. W. M. Greer, engineer/gunner
TSgt. D. J. Mertes, radio/gunner
SSgt. W. B. Satterfield, gunner

Briefing started at 0600 hrs. and ended 0700 hrs.

T/off: 0831 hrs.	Rendezvous: 0934 hrs.	Landfall: 0942½ hrs.
Target: 0958 hrs.	Coast Out: 1022 hrs.	Return: 1123 hrs.

Mission Narrative

Thirty-five aircraft dispatched; the 1st Box was led by Capt. G. H. Watson with Capt. R. A. Porter. The 2nd Box was led by Maj. F. E. Fair with Capt. T. W. Nestlerode.

Route was Base to Splasher Beacon No. 8 to a line en route to Dungeness, for rendezvous with the 386th BG, who were to lead; rendezvous with RAF Spitfires was made at Dungeness, to 4 miles south of Hardelot to 4 miles north of Bethune to target.

Thirty-two aircraft attacked the primary, for fair results, releasing 317 × 300 GPs from 11,500 ft. One aircraft abortive because tail guns were out, and another because a parachute was accidentally deployed; both were early return; one aircraft did not release because of an intervalometer failure. A total of 30 × 300 GPs were returned, and another 3 × 300 GPs were jettisoned because of rack failure.

Weak inaccurate HFF first encountered from the Lillers/Merville area. Weak inaccurate HFF and LFF tracers bursting low at the IP, 4 miles north of Bethune. HFF at target, weak and accurate for height only. Weak inaccurate HFF from Aire and 25 to 30 bursts of inaccurate HFF, fired in salvoes of four, from northeast of Fruges. No aircraft were damaged.

Return was a right turn to 3 miles north of Lens to 4 miles south of Hardelot to Dungeness to Base.

Interrogation of crews began at 1115 hrs. and finished at 1220 hrs.

Mission Notes and "Flak-Bait" Crew Debrief Comments

"Flak-Bait" was No. 2 in the low flight of the 2nd Box. Takeoff was at 0840 hrs. and landing at 1125 hrs.

10 × 300 GP dropped for good results.

Fw 190 observed at 6,000 ft. over the target, but no attack made.

Take fixed nose gun out of the nose.

Food is generally cold when coming back from combat missions at the combat mess. Water for washing mess kits is greasy and unsuitable for the washing of mess kits.

Temporary Change of Command

In December 1943, Col. Glenn C. Nye, along with Brig. Gen. Curtis Le May and Col. Herbert Zemke, was chosen to return to the US to inform the Congress Committee, war workers, and students of the success and tribulations of American bombers and fighters in the ETO. Col. Nye's chief subject was the B-26, and all station section heads prepared data for his benefit.

Taking temporary command of the 322nd BG in his absence was Lt. Col. Grover C. Brown, assistant operations officer at 9th Bomber Command. Col. Nye returned on January 14, 1944, at which point Lt. Col. Grover C. Brown was promoted to full colonel and became the air executive of the 98th CBW. Later, in July 1944, he would take command of the 387th BG.

"Flak-Bait" Crew

1Lt. J. J. Farrell, pilot
F/O T. F. Moore, copilot
2Lt. O. J. Redmond, navigator/bombardier

TSgt. D. L. Tyler, engineer/gunner
SSgt. J. B. Manuel, radio/gunner
SSgt. N. E. Thielan, gunner

Briefing started at 1100 hrs. and ended 1205 hrs.
T/off: 1325 hrs.   Target: no attack   Return: 1551 hrs.

Mission Narrative

All four B-26 groups to provide a box of eighteen aircraft each to form composite formations.

Seventeen aircraft dispatched, led by Capt. G. B. Simler.

Briefed route was Base to Gravesend for rendezvous with the 386th BG to Splasher Beacon No. 8 to make rendezvous with the 323rd BG, who were to lead, to 50.40'N, 01.10'E (off Berck-sur-Mer), for fighter rendezvous then to 4 miles south of Hardelot to La Basse to target.

No attack; did not make proper rendezvous with the RAF Spitfire escort. Formation made a left turn 4 miles from enemy coast; the fighter escort was not seen until after the formation had turned back at 1452 hrs. Returned via Dungeness. Seventeen aircraft returned 510 × 100 GP bombs.

9/10th cloud plus stratocumulus with tops at 5/6,000 ft. obscured the target, causing an abort.

Weak to moderate HFF encountered from Hardelot and Boulogne; accurate for height but deflection inaccurate.

No interrogation timings recorded.

Mission Notes and "Flak-Bait" Crew Debrief Comments

"Flak-Bait" flew as No. 6 ship in the high flight.

Left English coast 1½ minutes later than briefed time; other groups were a full five minutes ahead of us.

Intense HFF from Boulogne; accurate for height but not course. Turned back off Hardelot.

Date: December 5, 1943
Target: XI/A/40 Ligescourt / Bois de St.-Saulve C/W, 36 a/c
XI/A/19 St.-Josse-au-Bois C/W, 18 a/c
Field Order: 9th BC F/O 153

"Flak-Bait" Crew

1Lt. J. J. Farrell, pilot
2Lt. W. F. Green, copilot
2Lt. O. J. Redmond, navigator/bombardier

TSgt. D. L. Tyler, engineer/gunner
SSgt. J. B. Manuel, radio/gunner
SSgt. N. E. Thielan, gunner

Briefing started at 0945 hrs.; no end time recorded.
T/off: 1217, 1230 & 1300 hrs.   Rendezvous: 1310 hrs.   Landfall: 1318, 1319 & 1349 hrs.
Target: 1322½, 1324 & 1352½ hrs.   Coast Out: 1325, 1326 & 1356 hrs.   Return: 1435 hrs.

Mission Narrative

Fifty-three aircraft dispatched; thirty-six-ship formation led by Maj. O. D. Turner with Capt. C. W. Hoover, with Maj. G. C. Celio and Col. J. J. Simpson (from 99th CBW) leading the 2nd Box. The eighteen-ship formation was led by Capt. R. A. Porter with Maj. E. Wursten.

Route was Base to Dungeness, for rendezvous with the 386th BG, who were to lead, to 50.40'N, 01.10'E (off Berck-sur-Mer), for fighter rendezvous with RAF Spitfire escort, to Berck-sur-Mer to target.

Thick haze was encountered at the target, with visibility down to 1 mile. 1st Box bombed Ligescourt, seventeen aircraft dropping 68 × 1,000 GPs from 12,000 ft. for fair to poor results; one aircraft had engine trouble and returned 4 × 1,000 GPs. 2nd Box lead bombardier could not pick out target, so no release was made; sixteen aircraft returned 64 × 1,000 GPs; one aircraft jettisoned 4 × 1,000 GPs. The 3rd Box attacked St. Josse, eighteen aircraft dropping 70 × 1,000 GPs for poor results from 11,000 ft.; one aircraft jettisoned 1 × 1,000 GP, and another returned 1 × 1,000 GP.

Weak inaccurate LFF between target and Berck-sur-Mer.

Return was a right turn to Rue, to Hastings and to Base.

Interrogation of crews began at 1430 hrs. and finished at 1545 hrs.

Mission Notes and "Flak-Bait" Crew Debrief Comments

"Flak-Bait" flew as No. 2 in the high flight, 2nd Box, of the thirty-six-ship formation.

Very uneventful trip; did not release; 4 × 1,000 GP bombs brought back.

Good formation.

Event: Luftwaffe Attacks against 9th Air Force Bases

On the night of December 10–11, 1943, approximately twenty Luftwaffe bombers sought out to attack several 9th Air Force bases in the northern part of Essex. Airfields that were attacked included Andrews Field, Earls Colne, Great Dunmow, and Gosfield. The damage was mostly minor, although eight persons were killed and a further twenty wounded at Gosfield, which, at this time, was still in the process of being completed. Only minor damage was experienced at Andrews Field.

```
Date: December 20, 1943
Target: XI/A/75 Le Meillard & XI/A/85 Bonnieres Noball, 36 a/c
XI/A/70 Cocove Noball, 18 a/c
Field Order: 9th BC F/O 160
```

"Flak-Bait" Crew

1Lt. J. J. Farrell, pilot
2Lt. W. F. Green, copilot
2Lt. O. J. Redmond, navigator/bombardier

TSgt. D. L. Tyler, engineer/gunner
SSgt. J. B. Manuel, radio/gunner
SSgt. N. E. Thielan, gunner

Briefing started at 0630 hrs. and ended 0900 hrs.

T/off: 0915 hrs.	Rendezvous: 1030 & 1040 hrs.	Landfall: 1046 & 1048 hrs.
Target: 1050 & 1055 hrs.	Coast Out: 1106 hrs.	Return: 1135 hrs.

Mission Narrative

Fifty-four plus two spare aircraft dispatched; thirty-six-ship formation led by Capt. G. H. Watson with Maj. E. Wursten; the 2nd Box was led by Lt. Col. G. C. Celio with Capt. D. L. Morrison. The eighteen-ship formation was led by Maj. F. E. Fair.

Route for thirty-six-ship formation was Base to rendezvous with the 386th BG on an assembly line from Gravesend to Hastings, the 386th to lead; rendezvous with RAF Spitfires was to be made at Hastings, to Ault to 8 miles southeast of Abbeville to target. Three aircraft were early returns.

Routing for the eighteen-ship formation was Base to rendezvous with the 386th BG on an assembly line from the Naze to Nth Foreland, the 322nd to lead, then to join up with a composite formation made up of aircraft from the 387th and 323rd BGs, on a line from Nth Foreland to Dungeness, the 387th to lead the whole formation. Fighter rendezvous to be made at Dungeness, to 4 miles north of Le Touquet to Desvres to target. RAF Spitfire escort was to be shared by all groups.

Cloud cover prevented bombing at all targets. One aircraft dropped 6 × 500 GPs at Agenvillers; remainder brought back 318 × 500 GPs; spares returned 12 × 500 GPs.

Flak for the thirty-six-ship formation was very slight inaccurate HFF at the IP, slight inaccurate LFF in Hesdin area, and weak inaccurate tracer fire, bursting low at exit near Berck-sur-Mer. The eighteen-ship formation encountered moderate accurate HFF from the Boulogne area; as the formation was turning to the right short of the coast, three aircraft received Cat. A damage.

Route back for thirty-six-ship formation was a left turn to Le Touquet, although actual exit was made at Berck-sur-Mer, after trying to attack as a target of last resort, to Hastings and Base. For the eighteen-aircraft formation it would have been a left turn to Gravelines to Nth Foreland to base, but formation turned back short of the coast due to weather.

All but eight aircraft landed at diversion airfields because of weather; all crews interrogated upon return to Base.

Interrogation of crews began at 1545 hrs. and finished at 1735 hrs.

Mission Notes and "Flak-Bait" Crew Debrief Comments

"Flak-Bait" flew as No. 4 in the low flight, 1st Box of the thirty-six-ship formation. Takeoff was at 0926 hrs., and landed at Thurleigh at 1235 hrs.

6 × 500 GP bombs brought back; target obscured by clouds; tried secondary but that wasn't clear.

Requested a QDM from Thurleigh and landed there.

Other Crew Comments

After the eighteen-ship formation turned back, a formation of Typhoons going into France came dangerously close to our formation—gunners nearly mistook them for e/a.

Date: December 21, 1943
Target: XI/A/83 Vacquerette Noball, 36 a/c
XI/A/70 Cocove Noball, 18 a/c
Field Order: 9th BC F/O 161

"Flak-Bait" Crew

1Lt. J. J. Farrell, pilot
F/O T. F. Moore, copilot
2Lt. O. J. Redmond, navigator/bombardier

TSgt. D. L. Tyler, engineer/gunner
SSgt. J. B. Manuel, radio/gunner
SSgt. N. E. Thielan, gunner

Briefing started at 0800 hrs. and ended 0915 hrs.

T/off: 0956 & 1020 hrs.	Rendezvous: 1101 & 1116 hrs.	Landfall: 1120 & 1126 hrs.
Target: 1137 & 1132½ hrs.	Coast Out: 1138 & 1137 hrs.	Return: 1305 hrs.

Mission Narrative

Fifty-four aircraft plus two spares dispatched to attack two V-1 sites. Thirty-six-ship formation led by Capt. G. B. Simler; the 2nd Box was led by Lt. Col. G. C. Celio with Maj. E. Wursten. The eighteen-ship formation was led by Capt. H. M. Posson.

Route for the thirty-six-ship formation was Base to rendezvous with the 386th BG, on an assembly line from Gravesend to Hastings for fighter rendezvous with RAF Spitfires, to Ault to 8 miles southeast of Abbeville to target.

The thirty-six-ship formation found the primary obscured by cloud; eighteen aircraft attacked Berck-sur-Mer A/D, at 1137 hrs. as a target of opportunity, dropping 102 × 500 GPs from 9,000 ft. Twenty aircraft brought back 111 × 500 GPs, which includes the two spare aircraft and one aircraft that was a mechanical abort; two aircraft jettisoned 3 × 500 GPs.

Slight to moderate inaccurate LFF, bursting 2,000 ft. below, at Ault, slight to moderate inaccurate LFF southeast of Abbeville. Slight to moderate LFF and slight HFF both inaccurate from Berck-sur-Mer.

Return was left turn to Le Touquet to Hastings, although route was flown to the right of briefed course, to Base.

Route for eighteen-ship formation was Base to rendezvous with 386th BG on an assembly line from Nth Foreland to Dungeness, where RAF Spitfire escort was met, to 4 miles north of Le Touquet to Desvres to target.

Seventeen aircraft dropped 102 × 500 GPs at 1132½ hrs. from 8,200 ft., for good results. One aircraft had rack failure and returned 6 × 500 GPs.

Slight to moderate inaccurate LFF and HFF at landfall; moderate inaccurate HFF from Boulogne; inaccurate barrage-type HFF from Foret d'Eperlecques, Watten and St.-Omer area. Weak inaccurate LFF from Gravelines on exit.

Return was a left turn to Gravelines to Nth Foreland to Base.

Interrogation of crews began at 1210 hrs. and finished at 1400 hrs. for the thirty-six-ship formation, while for the eighteen-ship formation this was begun at 1146 hrs. and finished at 1320 hrs.

Mission Notes and "Flak-Bait" Crew Debrief Comments
"Flak-Bait" flew as No. 2 high flight, 1st Box, of the thirty-six-ship formation.

Light flak from Ault.

Brought back 6 × 500 GPs.

Let's have transportation from squadron to mess hall and mess hall to briefing room for combat crews, especially when they are given short notice of briefing time.

Date: December 22, 1943
Target: XI/A/94 Audincthun Noball, 18 a/c
XI/A/85 Bonnieres Noball, 35 a/c
XI/A/57 Cormette Noball, 4 a/c (with 323rd BG)
Field Order: 9th BC F/O 162

"Flak-Bait" Crew

2Lt. K. W. Reed, pilot
1Lt. D. W. Allen, copilot
1Lt. J. C. Dick, navigator/bombardier

TSgt. A. M. Kondrasky, engineer/gunner
SSgt. E. V. McWilliams, radio/gunner
Sgt. B. D. Stoddard, gunner

Briefing started at 0640 hrs. and ended 0850 hrs.

T/off: 1120 & 1130½ hrs.	Rendezvous: 1233½ & 1245 hrs.	Landfall: 1240 & 1303 hrs.
Target: 1246 hrs.	Coast Out: 1255 & 1310 hrs.	Return: 1335 & 1330 hrs.

Mission Narrative
A total of fifty-seven aircraft dispatched to attack V-1 sites.

Eighteen-ship formation, to Audincthun, led by Capt. H. V. Smythe.

Route was Base to assembly line from Clacton to Nth Foreland, where rendezvous with the 386th BG was made; to Hythe, where the RAF Spitfire escort was met; and then on an assembly line from Hythe to Dungeness, where rendezvous with the 387th and 323rd BGs was made; the 322nd to lead entire formation, to 5 miles south of Hardelot to target. The third flight of the 322nd turned back prior to reaching the enemy coast since they were unable to catch the formation.

Target obscured by 10/10th cloud at 3–7,000 ft., so no attack made; 108 × 500 GPs brought back. Return was a left turn to 5 miles south of Hardelot to Dungeness to Base.

Inaccurate LFF from Hardelot at landfall, bursting at 6–7,000 ft.

Thirty-five-ship formation, to Bonnieres, led by Capt. R. A. Porter, with Capt. H. E. Lamb leading the 2nd Box.

Route was Base to assembly line from Gravesend to Hastings, where rendezvous with the 386th BG was made; the 386th were to lead. Fighter rendezvous was made at Hastings, to 6 miles southwest of Treport to 1½ miles inside enemy coast, where they turned back toward Cayeaux, then to Dungeness to Base. (Briefed route was to 10 miles southeast of Abbeville to target to Berck-sur-Mer to Dungeness.) Thirty-three aircraft returned 198 × 500 GPs; two aircraft jettisoned 12 × 500 GPs in the Channel.

Weak inaccurate HFF encountered from Le Treport, Ault, and Cayeux but was well below formation.

In addition, a flight of four aircraft, led by 1Lt. A. R. Jordan, was briefed to rendezvous with the 323rd BG over Earls Colne Airfield to join them on an attack against Cormette V-1 site (XI/A/57). Takeoff was at 1115 hrs. Route was Base assembly line Southend to Nth Foreland, for rendezvous with the 387th BG, to Hythe to Dungeness to 5 miles south of Hardelot to Lumbres. The target was reached at 1248 hrs. but was obscured, so no release made; one aircraft was an early return due to a lack of manifold pressure; a total of 24 × 500 GPs returned. As the formation made a left turn in the target area, about twenty bursts of HFF were seen far to the right, several miles away, believed from the Lumbres area. Return was a left turn to Desvres to 5 miles south of Hardelot to Dungeness to Base.

No interrogation times recorded.

Mission Notes and "Flak-Bait" Crew Debrief Comments
"Flak-Bait" flying No. 3 in the lead flight of the eighteen-ship formation.

From landfall onward, 10/10th cloud; 6 × 500 GPs brought back.

Other Crew Comments
Eighteen-ship formation flying through 4,000 ft. of cloud is not good.

```
Date: December 24, 1943
Target: XI/A/94 Audincthun Noball, 18 a/c
        XI/A/85 Bonnieres Noball, 36 a/c
Field Order: 9th BC F/O 164
```

"Flak-Bait" Crew

2Lt. V. N. Liniger, pilot	SSgt. M. D. Enlow, engineer/gunner
2Lt. C. A. Forrester, copilot	SSgt. R. F. Stickney, radio/gunner
2Lt. R. W. Fletcher, navigator/bombardier	SSgt. J. B. Mitchell, gunner

Briefing started at 0945 hrs. and ended 1030 hrs.

T/off: 1050½ & 1119 hrs.	Rendezvous: 1200 hrs.	Landfall: 1209 hrs.
Target: 1215½ hrs. & no attack	Coast Out: 1224 hrs.	Return: 1255 & 1258 hrs.

Mission Narrative
Fifty-four aircraft dispatched to attack V-1 sites.

Eighteen-ship formation plus two spares, to Audincthun, led by Capt. G. H. Watson with Capt. P. Shannon.

Route was Base to assembly line from Clacton to Nth Foreland and rendezvous with the 386th BG, the 322nd to lead. Rendezvous with the 387th and 323rd BG formations at Nth Foreland, to Hythe for rendezvous with RAF Spitfires, to 5 miles south of Hardelot to target.

Eighteen aircraft attacked, dropping 108 × 500 GPs, from 12,000 ft. for good results; weather was 6–7/10th cloud at 3–5,000 ft. with thick haze, but with a good break on the approach. Spares returned as briefed.

Slight to moderate inaccurate HFF encountered as formation made a 180-degree turn to the left after passing over the target. This came from the Lumbres and St.-Omer area; most burst well below.

Return was a left turn off the target to 5 miles south of Hardelot to Dungeness to Base.

Thirty-six-ship formation, plus four spares, to Bonnieres, was led by Lt. Col. G. C. Celio with Maj. E. Wursten; the 2nd Box was led by Capt. F. V. Pursel with Maj. O. D. Turner.

Routing was to a line from Gravesend to Hastings to rendezvous with the 386th BG; the 386th was supposed to lead, to 2 miles east of Hastings for fighter rendezvous. Rendezvous not made with either the 386th or fighters; visibility about ½ to 1 mile on the way out. Formation turned back at 1229 hrs., while 32 miles off the coast, and reentered 2 miles east of Hastings and returned to Base. 216 × 500 GP bombs returned. Spare aircraft returned as briefed.

No interrogation times recorded.

41-32010 PN-L, "the Cock in Hand," had an accidental discharge from the flexible nose gun on Christmas Eve 1943; fortunately no one was injured in the incident. *Author's collection*

Mission Notes and "Flak-Bait" Crew Debrief Comments

"Flak-Bait" flew as the No. 5 aircraft in the low flight of the 1st Box in the thirty-six-ship formation.

Saw no escort; 6 × 500 GP bombs brought back. Turned back at 1231 hrs., when about 10–12 minutes from the enemy coast.

Turret position interphone out; wire torn loose from jack box.

Other Crew Comments

An unidentified A-20 zoomed up in front of the formation twice, about five minutes out from English coast. Aircraft 41-32010 PN-L, "the Cock in Hand," accidentally fired ten rounds from the flexible nose gun while taxiing around perimeter track after landing.

```
Date: December 30, 1943
Target: XI/A/75 Le Meillard Noball, 36 a/c, 1st Box
XI/A/85 Bonnieres Noball, 36 a/c, 2nd Box
XI/A/57 Cormette Noball, 18 a/c
Field Order: 9th BC F/O 166
```

"Flak-Bait" Crew

1Lt. J. J. Farrell, pilot
2Lt. W. F. Green, copilot
2Lt. O. J. Redmond, navigator/bombardier

TSgt. D. L. Tyler, engineer/gunner
SSgt. J. B. Manuel, radio/gunner
Sgt J. L. Harding Jr., gunner

Briefing started at 1035 hrs. and ended 1200 hrs.

T/off: 1307, 1300 & 1251 hrs.   Rendezvous: 1405, 1405 & 1400 hrs.Landfall: 1414, 1414 & 1410 hrs.

Target: 1425, 1426 & 1418 hrs.   Coast Out: 1437, 1437 & 1428 hrs.   Return: 1520, 1534 & 1507 hrs.

Mission Narrative

Fifty-seven aircraft plus two spare aircraft dispatched.

Thirty-six plus two spare aircraft formation; the 1st Box was led by Capt. H. M. Posson with Maj. O. D. Turner, to attack Le Meillard. The 2nd Box was led by Lt. Col. G. C. Celio, with Maj. E. Wursten, to attack Bonnieres.

Route was Base to assembly line Gravesend to Hastings, for rendezvous with the 386th BG, who were to lead; rendezvous with RAF Spitfires was made at Hastings, to Ault to 49.58'N, 00.38'E (Parc-d'Anxtot), to 10 miles southeast of Abbeville to target.

1st Box released 106 × 500 GPs at Le Meillard, from 12000 ft. at 1425 hrs., for good results; one aircraft had rack failure and brought back 2 × 500 GP bombs. The 2nd Box released 108 × 500 GPs, on Bonnieres, from 12,500 ft. at 1426 hrs., for fair results.

Weak inaccurate LFF and HFF from Ault to the target and weak inaccurate LFF and HFF from Frevent area, which was thought to be railway-mounted flak; no damage received.

Return route was a left turn off the target to Berck-sur-Mer to Hastings to Base.

Eighteen-ship formation, plus three aircraft in a composite formation, led by Maj. B. G. Willis.

Routing was Base to a line from Bradwell Bay to Dungeness, for rendezvous with the 386th BG; the 322nd were to lead and joined up with a formation of the 387th and 323rd BGs on way to Dungeness, where the RAF Spitfire escort was met; the 387th BG to lead entire formation. To 4 miles south of Hardelot to target.

Formation did not bomb since it was cut off by a formation attacking another V-1 site.

A total of 121 × 500 GPs returned (figure includes aircraft in the composite formation mentioned below).

Slight inaccurate HFF from the St.-Omer area, but far to the right of the formation, as it turned in the target area; no damage received.

Return was a left turn to Desvres to 4 miles south of Hardelot to Dungeness to Base.

Three aircraft, part of a composite formation (made up of six aircraft from the 386th and 387th BGs and four from the 322nd), followed a box ahead, but that formation turned back in vicinity of Tingry at 1432 hrs. and exited coast 5 miles north of Le Touquet at 1434 hrs.; one aircraft was an early return. (Bomb disposition of these aircraft included in eighteen-ship formation above.)

No interrogation times recorded.

Mission Notes and "Flak-Bait" Crew Debrief Comments

"Flak-Bait" flew as No. 2 in the low flight of the 2nd Box of the thirty-six-ship formation.

6 × 500 GPs dropped, for fair results.

```
Date: December 31, 1943
Target: XI/A/81 Montorgueil Noball, 18 a/c
XI/A/72 Linghem Noball, 36 a/c
Field Order: 9th BC F/O 167
```

"Flak-Bait" Crew

1Lt. J. J. Farrell, pilot   TSgt. D. L. Tyler, engineer/gunner

F/O T. F. Moore, copilot   SSgt. J. B. Manuel, radio/gunner

2Lt. O. J. Redmond, navigator/bombardier   SSgt. J. L. Harding Jr., gunner

Briefing started at 1000 hrs. and ended 1100 hrs.

T/off: 1210 & 1222 hrs.   Rendezvous: 1300 & 1319 hrs.   Landfall: 1314 & 1331 hrs.

Target: 1334 & 1355 hrs.   Coast Out: 1341 & 1359 hrs.   Return: 1427 & 1450 hrs.

Mission Narrative

Fifty-five aircraft dispatched.

Eighteen-ship formation led by Maj. E. Wursten. Route was Base to Splasher Beacon No. 9 to Beachy Head, for rendezvous with RAF Spitfires, to 5 miles southwest of Le Touquet to 49.53'N, 01.43'E (vicinity of La Rondine), to 8 miles northwest of Amiens to target.

All eighteen aircraft attacked from 11,400 ft., releasing 108 × 500 GPs for good results; no flak encountered.

Return was a left turn to 8 miles north of Cayeux to Hastings to Base.

Thirty-six- plus one-spare-aircraft formation was led by Capt G. B. Simler; the 2nd Box was led by Capt. H. M. Posson.

Route was Base to an assembly line at Nth Foreland to Dungeness, where rendezvous with the 386th BG was made, the 322nd to lead. RAF Spitfire escort was met at Dungeness, to Cayeux to Frevent to target, then turned left to Aire to 5 miles south of St.-Omer to secondary target.

A small patch of cloud obscured the target, so secondary target, at Clety, was attacked at 1355 hrs. by nineteen aircraft, releasing 112 × 500 GPs for poor results. Seventeen aircraft were abortive (2nd Box) and one had an accidental release, when the bomb bay doors wouldn't open in time, and fifteen who did not see the leader drop. Five aircraft jettisoned a total of 25 × 500 GP bombs, and fifteen returned 85 × 500 GPs (includes spare aircraft).

Weak inaccurate LFF and HFF encountered from Frevent bursting low, and moderate accurate HFF from southwest of Aire just after passing over the primary. Very accurate and intense HFF from St.-Omer and Lumbres and continuing intermittently to Desvres, which was moderate and was particularly accurate. Twenty-seven aircraft received Cat. A damage, with two men wounded: Sgt. R. F. Wittling and 2Lt. P. E. Ross, both from the 449th BS.

Lead aircraft of formation received a direct hit on the left engine, approximately 3 miles west of Aire; continued on to bomb secondary, then dropped out and returned to Base on single engine.

Return was from secondary target to Le Touquet to Dungeness to Base.

Interrogation of crews began at 1430 hrs. and finished at 1630 hrs.

Mission Notes and "Flak-Bait" Crew Debrief Comments

"Flak-Bait" flew as No. 3 in the high flight, 2nd Box, of the thirty-six-ship formation.

Cat. A flak damage received.

Brought back 6 × 500 GPs since lead ship did not release.

Other Crew Comments

Formation should have avoided the St.-Omer area.

```
Date: January 4, 1944
Target: XI/A/53 Bois Rempre Noball, 18 a/c
XI/A/85 Bonnieres Noball, 35 a/c, 1st Box
XI/A/15A Croisette Noball, 35 a/c, 2nd Box
Field Order: 9th BC F/O 169
```

"Flak-Bait" Crew

1Lt. J. J. Farrell, pilot
F/O T. H. Rivenbark, copilot
2Lt. O. J. Redmond, navigator/bombardier
Sgt. O. F. Burton, passenger

TSgt. D. L. Tyler, engineer/gunner
SSgt. J. B. Manuel, radio/gunner
Sgt. J. L. Harding Jr., gunner

Briefing started at 0610 hrs. and ended 0715 hrs.

T/off: 0838 & 0904 hrs.
Target: 1005 & 1030 hrs.

Rendezvous: 0935 & 0955 hrs.
Coast Out: 1006 & 1037 hrs.

Landfall: 0947 & 1008 hrs.
Return: 1110 & 1124 hrs.

Mission Narrative

Fifty-three aircraft dispatched.

Thirty-five-ship formation, led by Capt. F. V. Pursel with Maj. O. D. Turner, to attack Bonnieres, and the 2nd Box, led by Capt. G. H. Watson, to attack Croisette.

Route was Base to Splasher Beacon No. 9 to rendezvous with the 386th BG, who were to lead, to Hastings, for fighter rendezvous with RAF Spitfires, to 50.30'N, 01.10'E (off the Somme estuary), to Berck-sur-Mer to target.

Position of the sun interfered with target recognition; both boxes bombed the secondary, Ligescourt, releasing 206 × 500 GPs, although results were poor. One aircraft from the 2nd Box returned 4 × 500 GP bombs.

Both boxes encountered weak inaccurate LFF from Berck-sur-Mer on landfall; the 2nd Box also reported weak inaccurate LFF in the secondary target area.

Return was via Berck-sur-Mer to Dungeness to Base.

Eighteen-ship formation, to attack Bois Rempre, led by Capt. H. V. Smythe.

Route was Base to Canterbury, for rendezvous with the 386th BG, the 322nd to lead. To Splasher Beacon No. 8, to rendezvous with a formation made up of the 387th and 323rd BGs, to Hastings, where the RAF Spitfire escort was met, to 50.30'N, 01.10'E (off the Somme estuary), to 2 miles south of Le Touquet to target. Because of difficulty in seeing the target due to glare from the sun, formation exited enemy coast 4 miles south of Hardelot and reentered at Le Touquet to attack.

A total of three passes were made at the target; seventeen aircraft attacked at 1030 hrs. from 11,000 ft., dropping 100 × 500 GPs on the primary for good results; one aircraft had a rack malfunction and jettisoned 1 × 500 GP; and two others returned a total of 7 × 500 GPs.

Weak inaccurate LFF encountered from Le Touquet at landfall and exit, bursting below the formation; no damage received.

Return route was a left turn to 2 miles south of Le Touquet to Dungeness to Base.

Interrogation of crews began at 1100 hrs. and suspended at 1150 hrs. due to the short amount of time between missions. Restarted at 1730 hrs. and finished at 1825 hrs.

Mission Notes and "Flak-Bait" Crew Debrief Comments

"Flak-Bait" flew as No. 3 aircraft of the high flight of the eighteen-ship formation to attack Bois Rempre.

6 × 500 GPs released on the primary.

Explosion seen in woods where target located.

Building construction and two tunnels seen running into woods at 50.38'N, 01.40'E; photographs taken. (Coordinates given are actually just off the coast at Berck-sur-Mer; sighting was probably made in the Berck area.)

> Date: January 4, 1944
> Target: XI/A/63 Longuemont Noball, 1st Box
> XI/A/59 Behen Noball, 2nd Box
> Field Order: 9th BC F/O 170

"Flak-Bait" Crew

1Lt. J. J. Farrell, pilot
F/O T. H. Rivenbark, copilot
2Lt. O. J. Redmond, navigator/bombardier
Sgt. O. F. Burton, passenger

TSgt. D. L. Tyler, engineer/gunner
SSgt. J. B. Manuel, radio/gunner
Sgt. J. L. Harding, gunner

Briefing started at 1205 hrs. and ended 1250 hrs.

T/off: 1423 & 1430 hrs.	Rendezvous: 1518 hrs.	Landfall: 1533 & 1601 hrs.
Target: 1606 hrs.	Coast Out: 1558 & 1607 hrs.	Return: 1651 & 1705 hrs.

Mission Narrative

Thirty-six aircraft plus two spares dispatched to attack two V-1 sites, 1st Box, led by Capt. H. M. Posson with Maj. O. D. Turner to attack Longuemont, and the 2nd Box led by Capt. G. H. Watson to Behen.

Routing was Base to assembly line from Splasher Beacon No. 9 to Beachy Head, for rendezvous with 386th BG, the 322nd to lead; the RAF Spitfire escort was met at Beachy Head, to 8 miles northeast of Dieppe to Neufchatel to 49.46'N, 01.46'E (La Porcherie), to target.

1st Box could not pick out primary due to haze, so they attacked a target of opportunity near Cayeaux. Seventeen aircraft released 102 × 500 GPs from 11,000 ft.; one aircraft had a rack malfunction and jettisoned 6 × 500 GPs. One aircraft got separated and joined the 386th BG formation. This aircraft was attacked by three Fw 190s in the Abbeville/Cayeaux area, who made only the one pass, receiving Cat. A damage, the tail turret being damaged and the gunner, SSgt. J. R. Dana of the 450th BS, wounded. One spare aircraft returned 6 × 500 GPs.

Climbing out on the afternoon mission of January 4, 1944, this is the first box that was briefed to attack Longuemont V-1 site but attacked Cayeaux as a target of opportunity. The aircraft at lower right is 41-31914 SS-S, "Druther Not," which was MIA on March 20, 1944. *Trevor J. Allen collection*

Weak inaccurate LFF and weak but fairly accurate HFF from Dieppe area on landfall. Weak inaccurate LFF encountered 5–8 miles southwest of Abbeville.

2nd Box could not pick up target so exited the enemy coast at Cayeaux and reentered at Ault for a second attempt, but target not identified, so formation exited again at Ault and returned. Seventeen aircraft brought back 102 × 500 GPs; one aircraft jettisoned 6 × 500 GPs. The spare aircraft returned 6 × 500 GPs.

Weak to moderate HFF from northeast of Dieppe; four aircraft received Cat. A damage.

Interrogation of crews began at 1730 hrs. and finished at 1845 hrs.

Mission Notes and "Flak-Bait" Crew Debrief Comments

"Flak-Bait" flew as No. 3 aircraft, low flight of the 2nd Box.

6 × 500 GPs returned; a good concentration of bombs observed from 1st Box at Cayeaux.

Heard a message on VHF channel D supposedly from a B-26 that went down.

Other Crew Comments

Box 1: Too much circling after missing target. Flight got mixed up; formation too large.

One crew reported a Fw 190 going down smoking, with a Spitfire on its tail.

Box 2: Formation flew around France with bomb bay doors open too long.

Two crews from Box 2 reported that they thought a flak ship was firing from off the shore.

```
Date: January 7, 1944
Target: XI/A/93 La Sorellerie 2 Noball, 36 a/c, 1st Box
XI/A/103 La Sorellerie 1 Noball, 36 a/c, 2nd Box
XI/A/103 La Sorellerie 1 Noball, 18 a/c
Field Order: 9th BC F/O 172
```

"Flak-Bait" Crew

2Lt. V. N. Liniger, pilot
2Lt. C. A. Forrester, copilot
2Lt. R. W. Fletcher, navigator/bombardier

TSgt. H. D. Coulson, engineer/gunner
SSgt. R. F. Stickney, radio/gunner
SSgt. J. B. Mitchell, gunner

No briefing or interrogation timings recorded.

T/off: 1004 & 1023 hrs.   Rendezvous: 1054 hrs.   Landfall: 1138 & 1151 hrs.
Target: 1144½ & 1158½ hrs.   Coast Out: 1148 & 1200 hrs.   Return: 1330 hrs.

Mission Narrative

Thirty-six-ship formation; 1st Box led by Capt. H. E. Lamb to La Sorellerie No. 2, and the 2nd Box was led by Capt. D. L. Morrison to La Sorellerie No. 1.

Route was Base to an assembly line between Dungeness and Beachy Head for rendezvous with the 386th BG, the 386th to lead. To 49.50'N, 00.40'W (off Courseulles-sur-Mer), for rendezvous with the RAF Spitfire escort to 49.30'N, 01.00'W (Colombieres), to 49.26'N, 01.14'W (La Raye), to targets.

A large cloud, base 3,000 ft. and tops 5,000 ft., obscured the target; thirty-seven aircraft abortive (spare aircraft accompanied formation) returning 210 × 500 GPs; two aircraft from the 1st Box jettisoned 12 × 500 GPs in the Channel.

Weak inaccurate HFF at the IP, over the target and Cherbourg area.

Eighteen-ship formation, led by Maj. R. A. Porter to La Sorellerie No. 1.

Route was Base to a line from Maidstone to Dungeness to rendezvous with box from 386th BG to Beachy Head, where rendezvous with a formation from the 387th and 323rd BGs was made, then rest of routing was the same as the thirty-six-ship formation, as above.

Target obscured, so formation attacked Cherbourg-Maupertus A/D at 1158 hrs., fifteen aircraft releasing 88 × 500 GPs for fair results. Three aircraft abortive, two due to rack malfunction and one because of engine trouble. In total, 20 × 500 GP bombs were returned.

Moderate to intense LFF from Valognes bursting below; moderate inaccurate LFF mostly low from Cherbourg area, where moderate mainly inaccurate HFF was encountered, particularly over Maupertus A/D. One aircraft received Cat. A damage.

Return was to be a right turn off the target, but formation carried straight on from Cherbourg-Maupertus A/D and exited at Pointe de Barfleur to Selsey Bill to Base.

Mission Notes and "Flak-Bait" Crew Debrief Comments

"Flak-Bait" flew as No. 3 aircraft of the lead flight, 2nd Box, in the thirty-six-ship formation.

Brought back 6 × 500 GPs; solid cloud over the target only.

Three to four bursts of HFF about 4 miles to right from area of IP, inaccurate for height.

Nose gun jammed and left wheel position indicator inoperative.

Comment made that they should have cable splicers in back of the ship.

Other Crew Comments

High flight of the 1st Box flew right through the low flight of the 2nd Box just before the enemy coast, breaking up the flight.

3rd Box had to circle field for forty minutes before the base was cleared for landing—too many aircraft over the base.

41-34859 PN-X, "Rat Poison," flew her last mission on January 7, 1944; she was written off in a belly landing at Stansted, three days later. *Roger A. Freeman collection*

Date: January 14, 1944
Target: XI/A/70 Cocove Noball, 36 a/c, 1st Box
XI/A/57 Cormette Noball, 36 a/c, 2nd Box
XI/A/11C Bois d'Esquerdes Noball, 18 a/c
Field Order: 9th BC F/O 177

"Flak-Bait" Crew

2Lt. R. E. Moninger, pilot	SSgt. J. L. Kuhl, engineer/gunner
1Lt. J. J. Farrell, copilot	SSgt. J. B. Manuel, radio/gunner
2Lt. O. J. Redmond, navigator/bombardier	SSgt. N. E. Thielan, gunner

Briefing started at 0730 hrs.; no end time recorded.

T/off: 1020, 1027 & 1013 hrs.   Rendezvous: 1115 hrs.   Landfall: 1125, 1126 & 1124 hrs.
Target: 1134½, 1135 & 1133 hrs.   Coast Out: 1138, 1144 & 1150 hrs.   Return: 1332 hrs.

Mission Narrative

Fifty-four aircraft dispatched.

Thirty-six-ship formation led by Capt. N. L. Harvey with Maj. O. D. Turner; 1st Box attacking Cocove V-1 site. The 2nd Box was led by Maj. E. Wursten, to attack Cormette.

Routing was Base to Dungeness for rendezvous with RAF Spitfires, to 3 miles south of Le Touquet, although actual entry was made at Berck-sur-Mer, to Desvres to targets.

1st Box: eighteen aircraft attacked Cocove, releasing 108 × 500 GPs from 11,500 ft. at 1134½ hrs. Moderate inaccurate HFF was encountered from east of Desvres. Moderate HFF accurate for height, from the St.-Omer area, was bursting into other formations. Moderate inaccurate HFF 7 miles from target, and both weak inaccurate LFF and moderate accurate HFF from Watten and weak inaccurate LFF from Gravelines upon exit. No aircraft damaged.

Return route was to Gravelines to Nth Foreland to Base.

2nd Box: seventeen aircraft attacked from 11,000 ft., releasing 100 × 500 GPs at 1135 hrs. One aircraft unaccounted for, since it was MIA. Intense accurate HFF from St.-Omer, intense and very accurate HFF southwest of Lumbres, intense but inaccurate HFF at Bourbourg-Ville. Inaccurate and scattered, low, HFF from Gravelines. One aircraft returned 2 × 500 GPs through rack failure. Two aircraft MIA; fifteen aircraft Cat. A and one Cat. E in a crash landing at Newmarket. Thirteen men MIA and six men wounded: SSgt. R. E. Allen, Capt. P. Bridges, SSgt. E. Ivy, SSgt. K. W. McKeague, SSgt. G. F. Christianson, and F/O J. Szollosy; the last two were in the aircraft that crash-landed at Newmarket. All were members of the 452nd BS.

Return was from the target to Wormhout to Gravelines to Nth Foreland to Base.

Eighteen-ship formation, 3rd Box, led by Maj. F. E. Fair to attack Bois d'Esquerdes. Route out was Base to Dungeness, for fighter rendezvous, to 3 miles from Le Touquet, although actual landfall was at Berck-sur-Mer, to Desvres to Hucqueliers to target.

Target could not be identified, so attacked a target of opportunity 6 miles southeast of St.-Omer; all eighteen aircraft released 100 × 500 GPs, from 12,000 ft., at 1133 hrs. Formation encountered intense very accurate HFF from St.-Omer and woods at Watten. Railway flak reported from a track northwest of St.-Omer and moderate railway flak from Gravelines, and some from a flak boat. One crew reported weak HFF from Berck-sur-Mer on landfall. All eighteen aircraft received Cat. A damage; one aircraft landed at Gosfield, with hydraulic system and left engine instrument shot out.

Return was target to Gravelines to Nth Foreland to Base.

No interrogation timings recorded.

Mission Notes and "Flak-Bait" Crew Debrief Comments

"Flak-Bait" flew as No. 2 in the low flight of the 1st Box, in the thirty-six-ship formation.

6 × 500 GPs dropped, seen to be concentrated in woods in target area.

Observed two trains heading north on railroad between Abbeville and Le Touquet, about thirty cars in each.

MIA Information
41-31948 PN-K
Lead ship of the low flight, 2nd Box, hit by flak in the target area; peeled out of formation to the left, with fuel coming from the left engine, and observed to spiral into woods; six chutes observed.

1Lt. S. A. Walker, pilot	POW
2Lt. J. D. Pearson, copilot	POW
2Lt. P. L. Wolff, navigator/bombardier	evaded
TSgt. J. J. Perhart, engineer/gunner	POW
SSgt. L. I. Creason, radio/gunner	evaded: returned to the UK on May 5, 1944
SSgt. W. J. Brogle, gunner	evaded
SSgt. E. J. Riegelhuth, passenger	POW

41-31880 SS-T
No. 4 aircraft in low flight, 2nd Box, went down at 1138/1140 hrs., after previous flak hit; seen to lose altitude and went into a spiral dive and crash in an open field 5–10 miles south of Gravelines. Four to five chutes reported.
449th BS crew:

1Lt. D. Isgrig, pilot	POW
2Lt. C. J. Gemmell, copilot	POW
2Lt. G. S. Goldstein, navigator/bombardier	POW
SSgt. W. M. Greer, engineer/gunner	evaded
TSgt. D. J. Mertes, radio/gunner	evaded
SSgt. W. B. Satterfield, gunner	evaded

Category E Information:
41-31905 DR-L
Pilot F/O R. S. Tate, flying in the No. 4 position in the high flight of the 2nd Box, was written off in a crash landing at Newmarket; two crew seriously injured—first-aid kit was minus morphine. Aircraft left formation 10 miles after the enemy coast and made landfall at Dover. Hydraulics system was shot out; fifteen large and many small holes in the aircraft.

Date: January 21, 1944
Target: XI/A/68 Lostebarnes/Ardres Noball, 1st Box
XI/A/112 Notre Dame Ferme Noball, 2nd Box
Field Order: 9th BC F/O 180

"Flak-Bait" Crew

1Lt. S. M. Chase, pilot	SSgt. W. T. Guyette, engineer/gunner
2Lt. L. E. Stanford, copilot	SSgt. R. G. Baum, radio/gunner
2Lt. E. I. Baughman, navigator/bombardier	Sgt. J. O. Hartsell, gunner

Briefing started at 0900 hrs. and ended 0935 hrs.

T/off: 1110 & 1117 hrs.	Rendezvous: 1215 hrs.	Landfall: 1227 hrs.
Target: 1236 & 1235½ hrs.	Coast Out: 1237 & 1240 hrs.	Return: 1343 hrs.

Mission Narrative
A total of forty-one plus three spare aircraft dispatched against two V-1 sites.

Routing was Base to assembly line Gravesend to Hastings for rendezvous with the 386th BG, the 322nd to lead, to rendezvous with RAF Spitfire escort at Hastings, to Berck-sur-Mer to targets.

1st Box led by Lt. Col. G. C. Celio to attack Lostebarne/Ardres V-1 site.

Twenty-one plus one spare aircraft dispatched; twenty aircraft attacked from 12,000 ft., dropping 120×500 GPs for good results; no opposition met. One a/c returned a total of 6×500 GP bombs; spare returned 6×500 GPs.

2nd Box, led by Capt. F. V. Pursel with Maj. O. D. Turner, to attack Notre Dame Ferme V-1 site.

Twenty aircraft plus two spares dispatched; twenty-one attacked, releasing 126×500 GPs from 11,500 ft. for fair to poor results; spares went with the formation; one aircraft was abortive due to a fuel leak, returning 6×500 GPs.

Weak inaccurate HFF encountered in target area and to north of the target. Railroad flak encountered 5 miles north of Audruicq. No damage received.

Return routing was a left turn to Gravelines to Nth Foreland to Base.

Interrogation of crews began at 1330 hrs. and finished at 1500 hrs.

Mission Notes and "Flak-Bait" Crew Debrief Comments
"Flak-Bait" flying as No. 6 aircraft in the high flight of the 1st Box.

6×500 GPs released; good results observed.

Improve the latrines at crew room no. 1.

Other Crew Comments
Do not fly seven-ship flights; No. 7 is by himself and has to do too much jockeying to keep out of the way of the No. 5 and No. 6 ships yet still stay in formation.

Box 2 did too-violent evasive action close to the target; spoiled bombardier's aim.

Date: January 23, 1944
Target: XI/A/95 Le Grismont Noball, 1st Box
XI/A/99 Bois d'Enfer Noball, 2nd Box
XI/A/102 (II) Bois de Renty Noball, 3rd Box
Field Order: 9th BC F/O 181

"Flak-Bait" Crew

1Lt. J. J. Farrell, pilot	SSgt. W. L. Moore, engineer/gunner
F/O T. F. Moore, copilot	SSgt. J. B. Manuel, radio/gunner
2Lt. O. J. Redmond, navigator/bombardier	SSgt. N. E. Thielan, gunner

Briefing started at 1230 hrs. and ended 1315 hrs.

T/off: 1412, 1419 & 1405 hrs.	Rendezvous: 1510 hrs.	Landfall: 1521½ hrs.
Target: 1528, 1528 & 1527 hrs.	Coast Out: 1619½ hrs.	Return: 1650 hrs.

Mission Narrative
Fifty-four aircraft dispatched in three boxes, to attack three V-1 sites.

Routing was Base to Hastings for fighter rendezvous with RAF Spitfires, to Le Touquet to targets.

Box 1, led by Capt. G. B. Simler, to attack Le Grismont V-1 site. Seventeen aircraft attacked, dropping 102×500 GPs from 12,000 ft.—results poor; bombs fell to the right of the target. One aircraft could not open bomb bay doors and returned 6×500 GPs. Weak inaccurate LFF from Berck-sur-Mer and weak to moderate, fairly accurate HFF over target. No damage received.

Box 2, led by Capt. L. J. Sebille, to attack Bois d'Enfer V-1 site. Seventeen aircraft attacked, dropping 102×500 GPs from 11,500 ft.; results fair to good. One aircraft returned early with 6×500 GPs because of an electrical problem. Slight inaccurate HFF at landfall south of Le Touquet, and slight to moderate mostly inaccurate HFF from the target, Aire and Fruges. One aircraft received Cat. A damage ("Flak-Bait").

Box 3, led by Capt. G. H. Watson, to attack Bois de Renty II V-1 site. Seventeen aircraft attacked, dropping 102×500 GPs from 12,500 ft. for good results. One aircraft abortive—oil congealed and returned 6×500 GPs. No flak encountered.

Return route was a right turn to Berck-sur-Mer to Hastings to Base.

Interrogation of crews began at 1635 hrs. and finished at 1740 hrs.

Mission Notes and "Flak-Bait" Crew Debrief Comments

"Flak-Bait" flew as No. 6 ship in the low flight of the 2nd Box to Bois d'Enfer.

Cat. A damage; one small hit in the left flap.

6 × 500 GP in target area; results unobserved but pattern very good.

Gunners request flak helmets.

Get bigger stoves in the briefing room to keep it warm.

Very good leadership and evasive action.

```
Date: January 24, 1944
Target: XI/A/81 Montorgueil Noball, 36 a/c, 1st Box
XI/A/76 Eclimeux Noball, 36 a/c, 2nd Box
XI/A/15A Croisette Noball, 18 a/c
Field Order: 9th BC F/O 182
```

"Flak-Bait" Crew

1Lt. J. J. Farrell, pilot

F/O T. F. Moore, copilot

2Lt. O. J. Redmond, navigator/bombardier

SSgt. N. E. Thielan, engineer/gunner

SSgt. J. B. Manuel, radio/gunner

SSgt. W. L. Moore, gunner

Briefing started at 0630 hrs. and ended 0730 hrs.

T/off: 0814, 0821 & 0840 hrs.   Rendezvous: 0915, 0918 & 0937 hrs.   Landfall: 0934 & 0954 hrs.

Target: 0957, 0955 & 1018 hrs.   Coast Out: 1002, 1004 & 1026 hrs.   Return: 1055 hrs. (Feltwell)

Mission Narrative

Fifty-four aircraft dispatched in three boxes, to attack three V-1 sites.

Thirty-six-ship formation. Route was Base to rendezvous with the 386th BG on line from Splasher Beacon No. 8 to Beachy Head, the 322nd to lead. RAF Spitfire escort met at Beachy Head, to 10 miles southwest of Treport to 8 miles north of Poix to 8 miles north of Amiens to targets.

Box 1, led by Capt. H. V. Smythe, to attack Montorgueil V-1. Seventeen aircraft attacked secondary target, the V-1 site at Hesdin (XI/A/34), dropping 101 × 500 GPs from 11,000 ft. for fair results. One aircraft had an accidental release, dropping 6 × 500 GPs prior to the target, and one other aircraft had 1 × 500 GP hang up and was returned. Slight inaccurate HFF from primary area and Hesdin; slight inaccurate HFF from Amiens, Crecy, and Abbeville. No damage received.

Box 2, led by Lt. Col. G. C. Celio, to attack Eclimeaux V-1 site. Sixteen attacked, releasing 93 × 500 GPs from 10,500 ft. for good results. Three aircraft had rack malfunctions and jettisoned a total of 15 × 500 GP bombs in the Channel. No flak encountered.

Eighteen-ship formation, led by Maj. O. D. Turner, to attack Croisette V-1 site. Routing was Base to rendezvous, with boxes from the 387th and 323rd BGs on a line from Splasher Beacon No. 8 to Beachy Head; the rest of the routing as the thirty-six-ship formation. Eighteen aircraft attacked, releasing 106 × 500 GPs from 11,500 ft. for good results. One aircraft had 2 × 500 GPs hang up, so released them on a military objective at Berck-sur-Mer. HFF was observed at the IP, St.-Pol, 5 miles west of the target, Crecy, Hesdin, and Abbeville. LFF observed at Berck-sur-Mer. No damage received. 386th and 323rd BGs ahead were off course at Dieppe, and instead of taking a heading for the IP held a course to the southeast; on advice from the flight commander, our formation took up correct heading for the IP and lost them.

Return route was from targets to Berck-sur-Mer to Dungeness to Base, but formations diverted to Feltwell due to poor visibility.

Interrogation of crews began at 1150 hrs. and finished at 1230 hrs. for the 3rd Box and began at 1500 hrs. and finished at 1600 hrs. for 1st and 2nd Boxes.

Mission Notes and "Flak-Bait" Crew Debrief Comments
"Flak-Bait" flew as No. 5 in the lead flight of the 1st Box in the thirty-six-ship formation.

6 × 500 GPs dropped; observed good results.

Haze over Base on return, but believe landing could have been made. Landed at Feltwell at 1055 hrs.

Other Crew Comments
1st and 2nd Box aircraft could have landed at base; have landed in worse weather conditions.

Aircraft had to circle Feltwell for thirty minutes before starting landing procedure.

```
Date: January 29, 1944
Target: XI/A/89 Les Petits Moraux Noball, 1st Box
XI/A/56 Pommereval Noball, 2nd Box
Field Order: 9th BC F/O 186
```

"Flak-Bait" Crew
1Lt. J. J. Farrell, pilot

F/O T. F. Moore, copilot

1Lt. O. J. Redmond, navigator/bombardier

TSgt. D. L. Tyler, engineer/gunner

SSgt. J. B. Manuel, radio/gunner

SSgt. N. E. Thielan, gunner

Briefing started at 0935 hrs. and ended 1030 hrs.

T/off: 1152 & 1252 hrs.	Rendezvous: 1315 & 1415 hrs.	Landfall: 1321 & 1421 hrs.
Target: 1339½ & 1443 hrs.	Coast Out: 1346 & 1449 hrs.	Return: 1445 & 1527 hrs.

Mission Narrative
Thirty-six aircraft to attack two V-1 sites.

Routing was Base to Splasher Beacon No. 8, for rendezvous with 386th BG, who were to lead, to rendezvous with RAF Spitfire escort at 50.10'N, 00.30'E, to 6 miles west of St.-Valery-en-Caux to Barent to targets.

Box 1, led by Lt. Col. G. C. Celio, to attack Les Petits Moraux V-1 site. Eighteen aircraft dispatched, one abortive when VHF began smoking; jettisoned 6 × 500 GPs in Channel and turned back. Seventeen attacked last-resort targets as primary cloud covered. Lead flight bombed 1 mile west of Ardouval, second flight misidentified target and bombed similar area, 1 mile southeast of the primary. Third flight identified target but dropped on the second flight's release; 102 × 500 GPs dropped. No flak encountered.

Box 2, led by Maj. E. Wursten, to attack Pommereval V-1 site. One aircraft had a fire in the VHF radio in the cockpit; returned early but took off again but couldn't catch the formation so jettisoned 6 × 500 GPs in the Channel. Twelve aircraft attacked from 12,000 ft., dropping 72 × 500 GP, but results were poor. Second flight did not drop, since leader didn't release since he could not identify the target after two runs; two aircraft jettisoned 6 × 500 GPs in Channel; four brought back 24 × 500 GPs. Third flight misidentified target after a second run. No flak encountered.

Return was a left turn off the target to Ault to Hastings to Base.

Interrogation of crews began at 1435 & 1520 hrs. and finished at 1525 & 1620 hrs.

Mission Notes and "Flak-Bait" Crew Debrief Comments
"Flak-Bait" flew as No. 4 in the low flight, in the 1st Box.

6 × 500 GP released; bombs seen to drop just short of the target.

4–5/10th scattered cloud in target area. Five balloons seen at Rouen at approx. 1,500 ft.

High flight should be careful in dropping bombs; bombs missed flight by less than 100 ft.

Date: February 3, 1944
Target: XI/A/95 Le Grismont Noball, 36 a/c
XI/A/11C Bois d'Esquerdes Noball, 18 a/c
Field Order: 9th BC F/O 189

"Flak-Bait" Crew

1Lt. J. J. Farrell, pilot
F/O T. F. Moore, copilot
1Lt. O. J. Redmond, navigator/bombardier

TSgt. D. L. Tyler, engineer/gunner
SSgt. J. B. Manuel, radio/gunner
SSgt. N. E. Thielan, gunner

Briefing started at 1000 hrs. and ended 1035 hrs.

T/off: 1140 & 1147 hrs.
Rendezvous: 1242 & 1245 hrs.
Landfall: 1253 hrs.

Target: 1259 & 1313 (S) hrs.
Coast Out: 1305 & 1313 hrs.
Return: 1350 & 1403 hrs.

Mission Narrative

Fifty-four aircraft dispatched to attack two V-1 sites.

Routing was Base to Dungeness, and rendezvous with RAF Spitfire escort, to 3 miles north of Le Touquet to targets.

Eighteen-ship formation, to attack Bois d'Esquerdes V-1 site, led by Maj. E. Wursten. 10/10th cloud prevented bombing; recalled because of the weather. A heavy concentration of HFF at St.-Omer and Lumbres area, apparently barrage-type fire, accurate for altitude but mostly behind the formation. Fifty bursts of HFF seen to right and below formation at exit north of Le Touquet. 108 × 500 GPs returned.

Thirty-six-ship formation, to attack Le Grismont V-1 site, led by Lt. Col. G. C. Celio, with Maj. F. E. Fair leading the 2nd Box. 7–10/10th cloud tops 6,000 ft. prevented attack on primary, so formation attacked secondary target Dannes C/Ws (XI/A/8) near Hardelot. 212 × 500 GPs released from 12,000 ft. for fair to poor results. 2 × 500 GPs jettisoned due to rack failure, and 1 × 500 GP returned. Moderate HFF accurate for the 2nd Box from St.-Omer/Aire area; moderate LFF very inaccurate and low from Le Touquet on exit, and weak to moderate HFF, very accurate, from Hardelot/Boulogne area continuous for one minute after exit from coast. Six aircraft received Cat. A damage.

Return route was a right turn off the targets to 3 miles north of Le Touquet to Dungeness to Base.

Interrogation of crews began at 1415 hrs. and finished at 1530 hrs.

Mission Notes and "Flak-Bait" Crew Debrief Comments

"Flak-Bait" flew as No. 4 aircraft, high flight, 1st Box of the thirty-six-ship formation. Actual takeoff time was 1150 hrs., and landed at 1411 hrs.

6 × 500 GPs released on secondary near Hardelot; hit in south-center part of woods, good concentration in target area.

HFF at Hardelot, inaccurate below; HFF between Hardelot and Boulogne accurate for height but inaccurate for course. Inaccurate HFF in vicinity of St.-Omer. No damage received.

Should have a list of alerted combat crews at the mess hall, so mess officer can check off names to prevent arguments or confusion.

Other Crew Comments

Have aircraft from other groups fly with their own group and not in our formation.

Thirty-six-ship formation: leader should fly high enough to keep low flight out of the overcast.

Date: February 5, 1944
Target: XI/A/53 Bois Rempre Noball, 1st Box
XI/A/54 Embry Bois Pottier Noball, 2nd Box
XI/A/65C Ruisseauville Noball, 3rd Box
Field Order: 9th BC F/O 191

"Flak-Bait" Crew

F/O T. H. Rivenbark, pilot
2Lt. G. E. Stone, copilot
1Lt. R. E. Palmer, navigator/bombardier

Sgt. W. L. Moore, engineer/gunner
SSgt. P. E. McManes, radio/gunner
Sgt. C. B. Hill, gunner

Briefing started at 1030 hrs. and ended 1120 hrs.

T/off: 1231, 1245 & 1238 hrs.	Rendezvous: 1335 & 1336 hrs.	Landfall: 1352 & 1353 hrs.
Target: 1429, 1409 & 1422 hrs.	Coast Out: 1430, 1425 & 1415 hrs.	Return: 1512, 1454 & 1523 hrs.

Mission Narrative

Fifty-four plus four spare aircraft in three boxes dispatched to attack V-1 sites in Pas des Calais area.

Routing was Base to Beachy Head, for rendezvous with RAF Spitfire escort, to 3 miles south of Berck-sur-Mer to Auxi-le-Chateau to Frevent to targets.

Box 1, led by Capt. H. V. Smythe, to attack Bois Rempre V-1. 6–8/10th cloud prevented bombing of primary; eighteen aircraft attacked secondary, XI/B/6 Dannes/Rouart C/Ws, from 10,500 ft., releasing 108 × 500 GPs for poor results. Thirteen aircraft received Cat. A damage.

Box 2, led by Capt. H. M. Posson, to attack Embry Bois Pottier V-1 site. All eighteen attacked primary, dropping 105 × 500 GPs from 10,000 ft. for poor results. 3 × 500 GPs returned through rack failures. Five aircraft received Cat. A damage.

Box 3, led by Capt. G. H. Watson, to attack Ruisseauville V-1. Primary was cloud covered, so attacked secondary, XI/C/6 Enocq, from 11,000 ft., releasing 105 × 500 GPs for fair results. One aircraft had an accidental release; bombs dropped when doors were opened, and 6 × 500 GPs released between the IP and the target. Fourteen aircraft damaged Cat. A; one man slightly wounded: SSgt. J. V. Pogue, 452nd BS.

Four spare aircraft returned 6 × 500 GPs.

All formations encountered intense to moderate, accurate HFF on route in at Crecy-en-Ponthieu, Auxi-le-Chateau, Frevent, and St.-Pol areas.

Return route was a left turn off the targets to 3 miles south of Hardelot to Dungeness to Base.

Interrogation of crews began at 1525 hrs. and finished at 1625 hrs.

Mission Notes and "Flak-Bait" Crew Debrief Comments

"Flak-Bait" flew as No. 2 in the high flight, of the 1st Box.

6 × 500 GP released.

Other Crew Comments

Heavy jamming of special navigation equipment (GEE).

Date: February 6, 1944
Target: XI/A/115 Beaumont-le-Hareng Noball, 18 a/c
Cormeilles-en-Vixen A/D, 36 a/c
Field Order: 9th BC F/O 192

"Flak-Bait" Crew

F/O T. H. Rivenbark, pilot
2Lt. G. E. Stone, copilot
1Lt. R. E. Palmer, navigator/bombardier

Sgt. W. L. Moore, engineer/gunner
SSgt. P. E. McManes, radio/gunner
Sgt. C. B. Hill, gunner

Briefing started at 1000 hrs. and ended 1100 hrs.

T/off: 1229 & 1242 hrs.	Rendezvous: 1300 hrs.	Landfall: 1354 hrs.
Target: 1358 & 1413 hrs.	Coast Out: 1400 & 1148 hrs.	Return: 1512 hrs. (Horsham St. Faith)
		1530 hrs. (Base 36 a/c)

Mission Narrative

Eighteen plus one spare aircraft, led by Capt. G. B. Simler, to attack Beaumont-le-Hareng V-1. Route was Base to rendezvous with 387th and 323rd BGs on an assembly line from Crowborough to Hastings, where RAF 11 Group escort was met, the 322nd to lead, to Ault to Grandvilliers to Gournay to target. Eighteen aircraft attacked primary from 11,500 ft., dropping 108 × 500 GPs. No flak encountered. Return was a right turn to Tocqueville to Hastings to Base; all aircraft landed at Horsham St. Faith, returning to Base the next day. The spare aircraft joined the 323rd BG formation, since they were an aircraft short, and dropped 6 × 500 GPs on their target the Noball at XI/A/101; this aircraft landed at Metfield short of fuel.

Thirty-six aircraft plus one spare, formation led by Maj. E. Wursten, to attack Cormeilles-en-Vixen A/D. Route was Base to assembly line between Lewes and Beachy Head for rendezvous with 386th BG, the 322nd to lead. RAF 11 Group fighters met at Beachy Head, to 8 miles east of St.-Valery-en-Caux to 49.07'N, 01.40'E (St.-Vincent-des-Bois), to target. Sixteen aircraft attacked primary, dropping 449 × 100 GPs from 10,400 ft. Nineteen aircraft attacked target of opportunity, a factory near Grandvilliers, from 11,000 ft., dropping 568 × 100 GPs. Results unobserved. Two aircraft were early return: "Flak-Bait" and one other that had a fuel leak when the fuel cap had not been installed properly. Weak inaccurate LFF at landfall and fifteen bursts of HFF from Quiberville area, mainly inaccurate; two aircraft received Cat. A damage. A total of 83 × 100 GPs brought back: sixty by early returns and the rest through rack failures.

Return route was a left turn to Tocqueville to Beachy Head to Base.

Interrogation of crews began at 1600 hrs. and finished at 1650 hrs.

Mission Notes and "Flak-Bait" Crew Debrief Comments

Abortive: "Flak-Bait" was to fly as No. 5 aircraft in low flight of the 1st Box to attack Cormeilles-en-Vixen A/D but was abortive when the tail guns jammed; turned back over the Channel at 1351 hrs., 15 miles off the enemy coast, and returned 30 × 100 GPs.

Other Crew Comments

Much criticism of the 100 GP bombloads. Thirty too many; they are hard to get rid of and they do not drop properly because of wiring; fell in different directions.

```
Date: February 8, 1944
Target: XI/A/95 Le Grismont Noball, 1st Box
       XI/A/99 Bois d'Enfer Noball, 2nd Box
Field Order: 9th BC F/O 194
```

"Flak-Bait" Crew

1Lt. G. B. Backes, pilot	SSgt. M. D. Enlow, engineer/gunner
F/O J. L. Hancock, copilot	TSgt. W. Lopatin, radio/gunner
1Lt. H. C. Huber, navigator/bombardier	SSgt. C. T. Duke, gunner

Briefing started at 1130 hrs. and ended 1205 hrs.

T/off: 1326 & 1319 hrs.	Rendezvous: 1415 & 1417 hrs.	Landfall: 1426 & 1425 hrs.
Target: 1451 (S) & 1454 hrs.	Coast Out: 1451 & 1456 hrs.	Return: 1526 & 1547 hrs.

Mission Narrative

Thirty-six aircraft plus three spares ("Flak-Bait" was one of the spare aircraft) dispatched; the 1st Box was led by Capt. L. J. Sebille, and the 2nd Box by Capt. C. Cordill.

Routing was Base to Dungeness, for rendezvous with RAF Spitfire escort, to 5 miles south of Berck-sur-Mer to Fillievres to Auchel to targets.

Clouds covered the primary targets, so the secondary, a labor camp at Dannes/Rouart (XI/B/6), was attacked by both boxes. Thirty-four aircraft dropped 202 × 500 GP bombs. Spares returned 18 × 500 GPs.

1st Box encountered moderate fairly accurate HFF from Hesdin, Auxi-le-Chateau, Frevent, and St.-Pol areas. In the immediate primary area, moderate fairly accurate HFF and weak to moderate, mostly inaccurate, HFF was encountered from the Samer/Desvres areas. Weak inaccurate HFF from Hardelot. 2nd Box reported the same but also reported moderate accurate HFF from St.-Omer/Lumbres area and weak inaccurate LFF and HFF from Le Touquet. A total of sixteen aircraft received Cat. A flak damage.

Return route was to 5 miles south of Hardelot to Dungeness to Base.

Interrogation of crews began at 1600 hrs. and finished at 1710 hrs.

Mission Notes and "Flak-Bait" Crew Debrief Comments

"Flak-Bait" flew as a spare aircraft for the 2nd Box; briefed to attack Bois d'Enfer V-1 site.

Went to English coast; formation was intact so returned to Base; brought back 6 × 500 GPs.

```
Date: February 9, 1944
Target: Tergnier M/Y, 36 a/c
XI/A/89 Les Petit Moraux Noball, 18 a/c
Field Order: 9th BC F/O 195
```

"Flak-Bait" Crew

F/O T. H. Rivenbark, pilot
2Lt. G. E. Stone, copilot
1Lt. P. E. Ross, navigator/bombardier

Sgt. W. L. Moore, engineer/gunner
SSgt. P. E. McManes, radio/gunner
Sgt. C. B. Hill, gunner

Briefing started at 0600 hrs. and ended 0700 hrs.

T/off: 0746, 0752½ & 0830 hrs.	Rendezvous: 0845 & 0919 hrs.	Landfall: 0900 & 0935 hrs.
Target: 0939, 0927 & 1003 hrs.	Coast Out: 1006 & 1005 hrs.	Return: 1048, 1038 & 1052 hrs.

Mission Narrative

Thirty-six-ship formation, led by Lt. Col. G. C. Nye with Brig. Gen. R. G. Nugent from 9th AF HQ as copilot; the 2nd box was led by Lt. D. W. Allen with Capt. J. W. Seale.

Route was Base to an assembly line from Tunbridge Wells to Hastings, for rendezvous with the 386th BG, who were to lead, to Hastings, for rendezvous with RAF Spitfire escort, to Ault to 49.45'N, 02.21'E (Fouquerolles), to 49.32'N, 03.08'E (Longavesne), to target.

Thirty-five aircraft attacked, dropping 210 × 500 GPs from 11,500 and 12,000 ft. One aircraft failed to release when the bomb bay doors failed to open in time, so jettisoned 6 × 500 GPs in the Channel.

Moderate HFF, very accurate for both course and height, encountered from the Oisemont/Horney area, south of Abbeville and Poix areas. Moderate fairly accurate HFF south of Amiens. Moderate fairly accurate HFF from approximately 6 miles north and 8 miles northwest of the target. Slight inaccurate HFF from Le Treport, very slight inaccurate HFF from Montdidier. Slight inaccurate LFF from aerodrome 6 miles south of St.-Quentin and just east of Noyen. Fourteen aircraft received Cat. A damage; one man slightly wounded (name not identified in the records).

Return route was a left turn to 49.45'N, 02.21'E (Fouquerolles), to Ault to Hastings to Base.

Eighteen-ship formation, led by Lt. Col. E. Wursten.

Route was Base to assembly line Lewes to Beachy Head for rendezvous with the 387th BG, who were to lead. RAF Spitfire escort was met at Beachy Head to Ault to 6 miles east of Serqueux to 6 miles south of Serqueux to target.

Clouds prevented bombing of primary, so target of opportunity near Ault or Le Treport (approx. midway between Ault and Cayeaux) attacked. Thirteen aircraft dropped 78 × 500 GPs from 12,000 ft. Three aircraft were not prepared for release at the target of opportunity, so returned 18 × 500 GPs. Very slight and inaccurate HFF from Le Treport and Creil areas.

Briefed return was to Tocqueville to Beachy Head and Base.

Interrogation of crews began at 1110 hrs. and finished at 1215 hrs.

Mission Notes and "Flak-Bait" Crew Debrief Comments
"Flak-Bait" flew as No. 4 ship in the low flight of the eighteen-ship formation to attack Les Petit Moraux V-1 site.

Clouds at primary; 6 × 500 GPs dropped on target of last resort.

Observed three ships going out to sea at Le Treport.

```
Date: February 10, 1944
Target: XI/A/85 Bonnieres Noball, 1st Box
XI/A/79 Beauvoir Noball, 2nd Box
XI/A/71 Vacquerie-de-le-Bocq Noball, 3rd Box
Field Order: 9th BC F/O 196
```

"Flak-Bait" Crew
F/O T. H. Rivenbark, pilot
2Lt. G. E. Stone, copilot
1Lt. P. E. Ross, navigator/bombardier

Sgt. W. L. Moore, engineer/gunner
SSgt. P. E. McManes, radio/gunner
Sgt. C. B. Hill, gunner

Briefing started at 0630 hrs. and ended 0730 hrs.

T/off: 0829, 0836 & 0845 hrs.	Rendezvous: 0930 hrs.	Landfall: 0944, 0942 & 0943 hrs.
Target: 1010, 1008½ & 1000 hrs.	Coast Out: 1011, 1009 & 1011 hrs.	Return: 1058, 1105 & 1055 hrs.

Mission Narrative
Three boxes, of eighteen aircraft each, to attack three separate V-1 sites.

Route was Base to Dungeness, for rendezvous with RAF Spitfire escort, to Ault to 49.53'N, 01.59'E (Le Hideux), to 50.00'N, 02.15'E (west of Vignacourt), to targets.

Box 1, led by1Lt. D. W. Allen with 1Lt. K. L. Bayles, to attack Bonnieres V-1 site. No attack; target was cloud covered. Seventeen aircraft returned 90 × 500 GPs. One aircraft was an early return when the pilot's hatch blew open. A total of 12 × 500 GPs jettisoned in Channel. Five aircraft received Cat. A damage.

Box 2, led by Lt. Col. G. C. Celio with 1Lt. J. E. Haley, to attack Beauvoir V-1 site. 8–10/10th cloud over the target, so attacked Crotoy as a target of opportunity. Thirteen aircraft released 75 × 500 GPs for poor results, one aircraft jettisoned 7 × 500 GPs in the Channel, and 26 × 500 GPs returned by five aircraft when leader's bomb bay doors failed to open in time. One aircraft received Cat. A damage.

Box 3, led by Capt. H. M. Posson with 1Lt. A. W. Bouquet, to attack Vacquerie-de-le-Bocq. Seventeen aircraft attacked the primary, releasing 100 × 500 GPs, although results were unobserved. One aircraft jettisoned 8 × 500 GPs in Channel due to rack failure. Three aircraft received Cat. A damage.

Flak for all three boxes was moderate, fairly accurate, HFF from Abbeville, Crecy-en-Porthieu, Hesdin, Doullens, Frevent, and Auxi-le-Chateau areas.

Return route was a right turn off the target to 3 miles south Le Touquet to Dungeness to Base.

Interrogation of crews began at 1200 hrs. and finished at 1300 hrs.

Mission Notes and "Flak-Bait" Crew Debrief Comments
"Flak-Bait" flew as No. 6 in the lead flight of the 1st Box to attack Bonnieres V-1 site.

Brought back 6 × 500 GPs, since leader did not drop.

Cat. A damage, holes in wing.

Date: February 11, 1944
Target: Amiens-Longeau M/Y, 36 a/c
         Tergnier M/Y, 18 a/c
Field Order: 9th BC F/O 198

"Flak-Bait" Crew

F/O T. H. Rivenbark, pilot
2Lt. G. E. Stone, copilot
1Lt. P. E. Ross, navigator/bombardier

Sgt. W. L. Moore, engineer/gunner
SSgt. P. E. McManes, radio/gunner
Sgt. C. B. Hill, gunner

Briefing started at 0600 hrs. and ended at 0645 hrs.

T/off: 1005 & 1011 hrs. Rendezvous: 1125 & 1124 hrs. Landfall: 1132 hrs.
Target: 1206 hrs. Coast Out: 1207 hrs. Return: 1307 & 1252 hrs.

Mission Narrative

Thirty-six-ship formation; 1st Box led by Capt. G. H. Watson, and the 2nd Box was led by Capt. H. M. Posson with Maj. F. P. Taylor.

Routing was Base to rendezvous with 386th BG on an assembly line Splasher Beacon No. 9 to Beachy Head; the 322nd were to lead. RAF Spitfire escort was met at 50.20'N, 00.50'E (off St.-Valery-en-Caux), to Toucqueville to 49.42'N, 01.58'E (Bosquentin), to 49.44'N, 02.16'E (east of Beauvais), to target.

Cloud prevented bombing at primary; eighteen aircraft (2nd Box) attacked a target of opportunity, Berneval-le-Grand, near Ault, for poor results. 107 × 500 GPs released from 12,000 ft.; 109 × 500 GPs returned by aircraft of the 1st Box; one aircraft was an early return because the turret was out, the other seventeen because of weather.

Weak inaccurate LFF from Tocqueville at landfall and weak inaccurate HFF from Oisemont, Horney, Poix, and Amiens areas; no damage received.

Eighteen-ship formation, led by Capt. G. B. Simler.

Routing was Base to rendezvous with 386th on line from Guildford to Splasher Beacon No. 9, the 386th to lead, and with 387th and 323rd BG formation on line Splasher Beacon No. 9 to Beachy Head. Remainder of routing the same as thirty-six-ship formation as related above.

Mission recalled because of weather; 108 × 500 GPs returned.

Return route was to Tocqueville to Beachy Head to Base.

No interrogation timings recorded.

Mission Notes and "Flak-Bait" Crew Debrief Comments

"Flak-Bait" flew as No. 2 ship, low flight, 2nd Box, of the thirty-six-ship formation.

6 × 500 GP dropped on box leader.

No damage received.

Tail guns out.

Flashlight requested for engineers.

"Flak-Bait" Crew

1Lt. S. M. Chase, pilot
2Lt. B. T. Belleson, copilot
2Lt. E. I. Baughman, navigator/bombardier

SSgt. W. T. Guyette, engineer/gunner
SSgt. R. G. Baum, radio/gunner
Sgt. J. O. Hartsell, gunner

Briefing started at 1215 hrs. and ended 1300 hrs.

T/off: 1416, 1423 & 1440 hrs.   Rendezvous: 1520, 1520 & 1542 hrs.Landfall: 1525, 1525 & 1548 hrs.

Target: 1537, 1538 & 1601 hrs.   Coast Out: 1543, 1544 & 1607 hrs.   Return: 1621, 1640 & 1653 hrs.

Mission Narrative

Three boxes dispatched to attack two V-1 sites; 1st Box, led by Capt. L. J. Sebille, to attack Les Petits Moraux; 2nd Box, led by Capt. G. B. Simler, to Pommereval; and the 3rd Box, led by Capt. H. V. Smythe, also to attack Les Petits Moraux.

Route for thirty-six-ship formation was Base to assembly line between Beachy Head and position 50.10'N, 00.25'E (off Fecamp), for rendezvous with 386th BG, who were to lead. RAF Spitfire escort to be met at the same coordinates. To 49.50'N, 00.32'E (Sandouville), to Yvetot to Pavilly to targets. Eighteen-ship formation formed up with 386th on a line from Hastings to Beachy Head, 322nd to lead, and formed up with 323rd and 387th BG formation on line to fighter rendezvous, otherwise routing as before.

Of the thirty-six aircraft dispatched to Les Petits Moraux (1st and 3rd Boxes), thirty-three attacked releasing 198 × 500 GPs, from 11,500 ft.; 1st Box achieved fair to good results; 3rd Box results were assessed as poor. Two aircraft had engine problems and returned early, and another had an intervalometer-setting error. 12 × 500 GPs jettisoned over Channel, and 6 × 500 GPs returned. No damage received.

Box 2 attacking Pommereval; seventeen released on the primary, from 12,000 ft. dropping 102 × 500 GPs for good to fair results. Slight inaccurate LFF was encountered in the target area; no damage received. One aircraft had engine trouble and returned 6 × 500 GPs.

Return route was to Tocqueville to Hastings to Base.

Interrogation of crews began at 1700 hrs. and finished at 1805 hrs.

Mission Notes and "Flak-Bait" Crew Debrief Comments

Abortive: "Flak-Bait" was to fly No. 3 in the high flight, 3rd Box, but was abortive due to a loss of power in the right engine; turned back over the river Thames and landed back at base at 1545 hrs.; 6 × 500 GPs returned.

```
Date: February 15, 1944
Target: XI/A/26B La Glacerie Noball, 1st Box
XI/A/26C La Glacerie Noball, 2nd Box
XI/A/18 Sottevast Noball, 3rd Box
Field Order: 9th BC F/O 202
```

"Flak-Bait" Crew
452nd BS crew

1Lt. L. L. Holmes, pilot

1Lt. W. F. Groman, copilot

2Lt. R. L. Roland, navigator/bombardier

SSgt. J. Docca, engineer/gunner

TSgt. C. Leja, radio/gunner

Sgt. J. W. Venable, gunner

Briefing started at 0715 hrs. and ended 0815 hrs.

T/off: 0856, 0903 & 0910 hrs.   Rendezvous: 1009, 0949 & 1010 hrs.Landfall: 1021, 1022 1019 hrs.

Target: 1024, 1029 & 1025 hrs.   Coast Out: 1028, 1031 & 1031 hrs.   Return: 1121, 1149 & 1210 hrs.

Mission Narrative

Fifty-four aircraft dispatched to attack three V-1 sites.

Routing was Base to Beachy Head, to fighter rendezvous at 49.50'N, 00.40'W (off Courcelles-sur-Mer), to 49.26'N, 01.14'W (La Raye), to targets.

Thirty-six-ship formation to attack two sites at La Glacerie. 1st Box led by Lt. Col. G. C. Nye with Maj. F. P. Taylor; the 2nd Box was led by Capt. H. V. Smythe.

1st Box to attack La Glacerie B. Eighteen aircraft off; seventeen attacked, dropping 102 × 500 GPs from 11,500 ft. for good results. On one aircraft the bomb bay doors wouldn't open in time, so jettisoned 6 × 500

GPs in the Channel. Formation encountered continuous accurate HFF from Valognes and Cherbourg; became inaccurate after Maupertus had been passed. Seventeen aircraft with Cat. A damage; one man wounded: 2Lt. R. D. Farrens, 451st BS.

2nd Box to attack La Glacerie C. Eighteen aircraft off; seventeen attacked secondary, Cherbourg/Maupertus A/D, dropping 102 × 500 GPs from 11,500 ft. for fair results. One aircraft jettisoned 6 × 500 GPs, after bombardier was hit by flak on the bomb run. Intense accurate HFF from Ecausseville to the primary and following to Cherbourg/Maupertus A/D and continuing up until one minute before exit. All eighteen aircraft damaged Cat. A; two men injured: one seriously, 1Lt. R. G. Caldwell, a bombardier from the 449th BS who was on his first mission and was flown to the General Hospital, and one slight, SSgt. P. Crovin, 450th BS.

Eighteen-ship formation, 3rd Box, led by Lt. Col. E. Wursten, to attack Sottevast V-weapon site. Eighteen dispatched, fifteen attacking the primary, releasing 90 × 500 GPs from 11,000 ft. for fair results. Three aircraft were late takeoffs and failed to make formation; one jettisoned 6 × 500 GPs and two returned 12 × 500 GPs. Encountered continuous, intense accurate, HFF from Briequebec and Cherbourg areas, continuing almost to coast. Eleven aircraft with Cat. A damage.

Return was a right turn off the targets to 49.42'N, 01.15'W (La Grande Dune), to Selsey Bill to Base.

Interrogation of crews began at 1220 hrs. and finished at 1345 hrs.

Mission Notes and "Flak-Bait" Crew Debrief Comments
"Flak-Bait" flew as No. 6 in the high flight, in the 3rd Box.

No damage; 6 × 500 GPs dropped on target.

```
Date: February 15, 1944
Target: XI/A/56 Pommereval Noball, 1st Box
XI/A/101 Ecalles-sur-Buchy Noball, 2nd Box
Field Order: 9th BC F/O 203
```

"Flak-Bait" Crew
1Lt. R. E. Moninger, pilot	SSgt. W. S. Jones, engineer/gunner
1Lt. C. M. Foster, copilot	TSgt. S. Einbinder, radio/gunner
1Lt. R. E. Palmer, navigator/bombardier	SSgt. K. A. Ottocrans, gunner

Briefing started at 1315 hrs. and ended 1350 hrs.

T/off: 1446 & 1452 hrs.	Rendezvous:	Landfall: 1602 & 1602 hrs.
Target: 1614 & 1613 hrs.	Coast Out: 1619 & 1621 hrs.	Return: 1659 & 1716 hrs.

Mission Narrative
Thirty-four ships dispatched; 1st Box, led by Lt. Col. G. C. Nye with Maj. F. P. Taylor, to attack Pommereval V-1 site, and the 2nd Box, led by Capt. H. V. Smythe, to attack Ecalles-sur-Buchy V-1 site.

Route was Base to rendezvous with the 386th BG on a line from Lewes to Beachy Head, the 386th to lead. RAF Spitfire escort met at Beachy Head, to 4 miles northeast of Fecamp (although actual entry was made at St.-Valery) to 2 miles west of Yvetot to targets.

1st Box: seventeen dispatched, sixteen attacked, dropping 96 × 500 GPs from 12,000 ft. in CAVU conditions for good results. One aircraft returned early because of engine trouble; 6 × 500 GP bombs returned.

2nd Box: seventeen dispatched, sixteen attacking, dropping 96 × 500 GPs for poor results from 12,000 ft. in CAVU conditions. One aircraft ("Flak-Bait") returned 6 × 500 GPs; see below.

No opposition encountered. Return route was a left turn off the target to Tocqueville to Hastings to Base.

Interrogation of crews began at 1710 hrs. and finished at 1800 hrs.

Mission Notes and "Flak-Bait" Crew Debrief Comments

"Flak-Bait" flew as No. 2 in the high flight, 2nd Box.

6 × 500 GP brought back; bombardier probably forgot to switch the intervalometer to "on"—didn't know that the bombs hadn't released until back over the English coast.

Booster motor for right turret gun out.

Col. Nye's comments

386th went in over St.-Valery, way past IP; they came out as briefed ahead of us.

```
Date: February 20, 1944
Target: Gilze-Rijen A/D
Field Order: 9th BC F/O 205
```

"Flak-Bait" Crew

2Lt. H. C. Rodgers, pilot
2Lt. B. P. Burrage, copilot
2Lt. K. A. Brower, navigator/bombardier

SSgt. V. J. Mammolito, engineer/gunner
TSgt. O. D. Freeman, radio/gunner
Sgt. A. Christopher, gunner

Briefing started at 0700 hrs. and ended 0800 hrs.

T/off: 0905 hrs.	Rendezvous: 1025 hrs.	Landfall: 1027 hrs.
Target: 1049 hrs.	Coast Out: 1049½ hrs.	Return: 1141 hrs.

Mission Narrative

Twenty-nine aircraft dispatched; formation led by Maj. B. G. Willis, and the 2nd Box was led by Maj. E. Wursten.

Route was Base to rendezvous with the 386th BG on a line from the Naze to the fighter rendezvous, the 322nd to lead, to fighter rendezvous at 51.40'N, 03.25'E (off Knocke), to Roosendaal to target.

10/10th cloud at target and 7–8/10th at secondary, tops 6,000 ft., so formation attacked a casual target, an airfield near Haamstede, 5 miles NNW of Flushing. Seventeen aircraft dropped 448 × 100 GPs from 11,000 ft., although results were poor; most bombs fell in the water or on the edge of the target. Twelve aircraft were abortive, one couldn't catch the formation before leaving the English coast, and another five turned back for the same reason 4 miles off the English coast. Five aircraft turned back after reaching the enemy coast because of weather; 382 × 100 GPs returned.

Weak inaccurate HFF at landfall from Flushing and a few inaccurate HFF bursts at exit near Haamstede. One crew reported that when at 6,000 ft., on course at 0953 hrs., there were approximately fifty bursts of HFF off to the left of the formation from friendly gunners at the Naze, or possibly from vessels in the vicinity.

Briefed return route was a right turn to Roosendaal to 51.40'N, 03.25'E (off Knocke), to the Naze to Base.

Interrogation of crews began at 1135 hrs. and finished at 1300 hrs.

Mission Notes and "Flak-Bait" Crew Debrief Comments

"Flak-Bait" flew as No. 6 aircraft in the lead flight, 1st Box.

30 × 100 GPs dropped on target.

Other Crew Comments

Maj. Willis left base on course five minutes late, but 386th was late at rendezvous.

Too many bombs for stations, not safe, bombs fall everywhere.

"Flak-Bait" Crew

2Lt. H. C. Rodgers, pilot	SSgt. V. J. Mammolito, engineer/gunner
2Lt. B. P. Burrage, copilot	TSgt. O. D. Freeman, radio/gunner
2Lt. K. A. Brower, navigator/bombardier	Sgt. A. Christopher, gunner
Capt. J. P. Eckenrode, observer	

Briefing started at 0719 hrs. and ended 0800 hrs.

T/off: 1120 hrs.	Rendezvous: 1231½ hrs.	Landfall: 1257 hrs.
Target: 1257 hrs.	Coast Out: 1300 hrs.	Return: 1340 hrs.

Mission Narrative

First Pathfinder-led mission for the 9th Air Force.

Eighteen aircraft dispatched, led by Maj. R. Porter of the 1st PFF Squadron (P). Route was Base to fighter rendezvous with RAF Typhoons at the Naze, to 51.50'N, 02.08'E (mid-Channel off Margate), to target. All aircraft attacked; 516 × 100 GPs dropped from 12,000 ft., through 10/10th cloud with tops at 6,000 ft.; results unobserved; 14 × 100 GPs returned due to rack malfunction.

No opposition met. Return was a left turn to Nth Foreland to Base.

Interrogation of crews began at 1415 hrs. and finished at 1440 hrs.

The 9th Air Force's first PFF-led mission was on February 21, 1944. Each of the bomb groups then in England was ordered to supply aircraft and crews to provide the complement for this squadron. One of the aircraft handed over from the 322nd BG was 41-31847 ER-D, "Jolly Roger." *USAAF*

Mission Notes and "Flak-Bait" Crew Debrief Comments

"Flak-Bait" flew as No. 5 aircraft in the low flight.

30 × 100 GPs dropped; results unobserved.

Fighter support good.

Other Crew Comments

Someone in the high flight fired at a Typhoon on the way out from the coast.

Seventeen-minute bomb run would be too long for a heavily defended target.

"Flak-Bait" Crew

2Lt. H. C. Rodgers, pilot	SSgt. V. J. Mammolito, engineer/gunner
2Lt. B. P. Burrage, copilot	TSgt. O. D. Freeman, radio/gunner
2Lt. K. A. Brower, navigator/bombardier	Sgt. A. Christopher, gunner

Briefing started at 0744 hrs. and ended 0810 hrs.

T/off: 0935 hrs.	Rendezvous: 1040 hrs.	Landfall: 1045 hrs.
Target: 1108 hrs.	Coast Out: 1120 hrs.	Return: 1200 hrs.

Mission Narrative

Eighteen aircraft dispatched, led by Capt. G. H. Watson.

Route was Base to rendezvous with the 386th BG on assembly line from the Naze to the fighter rendezvous point, the 386th to lead. Rendezvous with RAF Spitfires at 51.40'N, 03.25'E (off Knocke), to Roosendaal to target.

Seventeen aircraft attacked, dropping 147 × 250 GPs and 20 × 300 demolition bombs from 12,500 ft.; results good, with fires and smoke observed from the target area. Ten × 250 GPs jettisoned by one aircraft with engine trouble, and 3 × 300 DBs were jettisoned because of rack failure.

Moderate inaccurate HFF in the target area and southwest of the target. Slight inaccurate HFF near Hoogstraeten and Breda area; no damage received.

Return was a right turn to Roosendaal to 51.40'N, 03.25'E (off Knocke), to the Naze to Base.

Interrogation of crews began at 1205 hrs. and finished at 1250 hrs.

Mission Notes and "Flak-Bait" Crew Debrief Comments

"Flak-Bait" flew as No. 2 aircraft in the low flight.

10 × 300 demolition bombs dropped.

At 1110 hrs., about 3 miles east of Gilze-Rijen, six chutes observed from a B-26, which fell like a leaf crashed and burst into flames (the 386th BG lost two aircraft this day).

Other Crew Comments

Formation should fly at briefed altitude; too much of this mission flown at 14,000 ft.

A pilot of a Spitfire seen to bail out at 1041 hrs.; aircraft seen to hit water.

Date: February 24, 1944
Target: Deelen A/D
Field Order: 9th BC F/O 211

"Flak-Bait" Crew

F/O T. H. Rivenbark, pilot
1Lt. S. M. Chase, copilot
2Lt. E. I. Baughman, navigator/bombardier

SSgt. P. E. McManes, engineer/gunner
SSgt. W. L. Moore, radio/gunner
Sgt. C. B. Hill, gunner

Briefing started at 0645 hrs. and ended 0715 hrs.

T/off: 0851 hrs.	Rendezvous: 1010 hrs.	Landfall: 1016½ hrs.
Target: 1037 hrs.	Coast Out: 1057½ hrs.	Return: 1141 hrs.

Mission Narrative

Fifty-two aircraft dispatched in three boxes, led by Lt. Col. G. C. Celio, Lt. Col. O. D. Turner, and 1Lt. D. W. Allen, respectively.

Route was Base to rendezvous with the 386th BG on a line from Orfordness, the 322nd to lead, to the rendezvous with RAF Spitfires at 52.10'N, 03.50'E (off The Hague), to 4 miles south of Katwijk to Vianen to Wageningen to target.

Fifty-one aircraft attacked the primary, dropping 540 × 100 GPs and 329 × 250 GPs from 11,500 ft. for good results, in clear skies. One aircraft jettisoned 10 × 250 GPs and returned early; one other 250 GP bomb returned due to rack failure.

Moderate inaccurate HFF and weak inaccurate LFF from the target area; twenty-four aircraft received Cat. A damage.

Return route was a left turn to Vianen to 4 miles south of Katwijk aan Zee to Base.

Interrogation of crews finished at 1245 hrs.; no start time recorded.

Mission Notes and "Flak-Bait" Crew Debrief Comments

"Flak-Bait" flew as No. 2 in the lead flight, 3rd Box.

10 × 250 GPs dropped for good results.

No damage received.

```
Date: February 24, 1944
Target: XI/A/53 Bois Rempre Noball
Field Order: 9th BC F/O 212
```

"Flak-Bait" Crew

451st BS crew

1Lt. C. B. Jones, pilot
1Lt. J. T. Masters, copilot
2Lt. R. E. Potratz, navigator/bombardier

SSgt. J. C. Ferrell, engineer/gunner
Sgt. T. E. Renfroe, radio/gunner
SSgt. G. N. Gibson, gunner

Briefing started at 1330 hrs. and ended 1400 hrs.

T/off: 1515 hrs.	Rendezvous: 1610 hrs.	Landfall: 1623 hrs.
Target: 1628½ hrs.	Coast Out: 1633 hrs.	Return: 1707 hrs.

Mission Narrative

Thirty-six plus two spare aircraft dispatched; formation led by Lt. Col. G. C. Celio with Capt. L. A. Tenold. The 2nd Box was led by Capt. L. J. Sebille.

Route was Base to Dungeness for rendezvous with RAF Spitfire escort, to 4 miles south of Le Touquet to target.

Thirty-five aircraft attacked the primary, in CAVU conditions, dropping 142 × 600 GPs and 102 × 500 GPs from 12,000 ft. for fair results. One aircraft failed to recognize the target and returned its load of 6 × 500 GPs and 2 × 600 GP bombs. Two spare aircraft returned 12 × 600 GP bombs.

Weak inaccurate LFF encountered from Montreuil.

Return route was a left turn to 4 miles south of Le Touquet to Dungeness to Base.

No interrogation times recorded.

Mission Notes and "Flak-Bait" Crew Debrief Comments

"Flak-Bait" flew as No. 2 in the high flight, 1st Box.

6 × 600 GPs dropped; crew reported good results. First flight hit short; ours were dropped accidentally but hit the target.

Unidentified objects in water 1 mile off coast, probably buoys.

Crew member reports that he had no transportation to mess hall between missions.

```
Date: February 25, 1944
Target: St. Trond—Brusthem A/D
Field Order: 9th BC F/O 213
```

"Flak-Bait" Crew

2Lt. H. C. Rodgers, pilot
2Lt. B. P. Burrage, copilot
2Lt. K. A. Brower, navigator/bombardier

SSgt. V. J. Mammolito, engineer/gunner
TSgt. O. D. Freeman, radio/gunner
Sgt. A. Christopher, gunner

Briefing started at 0700 hrs. and ended 0730 hrs.

T/off: 0850 hrs.	Rendezvous: 1015 hrs.	Landfall: 1019 hrs.
Target: 1051 hrs.	Coast Out: 1117 hrs.	Return: 1209 hrs.

Mission Narrative

Fifty-two aircraft dispatched in three boxes, led by Capt. L. J. Sebille, Capt. H. V. Smythe, and Lt. Col. E. Wursten, respectively.

Route was Base to rendezvous with the 386th BG on a line from the Naze to the fighter rendezvous point, the 386th to lead. RAF Spitfires met at 51.25'N, 03.00'E (north of Ostend), to Knocke to 51.04'N, 04.22'E (river Scheldt near Oude Briel), to 5 miles east of Louvain to target.

Fifty-one aircraft attacked, dropping 350 × 250 GPs and 320 × 100 frag bombs, in CAVU conditions from 11,500 ft., for good results. One aircraft had a fuel leak so returned early and brought back 10 × 250 GPs.

Slight to moderate inaccurate HFF from Knocke, Blankenberge, and Malines. Moderate accurate HFF from Louvain, Beauvechain A/D, Keerbergen, and at the target. Nineteen aircraft received Cat. A damage.

Return route was a left turn to 51.04'N, 04.22'E (river Scheldt near Oude Briel), to Knocke to the Naze to Base. No interrogation times recorded.

Mission Notes and "Flak-Bait" Crew Debrief Comments

"Flak-Bait" flew as No. 5 aircraft in the low flight, 3rd Box.

19 × 100 frag bombs dropped; good results.

Date: February 25, 1944
Target: XI/A/99 Bois d'Enfer Noball
Field Order: 9th BC F/O 215

"Flak-Bait" Crew

2Lt. L. U. Yount, pilot
1Lt. E. W. Goodwin, copilot
1Lt. R. G. Caldwell, navigator/bombardier

Sgt. R. J. Keating, engineer/gunner
SSgt. R. P. Bender, radio/gunner
SSgt. A. J. Sosenko, gunner

Briefing started at 1400 hrs. and ended 1440 hrs.

T/off: 1525½ hrs.	Rendezvous: 1630 hrs.	Landfall: 1648 hrs.
Target: 1659 hrs.	Coast Out: 1710 hrs.	Return: 1804 hrs.

Mission Narrative

Thirty-six plus one spare aircraft dispatched; formation led by Capt. H. M. Posson, and the 2nd Box was led by Capt. H. V. Smythe.

Route was to be Base to fighter rendezvous with RAF 11 Group fighters at Beachy Head, to 4 miles south of Berck-sur-Mer to 2 miles west of Fruges to target.

Formation recalled because of weather, 10/10th stratocumulus tops at 4,500 ft., at the target. 210 × 600 GPs returned; one aircraft jettisoned 6 × 600 GPs; the spare returned 6 × 600 GP bombs.

Briefed return was a right turn to 4 miles south of Berck-sur-Mer to Hastings to Base.

No interrogation times recorded.

Mission Notes and "Flak-Bait" Crew Debrief Comments

"Flak-Bait" flew as No. 2 aircraft in the lead flight, 2nd Box.

6 × 600 GP bombs returned.

Other Crew Comments

Only two aircraft reported seeing the escorting fighters.

The formation met two formations of B-17s, at the same altitude, one at five minutes and other at two minutes before reaching the enemy coast.

Weather forecast wrong about icing; severe icing today.

"Flak-Bait" Crew

2Lt. H. C. Rodgers, pilot
2Lt. B. P. Burrage, copilot
2Lt. W. Barbour, navigator/bombardier

SSgt. V. J. Mammolito, engineer/gunner
TSgt. O. D. Freeman, radio/gunner
Sgt. A. Christopher, gunner

Briefing started at 0900 hrs. and ended 1000 hrs.
T/off: 1249, 1256 & 1303 hrs.   Rendezvous: 1416, 1415 & 1415 hrs. Landfall: 1421 hrs.
Target: 1508½ 1510 & 1446 hrs.   Coast Out: 1509½, 1510 & 1509 hrs.   Return: 1556, 1550 & 1550 hrs.

Mission Narrative

Fifty-three aircraft dispatched in three boxes; formation led by Lt. Col. E. Wursten, the 2nd Box was led by Maj. G. B. Simler, and the 3rd Box by Lt. Col. O. D. Turner.

Briefed route was Base to rendezvous with the 391st BG on a line from Dungeness to the rendezvous with RAF 11 Group fighters at 50.10'N, 01.10'E (off Criel-sur-Mer), to 6 miles northeast of Dieppe to 5 miles southwest of Serqueux to Gisors to 49.05'N, 02.20'E (Frepillon), to target.

Two aircraft returned early with mechanical problems, and twenty-two others (mostly the 3rd Box) were abortive because of weather; 9/10th thin altostratus cloud with tops at 9,000 ft.

A total of twenty-nine aircraft from Boxes 1 and 2 attacked casual targets: sixteen on a coastal gun position at Biville-sur-Mer, dropping 223 × 300 GPs at 1508½ hrs. from 11,500 ft.; four on military huts at 50.19'N, 01.19'E, releasing 24 × 500 GPs and 5 × 600 GPs at 1510 hrs. from 11,000 ft.; and nine on an installation at Le Treport, dropping 54 × 500 GPs and 18 × 600 GPs, also at 1510 hrs., from 11,000 ft. A total of 132 × 500 GP, 45 × 600 GP, and 19 × 300 GP bombs were returned.

Weak inaccurate HFF from the Dieppe/Envermeu area, weak to moderate but accurate HFF from area around St.-Saens, and weak inaccurate HFF from Beaumont-sur-Oise on run over primary. Majority of the HFF appears to come from an area roughly bounded by Longueville, Totes, St.-Saens, and Londinieres. Several e/a were seen, but no encounters ensued. No damage received.

Briefed return route was a left turn to 7 miles northeast of Beauvais to Tocqueville to Dungeness to Base. Interrogation of crews began at 1615 hrs. and finished at 1730 hrs.

Mission Notes and "Flak-Bait" Crew Debrief Comments

"Flak-Bait" flew as No. 4 ship in the low flight, 2nd Box.

Primary and secondary covered by cloud; 6 × 500 GPs and 2 × 600 GPs dropped on a military installation at Ault.

Slight inaccurate HFF from St.-Saens.

English helmet is too large for tail gunners; need flak helmet.

"Flak-Bait" Crew

2Lt. H. C. Rodgers, pilot
2Lt. B. P. Burrage, copilot
2Lt. K. A. Brower, navigator/bombardier

SSgt. W. C. Upton, engineer/gunner
TSgt. O. D. Freeman, radio/gunner
Sgt. A. Christopher, gunner

Briefing started at 0745 hrs. and ended 0830 hrs.

T/off: 0920, 0927 & 0934 hrs.   Rendezvous: 1040 hrs.   Landfall: 1051, 1056 1050 hrs.

Target: 1121, 1122 & 1123½ hrs.   Coast Out: 1145, 1137 & 1144 hrs.   Return: 1218, 1218 & 1246 hrs.

Mission Narrative

Forty-nine aircraft dispatched in three boxes, led by Maj. G. B. Simler, 1Lt. A. W. Bouquet, and Capt. D. W. Allen, respectively.

Route was to rendezvous with the 386th BG on a line from the Naze to the fighter rendezvous, the 386th to lead; the RAF Spitfire escort was met at 51.45'N, 03.00'E (off Knocke), to Haamstede to St.-Annaland to target.

All forty-nine attacked, releasing 655 × 300 GPs from 11000 to 11980 ft., in CAVU conditions, for good results.

Weak inaccurate HFF from Eindhoven, Gilze-Rijen, Tilbury, and Breda and in the target area. LFF from Zierikzee, St.-Annaland, and Breda. No damage received.

Return was from target to Hertogenbosch to St.-Annaland to the Naze to Base.

No interrogation times recorded.

Mission Notes and "Flak-Bait" Crew Debrief Comments

"Flak-Bait" flew as No. 2 aircraft in the lead flight, 3rd Box.

Only 12 × 300 GPs loaded; hit in dispersal area; well concentrated.

Slight inaccurate HFF from Gilze-Rijen A/D.

Observed a lot of shipping activity in Dutch waters, and a train observed on railway near Hertogenbosch.

Other Crew Comments

Too much prop wash from the group ahead; suggest staggering the formations.

Crew of aircraft 41-31830 ER-K, pilot 2Lt. M. C. Simmons, had to go to the bomb dump and get bombs and load them.

Event: First Men of 449th BS Reach Fifty-Mission Mark

On March 12, 1944, the first men in the 449th BS to reach the fifty-mission mark were given two weeks of leave. While this was welcome news, the fact was that the crews had originally expected to be rotated once they reached the fifty-mission figure. In early March 1944, this number of missions to constitute a tour was rescinded, and no definite figure of missions was set. This did cause a drop in moral for the Marauder crews of the 9th Air Force, and eventually a figure of sixty-five missions was established as a tour.

Date: March 15, 1944
Target: Aulnoye M/Y
Field Order: 9th BC F/O 237

"Flak-Bait" Crew

1Lt. H. I. Lewter, pilot   SSgt. E. H. Young, engineer/gunner
2Lt. G. H. Lane, copilot   TSgt. W. E. Clark Jr., radio/gunner
SSgt. W. C. Upton, toggler   SSgt. S. Krykla, gunner

Briefing started at 0730 hrs. and ended 0815 hrs.

T/off: 0920 hrs.   Rendezvous: 1030 hrs.   Landfall: 1033 hrs.

Target: 1108½ (P) & 1118½ (S) hrs. Coast Out: 1138 hrs.   Return: 1212 hrs.

Mission Narrative

Thirty-six aircraft dispatched; 1st Box led by Lt. Col. G. C. Celio, and the 2nd Box by Capt. G. H. Watson with Maj. F. J. McGlynn.

Route was briefed as Base to rendezvous with the 386th BG on a line from Dungeness to the fighter rendezvous, the 322nd to lead. With RAF Spitfires at 50.10'N, 01.10'E (off Le Treport), to Tocqueville to 5 miles south of Amiens, although formation actually flew around the north of Amiens, to 50.00'N 03.50'E (to the south of Vaux-Andigny), to the target.

Formation encountered 6–8/10th cloud cover, tops at 7,000 ft.; 2nd Box attacked primary, thirteen aircraft releasing 52 × 1,000 GPs at 1108½ hrs. for poor results; bombs hit in open fields 500 yds. from the aiming point. On one aircraft the bomb bay doors failed to open in time, and one flight leader did not drop because of the weather; four others because leader did not drop. 24 × 1,000 GPs returned. The 1st Box found a small gap in the clouds over the secondary target, Chievres A/D; seventeen aircraft dropped 68 × 1,000 GPs at 1118½ hrs.; results were unobserved but believed to be poor to fair. No bomb hits showed on the photographs, although a dispersal area was visible through the clouds.

Moderate fairly accurate HFF from Amiens and Oisemont, moderate inaccurate from Peronne. Slight inaccurate HFF from woods south of Chievres, and weak fairly accurate HFF from Chievres A/D. Slight inaccurate HFF from Aulnoye, Tournai, La Bouverie, and Bernaville. Slight to moderate, inaccurate HFF southeast of Amiens. Slight inaccurate HFF from Albert, Poix, and Valenciennes. Five aircraft received Cat. A damage.

Return was a left turn to Waereghem to Nieuport to Nth Foreland to Base.

Interrogation of crews began at 1220 hrs. and finished at 1320 hrs.

Mission Notes and "Flak-Bait" Crew Debrief Comments

"Flak-Bait" flew as No. 5 aircraft in the low flight of the 1st Box.

4 × 1,000 GPs dropped, but results unobserved.

Crew reported weak inaccurate HFF near Amiens, about one minute before the IP, and moderate inaccurate HFF near Mons.

Other Crew Comments

A B-26 from the 386th BG seen to be hit by flak and crash. (No B-26s reported MIA on this day).

One crew reported seeing an e/a crashing at 1057 hrs., probably shot down by the Spitfire escort, near Bapaume.

Ten bursts of flak from a ship encountered approximately 6 miles off the English coast.

```
Date: March 17, 1944
Target: Creil M/Y
Field Order: 9th BC F/O 240
```

"Flak-Bait" Crew

Capt C. E. Davis, pilot
2Lt. D. L. Hunter, copilot
TSgt. C. L. Zearfoss, togglier

SSgt. S. B. Marcum, engineer/gunner
SSgt. A. I. Duncan, radio/gunner
SSgt. J. L. Smith, gunner

Briefing started at 1015 hrs. and ended 1046 hrs.

T/off: 1258 hrs.	Rendezvous: 1400 hrs.	Landfall: 1419 hrs.
Target: 1455 hrs.	Coast Out: 1515 hrs.	Return: 1601 hrs.

Mission Narrative

Thirty-six plus two spare aircraft dispatched; the 1st Box was led by Capt. D. E. Harnly with 1Lt. H. H. Herring, and the 2nd Box was led by Maj. F. P. Taylor.

The brief for the route was Base to rendezvous with the 344th BG on a line from Splasher Beacon No. 8 to Dungeness; however, the 344th mission was scrubbed. Rendezvous with P-47 fighter escort was at Dungeness to 5 miles southwest of Le Treport to Grandvilliers, to Compiegne to 49.12'N, 02.55'E (La Chapelle-en-Serval), to 49.06'N, 02.39'E (Les Mesnil-Aubry), to target.

Thirty-six aircraft attacked the primary, releasing 503 × 250 GPs from 11,500 ft. for fair results. One aircraft had a rack malfunction and returned 1 × 250 GP. The 2nd Box bombed before the 1st Box, which went around for a second run. One aircraft was an early return due to a fuel leak, returning 14 × 250 GPs; a spare filled in, and the other spare returned with its load of 14 × 250 GPs.

Moderate accurate HFF from Oisemont, Aumale, Hornoy, and Poix. A few bursts of weak inaccurate HFF from Beauvais-Tille. Moderate accurate HFF from outer defenses of Paris and Londinieres. Weak inaccurate HFF from Dieppe. Weak, fairly accurate LFF and moderate accurate HFF from Neufchatel and weak inaccurate HFF from Blangy area. Twelve aircraft received Cat. A damage; one man slightly wounded: Sgt. Blevens, 450th BS.

Briefed return was a left turn to Grandvilliers to 5 miles southwest of Le Treport to Dungeness to Base, although the actual route to Le Treport was flown to the south of the intended course.

Interrogation of crews began at 1635 hrs. and finished at 1720 hrs.

Mission Notes and "Flak-Bait" Crew Debrief Comments
"Flak-Bait" flew as No. 3 aircraft in the lead flight, 1st Box.

14 × 250 GP dropped.

P-47s' best escort yet.

Accurate HFF from Aumale both in and out; weak fairly accurate HFF from Paris area.

Observed four boats, at rest, 6 miles off the English coast on way back.

Date: March 20, 1944
Target: XI/A/100 Zudausques Noball
Field Order: 9th BC F/O 243

"Flak-Bait" Crew

1Lt. H. C. Rodgers, pilot
2Lt. B. P. Burrage, copilot
SSgt. J. L. Misarko, togglier

SSgt. V. J. Mammolito, engineer/gunner
TSgt. O. D. Freeman, radio/gunner
Sgt. A. Christopher, gunner

Briefing started at 0630 hrs. and ended 0655 hrs.

T/off: 0814 hrs.	Rendezvous: area cover	Landfall: 0917 hrs.
Target: 0927 hrs.	Coast Out: 0933 hrs.	Return: 1003 hrs.

Mission Narrative
Thirty-six plus one spare aircraft dispatched; formation led by Lt. Col. E. Wursten; the 2nd Box was led by 1Lt. U. T. Downs.

Route was Base to Dungeness to 3 miles south of Hardelot to the target. RAF fighters to provide an umbrella cover in the target area.

Thirty aircraft attacked; part of the 1st Box picked out Cormette, 1½ mile east of the briefed target, in error, and another section of the 1st Box dropped in the vicinity of Watten C/Ws. The 2nd Box attacked the primary, but results at all targets were poor, with no damage to any military installations. 240 × 500 GP bombs released. Low flight of the 2nd Box failed to pick out the target so did not release; 48 × 500 GPs returned. Spare aircraft returned 8 × 500 GPs.

From the IP to past the target area, the formation encountered intense accurate HFF; a short break of about thirty seconds after the target was followed by intense accurate HFF from the Watten wood area, and intense fairly accurate HFF from Gravelines on the way out. Two aircraft MIA, seven aircraft Cat. AC, and twelve aircraft Cat. A damage. Thirteen men MIA.

Return route was a left turn off the target to 4 miles west of Gravelines to Nth Foreland to Base.

Interrogation of crews began at 1010 hrs. and finished at 1125 hrs.

Mission Notes and "Flak-Bait" Crew Debrief Comments
"Flak-Bait" flew as No. 4 aircraft, low flight, 2nd Box.

8 × 500 GP bombs brought back; leader did not release.

Saw two chutes in vicinity of one B-26 that was shot down.

MIA Information
41-31849 ER-N, "Scotch and Soda"
No. 2 aircraft in low flight, 1st Box. Hit just past the target; left wing seen on fire; aircraft went into a dive and then spun down and exploded on the ground; two chutes seen.

1Lt. R. G. Thornton, pilot	KIA
2Lt. H. L. Lawrence, copilot	KIA
1Lt. C. M. Hall, navigator/bombardier	KIA
Sgt. J. O. Lampkins, engineer/gunner	POW
SSgt. K. W. Grigsby, radio/gunner	POW
Sgt. H. Fernous, gunner	KIA
Maj. C. W. Faust, observer	KIA (member of the 643rd BS, 409th BG, an A-20 unit)

41-31914 SS-S, "Druther Not"
No. 2 aircraft in lead flight of the 2nd Box. Hit two minutes after the above aircraft; seen to be hit by flak, and left wing caught fire. Aircraft suddenly pulled up and did two loops, after which it went spinning down and crashed in the vicinity of Audricq. Five chutes seen.

1Lt. C. W. Larson, pilot	evaded
1Lt. G. C. Fahnestock, copilot	POW
SSgt. J. Sanchez, toggler	evaded
SSgt. W. L. Hamilton, engineer/gunner	POW
Sgt. E. B. Jackson, radio/gunner	evaded
SSgt. C. R. Yingling, gunner	KIA

```
Date: March 23, 1944
Target: Creil M/Y
Field Order: 9th BC F/O 246
```

"Flak-Bait" Crew

1Lt. H. C. Rodgers, pilot	SSgt. V. J. Mammolito, engineer/gunner
2Lt. B. P. Burrage, copilot	TSgt. O. D. Freeman, radio/gunner
SSgt. J. L. Misarko, toggler	Sgt. A. Christopher, gunner

Briefing started at 0815 hrs. and ended 0905 hrs.

T/off: 1005 hrs.	Rendezvous: 1110 hrs.	Landfall: 1117 hrs.
Target: 1147½ & 1156 (S) hrs.	Coast Out: 1210½ hrs.	Return: 1255 hrs.

Mission Narrative
Thirty-six plus two spare aircraft dispatched; the 1st Box was led by Lt. Col. G. C. Nye, and the 2nd Box by Maj. G. B. Simler.

Route was to rendezvous with 386th BG on an assembly line from Tunbridge Wells to Hastings, the 322nd to lead; rendezvous with IX FC P-47 escort was at 50.20'N, 01.00'E (off Le Treport), to Tocqueville, to 49.43'N, 01.41'E (Foret Domaniale de Lyons), to 49.15'N, 02.53'E (Pontarme), to 49.02'N, 02.38'E (Ecouen) to target.

Twenty-eight aircraft attacked the primary in CAVU conditions, releasing 112 × 1,000 GPs from 11,500 ft., with a good concentration of bursts seen on the tracks. Lead flight of the 2nd Box bombs failed to release at the primary, so the seven aircraft in this flight dropped on the secondary, Beauvais-Tille A/D, releasing 28 × 1,000 GPs for fair results. One aircraft returned 4 × 1,000 GPs after a rack malfunction. Two aircraft were mechanical aborts: one had engine cut out over base and a spare filled in, and another had a fuel leak and returned early. Spare aircraft for 1st Box returned as briefed. Twelve × 1,000 GPs returned from these three aircraft.

Weak inaccurate flak from Beaumont-le-Roger, moderate inaccurate HFF from Neufchatel area, weak inaccurate HFF from vicinity of Neufchatel. Weak inaccurate HFF from woods south of Londonieres, moderate inaccurate from area near Rouen, and moderate inaccurate from Dieppe. No damage reported.

Return was a left turn off the target to 49.18'N, 02.04'E (Le Quoniam), to 49.43'N, 01.41'E (Foret Domaniale de Lyons), to Tocqueville, to Hastings to Base.

Interrogation of crews began at 1320 hrs. and finished at 1350 hrs.

Mission Notes and "Flak-Bait" Crew Debrief Comments

"Flak-Bait" flew as No. 3 in the lead flight, 1st Box.

4 × 1,000 GPs dropped; observed good results.

Escort OK.

Date: March 25, 1944
Target: Hirson M/Y
Field Order: 9th BC F/O 249

"Flak-Bait" Crew

2Lt. G. P. Jones, pilot
1Lt. T. W. Piippo, copilot
2Lt. R. W. Rodriguez, navigator/bombardier

SSgt. J. E. Corlew, engineer/gunner
SSgt. W. Goetz Jr., radio/gunner
Sgt. J. Palcich, gunner

Briefing started at 1115 hrs. and ended 1215 hrs.

T/off: 1320 hrs.	Rendezvous: 1420 hrs.	Landfall: 1420 hrs.
Target: 1459 hrs.	Coast Out: 1538 hrs.	Return: 1640 hrs.

Mission Narrative

Thirty-six plus two spare aircraft dispatched; 1st Box was led by Capt. G. H. Watson, with Capt. L. J. Sebille leading the 2nd Box ("Flak-Bait" was the spare for the 2nd Box).

Route was Base to rendezvous with the 344th BG on an assembly line from Beachy Head to the fighter rendezvous, the 322nd to lead. Rendezvous with IX FC P-47s at Tocqueville, to 49.45'N, 02.40'E (west of Avrechy), to the IP to target, although it was reported that the formation was off course for almost the entire route.

Thirty-six attacked, dropping 288 × 500 GPs for fair results.

Formation encountered moderate to intense accurate HFF and weak inaccurate LFF from Montdidier and moderate inaccurate HFF from Oisemont area. Two aircraft were MIA, and twenty-two received Cat. A damage. Personnel casualties included thirteen MIA, with one man slightly wounded: SSgt. T. Evans, 451st BS.

Return was from target to 3 miles north of Guise to Tocqueville to Beachy Head to Base.

Interrogation of crews began at 1630 hrs. and finished at 1730 hrs.

Mission Notes and "Flak-Bait" Crew Debrief Comments

"Flak-Bait" was the spare aircraft for the 2nd Box; not required, so returned with 8 × 500 GPs.

MIA Information
41-31906 DR-W

No. 4 aircraft of the lead flight, 1st Box, received a direct hit from flak in the midsection while in the vicinity of Montdidier at approx. 1518/1519 hrs. The aircraft was seen to explode immediately and break up, with the tail assembly separating completely. One chute was observed.

1Lt. J. P. Ryan, pilot	KIA
1Lt. H. E. Williams, copilot	KIA
1Lt. R. L. Roland, bombardier	KIA
2Lt. C. C. Carlson, navigator	KIA
SSgt. E. M. Olsen, engineer/gunner	KIA
TSgt. R. M. Stephens, radio/gunner	KIA
Sgt. T. N. Bentley, gunner	KIA

41-31798 DR-Q, "Utopia"

No. 3 aircraft of high flight, 1st Box. Hit immediately after aircraft 906 at 1519 hrs.; received a direct flak hit to the right engine nacelle; the aircraft went into a steep dive with smoke coming out of the crippled engine. When at about 1,000 ft. the ship was observed to blow up and hit the ground in flames. Some crews reported one chute coming out of the aircraft, but there is no certainty that the chute had anyone in it.

F/O R. S. Tate, pilot	KIA
F/O W. B. Lannin, copilot	KIA
Sgt. J. P. Amos, togglier	KIA
SSgt. W. B. Considine, engineer/gunner	KIA
Sgt. D. G. Maryott, radio/gunner	KIA
SSgt. G. W. Egbert, gunner	KIA

Date: March 26, 1944
Target Ijmuiden E/R Boat Pens
Field Order: 9th BC F/O 250

"Flak-Bait" Crew

1Lt. H. C. Rodgers, pilot	SSgt. V. J. Mammolito, engineer/gunner
2Lt. B. P. Burrage, copilot	TSgt. O. D. Freeman, radio/gunner
2Lt. W. Barbour, navigator/bombardier	Sgt. A. Christopher, gunner

Briefing started at 1115 hrs. and ended 1205 hrs.

T/off: 1235 hrs.	Rendezvous: 1400 hrs.	Landfall: 1407 hrs.
Target: 1408 hrs.	Coast Out: 1408 hrs.	Return: 1505 hrs.

Mission Narrative

Forty-four aircraft dispatched in three boxes; 1st Box led by Lt. Col. G. C. Celio with Capt. G. H. Watson, the 2nd Box was led by Capt. L. Sebille with Lt. Col. O. D. Turner, and the 3rd Box was led by Capt. H. M. Posson.

Routing was Base to rendezvous with the 344th BG on an assembly line from Southwold to the fighter rendezvous, the 322nd to lead entire formation. Rendezvous with the RAF 11 Group fighters at 52.27'N, 04.00'E (off Noordwijk), to the target.

Forty-three aircraft attacked, dropping 172 × 1,000 GPs from 12,200 ft., for good results. The 1st Box bombs fell largely to the right and short of the aiming point [AP]; the 2nd and 3rd Boxes hit the AP squarely with many bombs. One aircraft returned 4 × 1,000 GPs when the copilot became ill.

Intense accurate HFF encountered, starting immediately after bombs away, and continued for two minutes through the turn and for 2–3 miles out to sea. Four aircraft Cat. AC, fourteen Cat. A, and one Cat. E in a crash landing at Wattisham. One man wounded: SSgt. J. W. Freitas, 450th BS.

Return was a left turn to 52.35'N, 03.43'E (Nth Sea off Haarlem), to Lowestoft to Base, although actual landfall was made between Aldeburgh and Southwold.

Interrogation of crews began at 1530 hrs. and finished at 1645 hrs.

Mission Notes and "Flak-Bait" Crew Debrief Comments

"Flak-Bait" flew as No. 4 in the high flight, 2nd Box.

4 × 1,000 GPs dropped—good results.

Intense inaccurate HFF; some flak from boats outside the breakwater along the shore. Crew like the window equipment; it seemed to make the flak inaccurate.

Other Crew Comments

Several crews complained that they should be fed before taking off at this time of day.

Report of a P-47 that broke through and in front of the low flight, 2nd Box, while the aircraft were circling the field, and almost hit them.

Two submarines seen leaving the jetty inside the harbor.

The lead aircraft, piloted by Lt. Col. Celio, returned on single engine and landed at Framlingham. Extent of damage not known, but the aircraft (41-31967 SS-H "Johnny Zero") was out of service until late May.

Category E Information
41-34861 SS-M, "Eleanor B"
Pilot 1Lt. U. T. Downs, flying deputy lead of the 1st Box, seen to leave formation at 1408 hrs. with bad hydraulic leak. Belly-landed at Wattisham; six crew members bailed out over the field, after which the pilot and copilot, 2Lt. J. G. Brunsman, crash-landed the aircraft safely.

41-34861 SS-M, "Eleanor B," with Sgt. Giesler in the foreground. *Trevor J. Allen collection*

Ijmuiden Revenge Trip
Billed as a red-letter day, the mission of March 26, 1944, was a much-longed-for revenge trip to Ijmuiden, scene of the two low-level missions of May 1943. Three members of the lead crew were veterans on the May 14 mission, and eighteen other personnel from that mission were among the remaining aircraft in the formation.

All seven operational B-26 groups joined in the attack on the E/R boat pens, with the 322nd BG leading. The 9th Air Force launched 344 B-26s, of which 338 attacked the target, one aircraft from the 323rd BG was lost, and a further eighty-three received battle damage.

Event: Practice Move
The groups of the 9th Air Force were always made aware that they needed to be prepared to "stay mobile," since once the invasion had taken place, groups supporting the ground forces would have to move closer to the battle lines. With this in mind, a practice move was planned

The order was received on March 26, 1944, and ordered the 322nd BG to make a move to Station 166 Matching, home of the 391st BG. All excess personnel equipment was stored, and the equipment boxes were packed on the twenty-seventh. The reconnaissance echelon left at 0900 on the twenty-eighth, and the aircraft departed at 1330 hrs. the same day, the 449th BS dispatching fifteen aircraft. The rear echelon left Andrews Field at 1520 hrs.

"Eleanor B" after her crash landing at Wattisham. *Trevor J. Allen collection*

Upon arrival at Matching, the aircraft were prepared for a combat mission. The individual squadrons prepared meals, and the group CO ate with the 449th BS personnel. The squadron felt that it must have been a success, since he returned for breakfast the next morning!

On March 30, the return to Andrews Field was made, the reconnaissance echelon leaving at 0930 hrs., with the advance echelon at 1030 hrs. and the aircraft departing at 1330 hrs. The rear echelon left at 1415 hrs., and all were back at Andrews Field by 1615 hrs.

No missions were flown between March 26 and April 8 due to a prolonged period of bad weather.

"Flak-Bait" Crew

1Lt. K. W. Reed, pilot
1Lt. D. B. Barker, copilot
1Lt. W. L. Juneau, navigator
SSgt. G. W. Gueterman, togglier

SSgt. D. C. Mustain, engineer/gunner
SSgt. S. P. Smith, radio/gunner
Sgt. J. L. Harding, gunner

Briefing started at 1000 hrs. and ended 1050 hrs.

T/off: 1127 & 1134 hrs.	Rendezvous: 1145 hrs.	Landfall: 1250 & 1251 hrs.
Target: 1337 & 1332 hrs.	Coast Out: 1358 & 1334 hrs.	Return: 1439 & 1400 hrs.

Mission Narrative

Thirty-six plus one spare aircraft dispatched; the 1st Box was led by Maj. G. B. Simler, and the 2nd Box by Capt. H. V. Smythe.

Briefed routing was Base to rendezvous with the 344th BG at Nth Foreland, the 344th to lead, to rendezvous with IX FC P-47 escort at 51.12'N, 02.20'E (off Dunkirk), to Nieuport to 50.41'N, 03.56'E (Escautpont), to 50.41'N, 05.20'E (Libois), to the IP, 2 miles southeast of Tongres, to the target. The 322nd followed the 344th until the formation reached Lille, when the leader noticed that the 344th were off-course so changed course, leaving the 344th near Roubaix, 5 miles south of briefed course, and took his box to the primary. The 2nd Box continued to follow the 344th.

1st Box attacked the primary, eighteen aircraft dropping 142 × 500 GPs from 12,000 ft. for good results; hits seen on tracks and among cars and stores, with 2–3 direct hits on the AP and many near misses; tracks on all sides of AP put out. Two × 500 GPs jettisoned through rack failures.

The 2nd Box, who continued to follow the 344th BG, reported that both primary and secondary were obscured, so orbited to the left over Ghent and attacked Coxyde A/D as a casual target; seventeen aircraft released 136 × 500 GPs from 12,500 ft., for good results; bursts in center of airfield and across ESE/WNW runway and exited coast to intercept the return course. Two aircraft were mechanical aborts, so spare filled in; 16 × 500 GPs returned.

Moderate intense and accurate HFF from Lille, Roubaix, and Renaix for both boxes; in addition the 1st Box experienced moderate inaccurate flak in the Ath/Chievres area, from an airfield northwest of Liege, possibly Bierset, and weak inaccurate HFF from area between Malines and Antwerp. Six aircraft received Cat. A damage.

Briefed return was a left turn to Diest to 7 miles north of Aerschot to Malines to Knocke to Nth Foreland and Base.

Interrogation of crews began at 1430 hrs. and finished at 1545 hrs.

Mission Notes and "Flak-Bait" Crew Debrief Comments

"Flak-Bait" flew as No. 3 ship in the lead flight, 2nd Box.

Cloud prevented going farther than Renaix, so returned to Coxyde, hit runways. Released 8 × 500 GPs for good results.

Observed many trains and much activity in marshaling yards at Roubaix.

Other Crew Comments

Lead pilot of 1st Box did a good job despite being taken off course by lead group.

Long trip for evasive action—gas low.

"Flak-Bait" Crew

2Lt. R. R. Crusey, pilot
2Lt. A. F. Minich, copilot
SSgt. G. W. Gueterman, togglier

SSgt. W. S. Allen, engineer/gunner
Sgt. C. S. Walters, radio/gunner
SSgt. R. J. Buckles, gunner

Briefing started at 0600 hrs. and ended 0655 hrs.

T/off: 0750 hrs.	Rendezvous: 0923 hrs.	Landfall: 0927 hrs.
Target: 0927 hrs.	Coast Out: 0928 hrs.	Return: 1015 hrs.

Mission Narrative

Thirty-seven aircraft dispatched, led by Capt. C. W. Hoover; the 2nd Box was led by Capt. H. V. Smythe.

Route was Base to rendezvous with the 344th BG at Splasher Beacon No. 11, the 322nd to lead, to Selsey Bill to rendezvous with IX FC P-47s at 49.40'N, 00.27'W (off Ouistreham), to 49.24'N, 00.24'W (Breville-les-Monts), the IP, to the target.

Special instructions given to the formation: three A-20 aircraft, from the 416th BG, to rendezvous with the formation at takeoff and fly to a point 24 miles from the target, maintaining 1,000 ft. above the 1st Box. At 24 miles, with the formation on a definite heading toward the target, the formation leader to call the A-20 lead, telling him to "scramble," firing a green flare at the same time. Leader of the A-20s will increase speed to 230 mph and spread his element to a 300 ft. interval, dropping window up to and past the target.

Thirty-six aircraft attacked, dropping 144 × 1,000 GPs from 11,500 ft., achieving a poor concentration 1,000 yds. north of the target. One aircraft was an early return when the pilot became ill; 4 × 1,000 GPs returned.

Formation encountered weak inaccurate HFF over the target; appeared to be concentrated on the group following. Moderate to intense, inaccurate HFF 3–5,000 ft. below the formation, from 3 miles from the coast to landfall. One aircraft suffered Cat. A damage.

Return was a left turn from the target to Beachy Head to Base.

Interrogation of crews began at 1035 hrs. and finished at 1125 hrs.

Mission Notes and "Flak-Bait" Crew Debrief Comments

"Flak-Bait" flew as No. 5 in the low flight in the 1st Box.

4 × 1,000 GP dropped; fair results, hit to side of the target.

Very inaccurate HFF; six gun salvoes seen.

B-26 seen at approximately 7,000 ft. with black smoke coming from the left wing; seemed under control and heading home (see note below; possibly same aircraft).

Other Crew Comments

B-26 seen to ditch, or crash in water, at 49.50'N, 00.30'W (in the sea off Ouistreham abeam Le Havre), friendly fighter seen circling this spot.

Eighteen crews praised the use of the A-20 window aircraft.

"Flak-Bait" Crew

2Lt. R. R. Crusey, pilot
F/O G. H. Tharp, copilot
SSgt. J. B. Mitchell, togglier

Sgt. C. S. Walters, engineer/gunner
SSgt. W. S. Allen, radio/gunner
SSgt. R. J. Buckles, gunner

Briefing started at 1430 hrs. and ended 1505 hrs.

T/off: 1615 hrs.	Rendezvous: 1728 hrs.	Landfall: 1731 hrs.
Target: 1804½ hrs.	Coast Out: 1834 hrs.	Return: 1911 hrs.

Mission Narrative

Thirty-six plus one spare aircraft dispatched; the 1st Box was led by Capt. A. W. Bouquet, and the 2nd Box by Capt. D. W. Allen.

Route was Base to rendezvous with the 344th BG at Nth Foreland, the 322nd to lead, to rendezvous with IX FC P-47s at 51.10'N, 02.30'E (off Dunkirk), to Nieuport to Grammont to 50.17'N, 04.23'E (south of Court Tournant), to Florennes, the IP, to the target. A small deviation from the briefed route was made on the bomb run to avoid flak.

All aircraft attacked, dropping 144 × 1,000 GPs from 11,500 ft. in CAVU conditions for good results, with many direct hits observed, with a good concentration on the AP. The spare aircraft returned 4 × 1,000 GPs.

Moderate inaccurate HFF from Nieuport and Florennes, four aircraft receiving Cat. A damage. Pairs of e/a observed low down on the deck in the target area, and near Grammont and Roulers, but no encounters took place.

Return was a left turn to Gembloux to 50.59'N, 03.32'E (west of Tournai), to Nieuport to Nth Foreland to Base. Interrogation of crews began at 1930 hrs. and finished at 2015 hrs.

Mission Notes and "Flak-Bait" Crew Debrief Comments

"Flak-Bait" flew as No. 5 in the low flight, 1st Box.

4 × 1,000 GP dropped on target, with a good concentration around AP.

Ten barrage balloons observed at Thielt.

Other Crew Comments

Landfall was made at 9,500 ft.; the briefed altitude was 11,000 ft.

"Flak-Bait" Crew

1Lt. J. J. Farrell, pilot
F/O T. F. Moore, copilot
1Lt. O. J. Redmond, navigator/bombardier

TSgt. D. L. Tyler, engineer/gunner
SSgt. J. B. Manuel, radio/gunner
SSgt. N. E. Thielan, gunner

Briefing started at 0715 hrs. and ended 0745 hrs.

T/off: 0843 hrs.	Rendezvous: 1015 hrs.	Landfall: 1018 hrs.
Target: 1050 & 1101½ (S) hrs.	Coast Out: 1120 hrs.	Return: 1202 hrs.

Mission Narrative

Thirty-six plus two spare aircraft dispatched, led by Maj. F. Taylor; the 2nd Box was led by Capt. A. W. Bouquet.

Route was Base to rendezvous with the 344th BG at Nth Foreland, the 322nd to lead, to rendezvous with RAF Spitfires at 51.11'N, 02.30'E (off Dunkirk), to Nieuport to Waereghem to Aulnoye to 50.10'N, 04.24'E (east of Moustier-en-Fagne), the IP, to the target.

One large cloud obscured the primary target, so the secondary, Chievres A/D, was attacked by thirty-six aircraft. The 1st Box attacked northeast dispersal area but bombing was scattered, mostly in open fields; one small building hit and road cut in the dispersal area. The 2nd Box attacked the northwest dispersal area, two shelters receiving a direct hit, and three others had several near misses. Two Nissen-type huts hit, two hits to north–south runway, and a peri-track received several hits. 142 × 1,000 GPs dropped. One aircraft returned early with an oil leak, returning 4 × 1,000 GPs, one spare returned with 4 × 1,000 GPs, and 2 × 1,000 GPs returned through rack failures.

Moderate accurate HFF at Chievres and weak inaccurate HFF at Nieuport. Nineteen aircraft received Cat. A damage. Three crewman wounded: 1Lt. O. J. Redmond, 1Lt. R. E. Palmer, and TSgt. C. L. Zearfoss, all from the 449th BS.

Return was a left turn to the rally point at Nivelles to 8 miles southwest of Ghent to Nieuport to Nth Foreland to Base.

Interrogation of crews began at 1230 hrs. and no end time recorded.

Mission Notes and "Flak-Bait" Crew Debrief Comments

"Flak-Bait" flew as No. 2 in the lead flight, 1st Box.

Bombardier 1Lt. O. J. Redmond received flak wounds to face, hands, and right leg. Pilot pulled air bottle to release bombs after bombardier was hit over target; 4 × 1,000 GP bombs salvoed armed.

Over 100 flak holes, damage to hydraulic system, and damage to bomb bay cables.

Take more-evasive action, and bomb run too long.

Weak inaccurate HFF at Nieuport, and intense very accurate HFF tracked our bomb run over target.

Two unidentified e/a seen in target area, but they turned away from the flak.

```
Date: April 18, 1944
Target: Monceau-sur-Sambre M/Y
Field Order: 9th BC F/O 270
99th CBW F/O 13
```

"Flak-Bait" Crew

1Lt. H. C. Rodgers, pilot
2Lt. B. P. Burrage, copilot
2Lt. W. Barbour, navigator/bombardier

SSgt. V. J. Mammolito, engineer/gunner
TSgt. O. G. Freeman, radio/gunner
Sgt. A. Christopher, gunner

Briefing started at 1515 hrs. and ended 1555 hrs.

| T/off: 1709 hrs. | Rendezvous: 1815 hrs. | Landfall: 1816 hrs. |
| Target: 1847 hrs. | Coast Out: 1911 hrs. | Return: 2015 hrs. |

Mission Narrative

Thirty-eight aircraft off; the 1st Box was led by Capt. D. W. Allen, and the 2nd Box by Capt. G. H. Watson.

Routing was Base to rendezvous with the 344th BG at Nth Foreland, the 322nd to lead, to rendezvous with IX FC fighter escort at 51.11'N, 02.30'E (off Dunkirk), to Nieuport to Waereghem to Aulnoye to Beaumont (the IP) to target.

Thirty-five attacked, dropping 140 × 1,000 GPs from 11,500 ft. in CAVU conditions, with an excellent concentration on the AP, with main weight of bombs on engine repair sheds and adjacent tracks. Three aircraft returned early: on one the nosewheel doors would not close, one had an engine cut out immediately after takeoff, and another had the left engine cut out just before the enemy coast; 4 × 1,000 GPs jettisoned and 12 × 1,000 GPs brought back.

Weak inaccurate LFF and HFF from Nieuport on route in and out. No damage received.

Return was a left turn to the rally point at Nivelles to 8 miles southwest of Ghent to Nieuport to Nth Foreland to Base.

Interrogation of crews began at 2000 hrs. and finished at 2055 hrs.

Mission Notes and "Flak-Bait" Crew Debrief Comments
"Flak-Bait" flew as No. 4 ship in the low flight, 1st Box.

4 × 1,000 GPs dropped, for good results.

Railway traffic observed in Ostend to Dunkirk area and into Ghent.

```
Date: April 19, 1944
Target: Fecamp C/D
Field Order: 9th BC F/O 271
99th CBW F/O 14
```

"Flak-Bait" Crew
1Lt. H. C. Rodgers, pilot
2Lt. B. P. Burrage, copilot
SSgt. G. W. Gueterman, togglier

SSgt. V. J. Mammolito, engineer/gunner
TSgt. O. D. Freeman, radio/gunner
Sgt. A. Christopher, gunner

Briefing started at 0745 hrs. and ended 0815 hrs.

| T/off: 0925 hrs. | Rendezvous: area cover | Landfall: 1047 hrs. |
| Target: 1058 hrs. | Coast Out: 1058 hrs. | Return: 1208 hrs. |

Mission Narrative
Thirty-six plus two spare aircraft dispatched led by Maj. B. G. Willis; the 2nd Box was led by Maj. G. B. Simler.

Routing was Base to Beachy Head to Quiberville to Yvetot to Fauville (the IP) to target. RAF Spitfires provided umbrella support.

8/10th cloud over the target; the 1st Box found a quick gap in the clouds, and nineteen aircraft dropped 76 × 1,000 GPs from 11,500 ft., for fair results. The 2nd Box were unable to attack due to the cloud; nineteen aircraft returned 76 × 1,000 GPs. The spare aircraft accompanied the formation.

Weak inaccurate LFF and HFF at the target, to the left of course. No damage received.

Return was a right turn to Beachy Head to Base.

Interrogation of crews began at 1210 hrs. and finished at 1245 hrs.

Mission Notes and "Flak-Bait" Crew Debrief Comments
"Flak-Bait" flew as No. 6 ship in the lead flight, 1st Box.

4 × 1,000 GPs released.

LFF in target area 3,000 ft. below and LFF from Dieppe, below and inaccurate.

Other Crew Comments
Too many groups assembling at the same time; caused near collision of aircraft.

```
Date: April 19, 1944
Target: Malines M/Y and Repair Shops
Field Order: 9th BC F/O 272
99th CBW F/O 15
```

"Flak-Bait" Crew
F/O G. H. Tharp, pilot
2Lt. L. L. Peters, copilot
SSgt. J. B. Mitchell, togglier

SSgt. D. C. Mustain, engineer/gunner
SSgt. W. J. Whitesell, radio/gunner
SSgt. J. G. Morgan, gunner

Briefing started at 1530 hrs. and ended 1610 hrs.

T/off: 1710 hrs.	Rendezvous: 1814 hrs.	Landfall: 1830 hrs.
Target: 1852½ hrs.	Coast Out: 1916 hrs.	Return: 2000 hrs.

Mission Narrative

Thirty-six aircraft dispatched; the 1st Box was led by Capt. G. H. Watson, and the 2nd Box by Capt. H. M. Posson.

Route was Base to rendezvous with the 391st BG at Herne Bay, the 322nd to lead, to Nth Foreland for rendezvous with RAF Spitfire escort, to Furnes to Waereghem to Termonde to target.

All thirty-six aircraft attacked, dropping 144 × 1,000 GPs in CAVU conditions for excellent results. Bombs from the 1st Box hit the AP squarely, and all bombs within 2,000 ft., with direct hits to power station and tracks. The 2nd Box bombs fell within the target area, landing in the smoke from those of the 1st Box.

Weak inaccurate HFF at the primary, and weak inaccurate HFF at Roosendaal and western end of Schouwen Island. No more than 8–10 bursts in these areas. No damage received.

Return was a left turn to 5 miles west of Oostmalle to Roosendaal to 51.40'N, 03.34'E (off Cadzand), to the Naze to Base.

Interrogation of crews began at 2022 hrs. and finished at 2105 hrs.

Mission Notes and "Flak-Bait" Crew Debrief Comments

"Flak-Bait" flew as No. 5 aircraft in the low flight, 2nd Box.

4 × 1,000 GPs dropped, for good results.

```
Date: April 20, 1944
Target: XI/A/85 Bonnieres Noball
Field Order: 9th BC F/O 275
99th CBW F/O 17
```

"Flak-Bait" Crew

2Lt. B. P. Burrage, pilot	SSgt. V. J. Mammolito, engineer/gunner
1Lt. H. C. Rodgers, copilot	TSgt. O. D. Freeman, radio/gunner
TSgt. H. L. Gray, togglier	Sgt. A. Christopher, gunner

Briefing started at 1645 hrs. and ended 1710 hrs.

T/off: 1820 & 1827 hrs.	Rendezvous: 1929 hrs.	Landfall: 1942 hrs.
Target: 1950 & 1951 hrs.	Coast Out: 2000 & 2001 hrs.	Return: 2105 hrs.

Mission Narrative

Thirty-six aircraft dispatched; 1st Box was led by Maj. G. B. Simler with Lt. Col. F. E. Fair. The 2nd Box was led by Capt. L. R. Wade.

Route was Base to Hastings to Berck-sur-Mer to target. RAF Sitfires to provide umbrella cover.

Thirty-four aircraft abortive; 5–7/10th cloud and thick haze prevented sighting. Two aircraft dropped 8 × 1,000 GPs, one by a misunderstanding between pilot and bombardier. Pilot called, "Close the bomb bay," whereas bombardier thought he said, "Clear the bomb bay," and dropped. Another aircraft released on this aircraft. A total of 64 × 1,000 GPs and 288 × 250 GPs were returned. (1st Box carried 1,000 GP, and 2nd Box 250 GP bombs).

Moderate to intense, fairly accurate HFF experienced continuously, first from Auxi-le-Chateau area and tracking thereafter through turn off target and as far as Hesdin. Moderate inaccurate LFF from landfall to Nampont. Intense LFF from Crecy woods but burning out at 8–9,000 ft. Eighteen aircraft received Cat. A damage, fifteen of which were in the 1st Box. No injuries received.

Return was a left turn to Berck-sur-Mer to Hastings to Base.

Interrogation of crews began at 2100 hrs. and finished at 2135 hrs.

Mission Notes and "Flak-Bait" Crew Debrief Comments

"Flak-Bait" flew as No. 2 aircraft in the lead flight, 2nd Box.

16 × 250 GP returned; haze over all areas.

9th BC slipped up, sending planes over in such haze.

Other Crew Comments

B-17 observed spinning in flames, over Boulogne area.

B-26 from another group observed losing altitude, with both engines smoking.

B-26 hit by flak 3 miles west of Frevent and went down in flames. (the 394th BG lost three aircraft this day).

One unidentified fighter seen to go down in flames 5–6 miles north of Hesdin.

The 394th BG commented that an unidentified B-26 group cut across them at landfall, forcing them to make a 360-degree turn; although early reports thought it may have been the 386th BG, upon further investigation it indicated that it might have been the 322nd BG formation.

> Date: April 21, 1944
> Target: XI/A/7 Siracourt Noball
> Field Order: 9th BC F/O 276
> 99th CBW F/O 18

"Flak-Bait" Crew

1Lt. G. K. Eubank, pilot
1Lt. R. R. Murray, copilot
SSgt. J. L. Campbell, togglier

Sgt. G. G. Minter, engineer/gunner
Sgt. E. C. Schaefer, radio/gunner
SSgt. J. A. Pavesich, gunner

Briefing started at 0830 hrs. and ended 0905 hrs.

T/off: 1027½ hrs.	Rendezvous: area cover	Landfall: 1138 hrs.
Target: 1206½ hrs.	Coast Out: 1207 hrs.	Return: 1315 hrs.

Mission Narrative

Thirty-seven aircraft dispatched, led by Capt. H. M. Posson; the 2nd Box was led by Capt. L. R. Wade.

Routing was Base to Hastings to Berck-sur-Mer to 50.30'N, 02.29'E (Nuncq-Hautecote), to 50.18'N, 02.32'E (west of Haute Visee), the IP, to the target. RAF fighters to provide umbrella cover.

Primary obscured by haze and in shadow; two runs were made; cloud cover was 5–6/10th. Thirteen aircraft from the 1st Box attacked a casual target, a gun position at Rang-du-Fliers, 4 miles east of Berck-sur-Mer; 104 × 500 GPs were released, most of which fell in open fields and among some dwellings. Five aircraft from the 1st Box salvoed their bombs (40 × 500 GPs in total) when these aircraft were hit and on single engine; bombs fell at various locations. The 2nd Box did not release because the leader was in distress. 56 × 500 GPs jettisoned in the Channel, and 88 × 500 GPs brought back. Disposition of bombs on MIA aircraft unknown.

Intense accurate HFF from Auchel and Hesdin, and intense accurate HFF at the target. Fourteen aircraft received Cat. AC damage, fifteen were Cat. A, one Cat. E, and one MIA. A total of six aircraft returned on single engine; three aircraft landed at Hawkinge. One man KIA: SSgt. H. W. Gross, and one wounded: Sgt. J. A. Trainer, both from the 452nd BS, and six men were MIA.

Return route was a left turn off the target to 50.18'N, 02.00'E (Yvrench), to 4 miles south of Berck-sur-Mer to Hastings to Base.

Interrogation of crews began at 1325 hrs. and finished at 1430 hrs.

Mission Notes and "Flak-Bait" Crew Debrief Comments

"Flak-Bait" flew as No. 6 aircraft in the high flight, 1st Box.

Landed at Hawkinge at 1229 hrs.; Cat. AC damage.

8 × 500 GPs salvoed when hit by flak in right engine 5 miles south of Auchel, and returned on single engine. Turned off and left coast 4 miles north of Berck-sur-Mer.

Damage to aircraft included a large hole in the tail, large holes in the rear bomb bay, and one large hole in left engine nacelle, and other small holes.

Escort not seen.

Other Crew Comments
Use more window instead of using it sparingly.

MIA information
41-31767 PN-U, "Ginger"
Seen to be hit by flak in the left engine; aircraft fell back and to the left of the formation, salvoed bombs and dropped its wheels. Aircraft went down steeply near Auchel, close to the French coast. Three chutes observed.

F/O T. H. Rivenbark, pilot	POW
2Lt. G. E. Stone, copilot	POW
TSgt. J. L. Misarko, togglier	POW
SSgt. W. L. Moore, engineer/gunner	POW
SSgt. P. E. McManes, radio/gunner	POW
Sgt. C. B. Hill, gunner	POW

(This crew had flown "Flak-Bait" on a number of occasions.)

F/O T. H. Rivenbark and 2Lt. G. E. Stone in the cockpit of "Ginger." *USAAF*

41-31887 DR-F, "Mary," after her belly landing at Hawkinge. *USAAF*

The six pilots who returned on a single engine on April 21. *Left to right*: F/O G. Fuson, 1Lt. H. C. Rodgers, 1Lt. R. Wilson, 1Lt. G. Eubank, Capt. L. Wade, and 2Lt. McDonough. 1Lt. Rodgers would fly "Flak-Bait" on twenty-three occasions, and 1Lt. Eubank five times, including the single-engine landing this day. Capt. Wade made the belly landing at Hawkinge upon return. *USAAF*

Category E Information
41-31887 DR-F, "Mary"
Capt. L. R. Wade, leader of 2nd Box, had right engine knocked out by flak; came back on single engine, and with the hydraulic system shot out, belly-landed at Hawkinge, the engineer, SSgt. Harry W. Gross, having been killed by a flak wound to the head. In a cruel twist of fate, Sgt. Gross had just received orders for a period of leave in the United States and was due to depart imminently.

Event: Promotion for 449th BS CO
On April 24, 1944, the 449th BS CO, Maj. Benjamin G. Willis, was promoted to the rank of lieutenant colonel.

Event: Leave to the US
On April 25, 1944, the first six crew members of the 449th BS were returned to the Z of I for a thirty-day rest period; these were Capt. Smythe, Lt. Reed, Lt. Palmer, TSgt. Einbinder, TSgt. Evans, and SSgt. Manning.

Event: 322nd BG Taken off Operations for One Week
On April 25, 1944, the 322nd BG was taken off operations for one week to practice night flying; the 323rd BG had been stood down the week before. Other groups were due to follow suit shortly thereafter.

```
Date: May 4, 1944
Target: Etaples Railroad Battery
Field Order: 9th BC F/O 296
99th CBW F/O 37
```

"Flak-Bait" Crew

1Lt. W. F. Green, pilot	TSgt. S. P. Smith, engineer/gunner
1Lt. D. B. Barker, copilot	Sgt. R. J. Keating, radio/gunner
SSgt. G. W. Gueterman, togglier	Sgt. J. L. Harding Jr., gunner

Briefing started at 0630 hrs. and ended 0700 hrs.

T/off: 0850 & 0905 hrs.	Rendezvous: area cover	Landfall: not recorded
Target: 1002 & 1016 hrs.	Coast Out: 1020 hrs.	Return: 1101 hrs.

Mission Narrative
Thirty-six plus two spare aircraft dispatched; formation led by Lt. Col. B. G. Willis; the 2nd Box was led by Capt. K. L. Bayles.

Route was Base to Dungeness to 4 miles south of Berck-sur-Mer to 50.31'N, 01.54'E (Quend-Rage), the IP, to the target. RAF fighters to provide umbrella cover.

Bombing was by flights, thirty-three aircraft releasing a total of 65 × 2,000 GPs; results fair to good—initial bursts fell short but carried over and into target area. Five aircraft abortive: three aircraft had mechanical failures, two for other reasons; leader of low flight, 2nd Box, peeled out of formation because of an oil leak and failed to signal the rest of the flight. This flight became scattered; two followed him and were too late to catch up with rest of the formation. Two aircraft jettisoned a total of 3 × 2,000 GPs in Channel, and 8 × 2,000 GPs were returned.

Weak to moderate, fairly accurate, HFF and LFF from the IP and continuing to the target. Five aircraft received Cat. A damage.

Return was a right turn to Dungeness to Base.

Interrogation of crews began at 1107 hrs. and finished at 1140 hrs.

Mission Notes and "Flak-Bait" Crew Debrief Comments

"Flak-Bait" flew as No. 3 aircraft in the lead flight, 2nd Box.

2 × 2,000 GPs dropped; hit in forest east of the target.

Went in south of course and made left turn.

HFF inaccurate on bomb run.

Quite a lot of shipping activity in harbor at Berck-sur-Mer and Le Touquet.

Other Crew Comments

Visibility good at target, and target plainly visible; difficult to differentiate between craters and gun positions, which may account for why bombing was scattered.

Observed two Fw 190s on bomb run, at 5,000 ft. going in opposite direction.

A B-26 observed out of formation and losing altitude, heading for France (no aircraft were reported MIA this day).

Too long an interval between briefing and takeoff.

```
Date: May 6, 1944
Target: Barfleur C/D
Field Order: 9th BC F/O 299
99th CBW F/O 41
```

"Flak-Bait" Crew

1Lt. A. F. Byrd Jr., pilot
1Lt. R. M. Cooper Jr., copilot
SSgt. J. L. Campbell, togglier

SSgt. E. M. Winstead, engineer/gunner
SSgt. G. F. Van Meter, radio/gunner
SSgt. P. A. Davis, gunner

Briefing started at 1600 hrs. and ended 1640 hrs.

T/off: 1800 & 1830 hrs.	Rendezvous: 1915 & 1945 hrs.	Landfall: 1927; 1st Box only
Target: No attack	Coast Out: 1931hrs.	Return: 2033 & 2048 hrs.

Mission Narrative

Thirty-six plus two spare aircraft dispatched; formation led by Lt. Col. G. C. Nye; the 2nd Box was led by Capt. H. M. Posson.

Routing was to be Base to Selsey Bill, to rendezvous with RAF 11 Group Spitfire escort at 50.20'N, 00.50'E (off Dieppe), to 49.31'N, 01.00'W (Hameau Minet), to 49.25'N, 01.19'W (Le Rotz), the IP, to the target.

No attack; thirty-eight aircraft abortive, recalled because of weather, 7–8/10th over the target with tops at 7,500 ft. 1st Box turned just past the IP and exited at St. Vaast. 2nd Box made turn six minutes before the IP and did not make landfall. 1st Box awarded a sortie. 76 × 2,000 GPs returned.

Three crews reported weak inaccurate HFF from St.-Mere-Eglise, and one crew reported the same from St.-Vaast. No damage received.

Return route was to Selsey Bill and Base.

Interrogation of crews began at 2045 hrs. and finished at 2120 hrs.

Mission Notes and "Flak-Bait" Crew Debrief Comments

"Flak-Bait" flew in the No. 4 position, high flight, 2nd Box.

No sortie, 2 × 2000 GPs returned.

"Flak-Bait" Crew

1Lt. D. B. Barker, pilot
1Lt. W. F. Green, copilot
SSgt. G. W. Gueterman, togglier

SSgt. K. M. Locke, engineer/gunner
TSgt. S. P. Smith, radio/gunner
Sgt. J. L. Harding Jr., gunner

Briefing started at 0615 hrs. and ended 0700 hrs.
T/off: 0802 & 0809 hrs.   Rendezvous: 0913 hrs.   Landfall: 0913 hrs.
Target: 1002½ & 1009 hrs.   Coast Out: 1044 hrs.   Return: 1146 hrs.

Mission Narrative

Thirty-six plus two spare aircraft dispatched, led by Lt. Col. G. C. Nye with Maj. C. W. Hoover. The 2nd Box was led by Capt. H. M. Posson.

Routing was Base to Splasher Beacon No. 8, for rendezvous with the 344th BG, who were to lead, to rendezvous with the P-38 fighter escort at Tocqueville, to St. Just to 49.31'N, 04.46'E (west of St. Pierre-a-Arnes), the IP, to the target.

Thirty-six aircraft attacked, by flights; cloud en route was 4–5/10th building to 10/10th, with tops at 8,000 ft. and some towering to 10,000 ft., but a clear spot over the target allowed bombing. Results for the 1st Box was poor to fair, while those from the 2nd Box were good to poor. A total of 69 × 2,000 GPs were dropped from 12,000 ft. 7 × 2,000 GPs returned, four by two aircraft aborting, one of which had cylinder head temperature problems, and the other the life raft inflated and damaged the rudder; three due to rack failure. The spares filled in.

Weak inaccurate HFF from 5 miles south of Laon, Courtrai area, and Ath. Weak inaccurate LFF between Dunkirk and Furnes. Intense inaccurate LFF from about 3 miles east of Marienbourg, bursting 1,000 ft. below, and moderate accurate HFF from 10–15 miles west of Dunkirk, while formation was over the Channel. No flak damage received.

Fourteen to twenty e/a (Fw 190s and Me 109s) circled the formation from the three o'clock position and attacked the low flight of the 1st Box while in the Charleroi area. Coming out of the clouds in the twelve o'clock position low, and in groups of three to four, successively. They made only one attack and peeled away low. One aircraft MIA, six crew MIA.

Return was to rally point at Roubaix to Furnes to Nth Foreland to Base. Lead group (the 344th BG) led the formation to the left of briefed course after Roubaix.

Interrogation of crews began at 1140 hrs. and finished at 1300 hrs.

Mission Notes and "Flak-Bait" Crew Debrief Comments

"Flak-Bait" flew in the No. 4 position of the high flight, 2nd Box.

2 × 2,000 GPs released, falling on lower part of target area; good results.

15–20 Fw 190s passed 500–600 ft. below, going in the opposite direction; went into cloud and did not attack. One crew member reported tracer coming about 100 ft. from the ship, but did not see where it came from.

Just off the rally point, a B-26 was observed losing altitude and bursting into flames; definitely saw four chutes. Observed to crash and blow up.

41-31845 DR-Q, "Patches," seen after a previous landing mishap, was MIA on May 7, 1944. *Author's collection*

Other Crew Comments

Wing of a P-38 seen to break off after attack by eight Fw 190s; pilot seen to bail out.

P-38 escort reported the FW-190s to be the long-nose variant. Although no claims were made by the 322nd BG, the P-38 escort reported that the B-26s destroyed one of the Me 109s, seen to be descending in flames. Credit for this destroyed e/a was awarded to Sgt. L. E. White, tail gunner of the missing aircraft, who was seen firing continuously at the e/a as they broke away.

MIA Information
41-31845 DR-Q, "Patches"

Flying No. 3 in the low flight, 1st Box attacked by e/a at about 1014 hrs., south of Charleroi; flames and fuel seen to be coming from the bomb bay area. Aircraft seen to lower wheels and break in two; 5–6 chutes observed.

1Lt. J. W. Wright, pilot	POW, repatriated (lost lower half of right leg)
1Lt. M. W. Kautz, copilot	POW
1Lt. L. L. Adams, navigator/bombardier	POW
SSgt. M. Hannesson, engineer/gunner	evaded, liberated by US Army on September 3, 1944
TSgt. C. F. Steele, radio/gunner	POW
Sgt. L. E. White, gunner	evaded, liberated by US Army on September 3, 1944

> **Date: May 7, 1944**
> **Target: Marquise C/D**
> **Field Order: 9th BC F/O 301**
> **99th CBW F/O 43**

"Flak-Bait" Crew

1Lt. W. F. Green, pilot	SSgt. K. M. Locke, engineer/gunner
1Lt. D. B. Barker, copilot	Sgt. J. L. Harding Jr., radio/gunner
SSgt. G. W. Gueterman, togglier	TSgt. S. P. Smith, gunner

Briefing started at 1615 hrs. and ended 1645 hrs.

T/off: 1833 & 1848 hrs.	Rendezvous: area cover	Landfall: 1936 & 1954 hrs.
Target: 1937 & 1955 hrs.	Coast Out: 1938 & 1957 hrs.	Return: 2022 hrs.

Mission Narrative

PFF mission; thirty plus six aircraft carrying window and two PFF ships dispatched; 1st Box led by Lt. Col. F. E. Fair, and the 2nd Box was led by Capt. R. H. Schmidt.

Route was Base to Rye to 50.53'N, 00.57'E (mid-Channel off Eastbourne), the IP, to the target. RAF 11 Group Spitfires provided top cover.

Thirty-one aircraft attacked the primary in clear conditions from 12,000 to 12,100 ft.; the 1st Box achieved poor results, the 2nd Box fair results. A total of 58 × 2,000 GPs and 8 × 500 GPs (PFF a/c) released. One aircraft returned early after a spark plug blew out, returning 2 × 2,000 GP bombs.

1st Box encountered moderate, fairly accurate HFF just before the target, continuing to the exit. The 2nd Box reported moderate to intense, accurate HFF from landfall, continuing over target and to extreme range at exit. Also some moderate HFF until about 2–3 miles from exit, possibly from a flak boat. Ten aircraft received Cat. A damage, all in the 2nd Box.

Return was a left turn to Dungeness to Base.

Interrogation of crews began at 2010 hrs. and finished at 2115 hrs.

Mission Notes and "Flak-Bait" Crew Debrief Comments

"Flak-Bait" flew in the No. 4 position in the low flight, 1st Box.

2 × 2000 GP dropped, for fair results. Saw some hits in the target area. Saw a fire in buildings north of the AP.

Asked for enough "poop" (information) sheets at briefing; ran out of these at last three briefings.

Procedure to Be Employed by Window Aircraft

Instructions as to the method of operating window-dropping aircraft were that three aircraft were to accompany each box, preceding the boxes on the bomb run by 400 yds. and 1,000 ft. above, to drop window in the target area, from 3 miles before the coast to three minutes after the enemy coast.

The window was highly effective for the 1st Box, but crews in the 2nd Box reported that the window was dropped to the south of course, and the wind, from 10 degrees, blew it too far south to be effective.

```
Date: May 8, 1944
Target: Neufchatel C/D
Field Order: 9th BC F/O 302
99th CBW F/O 44
```

"Flak-Bait" Crew

1Lt. A. F. Minich, pilot
1Lt. D. B. Barker, copilot
SSgt. G. W. Gueterman, togglier

TSgt. S. P. Smith, engineer/gunner
SSgt. W. C. Upton, radio/gunner
Sgt. J. L. Harding Jr., gunner

Briefing started at 0615 hrs.; no end time recorded.

T/off: 0824 & 0844 hrs.	Rendezvous: area cover	Landfall: 0949 hrs.
Target: 0938 & 1000 hrs.	Coast Out: 1000 hrs.	Return: 1037 hrs.

Mission Narrative

Thirty-six plus two spare aircraft off; the 1st Box was led by Lt. Col. F. E. Fair, and the 2nd Box was led by Capt. R. H. Schmidt.

Route was Base to Rye, to 4 miles south of Berck-sur-Mer to 50.32'N, 01.54'E (Belle Dune), the IP, to the target. RAF 11 Group to provide top cover.

Bombing was done by flights, and thirty-seven aircraft attacked, dropping 148 × 1,000 GPs from 11,900 to 12,000 ft., in clear conditions. Results were mainly poor to fair, although those of the low flight, 2nd Box, were good. The leader of the low flight, 1st Box (flown by 1Lt. J. J. Farrell, the original pilot of "Flak-Bait"), was hit by flak and on single engine; the deputy took over, and one aircraft failed to bomb when flight split up, returning 4 × 1,000 GPs.

Weak to moderate HFF fire began on bomb run and continued beyond the target; two aircraft received Cat. A damage.

Return was from target to Dungeness to Base.

Interrogation of crews began at 1030 hrs. and finished at 1130 hrs.

Mission Notes and "Flak-Bait" Crew Debrief Comments

"Flak-Bait" flew as No. 5 in the low flight, 2nd Box.

4 × 1,000 GP dropped; saw an explosion on the beach where bombs hit; believe a mine going off.

HFF was accurate for altitude; bursts to the right and tracking from the target area.

Other Crew Comments

Control tower landed the aircraft on Runway 27 when there was an aircraft parked on it. Landing aircraft had to go onto the grass to avoid it.

"Flak-Bait" Crew

1Lt. S. M. Chase, pilot
2Lt. M. F. Dombrowski, copilot
2Lt. E. I. Baughman, navigator/bombardier

SSgt. W. T. Guyette, engineer/gunner
Sgt. E. C. Malone, radio/gunner
Sgt. J. O. Hartsell, gunner

Briefing started at 1700 hrs.; no end time recorded.

T/off: 1825 & 1840 hrs.	Rendezvous: 1920 & 1935 hrs.	Landfall: 1936 & 1952 hrs.
Target: 1955 & 2013 hrs.	Coast Out: 2017 & 2032 hrs.	Return: 2122 hrs.

Mission Narrative

PFF mission. Thirty-four plus two spare and two PFF aircraft dispatched. The 1st Box was led by Lt. Col. E. Wursten, and the 2nd Box by Capt. J. E. Haley.

Route was Base to rendezvous with RAF fighters at Beachy Head, to Ault to 49.31'N, 01.42'E (Ecouis), to the target.

Thirty-four attacked, bombing on PFF equipment, dropping 473 × 250 GPs and 8 × 500 GPs (PFF a/c) from 13,000 ft. Weather was CAVU down sun, but visibility 3½ miles up sun. Results for the 1st Box were poor; hits were on the landing ground but not in the designated area, causing no apparent damage. Box 2 achieved good results; bombs walked across eastern dispersal area in a good concentration. One aircraft jettisoned 1 × 250 GP through rack failure; two aircraft returned early (with 32 × 250 GPs) because of fuel problems, one of which was one of the spares. A further 6 × 250 GPs were brought back because of rack failures.

"Mild and Bitter" returning from her 100th mission, avoiding flak on crossing the coast.
Peter Dole

1st Box reported moderate accurate HFF from Blaney and tracking and continuing past Neufchatel for three minutes. The 2nd Box reported moderate fairly accurate HFF tracking from Forges to Gournay. One aircraft received Cat. AC damage (landed at Manston on single engine), and seven aircraft received Cat. A damage.

Return route was a right turn to Etretat to Beachy Head to Base.

Interrogation of crews began at 2125 hrs. and finished at 2215 hrs.

Mission Notes and "Flak-Bait" Crew Debrief Comments

"Flak-Bait" flew as No. 5 in the high flight, 1st Box.

16 × 250 GP on field, but not on AP, in a good concentration.

A flak train observed at 49.26'N, 00.37'E (northwest of Cormeilles).

"Mild and Bitter" Completes 100th Mission

41-31819 DR-X "Mild and Bitter" completed its 100th mission on this raid, the first Allied bomber based in Britain to reach such a feat. Pilot was Capt. Paul Shannon, the aircraft's original pilot. The aircraft's crew chief was Sgt. William L. Stuart.

Both "Mild and Bitter" and an aircraft named "Bingo Buster" (41-34863 RJ-P 323rd BG), which was the second aircraft to reach the 100-mission mark, on May 16, 1944, were returned to the United States for bond-raising tours.

Adorned with the names of many of the personnel of the 322nd BG, "Mild and Bitter" prior to returning to the United States for a war bond tour. *USAAF*

> **Date:** May 9, 1944
> **Target:** Sangatte C/D, 1st Box
> Calais M/Y, 2nd Box
> **Field Order:** 9th BC F/O 304
> 99th CBW F/O 46

"Flak-Bait" Crew

1Lt. T. W. Piippo, pilot
2Lt. R. R. Riggs, copilot
2Lt. R. W. Rodriquez, navigator/bombardier

SSgt. W. Goetz Jr., engineer/gunner
SSgt. J. E. Corlew, radio/gunner
Sgt. J. Palcich, gunner

Briefing started at 0745 hrs. and ended 0815 hrs.

T/off: 0930 & 0937 hrs.	Rendezvous: 1029 & 1045 hrs.	Landfall: 1055 & 1056 hrs.
Target: 1102 & 1101 hrs.	Coast Out: 1102 hrs.	Return: 1134 & 1126 hrs.

Mission Narrative

Thirty-six plus two spare aircraft dispatched; the 1st Box was led by Lt. Col. E. Wursten, the 2nd Box by Capt. J. E. Haley.

Route was to rendezvous with the 391st BG at Bradwell Bay, then to rendezvous with the 344th BG at Eastchurch, the 391st to lead the entire formation. To rendezvous with IX FC P-47s at Nth Foreland to 51.15'N, 02.10'E (off Gravelines), to 7 miles west of Dunkirk to 50.53'N, 02.01'E (south of Herly), the IP, to targets.

Four groups of P-47s to dive-bomb flak positions in the target area.

Weather was CAVU.

1st Box to attack Sangatte RR Battery; nineteen aircraft dropped 76 × 1,000 Comp B bombs, from 12,500 ft., for good results.

Encountered weak inaccurate HFF from 3 miles north of Ardres, and intense accurate HFF on the bomb run and over target; fire continued for 3–4 minutes. Six aircraft received Cat. AC damage, and ten aircraft Cat. A. One man wounded: SSgt. R. F. Lavigne, 452nd BS.

2nd Box to attack Calais M/Y; 17 aircraft attacked, dropping 66 × 1,000 GPs, from 12,600 ft., for fair to good results. 8 × 1,000 GPs returned by two aircraft, which were mechanical aborts, and 2 × 1000 GPs brought back because of rack failure.

Several crews reported 12–14 bursts of HFF at landfall; weak inaccurate HFF was encountered from 3 miles north of Ardres and weak to moderate HFF over the target.

Return was a left turn to Nth Foreland to Base.

Interrogation of crews began at 1148 hrs. and finished at 1245 hrs.

Mission Notes and "Flak-Bait" Crew Debrief Comments

"Flak-Bait" flew as No. 4 aircraft in the high flight, 1st Box, to attack Sangatte.

No damage received; 4 × 1,000 dropped, good concentration in target area, smoke and fire observed.

Link chutes and cases malfunction of ammo feed to gun (which one was not specified).

Other Crew Comments

Teamwork and cooperation of P-47 escort confused the flak gunners.

```
Date: May 9, 1944
Target: Crisbecq C/D
Field Order: 9th BC F/O 305
99th CBW F/O 47
```

"Flak-Bait" Crew

1Lt. R. R. Murray, pilot
1Lt. G. K. Eubank, copilot
Sgt. E. Montes de Oca, togglier

Sgt. G. G. Minter, engineer/gunner
Sgt. E. C. Schaefer, radio/gunner
SSgt. J. A. Pavesich, gunner

Briefing started at 1600 hrs. and ended 1620 hrs.

T/off: 1740 & 1755 hrs.	Rendezvous: area cover	Landfall: 1858 hrs.
Target: 1911 & 1923½ hrs.	Coast Out: 1911 & 1923½ hrs.	Return: 2031 hrs.

Mission Narrative

Thirty-six aircraft dispatched; the 1st Box was led by Lt. Col. G. C. Nye with Capt. H. H. Herring. The 2nd Box was led by Maj. D. E. Harnly.

Route was Base to Brighton to 49.24'N, 00.58'W (Martragny), to 49.12'N, 01.10'W (St. Lo), to 49.21'N, 01.28'W (La Varde), the IP, to the target. RAF 11 Group to provide top cover.

Thirty-four aircraft attacked by flights; a total of 130 × 1,000 GPs were dropped from 12,000 ft. Conditions were clear but with haze. Results varied from poor to good for the 1st Box and good to excellent for the 2nd Box. One aircraft MIA: jettisoned 4 × 1,000 GPs before the target, and one aircraft was an early return with 4 × 1,000 GPs. Two aircraft had rack malfunctions, 1 × 1,000 GP was jettisoned, and 1 × 1,000 GP returned.

Weak inaccurate LFF reported from St. Lo and Airel. Intense LFF reported from Isigny and St.-Jean-de-Daye, firing at the aircraft going down; six men MIA. No other damage received.

Return was a left turn from the target to Brighton to Base.

Interrogation of crews began at 2022 hrs. and finished at 2112 hrs.

Mission Notes and "Flak-Bait" Crew Debrief Comments

"Flak-Bait" flew as No. 2 in the lead flight, 1st Box.

4 × 1,000 GPs on primary; results unobserved.

At 1901½ hrs., when 3 miles southwest of Isigny, saw a B-26 with fire coming out of left engine. Aircraft went down in two big spirals and crashed and exploded. Two open chutes seen; one other crewman was seen, but chute not open when observed.

Suggest putting target picture on wall at enlisted crew room.

MIA Information
41-31954 ER-Z
Flying as No. 5 aircraft in high flight, 1st Box. Left engine caught fire; unknown cause, since no flak or fighters observed at the time. Four to five chutes observed. Aircraft seen to crash and explode in vicinity of Isigny. Some crews reported that as chutes neared ground, intense light flak was fired at them.

1Lt. L. G. McGlocklin, pilot	KIA
2Lt. W. F. Cook, copilot	POW
2Lt. T. M. Straka, navigator/bombardier	POW
Sgt. N. J. Huschka, engineer/gunner	POW
TSgt. R. Tomlinson, radio/gunner	POW
SSgt. J. R. Dana, gunner	POW

> **Date: May 10, 1944**
> **Target: Douai M/Y**
> **Field Order: 9th BC F/O 307**
> **99th CBW F/O 49**

"Flak-Bait" Crew

1Lt. G. K. Eubank, pilot	Sgt. G. G. Minter, engineer/gunner
1Lt. R. R. Murray, copilot	Sgt. E. C. Schaefer, radio/gunner
Sgt. G. W. Gueterman, togglier	SSgt. J. A. Pavesich, gunner

Briefing started at 1430 hrs. and ended 1505 hrs.

T/off: 1613 hrs.	Rendezvous: 1716 hrs.	Landfall: 1729 hrs.
Target: 1746 hrs.	Coast Out: 1826 hrs.	Return: 1900 hrs.

Mission Narrative
Thirty-seven dispatched; the 1st Box was led by Lt. Col. G. C. Celio and the 2nd Box by Capt. L. J. Sebille.

Briefed route was Base to rendezvous with 344th BG at Eastchurch, the 322nd to lead, to rendezvous with IX FC P-38s at Nth Foreland to Furnes to 50.32'N, 02.53'E (Izel-les-Hameau), the IP, to the target. However, bad visibility at landfall caused navigation errors; landfall was made at Gravelines and then picked up Cambrai; thinking it was the primary, turned to make a run and realized error and flew north and passed over primary too late to make a run.

No attack because of weather; 7–9/10th altocumulus cloud layer tops 9,000 ft., visibility 2–3 miles in thick haze. Twenty-two aircraft made landfall, seventeen from the 1st Box and five from the 2nd Box. Four aircraft were mechanical aborts and a further twelve from the 2nd Box failed to complete formation after the leader aborted with radio problems. Deputy took over but could not catch the formation; 116 × 1,000 GPs returned. A total of 20 × 1,000 GPs jettisoned in Channel by four aircraft; two were low on gas and two through battle damage. 12 × 1,000 GPs were jettisoned over enemy territory by three aircraft suffering battle damage.

Moderate inaccurate HFF at landfall; one crew counted forty-three bursts. Intense accurate HFF from Bourbourg-Ville, Watten, Aire, Merville, and Lillers, and intense accurate HFF from Lens and Arras. Eleven aircraft Cat. AC damage, ten aircraft Cat. A, and one aircraft Cat. E in crash landing at base; three injured, two by flak: SSgt. O. C. Brown, 450th BS, and Sgt. R. E. Johnson, 452nd BS, and one in a parachute landing: see under Category E information.

Briefed return was a left turn to Tournai to Waereghem to Furnes to Nth Foreland to Base.

Interrogation of crews began at 1920 hrs. and finished at 2015 hrs.

Mission Notes and "Flak-Bait" Crew Debrief Comments

"Flak-Bait" flew as No. 6 in low flight, 2nd Box.

4 × 1000 GP returned; turned back at Nieuport due to flight being scattered.

Let's get weather right.

Observed large boat anchored off Dunkirk.

Other Crew Comments

Why did flight leader of low flight, 2nd Box, enter France when not in a box and without escort?

Category E* Information
41-31888 ER-S, "War Eagle"

Pilot 1Lt. M. C. Simmons, flying No. 2 position in the lead flight, 1st Box. Damaged by flak and belly-landed at base. Nav/Bomb, 2Lt. D. W. Franklin, 450th BS, injured in a parachute landing.

"War Eagle" after her belly landing on May 10; she was later repaired and returned to service. *Peter Dole*

* Although initially declared as Cat. E, the aircraft was subsequently reassessed as Cat. B and was repaired and returned to service, as ER-H with the 450th BS, on November 30, 1944, and eventually declared missing in action on February 23, 1945.

Date: May 11, 1944
Target: St.-Quentin C/D
Field Order: 9th BC F/O 308
99th CBW F/O 51

"Flak-Bait" Crew

1Lt. T. W. Piippo, pilot
F/O T. F. Moore, copilot
2Lt. R. W. Rodriquez, navigator/bombardier
Capt. J. O. Eaton (387th BG), observer

SSgt. W. Goetz Jr., engineer/gunner
SSgt. J. E. Corlew, radio/gunner
Sgt. J. Palcich, gunner

Briefing started at 1200 hrs. and ended 1240 hrs.

T/off: 1352 & 1407 hrs.	Rendezvous: area cover	Landfall: 1508 & 1520 hrs.
Target: 1505 to 1508 hrs.	Coast Out: 1508 & 1524 hrs.	Return: 1602 hrs.
1521 to 1524 hrs.		

Mission Narrative

Thirty-six aircraft dispatched; the 1st Box was led by Lt. Col. G. C. Celio, and the 2nd Box by Capt. L. J. Sebille.

Route was Base to Beachy Head to 50.16'N, 01.13'E (off Le Treport), the IP, to the target. IX FC P-47s to provide umbrella support.

Thirty aircraft attacked primary, bombing by flights, from 12,000 ft. in clear conditions. 1st Box results poor for two flights, and fair for six aircraft that dropped on some underwater obstacles in error. 2nd Box results were good. 120 × 1,000 GPs dropped on primary, and 24 × 1,000 GPs on underwater obstacles.

Window was dropped by all aircraft from the IP until exit from enemy coast; no flak experienced.

Return was a left turn to Dungeness to Base.

Interrogation of crews began at 1605 hrs. and finished at 1645 hrs.

Mission Notes and "Flak-Bait" Crew Debrief Comments

"Flak-Bait" flew as No. 5 in the high flight, 2nd Box.

4 × 1,000 GPs dropped, with a good concentration on target.

"Flak-Bait" Crew

1Lt. A. F. Byrd Jr., pilot
1Lt. R. M. Cooper Jr., copilot
SSgt. J. L. Campbell, togglier

SSgt. E. M. Winstead, engineer/gunner
SSgt. G. F. Van Meter, radio/gunner
SSgt. P. A. Davis, gunner

Briefing started at 0730 hrs. and ended 0805 hrs.

T/off: 0915 & 0930 hrs.	Rendezvous: area cover	Landfall: 1036 & 1046 hrs.
Target: 1047 & 1100 hrs.	Coast Out: as per target	Return: 1146 hrs.

Mission Narrative

Thirty-six aircraft dispatched; the 1st Box was led by Lt. Col. G. C. Nye with Capt. U. T. Downs. The 2nd Box was led by Maj. G. B. Simler.

Route was Base to Beachy Head to Etretat to 49.32'N, 00.31'E (La Gohaigne), to 49.39'N, 00.36'E (La Bigrerie), the IP, to the target. IX FC P-47s provided umbrella support.

Thirty-six aircraft attacked, by flights, dropping 144 × 1,000 GPs from 12,000 ft. in clear conditions. Results for the 1st Box were fair to good, fair, and poor, respectively, and the 2nd Box was fair, poor, and poor, respectively.

Very weak LFF and 10–12 bursts of inaccurate HFF from the target area, bursting low. No damage received.

Return was a right turn from the target to Beachy Head to Base.

Interrogation of crews began at 1140 hrs. and finished at 1235 hrs.

Mission Notes and "Flak-Bait" Crew Debrief Comments

"Flak-Bait" flew as No. 4 aircraft in the low flight, 1st Box.

4 × 1,000 GPs dropped, for fair results; some hits in the southern part of target; others were in the water. Weak inaccurate HFF just after leaving target.

"Flak-Bait" Crew

1Lt. R. M. Cooper Jr., pilot
1Lt. A. F. Byrd Jr., copilot
SSgt. J. L. Campbell, togglier

SSgt. E. M. Winstead, engineer/gunner
SSgt. G. F. Van Meter, radio/gunner
SSgt. P. A. Davis, gunner

Briefing started at 1630 hrs. and ended 1700 hrs.

T/off: 1800 & 1807 hrs.	Rendezvous: 1900 hrs.	Landfall: 1917 & 1916 hrs.
Target: 1954 & 1955½ hrs.	Coast Out: 2029 & 2028 hrs.	Return: 2121 hrs.

Mission Narrative

Thirty-six aircraft dispatched; 1st Box led by Capt. G. H. Watson, and the 2nd Box by Lt. Col. E. Wursten.

Route was Base to Nth Foreland, and rendezvous, with IX FC P-47 support, to Furnes to Huy to target. Route was flown as briefed, but landfall made just north of Dunkirk; winds were not as briefed; formation turned left over Channel and reentered at approximately the briefed place.

Attacking by flights, twenty-nine aircraft attacked, dropping 116 × 1,000 GPs from 11,500 to 11,000 ft. Visibility was very poor, 3–4 miles in thick haze. 1st Box results were excellent, poor, and poor, respectively, and those for the 2nd Box were good, poor, and poor. Six aircraft were early return because of mechanical difficulties, and one aircraft failed to bomb because the bomb bay doors would not open. A total of 28 × 1,000 GPs returned.

Moderate to intense, fairly accurate HFF from just after bombs away and continuing on left turn off the target. Weak inaccurate HFF from Dunkirk. Eight aircraft received Cat. A damage.

Return was a left turn to Huy to Furnes to Nth Foreland to Base.

Interrogation of crews began at 2120 hrs. and finished at 2155 hrs.

Mission Notes and "Flak-Bait" Crew Debrief Comments

"Flak-Bait" flew as No. 5 aircraft in the high flight, 1st Box.

4 × 1,000 GP dropped on bridge below the briefed railroad bridge; landed short and to the right; the lead bombardier picked up wrong target and missed by 100 yds.

Looked like first flight hit the target.

Other Crew Comments

Briefed wind was 170 degrees at 26 mph, but actual was found to be 75 degrees at 22 mph.

Either the high flight, Box 1, was too low, or the lead flight was too high, hit prop wash, and had to bomb to the left of lead flight instead of the right.

```
Date: May 13, 1944
Target: St.-Pierre-du-Mont C/D
Field Order: 9th BC F/O 313
99th CBW F/O 55
```

"Flak-Bait" Crew

1Lt. R. R. Murray, pilot
1Lt. G. K. Eubank, copilot
Sgt. G. W. Gueterman, togglier

Sgt. G. G. Minter, engineer/gunner
Sgt. E. C. Schaefer, radio/gunner
SSgt. J. A. Pavesich, gunner

Briefing started at 0815 hrs. and ended 0850 hrs.

T/off: 1023 & 1043 hrs.	Rendezvous: area cover	Landfall: 1127 & 1148 hrs.
Target: 1139½ & 1202½ hrs.	Coast Out: as per target	Return: 1258 hrs.

Mission Narrative

Thirty-five aircraft dispatched; the 1st Box was led by Capt. D. W. Allen, and the 2nd Box by Maj. D. E. Harnly.

Route was Base to Worthing to 49.21'N, 00.41'W (St.-Contest), to 49.06'N, 00.41'W (west of Le Bon Repos), to St. Lo to the target. The 2nd Box made landfall 4 miles east of the briefed route. IX FC P-47s provided umbrella support.

Bombing by flights, thirty-three aircraft dropped 64 × 2,000 GPs on the primary from 11,500 to 11,000 ft.; results for the 1st Box were poor, the bombs falling in the water. It appears that the wind drift, which was briefed as 3 degrees from the left, was actually 30 degrees from the right, and the bombardiers failed to correct for it. The 2nd Box achieved excellent results. Two aircraft from the low flight, 2nd Box, released between the IP and the target when a bomb accidentally fell out of the flight leader's aircraft, and they dropped on that, releasing a total of 5 × 2,000 GPs. One × 2,000 GP was jettisoned over the Channel.

The 1st Box reported no opposition; the 2nd Box reported weak inaccurate LFF at landfall, far below; no damage received.

Return was a right turn off the target to Worthing to Base.

Interrogation of crews began at 1304 hrs. and finished at 1350 hrs.

Mission Notes and "Flak-Bait" Crew Debrief Comments

"Flak-Bait" flew as No. 2 in the lead flight, 2nd Box.

1 × 2,000 GP released on target; one hung up due to rack failure, so was jettisoned over the Channel. Results poor—hit over and in the water.

Ten small vessels observed in the harbor at Grandcamp-les-Bains.

```
Date: May 15, 1944
Target: Beaumont-le-Roger A/D
Field Order: 9th BC F/O 315
99th CBW F/O 56
```

"Flak-Bait" Crew

1Lt. H. C. Rodgers, pilot
2Lt. R. R. Rigg, copilot
TSgt. H. L. Gray, togglier

SSgt. V. J. Mammolito, engineer/gunner
TSgt. O. D. Freeman, radio/gunner
Sgt. A. Christopher, gunner

Briefing started at 0630 hrs. and ended 0705 hrs.

T/off: 0803 & 0810 hrs.
Target: no attack

Rendezvous: 0900 & 0859 hrs.
Coast Out: 0954 & 0955 hrs.

Landfall: 0918 & 0919 hrs.
Return: 1100 hrs.

Mission Narrative

Thirty-six aircraft dispatched; the 1st Box was led by Lt. Col. G. C. Celio, and the 2nd Box by Maj. C. W. Hoover.

Route was Base to Brighton, for rendezvous with RAF 11 Group Spitfire escort, to Etretat to Beuzeville to Gace; formation turned back at Gace at 0935 hrs. due to weather. CAVU over Channel, but 7–9/10th cloud with base at 4,000 ft. and tops 5–6,000 ft. at coast and inland.

No opposition; 528 × 250 GPs returned and 32 × 250 GPs jettisoned over Channel by two aircraft with mechanical difficulties, one of which was on single engine. One aircraft was an early return with 16 × 250 GPs.

Return route was to Beuzeville and exited coast at Etretat to Beachy Head and Base.

Interrogation of crews began at 1120 hrs. and finished at 1145 hrs.

Mission Notes and "Flak-Bait" Crew Debrief Comments

"Flak-Bait" flew as No. 3 in the lead flight, 2nd Box.

Brought back 16 × 250 GPs; could not see target.

Event: More Personnel on US Leave

On May 18, 1944, seventeen members of the 449th BS returned to the US on a thirty-day leave; this included SSgt. Norman E. Thielan, who was a part of the original "Flak-Bait" crew.

```
Date: May 20, 1944
Target: Cambrai-Epinoy A/D
Field Order: 9th BC F/O 319
99th CBW F/O 60
```

"Flak-Bait" Crew

1Lt. W. F. Green, pilot
1Lt. W. A. Wagener, copilot
SSgt. G. W. Gueterman, togglier

TSgt. F. T. Ehrgood, engineer/gunner
SSgt. C. F. Van Meter, radio/gunner
SSgt. O. Hahn, gunner

Briefing started at 0600 hrs. and ended 0645 hrs.

T/off: 0942 hrs.
Target: 1127 hrs.

Rendezvous: 1045 & 1100 hrs.
Coast Out: 1205 & 1204 hrs.

Landfall: 1058 & 1124 hrs.
Return: 1237 hrs.

Mission Narrative

Thirty-six aircraft dispatched, led by Lt. Col. G. C. Nye; the 2nd Box was led by Lt. Col. F. E. Fair.

Route was Base to Eastchurch for rendezvous with the 344th BG, the 322nd to lead, to Nth Foreland for rendezvous with IX FC P-47 escort, to Furnes to Audenarde to 50.11'N, 03.30'E (Esnes), to target.

No attack; 8–10/10th cloud with tops 11,500–13,000 ft.; made target identification impossible. 276 × 500 GPs and two propaganda bombs returned. One aircraft accidentally released 8 × 500 GPs at the IP when bombardier accidentally hit the toggle switch when reaching to close the bomb bay doors.

Weak inaccurate HFF was reported from the Nieuport area.

Return was a right turn from the target to Somain to Audenarde to Furnes to Nth Foreland to Base.

Interrogation of crews began at 1305 hrs. and finished at 1335 hrs.

Mission Notes and "Flak-Bait" Crew Debrief Comments

"Flak-Bait" flew as No. 4 aircraft in the low flight, 1st Box.

6 × 500 GPs and one propaganda bomb returned (one a/c in each box carried a propaganda bomb).

Other Crew Comments

Criticism of mission by several crews: Why send them out when weather so bad?; flying at 14,000 ft. too high without oxygen.

```
Date: May 20, 1944
Target: Cormeilles-en-Vexin A/D
Field Order: 9th BC F/O 320
99th CBW F/O 61
```

"Flak-Bait" Crew

1Lt. H. C. Rodgers, pilot
1Lt. D. A. Palmer, copilot
1Lt. W. F. Vaughan, navigator/bombardier

SSgt. V. J. Mammolito, engineer/gunner
TSgt. A. W. Bradshaw, radio/gunner
Sgt. A. Christopher, gunner

Briefing started at 1600 hrs. and ended 1637 hrs.

T/off: 1734 & 1741 hrs.	Rendezvous: 1840 hrs.	Landfall: 1900 & 1901 hrs.
Target: 1930½ hrs.	Coast Out: 1958 hrs.	Return: 2100 hrs.

Mission Narrative

Thirty-six aircraft dispatched; the 1st Box was led by Capt. R. H. Schmidt, and the 2nd Box by Lt. Col. F. E. Fair.

Route was Base to rendezvous with the 344th BG at Splasher Beacon No. 8, the 344th to lead, to rendezvous with IX FC P-38 escort at Brighton, to Etretat to 49.10'N, 01.00'E (Quittebeuf), to 49.17'N, 01.48'E (east of La Grippiere), the IP, to the target.

Thirty-four aircraft attacked, by boxes, dropping 268 × 500 GPs and 2 × propaganda bombs in clear but very hazy conditions. 1st Box released from 12,000 ft. for poor results, the 2nd Box from 12,500 ft. for fair results, with one aircraft shelter and a taxi strip hit, although most bombs fell outside the target. Two aircraft returned early with mechanical problems; 16 × 500 GPs returned.

Weak inaccurate HFF from Ecquetot and Elbeuf. Weak moderate HFF, fairly accurate, from Pont-Audemer; weak inaccurate HFF from Le Havre. At the target, weak, moderate HFF was encountered, some of which came from Pontoise. One aircraft received Cat. A damage.

Briefed return was a right turn off the target to the rally point to 49.10'N, 01.00'E (Quittebeuf), to Etretat to Beachy Head to Base. Actual route flown was to the south of the briefed route, over Pont-Audemer, but exited as briefed.

Interrogation of crews began at 2107 hrs. and finished at 2130 hrs.

Mission Notes and "Flak-Bait" Crew Debrief Comments

"Flak-Bait" flew as the lead aircraft, low flight, 2nd Box.

8 × 500 GP dropped, for fair results—bombs hit a little over the target. One leaflet bomb also dropped, crew not told about the leaflet bomb, so no observation made.

Inaccurate HFF from left of target, Moderate accurate HFF at Evreaux to Beaumont, and slight inaccurate HFF from Le Havre.

Other Crew Comments

Use of command radio abused; language and singing heard; comments were heard as to position and mentioned time they should be over target.

Take flame dampers off aircraft for daylight operations; aircraft could not keep up.

```
Date: May 21, 1944
Target: Abbeville-Drucat A/D
Field Order: 9th BC F/O 321
99th CBW F/O 62
```

"Flak-Bait" Crew

1Lt. H. C. Rodgers, pilot
1Lt. D. A. Palmer, copilot
1Lt. W. F. Vaughan, navigator/bombardier

SSgt. V. J. Mammolito, engineer/gunner
SSgt. W. Goetz, radio/gunner
Sgt. A. Christopher, gunner

Briefing started at 1330 hrs. and ended 1355 hrs.

T/off: 1515 & 1522 hrs.	Rendezvous: 1629 & 1633 hrs.	Landfall: 1649 hrs.
Target: 1655½ & 1654½ hrs.	Coast Out: 1701 & 1700 hrs.	Return: 1816 hrs.

Mission Narrative

PFF led mission. Twenty-nine aircraft plus two PFF dispatched. 1st Box was led by Capt. L. R. Wade, and the 2nd Box by Capt. H. E. Short.

Route was Base to Beachy Head, for rendezvous with IX FC P-51 escort, to 50.10'N, 00.50'E (off St.-Valery-en-Caux), to the target. 1st Box was 2½ minutes late leaving Beachy Head; the 2nd Box reached the target first.

10/10th cloud, tops 5,000 ft.; at target, all attacked, dropping 174 × 500 GPs and 66 × 600 GPs (includes the PFF a/c) from 12,650 and 12,300 ft.; results unobserved.

One crew reported LFF two minutes after leaving the target; no aircraft battle damaged. One aircraft received Cat. A damage when a flak suit fell out of aircraft ahead, damaging the horizontal and vertical tail surfaces. One aircraft Cat. E in crash near Bottisham; six killed.

Return was a left turn to St.-Quentin to Dungeness to Base.

Interrogation of crews began at 1815 hrs. and finished at 1843 hrs.

Mission Notes and "Flak-Bait" Crew Debrief Comments

"Flak-Bait" flew as No 4 aircraft in the low flight, 2nd Box.

6 × 500 GPs and 2 × 600 GPs dropped.

Would rather have enlisted men's PW kit in crew room no. 2.

Category E Information
41-31885 SS-S

Flying No. 5 in the high flight, 2nd Box, crashed and destroyed 1 mile northeast of Bottisham; reported as being seen to break up in air and explode as it hit the ground. Aircraft came over base in formation upon return but made no attempt to land; there was no indication of any trouble, and had dropped on the target. Six killed.

2Lt. A. H. Ottley, pilot   KIA
2Lt. R. C. Grosskopf, copilot   KIA

Sgt. J. C. Anderson, togglier   KIA
SSgt. J. J. McDonald, engineer/gunner   KIA
SSgt. J. E. Bradford, radio/gunner   KIA
Sgt. F. K. Sapp, gunner   KIA

```
Date: May 22, 1944
Target: Beaumont-le-Roger A/D
Field Order: 9th BC F/O 322
99th CBW F/O 63
```

"Flak-Bait" Crew

1Lt. W. F. Green, pilot   TSgt. F. T. Ehrgood, engineer/gunner
1Lt. W. A. Wagener, copilot   Sgt. E. C. Malone, radio/gunner
2Lt. M. R. Schultz, navigator/bombardier   SSgt. O. Hahn, gunner

Briefing started at 1130 hrs. and ended 1200 hrs.
T/off: 1300 & 1307 hrs.   Rendezvous: 1408 & 1412 hrs.   Landfall: 1434 & 1437 hrs.
Target: 1500 & 1504 hrs.   Coast Out: 1516 & 1522 hrs.   Return: 1639 hrs.

Mission Narrative

PFF mission. Thirty aircraft plus two PFF dispatched; 1st Box led by Capt. J. E. Haley, and the 2nd Box was led by Capt. P. Shannon.

Route was Base to Brighton, where rendezvous with IX FC P-47 was made, to 49.17'N, 00.10'W (Hernetot), to 48.43'N, 00.10'W (Les Emondes), to 48.42'N, 00.07'E (Alencon), to the target.

The 1st Box dropped 34 × 600 GPs and 90 × 500 GPs on PFF from 12,500 ft.; cloud conditions were 7–8/10th cumulus; the results were assessed as fair. The 2nd Box failed to bomb after the PFF aircraft had equipment failure and the cloud prevented a visual attack. 34 × 600 GPs and 90 × 500 GPs returned. All aircraft except the PFF dropped window.

No flak reported, although one crew did say they saw three bursts of HFF far to the right at exit, possibly from Trouville.

Return was a right turn to 48.55'N, 00.45'E (Bozoches-sur-Hoene), to 49.17'N, 00.10'W (Hernetot), to Brighton to Base.

Interrogation of crews began at 1630 hrs. and finished at 1705 hrs.

Mission Notes and "Flak-Bait" Crew Debrief Comments

"Flak-Bait" flew as No. 2 in the high flight, 1st Box.

Some bombs on the target area; 6 × 500 GPs and 2 × 600 GPs released. Results fair to good.

Escort was good.

Event: 322nd Bomb Group Flies First Night Mission

On the night of May 22–23, 1944, the 322nd BG flew the first night mission by B-26 aircraft of the 9th Air Force, the target being the same as earlier in the day: Beaumont-le-Roger A/D.

Eighteen aircraft, including a PFF lead ship, were alerted, but two were NTO. Fifteen aircraft attacked on the target indicators (T/Is) dropped by the PFF aircraft. Two aircraft were attacked by night fighters, but they made only the one pass, and no damage was received.

Publicity shot of a B-26 Marauder preparing for takeoff on a night flight. *USAAF*

"Flak-Bait" Crew

1Lt. G. P. Jones, pilot
1Lt. T. W. Piippo, copilot
2Lt. R. W. Rodriquez, navigator/bombardier

SSgt. J. E. Corlew, engineer/gunner
SSgt. W. Goetz Jr., radio/gunner
Sgt. J. Palcich, gunner

Briefing started at 0645 hrs. and ended 0720 hrs.

T/off: 0910 & 0919 hrs.
Target: 1126 & 1126½ hrs.

Rendezvous: 1030 hrs.
Coast Out: 1156 & 1158 hrs.

Landfall: 1045 & 1046 hrs.
Return: 1301 hrs.

Mission Narrative

Thirty-six aircraft dispatched; the 1st Box was led by Lt. Col. G. C. Celio with Capt. N. L. Harvey. The 2nd Box was led by Lt. Col. E. Wursten.

Route was Base to Eastchurch, for rendezvous with the 344th BG, who were to lead, to Nth Foreland for rendezvous with IX FC P-47 escort, to Furnes to Audenarde to Le Cateau to 50.06'N, 03.08'E (Metz-en-Couture), the IP, to the target. However, formation was 2–3 miles north of briefed route on the way in.

Bombing by boxes, all aircraft attacked in clear conditions but with thick haze, dropping 211 × 500 GPs and 71 × 600 GPs from 12,000 and 12,500 ft. The 1st Box achieved good results, probably destroying four aircraft shelters and two buildings with four hits on the peri-track. The 2nd Box achieved excellent results, covering two shelters and near misses to another three, plus hits on the peri-track. One aircraft accidentally released 3 × 500 GPs at the IP. 2 × 500 GPs and 2 × 600 GPs were jettisoned over the Channel by aircraft having rack failures.

No opposition met.

Return was a right turn to Douai, the rally point, to Audenarde to Furnes to Nth Foreland to Base. Interrogation of crews began at 1252 hrs. and finished at 1331 hrs.

Mission Notes and "Flak-Bait" Crew Debrief Comments

"Flak-Bait" scheduled to fly as No. 2 aircraft in the high flight, 1st Box, but actually attached itself onto the high flight of the 2nd Box.

6 × 500 GPs and 2 × 600 GPs dropped; all bombs on the AP for good results.

Many vapor trails observed of unidentified aircraft high above.

A marshaling yard full of cars observed at Louvain.

Other Crew Comments

Poor navigation by the 344th BG, and not flying at the briefed altitude.

Escort had combat with six Fw 190s near Lille; observed one Fw destroyed and one P-47 lost.

On landing, there was too much deliberate cutting in and out of the traffic pattern.

"Flak-Bait" Crew

1Lt. W. A. Wagener, pilot
1Lt. W. F. Green, copilot
2Lt. M. R. Schultz, navigator/bombardier

TSgt. F. T. Ehrgood, engineer/gunner
Sgt. E. C. Malone, radio/gunner
SSgt. O. Hahn, gunner

Briefing started at 1430 hrs. and ended 1450 hrs.

T/off: 1629 hrs.　　　　　　　Rendezvous: 1715 hrs.　　　　　　Landfall: 1747 & 1749 hrs.

Target: 1815 & 1815½ hrs.　　Coast Out: 1845 & 1846 hrs.　　Return: 2002 hrs.

Mission Narrative

Thirty-four aircraft dispatched; 1st Box was led by Lt. Col. G. C. Nye, and the 2nd Box by Capt. D. W. Allen.

Route was Base to Splasher Beacon No. 8, for rendezvous with the 344th BG, who were to lead, to Brighton, for rendezvous, with IX FC P-47 escort, to 49.17'N, 00.09'W (Hernetot), to La Coupe (the IP) to the target.

Bombing was by flights, with thirty-four attacking, dropping 261 × 500 GPs and 10 × 600 GP bombs, from 12,000 and 12,500 ft. in CAVU conditions. Results were good, fair, and fair for the 1st Box and good, poor, and no photo coverage for the 2nd Box. 1 × 500 GP was returned through rack failure.

A barrage of intense to moderate, fairly accurate HFF from Chartres and in the target area. Intensity for this group was less than that for the 344th BG leading. Eight aircraft received Cat. A damage.

Return was a left turn to the rally point at La Coupe to 49.17'N, 00.09'W (Hernetot), to Brighton to Base. Interrogation of crews began at 1955 hrs. and finished at 2038 hrs.

Mission Notes and "Flak-Bait" Crew Debrief Comments

"Flak-Bait" flew as No. 2 in the lead flight, 1st Box.

6 × 500 GPs and 2 × 600 GPs dropped; bombs fell in target area to the right of the AP; saw hits on buildings.

Heavy inaccurate HFF to our flight over the target.

Cat. A damage, one small hole. Right prop out.

Marshaling yards at Mezidon with large number of freight cars and a large roundhouse observed.

```
Date: May 27, 1944
Target: Paris Maisons-LaFitte RR Br
Field Order: 9th BC F/O 331
99th CBW F/O 72
```

"Flak-Bait" Crew

1Lt. H. I. Lewter, pilot　　　　　　　　TSgt. S. P. Smith, engineer/gunner

1Lt. D. B. Barker, copilot　　　　　　　SSgt. W. C. Upton, radio/gunner

TSgt. G. W. Gueterman, toggler　　　　SSgt. J. L. Harding Jr., gunner

Briefing started at 1000 hrs. and ended 1035 hrs.

T/off: 1159 & 1206 hrs.　　　　　Rendezvous: 1304 hrs.　　　　　Landfall: 1321 hrs.

Target: 1348 & 1349½ hrs.　　　Coast Out: 1423 hrs.　　　　　　Return: 1530 hrs.

Mission Narrative

Thirty-five aircraft dispatched; the 1st Box was led by Capt. D. W. Allen, and the 2nd Box by 1Lt. R. C. Foote.

Route was Base to Splasher Beacon No. 8, for rendezvous with the 344th BG, the 322nd to lead, to Beachy Head for rendezvous with IX FC P-47 escort, to Etretat to 49.10'N, 00.56'E (Bernay), to 2 miles south of Mantes to target.

Twenty-nine aircraft attacked, bombing by flights, in clear conditions, releasing 56 × 2,000 GPs on the target. Two aircraft returned early with 4 × 2,000 GPs, one flight leader had a rack failure, and three others did not drop because the leader did not release—4 × 2,000 jettisoned and 6 × 2,000 GPs returned. Results varied; either unknown or gross for the 1st Box, because both the lead and deputy lead aircraft were knocked out of formation by flak. The 2nd Box achieved good, good, and poor results, respectively.

Flak began just before the target area and continued to track accurately to the Pontoise area. Fairly accurate HFF from Elbeuf; some off-course aircraft experienced moderate accurate HFF from Rouen, Cleres-St.-Saens area. Two rocket-type spirals from ground at Fecamp, which burst at approximately 12,000 ft. in two columns, similar but darker colored, from Dieppe at the same time. Two aircraft were Cat. E, one Cat. AC, and twelve

Cat. A damaged. One man killed—SSgt. S. V. Williams—and three MIA, all from the same 449th BS crew; see Category E details below. Two others received minor wounds from Plexiglas shards: SSgt. J. L. Campbell and 1Lt. B. N. Cooper, from the 449th BS.

Return was a left turn to 4 miles northeast of Pontoise to 49.10'N, 00.56'E (Bernay), to Etretat to Beachy Head to Base. The 1st Box took a shortcut on the way back, from Gaillon to outside Elbeuf, to exit at Etretat.

Interrogation of crews began at 1525 hrs. and finished at 1635 hrs.

Mission Notes and "Flak-Bait" Crew Debrief Comments
"Flak-Bait" flew as No. 2 aircraft in the lead flight, 1st Box.

$2 \times 2,000$ GPs dropped; fair results observed.

Approximately seven flak hits; control surfaces hit and upper turret out.

Lead aircraft left formation at 1411 hrs., with both engines smoking; P-47s gave escort.

Other Crew Comments
Encounters between P-47 escort and e/a observed in the Les Andelys area.

A P-47 released a drop tank through the formation.

Category E Information
42-43288 PN-V, "Vee Pack It II" / "Dolly"
Lead aircraft hit by flak and left formation at 1410 hrs.; P-47s gave escort. Three crew members bailed

42-43288 PN-V, "Vee Pack It II" / "Dolly," taxies out for a mission in early 1944; she crashed near Gravesend, Kent, after the remaining crew members bailed out. *Trevor J. Allen collection*

41-31788 PN-A, "Truman Committee," was the original aircraft of the 449th BS CO, Maj. Ben Willis. Note the flak patches covering the repairs after a mission on February 28, 1944, when flak killed the bombardier 1Lt. H. H. Heath and wounded the pilot 1Lt. F. M. Remmele. *Trevor J. Allen collection*

out over France in the target area; four bailed out over England. Rudder was shot away, causing severe vibration; the pilot originally ordered the crew to bail out, but upon the aircraft being slowed down to 180 mph, the vibration became less, so he rescinded the order and instructed remainder of crew to remain. When over England, he found that when nose was lowered for descent, the vibration rendered aircraft almost uncontrollable, so remainder of crew bailed over England. Aircraft seen to crash near Gravesend.

Capt. D. W. Allen, pilot	WIA, bailed out over England
1Lt. A. F. Minich, copilot	WIA, bailed out over England
Capt. J. L. Littwin, navigator/bombardier	bailed out over France, POW
1Lt. J. C. Dick, navigator/bombardier	bailed out over France, evaded
TSgt. R. G. Baum, radio/gunner	bailed out over France, POW
Sgt. R. L. Sylvester, tail gunner	bailed out over England
SSgt. E. V. McWilliams, engineer/gunner	wounded in foot and thrown out by Sgt. Sylvester, and

chute seen to open, but he was later reported as KIA

41-31788 PN-A, "Truman Committee"
Pilot 1Lt. F. M. Remmele, deputy lead aircraft; hydraulics shot out over target, and right tank hit over Oisemont. Peeled out of formation when 5 miles from Hastings, heading for emergency airfield in a gradual descent. Aircraft made a crash landing at Friston, landed without flaps or brakes; the air bottle worked momentarily and then quit. Pilot noticed cliffs and the English Channel ahead, and seeing a pillbox off to his left, he headed toward that and hit it, which took the undercarriage off. The aircraft sailed over the pillbox, and one prop dug in, spinning the aircraft around and bringing it to an abrupt halt. Crew safe.

```
Date: May 27, 1944
Target: Mantes-Gassicourt RR Br
Field Order: 9th BC F/O 332
99th CBW F/O 73
```

"Flak-Bait" Crew

2Lt. W. G. Fort, pilot	SSgt. S. J. Box, engineer/gunner
1Lt. C. M. Foster, copilot	SSgt. R. E. Richardson, radio/gunner
2Lt. W. D. Brearley, navigator/bombardier	Sgt. H. Brown, gunner

Briefing started at 1715 hrs. and ended 1740 hrs.

T/off: 1905 & 1912 hrs.	Rendezvous: 2007 & 2005 hrs.	Landfall: 2024 & 2026 hrs.
Target: 2053 & 2055 hrs.	Coast Out: 2115 & 2118 hrs.	Return: 2252 hrs.

Mission Narrative
Thirty-six aircraft dispatched; the 1st Box was led by Lt. Col. G. C. Celio with Capt. S. G. Rotkewicz. The 2nd Box was led by Maj. C. W. Hoover with 1Lt. F. E. Peters.

Route was Base to East Grinstead, for rendezvous with the 344th BG, who led, to Brighton for rendezvous with IX FC P-47 escort, to Etretat to 48.58'N, 01.19'E (St.-Maxime-Hauterive), the IP, to target.

Thirty-three aircraft attacked by flights, dropping 64 × 2,000 GPs from 12,000 and 12,400 ft.; conditions were CAVU over the target, with haze low down. Results were mostly poor; the low flight of the 2nd Box achieved an excellent result, with one or possibly two direct hits on bridge span, and on western approach. Three aircraft failed to release: one because trigger was not engaged, one because leader did not drop, and one because doors wouldn't open. 1 × 2,000 GP was jettisoned and 7 × 2,000 GPs returned.

Weak inaccurate LFF, bursting about 2,000 ft. below, about 4 miles southwest of Les Andelys; no damage received.

Return was a left turn to the rally point to Etretat to Brighton to Base.

Interrogation of crews began at 2220 hrs. and finished at 2315 hrs.

Mission Notes and "Flak-Bait" Crew Debrief Comments

"Flak-Bait" flew as No. 5 in the lead flight, 2nd Box.

2 × 2,000 GPs dropped; hit to right of target; poor results.

An A-20 or B-26 seen to explode in the air in the Paris area. (Three B-26s were lost this day: 42-96100 YA-O "Swamp Angel" from the 386th BG, and 41-31716 O8-O and 42-95827 O8-G from the 391st BG.)

Smoke seen from Conches to the coast, and a smoke screen started at Le Havre on way out.

What appeared to be a barrage balloon with a tail, but larger, seen on the ground at 49.22'N, 00.50'E (Lieurey).

Other Crew Comments

Poor formation and possibly going too fast.

Gunsights for night flying are poor for day use.

```
Date: May 28, 1944
Target: Mantes-Gassicourt RR Br
Field Order: 9th BC F/O 333
99th CBW F/O 74
```

"Flak-Bait" Crew

2Lt. D. L. Hunter, pilot
1Lt. C. E. Keenan, copilot
SSgt. J. L. Campbell, togglier

SSgt. K. M. Locke, engineer/gunner
SSgt. G. F. Van Meter, radio/gunner
SSgt. J. L. Smith, gunner

Briefing started at 0845 hrs. and ended 0910 hrs.

T/off: 1037 & 1044 hrs.	Rendezvous: 1150 hrs.	Landfall: 1156 hrs.
Target: 1227 & 1229 hrs.	Coast Out: 1249 hrs.	Return: 1358 hrs.

Mission Narrative

Thirty-six aircraft dispatched; 1st Box was led by Maj. G. B. Simler, and the 2nd Box by Capt. L. A. Tenold.

Route was Base to Brighton, to follow the 386th BG to rendezvous with RAF Spitfire escort at 50.00'N, 00.05'E (off Fecamp), to Etretat to 48.44'N, 01.40'E (Chartres), to 48.48'N, 01.52'E (St. Prest), the IP, to the target.

Bombing was by flights, thirty-five aircraft dropping 68 × 2,000 GPs from 11,500 ft. in CAVU conditions. Results were fair, good, and good for the 1st Box and poor, poor, and gross (lead bombardier misidentified the target) for the 2nd Box. 2 × 2,000 GPs jettisoned because of rack failures, and one aircraft failed to catch formation, having taken off late in a spare aircraft, and returned 2 × 2,000 GPs.

Weak to moderate, accurate HFF encountered about 5 miles south of Elbeuf; three aircraft received Cat. A damage. A high spiral of smoke topped by a large ball of gray smoke observed just inland from Fecamp, top at 12,500 ft.

Return route was a left turn to the rally point at 48.48'N, 01.52'E (St. Prest), to Etretat to Brighton to Base.

Interrogation of crews began at 1350 hrs. and finished at 1430 hrs.

Mission Notes and "Flak-Bait" Crew Debrief Comments

"Flak-Bait" flew as No. 3 aircraft in the low flight, 2nd Box.

2 × 2,000 GPs dropped—hit a highway bridge on northwest side of primary.

On way in a rocket seen between Fecamp and Dieppe, grayish burst.

Accurate HFF from woods off Elbeuf.

Brief the gunners on what temperatures to expect on mission.

"Flak-Bait" Crew

1Lt. B. P. Burrage, pilot
1Lt. H. C. Rodgers, copilot
1Lt. W. F. Vaughan, navigator/bombardier

Sgt. C. W. Coon, engineer/gunner
Sgt. E. C. Malone, radio/gunner
Sgt. T. J. Dumais, gunner

Briefing started at 1600 hrs.; no end time recorded.

T/off: 1734 & 1741 hrs.	Rendezvous: 1845 hrs.	Landfall: 1859 & 1900 hrs.
Target: 1907 & 1909 hrs.	Coast Out: 1915 & 1917 hrs.	Return: 2016 hrs.

Mission Narrative

Thirty-six aircraft dispatched; 1st Box was led by Capt. J. E. Haley, and the 2nd Box by Capt. L. R. Wade.

Briefed route was Base to rendezvous with IX FC P-47 escort at Nth Foreland, to Furnes to 51.00'N, 03.00'E (Luikhoek), to target. The formation leader, having received a message to change zero hour by fifteen minutes, unsuccessfully attempted to contact "Parade" (Bomber Command) to have the fighters vectored; mission was then flown as briefed but plus fifteen minutes; no escort was reported by either box.

Bombing by flights, thirty-two aircraft dropped 62 × 2,000 GPs from 11,500 and 11,000 ft.; conditions were CAVU with a 3–4/10th high cirrus. Results for Box 1 were excellent, gross (accidental release), and good; the low flight made a second run and dropped at 1915½ hrs. Those for the 2nd Box were fair, poor, and gross (bombardier failed to identify target). One aircraft dropped on Coxyde A/D as a casual target, after the salvo handle would not function over the primary. One aircraft had rack failure and two were early returns; 1 × 2,000 GP jettisoned and 7 × 2,000 GPs returned.

No opposition met.

Return was a right turn to 51.00'N, 03.00'E (Luikhoek), to Furnes to Nth Foreland to Base.

Interrogation of crews began at 2009 hrs. and finished at 2050 hrs.

Mission Notes and "Flak-Bait" Crew Debrief Comments

"Flak-Bait" flew as the No. 2 aircraft in the high flight, 1st Box.

2 × 2,000 GPs released—dropped short and to the right; the lead flight hit the target.

Escort not seen; called them but no reply.

At 1852 hrs. a small boat seen heading 280 degrees toward England; seemed to be taking evasive action since it was turning a great deal.

Other Crew Comments

Dinghy observed on way back; a fast surface vessel was seen heading toward it.

Fighters failed to rendezvous with us; called "Parade" to have fighters vectored, but none appeared; crew would like to know why.

"Flak-Bait" Crew

1Lt. J. J. Farrell, pilot
F/O T. F. Moore, copilot
1Lt. O. J. Redmond, bombardier
2Lt. A. D. Perkins, navigator

TSgt. D. L. Tyler, engineer/gunner
SSgt. J. B. Manuel, radio/gunner
SSgt. H. Brown, gunner

Briefing started at 0745 hrs. and ended 0820 hrs.

T/off: 0957 & 0950 hrs. Rendezvous: 1055 hrs. Landfall: 1112 & 1113 hrs.

Target: 1157½ & 1158 hrs. Coast Out: 1129 & 1240 hrs. Return: 1343 hrs.

Mission Narrative

Thirty-four aircraft dispatched; 1st Box was led by Lt. Col. B. G. Willis, and the 2nd Box by 1Lt. R. C. Foote.

Route was Base to Splasher Beacon No. 8, for rendezvous with the 386th BG, who were to lead, to rendezvous with IX FC P-47 escort at Brighton to 49.17'N, 00.05'W (Cheux), to L'Aigle to Etampes to 48.28'N, 02.32'E (Orveau-Bellesauve), to the target.

Bombing by flights, thirty-four aircraft attacked the primary, dropping 48 × 2,000 GPs from 12,000 and 12,500 ft.; weather was clear but with haze over the target; results for Box 1 were good, poor, and gross (bombardier sighted on wrong bridge); those for the 2nd Box were good, gross, and undetermined, but thought to be fair. The high flight lead bombardier could not synchronize on the target due to violent evasive action; the flight dropped their bombs in open fields because of fuel shortage; 12 × 2,000 GPs released. One aircraft accidentally dropped just after the IP. Three aircraft returned early with mechanical problems. 2 × 2,000 GPs jettisoned and 6 × 2,000 GPs returned. Smoke from preceding 386th BG partially obscured the target, which was still intact as we attacked.

Moderate to intense accurate HFF beginning about two minutes before the target, near the IP, and continued on turn off target for 2–3 minutes. Eight aircraft received Cat. A damage.

Return was a right turn off the target and retrace route in.

Interrogation of crews began at 1350 hrs. and finished at 1500 hrs.

Mission Notes and "Flak-Bait" Crew Debrief Comments

"Flak-Bait" flew as No. 4 aircraft in the lead flight, 2nd Box.

2 × 2,000 GP dropped; smoke over target made observation difficult, but it was believed that bombs were right in target area.

Intense accurate HFF over target and from Bretigny aerodrome after leaving target.

Large motor convoy observed on highway southwest of Dreux, stationary.

At 1300 hrs., while 30 miles south of Beachy Head, a B-26 was seen on the deck heading for Beachy Head; lost sight of aircraft but observed a large splash at 50.20'N, 00.10'W (mid-Channel).

Other Crew Comments

386th BG flew at our altitude, causing prop wash.

A B-26 escorted by four P-47s observed flying low and losing altitude just after leaving coast at Cabourg; the B-26 turned back toward France, and P-47s turned with him.

A 386th BG B-26 flying below this formation was smoking badly.

"They" (presumably the 386th BG) went past IP by 2½ minutes and therefore were not able to pick up the right bridge—reported by the bombardier of lead aircraft, low flight, 1st Box.

```
Date: May 30, 1944
Target: Rouen Hwy Br
Field Order: 9th BC F/O 338
99th CBW F/O 78
```

"Flak-Bait" Crew

1Lt. J. J. Farrell, pilot
F/O T. F. Moore, copilot
1Lt. O. J. Redmond, navigator/bombardier

TSgt. D. L. Tyler, engineer/gunner
SSgt. J. B. Manuel, radio/gunner
Sgt. H. Brown, gunner

Briefing started at 0816 hrs. and ended 0855 hrs.

T/off: 0958 & 1000 hrs.   Rendezvous: 1050 & 1049 hrs.   Landfall: 1109 & 1110 hrs.
Target: 1131½ & 1132½ hrs.   Coast Out: 1157 hrs.   Return: 1317 hrs.

Mission Narrative
Thirty-five aircraft dispatched; the 1st Box was led by Capt. A. Bouquet, the 2nd Box by Capt. S. G. Rotkewicz.

Route was Base to Beachy Head, where rendezvous to be made with IX FC P-47 escort, to Etretat to Quiterbeuf to Louvres (the IP) to target. The 322nd to follow fifteen minutes behind the 344th BG.

Attacking by flights, thirty-four dropped 67 × 2,000 GPs on the target from 11,500 and 11,000 ft. in clear conditions, but with haze. Box 1 results were fair, fair, and good, while those of the 2nd Box were poor, poor, and good, respectively. Bombing was in a good concentration, but a few hundred feet off. One aircraft failed to bomb when bomb bay doors wouldn't open, returning 2 × 2,000 GPs, and one aircraft jettisoned 1 × 2,000 GP in Channel through rack failure.

Some flights reported moderate accurate HFF, but inaccurate for others. Window was dropped from IP and continued during the turn off the target. Flak did not begin until formations were over the target. Eight aircraft received Cat. A damage; one man was wounded: SSgt. E. J. Inman, 450th BS.

Return was a right turn to the rally point at Louvres to Quiterbeuf to Etretat to Beachy Head to Base. Interrogation of crews began at 1308 hrs. and finished at 1400 hrs.

Mission Notes and "Flak-Bait" Crew Debrief Comments
"Flak-Bait" scheduled as No. 2 in the high flight; 2nd Box but took over the lead since the flight leader did not take off.

2 × 2,000 GPs on target for good results; time over target 1133 hrs.

HFF moderate accurate for height but not course at target.

Other Crew Comments
On return over the Channel, the flight leaders are breaking up too much; they don't keep formation.

```
Date: June 1, 1944
Target: Ault C/D
Field Order: 9th BC F/O 341
99th CBW F/O 81
```

"Flak-Bait" Crew
1Lt. H. C. Rodgers, pilot   SSgt. D. C. Mustain, engineer/gunner
1Lt. B. P. Burrage, copilot   SSgt. W. J. Whitesell, radio/gunner
1Lt. W. F. Vaughan, navigator/bombardier   SSgt. J. G. Morgan, gunner

Brifing started at 1445 hrs. and ended 1510 hrs.

T/off: 1625 & 1632 hrs.   Rendezvous: area cover   Landfall: 1802 & 1806 hrs.
Target: 1802½ & 1806 hrs.   Coast Out: 1805 & 1806 hrs.   Return: 1948 hrs.

Mission Narrative
PFF mission. Thirty-two plus two PFF aircraft off. 1st Box was led by Capt. J. E. Haley, the 2nd Box by 1Lt. J. H. Statts.

Route was Base to Beachy Head to 50.13'N, 00.30'E (off St.-Valery-en-Caux), to the target. IX FC P-47s provided area cover.

All thirty-four attacked; conditions were 8–10/10th cloud, tops 5–6,000 ft., with a patch of stratus directly over the target; 64 × 2,000 GPs and 8 × 600 GPs dropped on the target; results unobserved, but the PFF lead of 1st Box reported that the bombs were in the target area.

No opposition reported.

Return was a left turn to Hastings to Base.

Interrogation of crews began at 1925 hrs. and finished at 2010 hrs.

Mission Notes and "Flak-Bait" Crew Debrief Comments

"Flak-Bait" flew as No. 2 in the high flight, 1st Box.

2 × 2,000 GPs dropped; results unobserved due to cloud cover.

773 received a call on channel B that said, "Tell our little friends that we are changing course." Crew believes that call may have come from the enemy.

100th-Mission Press Release

"Roaring over Hitler's West Wall today, the veteran Marauder 'Flak-Bait' entered the select circle of Ninth Air Force medium bombers that have flown 100 bombing missions against the enemy.

"'Flak-Bait' is the second Marauder in 'Nye's Annihilators' pioneer Ninth Air Force Group in the ETO, and the third of the Ninth's B-26s to complete 100 missions. The first one was 'Mild and Bitter' of 'Nye's Annihilators' and the second was 'Bingo Buster' in another group (41-34963 RJ-P, 323rd BG).

"The pilot of 'Flak-Bait' on her 100th mission was 1st Lt. Horace C Rodgers, from Marshal[l], Texas.

"The three mechanics who care for "Flak-Bait" are TSgt. Charles F. Thompson, Yuba City, Calif., Crew Chief; SSgt. Clare Goodrich, Coldwater, Mich., Assistant Crew Chief, and Pvt. George Sangregorio, Brooklyn, NY, Mechanic."

Author's note: On the basis of photographic evidence, it appears that the 100th mission was celebrated after the completion of ninety-four combat sorties plus the six decoy missions as painted on the aircraft's nose. At some point in the future, the six decoy missions were excluded from the mission count.

Other 100-Mission Aircraft

The first B-26 aircraft to 100 missions was "Mild and Bitter," 41-31819 DR-X, on May 8, 1944; the second was the 323rd BG's "Bingo Buster," 41-34863 RJ-P, on May 16, 1944, both of which were returned to the United States in June 1944. The fourth aircraft to reach that figure was the 322nd BG's "Impatient Virgin II," 41-34951 SS-P, on June 4—this aircraft was lost on August 6, 1944, after 123 missions.

On June 8, "Lil Po'k Chop," 41-18250 SS-B (salvaged through battle damage on September 16, 1944); "Clark's Little Pill," 41-34959 SS-Q (abandoned over friendly territory on December 25, 1944); and "Bluebeard II," 41-34973 SS-R (salvaged through battle damage on August 10, 1944), all reached the 100-mission mark.

Later in June the following aircraft of the 322nd BG also reached the 100-mission mark: "Pickled Dilly," 41-18276 SS-C, reached that figure on the twenty-first (eventually lost on 105th mission, August 7, 1944); "Sarah E," 41-34762 SS-G, on the twenty-fifth (eventually crash-landed on November 11, 1944); and "Satan's Sister," 41-18277 SS-D, on a date unknown (to 361st Air Service Squadron due to battle damage on July 6, 1944; later returned to service and recoded as SS-Z).

"Impatient Virgin II" reached her 100th-mission milestone on June 4, three days after "Flak-Bait." She was MIA on the afternoon mission of August 6, 1944. *Peter Dole*

"Lil Po'K Chop" reached the 100-mission mark on June 8, 1944. *USAAF*

"Flak-Bait" Crew

1Lt. B. P. Burrage, pilot
2Lt. L. L. Peters, copilot
TSgt. J. L. Campbell, togglier

SSgt. D. C. Mustain, engineer/gunner
SSgt. W. J. Whitesell, radio/gunner
SSgt. J. G. Morgan, gunner

Briefing started at 1630 hrs.; no end time recorded.

T/off: 1825 & 1832 hrs.	Rendezvous: area cover	Landfall: 1941 & 1944 hrs.
Target: 1944 & 1944½ hrs.	Coast Out: 1950 & 1952 hrs.	Return: 2058 hrs.

Mission Narrative

Thirty-six plus three window ships dispatched. The 1st Box was led by Capt. G. H. Watson, and the 2nd Box by Lt. Col. E. Wursten.

Route was Base to Hastings to 50.30'N, 01.20'E (off the Somme estuary), to the target. IX FC P-47s provided area cover.

Bombing by flights, thirty-six aircraft released 70 × 2,000 GPs and one leaflet bomb over the target in clear conditions; results were generally unobserved. The results were rated as Box 1: gross, fair, and gross, and Box 2: poor, gross, and poor. 1 × 2,000 GP returned due to rack failure.

Moderate to intense accurate HFF at landfall, continuing to target and on course around to 4 miles south of Samer. Moderate HFF again experienced intermittently from Etaples area and continued on course to exit, with increased intensity and accuracy at Berck-sur-Mer. The 2nd Box reported that evasive action took them slightly north of Berck, where flak was less intense than that experienced by the 1st Box. Four aircraft received Cat. AC damage, twenty-two aircraft Cat. A, and one aircraft Cat. E, in a crash landing at Base. 3K and 4W. Killed were 1Lt. C. F. Crosier, who was killed by flak over the target, 1Lt. M. Saylor, and 2Lt. M. K. Brennan, on Capt. G. H. Watson's aircraft that crash-landed at base; rest of the crew were injured; all the casualties were from the 452nd BS. In addition, one man sitting on a vehicle was also killed when the crash-landing aircraft hit it.

Thirty-two P-47s, with 500 lb. bombs, were to dive-bomb flak positions or when flak was anticipated. Formation leader to call fighters on channel B and repeat "Bingo, Bingo, Bingo"; this will be their signal to start dive-bombing. If fighters do not hear signal, they will attack 1½ minutes before the time over target.

Return was a right turn to 50.26'N, 01.50'E (Somme estuary), to Berck-sur-Mer to Hastings to Base.

Interrogation of crews began at 2040 hrs. and finished at 2130 hrs.

Mission Notes and "Flak-Bait" Crew Debrief Comments

"Flak-Bait" flew as No. 5 aircraft in the high flight, 1st Box.

2 × 2,000 GPs dropped.

No damage received.

Other Crew Comments

Crews welcomed the dive-bombing, but they felt that it was too little too late, and they should have attacked sooner.

Three B-26s observed on single engine trailing the formation, but under control.

Category E Information

42-95935 DR-S

Pilot Capt. G. H. Watson was the formation leader; hydraulics were shot out; upon return and after circling the base for one hour in an effort to get the wheels down, they made a belly landing. The aircraft collided with a concrete spreader parked on the airfield, and the aircraft caught fire. 1Lt. M. Saylor, navigator, and 2Lt. M. K. Brennan, bombardier, were killed, with rest of crew injured; in addition, TSgt. Henry Miller, of the 819th

Chemical Company, who was sitting on the spreader, was killed when the aircraft collided with it.

Capt. G. H. Watson, pilot	injured
2Lt. G. F. Brentine, copilot	injured
1Lt. M. Saylor, navigator	KIA
2Lt. M. K. Brennan, bombardier	KIA
SSgt. D. E. Mabon, engineer/gunner	injured
TSgt. L. C. Tebeau, radio/gunner	injured; had one leg amputated
SSgt. C. A. O'Connell, gunner	injured

```
Date: June 4, 1944
Target: Courcelles-sur-Seine Hwy Br
Field Order: 9th BC F/O 346
99th CBW F/O 86
```

"Flak-Bait" Crew

1Lt. J. J. Farrell, pilot	TSgt. D. L. Tyler, engineer/gunner
F/O T. F. Moore, copilot	SSgt. J. B. Manuel, radio/gunner
1Lt. O. J. Redmond, bombardier	Sgt. H. Brown, gunner
1Lt. A. D. Perkins, navigator	

Briefing started at 1230 hrs. and ended 1255 hrs.

T/off: 1340 & 1346 hrs.	Rendezvous: 1500 hrs.	Landfall: 1522 & 1523 hrs.
Target: 1540 & 1541 hrs.	Coast Out: 1603 & 1604 hrs.	Return: 1712 hrs.

Mission Narrative

Thirty-six aircraft dispatched; the 1st Box was led by Lt. Col. G. C. Celio, with Maj. D. E. Harnly. The 2nd Box was led by Capt. R. C. Foote.

Route was Base to rendezvous with IX FC P-47s at Beachy Head to Etretat to 49.30'N, 00.40'E (Martainville), to 49.09'N, 00.55'E (Caorches-St.-Nicolas), the IP, to the target.

Bombing by flights, thirty-three aircraft attacked, dropping 64 × 2,000 GPs and one leaflet bomb, from 10,000 and 10,500 ft., in clear conditions. Results for the 1st Box were excellent, excellent, and poor, while those for the 2nd Box were excellent, poor, and excellent. The bridge was knocked out. The high flight of the 2nd Box made two runs. One aircraft did not bomb, since the doors would not open, and two others were early returns, one of which jettisoned 2 × 2,000 GPs because of a loss of power. 4 × 2,000 GPs returned.

Weak inaccurate HFF at target, beginning on bomb run and ceasing as formation made turn off the target. Two aircraft received Cat. A damage.

Return was a left turn and retrace route in.

Interrogation of crews began at 1710 hrs. and finished at 1755 hrs.

Mission Notes and "Flak-Bait" Crew Debrief Comments

"Flak-Bait" flew as No. 4 aircraft in the lead flight, 2nd Box.

2 × 2,000 GPs dropped; good results observed.

Three gun positions observed in area northwest of Etretat.

Three vessels, possibly barges, seen putting to sea.

Other Crew Comments

A P-47 and an unidentified single-engine aircraft seen 8 miles northwest of Etretat; the unidentified aircraft hit the water.

P-47 escort was making passes at our formation on this mission.

Fighters called formation, saying, "The bridge is in the water."

During briefing, the crews were ordered that in no case is any submarine to be attacked by any aircraft of this command on-route or returning.

"Flak-Bait" Crew

1Lt. H. C. Rodgers, pilot
2Lt. R. W. Page, copilot
1Lt. W. F. Vaughan, navigator/bombardier

SSgt. L. E. Parker, engineer/gunner
Sgt. J. Hastings, radio/gunner
Sgt. H. Brown, gunner

Briefing started at 0500 hrs. and ended 0535 hrs.
T/off: 1012 hrs.   Target: no attack   Return: 1209 hrs.

Mission Narrative

Thirty-six aircraft dispatched; the 1st Box was led by Maj. C. W. Hoover, and the 2nd Box by Capt. S. G. Rotkewicz.

Briefed route was Base to rendezvous with IX FC P-47 escort at Beachy Head, to Etretat to 49.12'N, 01.00'E (Ecauville), to 49.20'N, 01.45'E (Hennezis), to 49.20'N, 02.50'E (Vineuil-St.-Firmin), to 49.08'N, 02.49'E (Marly-la-Ville), to the target.

Formation recalled; solid overcast over England in the London area; formation leader instructed flights to climb individually through the overcast. Formation became scattered and was unable to re-form. Leader continued to within sight of the enemy coast, but only one other flight joined his, so he turned back. 288 × 500 GPs returned.

Fighter rendezvous not made even though at rendezvous point on time.

Interrogation of crews began at 1210 hrs. and finished at 1235 hrs.

Mission Notes and "Flak-Bait" Crew Debrief Comments

"Flak-Bait" flew as No. 2 in the high flight, 2nd Box.

Abortive: 8 × 500 GPs returned; turned around when flight leader did.

The official record card (AFLC card) for 41-31773; the aircraft that would be christened as "Flak-Bait." These record cards show movements only within the United States. This shows her acceptance date as April 26, 1943, at a cost of $191,131. *USAF/AFHSHRA*

1Lt. James J. Farrell with a canine friend at Andrews Field. He was responsible for christening her as "Flak-Bait" after his family's dog, which was known as "Flea Bait." *Smithsonian National Air and Space Museum, NASM 00068440*

Armorers pose with some of the bombs that would be loaded on "Flak-Bait," seen in the background at Andrews Field in the winter of 1943–44. *Smithsonian National Air and Space Museum, NASM 86-2150*

Sgt. Ted Simonaitis, who painted the nose art on "Flak-Bait"; he was the assistant crew chief on the aircraft "Sit 'N' Git" (42-43285 PN-K). *Trevor J. Allen collection*

"Flak-Bait" with ground crew members relaxing on top of the fuselage. Photo taken in the late summer at Andrews Field. The D-day stripes on the upper fuselage had already been removed. *Trevor J. Allen collection*

Publicity shot celebrating the aircraft's 100th mission, which was flown on June 1, 1944. Photo was taken on June 3 and shows, *front row, left to right*: 1Lt. Owen J. Redmond, F/O Thomas F. Moore, and 1Lt. Jim J. Farrell. Center rear is Sgt. Harold Brown; the other two gunners should be TSgt. Donald L. Tyler and SSgt. Joseph B. Manuel. Note the swastika e/a kill marking and the decoy symbols on the third row. *Author's collection*

Another photo taken of the Farrell crew on June 3, watching the ground crew working on the left engine. The mission tally at this time was ninety-four bombing missions and six decoy missions. *Author's collection*

Believed to be "Flak-Bait," with an unidentified ground crew member, possibly an armorer, posing with the tail guns; note the blast shields added for nighttime missions. *Mike Smith, B26.com*

TSgt. William L. Johnston, engineer/gunner on 1Lt. Henry "Hank" Bozarth's crew, standing by the waist position of "Flak-Bait." *Smithsonian National Air and Space Museum, NASM 00068390*

The D-day stripes being gradually removed from the fuselage of "Flak-Bait." *Smithsonian National Air and Space Museum, NASM 00068401*

The highest-ranking person to fly in "Flak-Bait" on a combat mission was Brig. Gen. Herbert B. Thatcher, who was the commanding officer of the 99th CBW and flew in the copilot's position on the August 1, 1944, mission to Cinq-Mars railroad bridge. *Trevor J. Allen collection*

The original ground crew of "Flak-Bait," showing 123 mission symbols but lacking the six decoy mission symbols. *Left to right*: Pvt. George Sangregorio, mechanic; TSgt. Charles F. Thompson, the original crew chief; and SSgt. Clare G. Goodrich, assistant crew chief, and later crew chief when TSgt. Thompson rotated. *Mike Smith, B26.com*

Another view of "Flak-Bait," with ground crew members, displaying 123 bomb symbols, which would date the photo from about mid-August 1944. *Author's collection*

Another crew that flew "Flak-Bait" on a number of occasions was, *left to right:* SSgt. William C. Upton, SSgt. Silas P. Smith, unconfirmed but believed to be 1Lt. Ken Reed, Sgt. John L. Harding Jr., and SSgt. George W. Gueterman. Sitting in the cockpit is 1Lt. Douglas B. Barker. The aircraft shown was abandoned over Kent by another crew (see operational history entry for May 27, 1944). *Douglas Robin Barker*

1Lt. Douglas B. Barker had joined the RCAF and flew a tour with RAF Coastal Command, flying Wellingtons and Hudson aircraft on antishipping patrols prior to transferring to the USAAF. Joining the 449th BS in early 1944, he flew seven missions on "Flak-Bait" among his sixty-five-mission tour with the squadron. *Douglas Robin Barker*

"Flak-Bait" now sporting 137 bomb symbols and with the six decoy mission symbols reapplied. Taken during the process of repainting them in red, sometime in September 1944. Note the nosewheel disk star symbol, and the early-style bomb bay door still in situ. *Mike Smith, B26.com*

Left to right: 2Lt. Thomas, 2Lt. Charles W. Spalty, 2Lt. Terrance J. O'Neill, Sgt. William L. Johnston (misspelled in photo), Sgt. McDonald T. Darnell Jr., and Sgt. Russell L. Bassler, upon completion of their training at Barksdale Field. All would fly "Flak-Bait," the three enlisted men as part of the Bozarth crew. *Randy Wells*

Taken at the same time as the photo at top, showing 137 bomb symbols, the white bomb fin markings and duck bills have yet to be applied. The aircraft still has the early-style bomb bay doors on the left-hand side. *Pima Air & Space Museum*

Unidentified crewman, believed to be TSgt. McDonald T. Darnell Jr., poses in front of "Flak-Bait"; photo taken in the late 1944, with the fins of every fifth bomb symbol and beaks of the decoy missions picked out in white. *Trevor J. Allen collection*

In a wintry scene at A-61 Beauvais-Tille. Note the later-style, open-ended bomb bay doors that are now fitted, and that the forward section of the package gun housings has been painted black. *Trevor J. Allen collection*

Taken at the same time as the previous photo, "Flak-Bait" in the harsh winter conditions of 1944–45, presenting extreme challenges for the ground crews who had to work outside in such poor weather. *Mike Smith, B26.com*

With 154 mission symbols displayed, the ground crew of "Flak-Bait" pose before the nose, with the crew chief, SSgt. Clare G. Goodrich, on the left. *Pima Air & Space Museum*

Another image of "Flak-Bait" during the extreme weather conditions experienced at the end of 1944. Because of the German Ardennes Offensive, missions continued whenever target opportunities allowed. *Douglas Robin Barker*

Standing, left to right: 1Lt. Sherman V. N. Best, copilot; 1Lt. Henry C. "Hank" Bozarth, pilot; and Sgt. Tom B. Gee, togglier. *Kneeling, left to right*: TSgt. William J. "Bill" Johnston, engineer/gunner; TSgt. McDonald T. "Mac" Darnell Jr., radio/gunner; and Sgt. Russell L. Bassler, tail gunner. This crew began flying "Flak-Bait" regularly starting in December 1944. *Smithsonian National Air and Space Museum, NASM-9A12266*

Another view of "Flak-Bait" in the winter of 1944–45. *Smithsonian National Air and Space Museum, NASM 9A12267*

Armorers leaning on a 2,000 lb. bomb, the largest ordnance carried by a B-26, with "Flak-Bait" in the background, displaying more than 145 bomb symbols. *Trevor J. Allen collection*

2Lt. Sherman Best, copilot on the Bozarth crew, flying a B-26 from the left-hand seat; either this was a checkout flight or, as sometimes happened, if the aircraft was on the left-hand side of a formation, the first pilot would, on occasion, prefer to sit in the right-hand seat for a better view. *Smithsonian National Air and Space Museum, NASM-9A12292*

TSgt. McDonald T. "Mac" Darnell Jr., radio operator, on the Bozarth crew, donated his A-2 jacket to the NASM. For many years this was hung over his seat in the nose section, when that was on display at the Mall in Washington, DC. *Smithsonian National Air and Space Museum, NASM 9A12275*

"Flak-Bait" with 164 plus missions showing, at A-61 Beauvais-Tille, in early 1945. *Trevor J. Allen collection*

1Lt. Henry C. "Hank" Bozarth flew on "Flak-Bait" on fifteen occasions; his last mission in her was on March 18, 1945. *Trevor J. Allen collection*

Togglier on the Bozarth crew was Sgt. Thomas B. Gee. *Trevor J. Allen collection*

"Flak-Bait" with at least 171 mission symbols showing, in the spring of 1945. *Trevor J. Allen collection*

The Bozarth crew pose before "Flak-Bait" in early March 1945, with 178 missions shown. *Standing, left to right*: TSgt. William L. Johnston, engineer/gunner; TSgt. McDonald T. Darnell Jr., radio/gunner; Sgt. Thomas B. Gee, togglier; Sgt. Russell L. Bassler, tail gunner. *Kneeling, left to right*: 2Lt. Sherman V. N. Best, copilot, and 1Lt. Henry C. Bozarth, pilot. *Pima Air & Space Museum*

Left-hand side of nose of "Flak-Bait," showing the distinctive flak patches located there; compare with the color photo section. *Trevor J. Allen collection*

"Flak-Bait" on her 200th mission, April 17, 1945, to Magdeburg, piloted by Capt. William G. Fort, with the 322nd Bomb Group CO, Col. John S. Samuel, in the copilot's seat. One of a series of photos taken by Sgt. Orval F. Burton, who was flying in the number 3 ship in the formation. *Trevor J. Allen collection*

"Flak-Bait" leading the group on her 200th mission; sadly, a failure of the PDI resulted in her dropping to the No. 4 position in the flight, with 1Lt. John H. Alderson, flying 42-107664 PN-A, "Je Reviens," taking over the flight lead, and the flight swapping places with the high flight. *Peter Dole*

With "Flak-Bait" leading, prior to the PDI fault, other aircraft visible are 43-34371 PN-X, "Belle of Bayou," flown by 1Lt. Edwin C. Pakish and crew; 42-107664 PN-A, "Je Reviens," flown by 1Lt. John H. Alderson; and 41-31823 PN-D, "No Compree," flown by 2Lt. Robert H. Pederson and crew. All of these pilots and their crews had flown in "Flak-Bait" at some point. *Trevor J. Allen collection*

The crew on the 200th mission pose upon their return. *Standing, left to right:* Col. John S. Samuel, 322nd BG CO, who flew as copilot; Capt. William G. Fort, pilot; and TSgt. William J. Hess, tail gunner. *Kneeling, left to right:* 1Lt. William D. Brearley, bombardier; TSgt. Kenneth M. Lock, engineer/gunner; TSgt. Cecil Fisher, radio/gunner; and 1Lt. Arthur D. Perkins, navigator. Also on board was war correspondent Oram C. "Bud" Hutton, from *Stars & Stripes* magazine. *Peter Dole*

The proud ground crew of "Flak-Bait" after the 200th mission. *Left to right:* Pvt. George Sangregorio, mechanic; SSgt. Clare G. Goodrich, crew chief; and Cpl. Dave Rich, assistant crew chief, with the temporarily placed 200th symbol. *Pima Air & Space Museum*

449th BS CO, Maj. John C. Ruse, congratulates the crew chief, SSgt. Clare Goodrich, on the remarkable record set by "Flak-Bait." Note the position of the temporary 200th bomb symbol, believed to have been painted on card, before the permanent 200 symbol was applied to the lower nose later. *Trevor J. Allen collection*

1Lt. Warren Langer, *standing second from right*, and crew, who flew "Flak-Bait" on her 201st and final mission of the war. This late replacement crew flew her on a total of five missions, all in April 1945. *Mark Copeland*

With her notoriety, many people were photographed standing in front of "Flak-Bait." This photo, taken just after the 200th mission, shows propeller specialists TSgt. John R. Sharpe on the left and Sgt. Ronald E. Heyn. *Mike Smith, B26.com*

Taken at a similar time period, this time with ground personnel identified as Blank, May, and Saletta. Note the late-style bomb bay doors clearly visible. *Trevor J. Allen collection*

Posing with "Flak-Bait" are members of the armaments section, who helped load the munitions; Cpl. Eugene Maglietta is in the center. *Trevor J. Allen collection*

Another picture of ground personnel posing with "Flak-Bait" at station A-89 Le Culot, Belgium. *Trevor J. Allen collection*

It seems everybody wanted to have a photo taken in front of the famous bomber; more ground crew members pose with her shortly after the 200th mission. *Pima Air & Space Museum*

"Flak-Bait" now with the permanent 200th bomb symbol applied; photo taken at A-89 Le Culot in the late spring of 1945. *Trevor J. Allen collection*

322nd Bomb Group CO, Col. John S. Samuel, showing "Flak-Bait" to some high-ranking officials from the RAF, French air force, US Army Air Corps, and local community. *Pima Air & Space Museum*

Another view of "Flak-Bait" in the spring/summer of 1945. *Author's collection*

Photo taken at the same time as the previous photo. *Author's collection*

Unidentified ground crew member posing with "Flak-Bait." *Author's collection*

Another view of ground crews posing with "Flak-Bait" after the end of hostilities; the 201st bomb symbol was never applied to the airframe. *Trevor J. Allen collection*

Color photo of "Flak-Bait" parked at A-69 Le Culot, in the early summer of 1945. *Pima Air & Space Museum*

"Flak-Bait" photographed at R-6 Kitzingen in the late summer of 1945, having been transferred to this base, which was home to the 394th BG. *Trevor J. Allen collection*

"Flak-Bait" being refueled for her final flight to Oberpfaffenhofen, in March 1946. *Smithsonian National Air and Space Museum, NASM 80-1901*

"Flak-Bait" photographed in a hangar at either A-69 Le Culot, Belgium, or R-6 Kitzingen, Germany, in the summer of 1945. *Pima Air & Space Museum*

Maj. John L. Egan, with copilot Capt. Norman Schloesser, ready to taxi out for the final flight to Oberpfaffenhofen, on March 18, 1946. *Trevor J. Allen collection*

Color photograph of "Flak-Bait" at Kitzingen, awaiting her final flight. *Clarence Lunnemann via Roger Freeman*

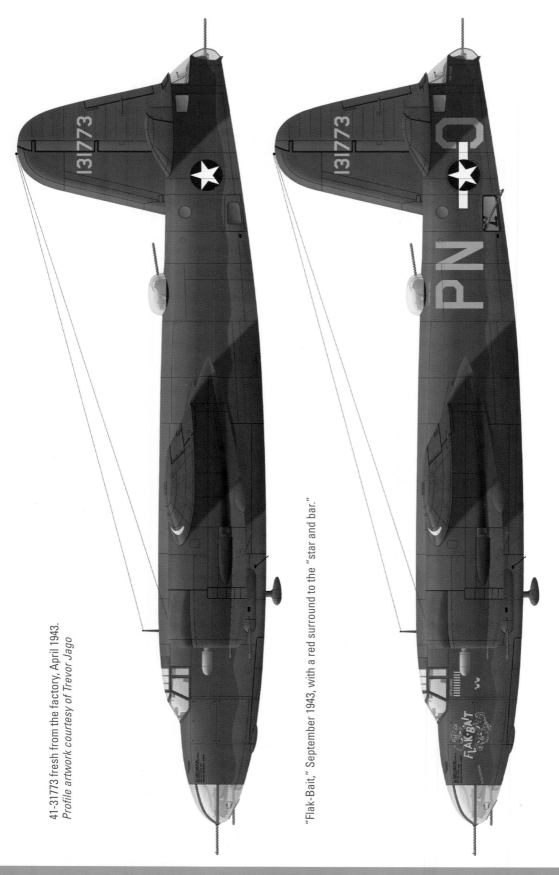

41-31773 fresh from the factory, April 1943.
Profile artwork courtesy of Trevor Jago

"Flak-Bait," September 1943, with a red surround to the "star and bar."

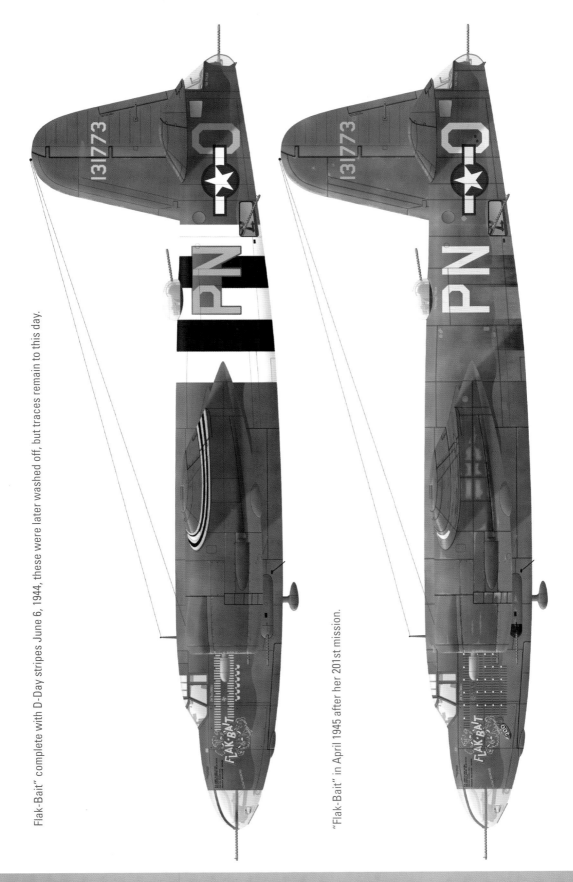

Flak-Bait" complete with D-Day stripes June 6, 1944, these were later washed off, but traces remain to this day.

"Flak-Bait" in April 1945 after her 201st mission.

Date: June 6, 1944
Target: Ouistreham (69) C/D, 1st Box
Ouistreham (74) C/D, 2nd Box
Montfarville (308) C/D, 3rd Box
Field Order: 9th BC F/O 348
99th CBW F/O 88

"Flak-Bait" Crew

1Lt. J. J. Farrell, pilot
F/O T. Hunt, copilot
1Lt. O. J. Redmond, navigator/bombardier

TSgt. D. L. Tyler, engineer/gunner
SSgt. J. B. Manuel, radio/gunner
Sgt. H. Brown, gunner

Briefing started at 0145 hrs. for targets 69 & 74 and 0300 hrs. for target 308 and ended 0240 & 0340 hrs., respectively.

T/off: 0345, 0400 & 0500 hrs.   Target: 0520, 0555 & 0627 hrs.   Return: 0707½, 0757 & 0759 hrs.

Mission Narrative

PFF mission; three boxes of fifteen aircraft plus one PFF aircraft in each. Led by Col. G. C. Celio, Maj. G. B. Simler, and Lt. Col. E. Wursten, respectively.

For the 1st Box, routing was Base to Dartford to Worthing to 49.31'N, 01.16'W (Les Veys), to targets. For the 2nd Box, the route was from Worthing to 49.31'N, 01.14'W (La Blanche), to the target, and for the 3rd Box from Worthing to 50.00'N, 00.40'W (mid-Channel), to the target. 9th FC to provide area cover.

Very pistol cartridges were used by all groups in the assembly of the formations, only to be fired by the formation leader. Colors for the 322nd Group were red/green.

No bombs were to be dropped after zero hour minus five minutes (zero hour was 0630 hrs.).

The leader of the 1st Box was instructed to make a weather report in the clear to Bomber Command immediately after leaving the target area.

1st Box: fifteen aircraft plus 1PFF; only the box leader and PFF aircraft bombed on Gee, the PFF on its equipment only. 4 × 2,000 GPs on primary, from 9,500 ft. through 8–9/10th multilayered cloud. Fourteen aircraft brought back 28 × 200 GPs because of weather. Took off in frontal weather with base at 1,500 ft.

2nd Box: fifteen aircraft plus one PFF; nine aircraft attacked primary, dropping 18 × 2,000 GPs from 12,300 ft., through 7–9/10th multilayered cloud. Bombed on Gee after PFF equipment failure. Seven aircraft returned early because of weather, returning 14 × 2,000 GPs. Leader complained that weather forecast was wrong: 35 mph predicted, actual was 65 mph.

3rd Box: fifteen aircraft plus one PFF; all attacked, dropping 32 × 2,000 GPs from 10,000 ft., bombed on PFF. Encountered 10/10th cloud cover en route and 5/10th at the target. Bombs fell in two groups; the larger completely covered target area for excellent results, and the other fell 2,100 ft. ESE in fields.

Return routing was a right turn to 49.13'N, 01.36'W (Le Mesnilbus), to 49.40'N, 02.30'W (east of Sark), to Portland to Base.

No interrogation times recorded.

Mission Notes and "Flak-Bait" Crew Debrief Comments

"Flak-Bait" was to fly as No. 4 ship in the low flight of the 2nd Box but moved up to the No. 2 position in the lead flight when others aborted.

2 × 2,000 GPs dropped on Gee; results unobserved; complete cloud cover.

One burst of flak seen about 1 mile right of formation as we left the enemy coast.

Saw battleships laying down barrage and landing craft heading south.

41-18277 SS-D "Satan's Sister" adorned with D-day stripes. *Trevor J. Allen collection*

```
Date: June 6, 1944
Target: Gatteville (258) C/D
Field Order: 9th BC F/O 349
99th CBW F/O 89
```

"Flak-Bait" Crew

1Lt. H. C. Rodgers, pilot
2Lt. R. W. Page, copilot
1Lt. W. F. Vaughan, navigator/bombardier

SSgt. J. E. Corlew, engineer/gunner
SSgt. W. Goetz Jr., radio/gunner
Sgt. J. Palcich, gunner

Briefing started at 1202 hrs. and ended 1205 hrs.
T/off: 1234 hrs.   Target: 1350½ & 1352 hrs.   Return: 1521 hrs.

Mission Narrative

Thirty-six aircraft dispatched; the 1st Box was led by Maj. C. W. Hoover, and the 2nd Box by Lt. Col. B. G. Willis.

Routing was Base to Selsey Bill to 49.40'N, 01.00'W (Pointe du Hoc), to the target. VIII & IX FC to provide area cover.

Bombing by flights, thirty-two aircraft dropped 61 × 2,000 GPs and one leaflet bomb from 6 and 7,000 ft., through a large gap in the clouds over the Cherbourg peninsula. 8–10/10th cloud encountered till mid-Channel. Results for all flights in the 1st Box were excellent, while those for the 2nd Box were excellent, good, and poor. The leader of the low flight, 1st Box, had a rack failure and couldn't release; another aircraft in the same flight failed to release when the bomb bay doors wouldn't open, and two others did not drop because the leader did not release; the remaining two aircraft in the flight dropped on the lead flight. 8 × 2,000 GPs returned; 2 × 2,000 GPs jettisoned through rack malfunctions.

No opposition met.

Return was a right turn off the target to St. Catherine's Point to Base.

Interrogation of crews began at 1515 hrs. and finished at 1552 hrs.

Mission Notes and "Flak-Bait" Crew Debrief Comments

"Flak-Bait" flew as No. 2 in the high flight, 2nd Box.

1 × 2,000 GP dropped on target; 1 × 2,000 GP jettisoned in Channel through rack malfunction.

Event: Three-Man Crew Fly D-day Mission

On the second mission of the day, the pilots of the aircraft 41-18276 SS-C, "Pickled Dilly," found that

41-18276 SS-C, "Pickled Dilly," flew the second D-day mission with a three-man crew. *Trevor J. Allen collection*

they did not have any gunners. Eager to fulfill the mission, the three men elected to fly the aircraft; the pilot was 1Lt. William L. Adams, the copilot was 1Lt. Carl O. Steen, who acted as the bombardier and the togglier, and SSgt. C. W. Holland acted as a gunner.

```
Date: June 6, 1944
Target: Caen Hwy Br
Field Order: 9th BC F/O 352
99th CBW F/O 92
```

"Flak-Bait" Crew

1Lt. V. N. Liniger, pilot
2Lt. H. C. Bozarth, copilot
1Lt. R. W. Fletcher, navigator/bombardier

SSgt. J. O. Mullen, engineer/gunner
SSgt. R. F. Stickney, radio/gunner
Sgt. B. D. Stoddard, gunner

Briefing started at 1845 hrs. and ended 1853 hrs.

T/off: 1940 & 1947 hrs.	Rendezvous: area cover	Landfall: 2054 hrs.
Target: 2105 & 2105½ hrs.	Coast Out: 2108 hrs.	Return: 2238 hrs.

Mission Narrative

Thirty-six aircraft dispatched; 1st Box was led by Capt. J. E. Haley, the 2nd Box by Col. G. C. Nye.

Route was Base to Brighton to Cabourg to Mezidon to 49.00'N, 00.16'W (Maizieres), to the target. Allied aircraft to provide area cover.

Bombing by flights, thirty-five aircraft dropped 69 × 2,000 GPs; on one aircraft the doors would not open, and another had one bomb hang up. 3 × 2,000 GPs returned. Bombed from 5–6,000 ft., in haze and smoke that obscured the target. Results were gross for all flights except the low flight, 2nd Box, whose results were poor. Bombing order was Box 1, flights 1 and 3; then Box 2, flights 1, 3, and 2; and finally Box 1, flight 2, who made a second run and bombed the town. Apparently, Box 1 aimed at the wrong bridges, choosing two RR bridges over the Orne River, which were 2½ miles northeast of the target. Box 2 bombs fell from 1,500 ft. to 1,000 yds. away, aiming on a crossroads in the town.

Weak to moderate LFF at target; fairly accurate for the 1st Box, inaccurate for the 2nd Box. A few bursts of HFF were reported. Intermittent weak and inaccurate LFF between Mezidon and the target, some of it from mobile transport guns between Ouilly, Le-Treport, and Rocquancourt. Two aircraft received Cat. A damage.

Return was a right turn to Cabourg to Brighton to Base.

Interrogation of crews began at 2225 hrs. and finished at 2315 hrs.

Mission Notes and "Flak-Bait" Crew Debrief Comments

"Flak-Bait" flew as No. 2 in the high flight, 2nd Box.

2 × 2,000 GPs in the city; visibility poor; dropped on flight leader.

LFF inaccurate from Mezidon and slight inaccurate HFF from Caen.

Other Crew Comments

2101 hrs., unidentified aircraft seen to crash on road just west of Ouilly.

2104 hrs., large Allied aircraft went down and crashed 5 miles northeast of Caen; two chutes seen.

2107 hrs., Spitfire seen to spin in and crash just north of Caen.

2115 hrs., Stirling aircraft seen to crash in water among landing barges, just offshore from Cabourg.

Event: Aircraft Flying All Three Missions On D-day

Of the three formations that attacked targets on D-day, fourteen of the 322nd BG's aircraft flew on all three missions, including "Flak-Bait."

"Flak-Bait" Crew

1Lt. J. J. Farrell, pilot
F/O T. F. Moore, copilot
1Lt. O. J. Redmond, navigator
2Lt. L. Karlinsky, bombardier

TSgt. D. L. Tyler, engineer/gunner
SSgt. J. B. Manuel, radio/gunner
Sgt. H. Brown, gunner

Briefing started at 1245 hrs. and ended 1255 hrs.

T/off: 1327 hrs.	Rendezvous: area cover	Landfall: 1431 hrs.
Target: 1448 & 1513 hrs.	Coast Out: 1508 hrs.	Return: 1653 hrs.

Mission Narrative

Thirty-six aircraft dispatched; the 1st Box was led by Capt. R. C. Foote, and the 2nd Box by Maj. D. E. Harnly.

Route was Base to Beachy Head to 49.24'N, 00.54'W (Cully), to St. Lo to 48.50'N, 01.25'W (La Grande Tournicotiere), to the target. Allied fighters to provide area cover.

Bombing by flights, all thirty-six attacked; cloud en route was 8–9/10th at 7–10,000 ft., but at the target, 10/10th between 1,700 ft. and 2,000 ft. was encountered. Results for Box 1 were excellent, poor, and poor; those for the 2nd Box were fair, gross, and fair. The 2nd Box approached at 10,000 ft. and made a 360-degree descending turn down to 1,600–2,000 ft., and bombed on second run. 183 × 500 GPs and 192 × 250 GPs plus one leaflet bomb released. 2 × 500 GPs returned through rack failure.

Weak inaccurate LFF between Folligny and target, and some LFF from Villedieu-les-Poeles (6 miles east of IP). Machine gun fire encountered on bomb run, and weak inaccurate LFF and MG fire from sidings at the target. 2nd Box made initial run on target at 10,000 ft. and encountered weak inaccurate HFF between Folligny and target. One aircraft received Cat. A damage from MG fire.

Briefed return was to turn left to St. Lo to 49.24'N, 00.04'W (Angerville), to Beachy Head to Base. Two flights of the 1st Box deviated from this route; they turned right off the target and exited between the peninsula and Jersey, then to the east of Guernsey to Newhaven to Base.

Interrogation of crews began at 1625 hrs. and finished at 1715 hrs.

Mission Notes and "Flak-Bait" Crew Debrief Comments

"Flak-Bait" as No. 4 in the lead flight, 2nd Box.

8 × 500 GPs dropped; fell into town.

Weak inaccurate HFF from La Baudriere.

At 1611 hrs., 30 miles off Beachy Head, saw a dinghy, while at 3,000 ft., position 50.40'N, 00.06'W.

Other Crew Comments

Not necessary for A-20s (409th BG) to fly through our formation on course.

A formation of A-20 aircraft were circling all around our traffic pattern, disrupting our landing procedure.

"Flak-Bait" Crew

2Lt. R. W. Page, pilot
1Lt. H. C. Rodgers, copilot
1Lt. W. F. Vaughan, navigator/bombardier

SSgt. V. J. Mammolito, engineer/gunner
SSgt. W. Goetz Jr., radio/gunner
Sgt. J. Palcich, gunner

Briefing started at 1930 hrs. and ended 1935 hrs.

T/off: 2012 hrs.   Target: 2155 hrs.   Return: 2340 hrs.

Mission Narrative

Thirty-six aircraft dispatched; the 1st Box was led by Lt. Col. E. Wursten, and the 2nd Box by Lt. Col. B. G. Willis.

Briefed route was Base to Dungeness to Villers to St. Lo to target. Allied fighters to provide area cover.

Formation encountered 10/10th cloud at 3,000 ft. The low flight, 1st Box, dropped 82 × 250 GPs on the primary, for fair to good results from 4,700 ft. Twenty-one aircraft were recalled because of the weather. Eighteen from the 2nd Box while still over the Channel, and eleven from the 1st Box while over enemy territory and on the bomb run at 4,500 ft. 14 × 250 GPs returned by two aircraft with rack failures, and 96 × 250 GPs and 192 × 500 GPs returned by weather recall. One aircraft failed to catch formation, having taken off late as a spare.

Weak to moderate inaccurate HFF from Evrecy area. Also moderate to intense inaccurate LFF from this area and extending farther southwest. Moderate inaccurate LFF from Caumont.

Briefed return was from target to Dungeness to Base. Twelve aircraft landed away, eight of which landed at Manston, two at Earls Colne, one at Boreham, and one at Kingsnorth.

Interrogation of crews began at 2210 hrs. and finished at 2350 hrs.

Mission Notes and "Flak-Bait" Crew Debrief Comments

"Flak-Bait" flew as No. 4 in the high flight, 2nd Box.

16 × 250 GPs brought back.

Other Crew Comments

Considerable confusion over recall existed because enemy was sending false messages on our frequency.

Circular raft, grayish color, with five or six men in it, observed 15 miles northwest of Le Havre.

Date: June 10, 1944
Target: Caumont R/J
Field Order: 9th BC F/O 359
99th CBW F/O 99

"Flak-Bait" Crew

1Lt. H. C. Rodgers, pilot   SSgt. V. J. Mammolito, engineer/gunner
2Lt. R. W. Page, copilot   TSgt. O. D. Freeman, radio/gunner
1Lt. W. F. Vaughan, navigator/bombardier   Sgt. A. Christopher, gunner

Briefing started at 0710 hrs. and ended 0720 hrs.

T/off: 0745 & 0752 hrs.   Rendezvous: area cover   Landfall: 0900 hrs.

Target: 0932 & 0935 hrs.   Coast Out: 0940 hrs.   Return: 1049 hrs.

Mission Narrative

Thirty-six aircraft dispatched; the 1st Box was led by Maj. G. B. Simler, and the 2nd Box by Capt. S. G. Rotkewicz.

Route was Base to Beachy Head to Bayeux to target. Allied fighters to provide area cover.

Bombing by flights, all flights made three or four runs at the target; 8–10/10th cloud with base at 7,000 ft. was encountered. The 1st Box dropped from 6,000 ft. for poor, poor, and undetermined results. The 2nd Box came down to 1,800 ft. to release; results were undetermined, good, and gross. Low-flight leader jettisoned his bombs after a flak hit, which killed the copilot; he had tried to signal rest of flight, but they did not hear and released on him; 78 × 500 GPs bombs fell 8 miles south of Bayeux. Thirty aircraft dropped 190 × 500 GPs, 93 × 250 GPs and one ZG-1 leaflet bomb. 1 × 250 GP jettisoned in Channel, clear of any shipping, and 20 × 250 GPs returned, four through rack failure and sixteen by an aborting aircraft.

Moderate HFF 3 miles south of Bayeux to area of Tilly-sur-Seulles to 3 miles south of Tilly. Twelve aircraft sustained Cat. A damage, and three aircraft damaged from own blast fragments. One man KIA by flak hit: 2Lt.

G. F. Brentine, 452nd BS (2Lt. Brentine had survived the crash landing of 42-95935 on June 2).

Return was a right turn off the target to Bayeux to Beachy Head to Base.

Interrogation of crews began at 1040 hrs. and finished at 1130 hrs.

Mission Notes and "Flak-Bait" Crew Debrief Comments

"Flak-Bait" flew as No. 2 in the low flight, 1st Box.

16 × 250 GPs dropped; hit southeast of crossroads; results fair to poor.

Slight accurate HFF 4 miles inland from Tilly area. Cat. A damage: holes in side, wings, and rudder.

Other Crew Comments

2nd Box crews complained that bombing height was too low.

A pair of B-26s from the 449th BS depart the Normandy beachhead area; note the D-day stripes that wrap around the entire fuselage. This is how "Flak-Bait" would have appeared at this time. *Trevor J. Allen collection*

```
Date: June 12, 1944
Target: Falaise R/J
Field Order: 9th BC F/O 363
99th CBW F/O 103
```

"Flak-Bait" Crew

1Lt. L. U. Yount, pilot
2Lt. R. R. Rigg, copilot
SSgt. P. A. Davis, togglier

Sgt. R. J. Keating, engineer/gunner
SSgt. D. N. West, radio/gunner
Sgt. D. W. Hone, gunner

Briefing started at 0330 hrs. and ended 0355 hrs.

T/off: 0527 & 0534 hrs.	Rendezvous: area cover	Landfall: 0646 hrs.
Target: 0708, 0710 & 0717 hrs.	Coast Out: 0716 & 0727 hrs.	Return: 0837 hrs.

Mission Narrative

Thirty-six aircraft dispatched; the 1st Box was led by Lt. Col. E. Wursten, and the 2nd Box by Capt. R. C. Foote.

Route was Base to Newhaven to 49.18'N, 00.08'W (Hotot-en-Auge), to Lisieux to 48.55'N, 00.12'E (Chahains), to target. Allied fighters to provide area cover.

Thirty-four aircraft attacked from 6,000 to 5,500 ft., bombing by flights in clear conditions, all of which made two runs, dropping 166 × 500 GPs and 184 × 250 GPs. All flights achieved fair results except third flight, 2nd Box, which scored good results. Two aircraft were mechanical aborts, one of which jettisoned 8 × 500 GPs bombs over England "safe" after engine failure. 2 × 500 GPs jettisoned through rack failures, and a total of 10 × 500 GP and 8 × 250 GP bombs were returned by aborting aircraft and rack failures.

Weak and inaccurate HFF and LFF between Troarn and Mezidon; no damage received.

Return was a right turn to Newhaven to Base.

Interrogation of crews began at 0820 hrs. and finished at 0915 hrs.

Mission Notes and "Flak-Bait" Crew Debrief Comments

"Flak-Bait" flew as No. 6 in the high flight, 2nd Box.

8 × 500 GPs dropped; hits observed in the town.

Observed a tank on the road at position Q-4562.

"Flak-Bait" Crew

1Lt. D. A. Palmer, pilot

1Lt. Jone*, copilot

2Lt. T. J. O'Neill, navigator/bombardier

SSgt. J. E. Corlew, engineer/gunner

SSgt. W. Goetz Jr., radio/gunner

Sgt. J. Palcich, gunner

* Name is shown as presented on crew roster and interrogation form. Thought to be 1Lt. G. P. Jones; details entered under his name in the crew member listing in Appendix 2.

Briefing started at 0400 hrs. and ended 0420 hrs.

T/off: 0535 hrs.

Target: 0721 to 0727 hrs. (P)

0728 to 0748 hrs. (T/Ops)

Rendezvous: area cover

Coast Out: 0744 hrs.

Landfall: 0659 hrs.

Return: 0915 hrs.

Mission Narrative

Thirty-seven aircraft dispatched; 1Lt. J. T. Flemming led the 1st Box, and 1Lt. M. C. Simmons, with Maj. C. W. Hoover, led the 2nd Box. Considerable disruption during the join-up procedure meant that many aircraft flew in positions other than that briefed.

Routing was Base to Brighton to Cabourg to Lisieux to Argentan to target. P-51s to provide area cover.

A stratus with base at 900–1,500 ft. in the target area and 8–10/10th at 8,000 ft. in the Caen area. Some aircraft flew as low as 900 ft. in the target area. Primary attacked by one aircraft that had an accidental release, dropping 6 × 250 GPs. Twenty-three were abortive because of the weather. A further ten attacked targets of opportunity as follows: five aircraft on a railroad intersection at Monlins-sur-Orne, dropping 76 × 250 GPs for excellent results, and five on a factory and small marshaling yard at Mace, dropping 15 × 250 GPs and 80 × 100 IBs for good results. 20 × 00 IBs were jettisoned near Villiers after an aircraft received flak damage, and 20 × 100 IBs were jettisoned in channel by an aircraft on single engine. One aircraft found that the undercarriage would not retract, so returned early. In total, 340 × 100 IBs and 62 × 250 GPs were returned. Bomb disposition of two aircraft MIA unknown (40 × 100 IBs).

One aircraft reported weak inaccurate LFF between Argentan and target. Intense accurate HFF; accurate LFF and MG fire experienced from Evrecy to Creully. Fire came from area of Caen/Carpiquet A/D and from vicinity of Tilly-sur-Seulles; the aircraft was at 3,500 ft. at this time. Eleven aircraft suffered Cat. AC damage, and fifteen Cat. A damage; two were MIA. Casualties were three injured: Maj. C. W. Hoover, CO of the 450th BS; SSgt. J. A. Arnold, 452nd BS; and SSgt. R. M. Jones, 449th BS, with twelve crewmen MIA.

41-107685 ER-V over shipping during the Normandy campaign; she received over 200 flak holes on the June 12 mission. *Author's collection*

Briefed return was a right turn to 49.30'N, 00.50'W (Colombiers-sur-Seulles), to Brighton to Base, but deviations occurred; both boxes exited the coast near Ver-sur-Mer.

Interrogation of crews began at 0855 hrs. and finished at 0955 hrs.

Mission Notes and "Flak-Bait" Crew Debrief Comments

"Flak-Bait" briefed to fly No. 5 position in the low flight, 1st Box. Considerable disruption during the join-up procedure meant that many aircraft flew in positions other than that briefed, so actual position flown not known.

Made three passes at primary; 20 × 100 IBs dropped on yard in Argentan.

Intense accurate HFF and LFF from Caen-Carpiquet A/F for two minutes while at 3,000 ft.

Flak-damaged; hit in left engine and three holes in right wing.

Saw a B-26 break up—no chutes, hit in right wing.

MIA Information
42-43286 DR-L

Flying in No. 4 position, low flight, 2nd Box. Seen to be hit in bomb bay and tail by flak. On return, near Audrieu, aircraft was seen to disintegrate in midair while at about 3,500 ft. and went down in flames at 0740 hrs. No chutes seen.

1Lt. L. L. Holmes, pilot	KIA
2Lt. J. M. Shoop, copilot	KIA
2Lt. J. G. Corones, navigator/bombardier	KIA
Sgt. G. D. Dawson, engineer/gunner	KIA
SSgt. I. Fischer, radio/gunner	KIA
Sgt. G. H. Pustelnik, gunner	KIA

42-107746 PN-D, "Luftwaffe's Lament"

No. 4 in the low flight, 1st Box; hit by flak in the Tilly-sur-Seulles area, at 0745 hrs. Severely damaged, with one engine shot out. All of the crew, except the pilot, bailed out from low level; the pilot crash-landed the aircraft but was knocked unconscious in the impact. Sgt. Fox was killed when his parachute failed to open; the rest of the crew were picked up by advanced Allied troops. German troops were reported as firing at the descending parachutes.

1Lt. R. E. Moninger, pilot	returned to UK after having been unconscious for ten days
1Lt. R. D. Messer, copilot	returned to UK; fractured ankle upon landing
SSgt. E. Montes de Oca, togglier	returned to UK
SSgt. J. L. Kuhl, engineer/gunner	returned to UK
Sgt. S. Fox, radio/gunner	KIA; parachute failed to open
SSgt. S. Krykla, gunner	returned to UK

Four members of this crew had previously flown in "Flak-Bait," and SSgt. de Oca would go on to fly in her four more times after his return to the unit.

In addition, the lead aircraft of the 2nd Box, 42-107685 ER-V, received over 200 flak holes. Maj. C. W. Hoover, flying as the copilot, was wounded by flak. The aircraft was repaired and returned to service on July 18, 1944. This aircraft would eventually be transferred to the 387th BG.

```
Date: June 13–14, 1944
Target: Coutances RR Jct, Night Mission
Field Order: 9th BC F/O 369
99th CBW F/O 109
```

"Flak-Bait" Crew

1Lt. H. C. Rodgers, pilot	SSgt. V. J. Mammolito, engineer/gunner
2Lt. R. W. Page, copilot	TSgt. O. D. Freeman, radio/gunner
1Lt. W. F. Vaughan, navigator/bombardier	Sgt. A. Christopher, gunner

Briefing started at 2200 hrs. and ended 2320 hrs.

T/off: 0046 hrs.   Target: 0216 to 0230 hrs.   Return: 0455 hrs.

Mission Narrative

322nd Bomb Group's 2nd night mission.

Thirty-five plus nine PFF aircraft dispatched, each aircraft bombing individually from staggered heights between 4,500 and 7,000 ft.

Routing was Base to Splasher Beacon No 13, to 49.44'N, 02.23'W (east of Sark), to target.

Thirty-two aircraft attacked, dropping 167 × 500 GPs and 192 × 250 GPs plus one ZG-5 leaflet bomb. The PFF aircraft dropped T/Is and 47 × 500 GPs. Two aircraft aborted, returning 8 × 500 GPs and 16 × 250 GPs since they could not see the T/Is.

Weak inaccurate LFF from Sark and area near Lessay. Moderate inaccurate HFF from Cap-de-la-Hague, Jersey Island, Chausey Isle, and Guernsey. One aircraft, well off course, flew directly over Cherbourg and received intense accurate HFF; this same aircraft upon reaching England was fired on by British HFF. A number of searchlights were reported, but no aircraft were coned. One aircraft received Cat. A damage. One aircraft landed at Exeter upon return.

Return routing was a right turn to 49.17'N, 02.52'W (west of Jersey), to Splasher Beacon No. 13 to Base.

Interrogation of crews began at 0415 hrs. and finished at 0530 hrs.

Mission Notes and "Flak-Bait" Crew Debrief Comments

Saw green flare drop. Twenty seconds later saw T/Is; bombs dropped just to the right; 8 × 500 GPs released from 6,500 ft. at 0215 hrs.

Moderate to slight inaccurate HFF in target area.

More time required for navigational briefing (reported by several crews).

Searchlights seen from Cherbourg tip, Jersey, Guernsey, and Brest peninsula. Flares observed from Guernsey, double red and some white ones.

Other Crew Comments

Excellent placing of T/Is by PFF; later crews reported large fires and explosions in the target area.

```
Date: June 15, 1944
Target: Jurques HQ Town
Field Order: 9th BC F/O 373
99th CBW F/O 113
```

"Flak-Bait" Crew

1Lt. W. A. Wagener, pilot   TSgt. F. T. Ehrgood, engineer/gunner
1Lt. W. F. Green, copilot   SSgt. J. H. Urbanovsky, radio/gunner
TSgt. G. W. Gueterman, toggler   SSgt. O. Hahn, gunner

Briefing started at 0600 hrs. and ended 0630 hrs.

T/off: 0742 & 0749 hrs.   Rendezvous: area cover   Landfall: 0855 & 0856 hrs.
Target: 0916 & 0918 hrs.   Coast Out: 0923 & 0926 hrs.   Return: 1052 hrs.

Mission Narrative

Thirty-six aircraft dispatched; the 1st Box was led by Col. G. C. Nye with Maj. D. E. Harnly, and the 2nd Box was led by Lt. Col. E. Wursten.

Routing was Base to Brighton to Cabourg to 48.42'N, 00.15'W (La Blardiere), to target. Allied fighters to provide area cover.

Bombing by flights, from 8,000 to 8,500 ft. Weather was 3–4/10th, tops 4,000 ft. All aircraft dropped. Results for Box 1 were good, poor after two runs, and gross. For the 2nd Box they were excellent, gross, and good. The high flight of the 2nd Box picked out wrong target and bombed Conde-sur-Noireau in error, bombs falling across railway lines and junction plus buildings nearby. 280 × 250 GPs and 96 × 500 GPs on primary, 96 × 250 GPs on Conde-sur-Noireau. 8 × 250 GPs brought back through rack failures.

Moderate inaccurate HFF from Villers and weak inaccurate HFF from Caumont; no damage received.

Return was a right turn to 49.22'N, 00.58'W (Loucelles), with exit from enemy coast at Grandcamp to Selsey Bill to Base.

Interrogation of crews began at 1050 hrs. and finished at 1140 hrs.

Mission Notes and "Flak-Bait" Crew Debrief Comments

"Flak-Bait" flew as No. 2 in the lead flight, 1st Box.

16 × 250 GPs on target; fair results observed.

Military installation consisting of Nissen huts and two high towers, observed just west of Jurques.

Other Crew Comments

A crash-landed B-26 looked like it had burned; observed on the ground at location U-2569.

> **Date: June 15, 1944**
> **Target: Foret d'Ecouves F/D**
> **Field Order: 9th BC F/O 375**
> **99th CBW F/O 114**

"Flak-Bait" Crew

2Lt. W. G. Fort, pilot
2Lt. S. V. N. Best, copilot
2Lt. J. F. Toscano, navigator/bombardier

SSgt. K. M. Locke, engineer/gunner
SSgt. M. T. Darnell Jr., radio/gunner
Sgt. H. W. Burgoyne, gunner

Briefing started at 1500 hrs.; no end time recorded.

T/off: 1619 & 1626 hrs.	Rendezvous: not recorded	Landfall: 1737 hrs.
Target: 1800 & 1800½ hrs.	Coast Out: 1818 hrs.	Return: 1940 hrs.

Mission Narrative

Thirty-six aircraft dispatched; the 1st Box was led by Capt. S. G. Rotkewicz, and the 2nd Box by Capt. R. H. Schmidt.

Routing was Base to Brighton to Cabourg to 48.42'N, 00.16'W (La Noe Petite), the IP, to the target. IX FC to provide P-47 escort.

Area bombing, bombing by flights. Thirty-three attacked, dropping 80 × 500 GPs and 365 × 250 GPs from 4,000 ft. and 2,500 ft. through 5/10th patchy cumulus from 3,500 to 7,000 ft. Poor visibility resulted in the target being misidentified; no bombs were closer than 2,000 ft. from designated target area, landing in fields and woods. One flight bombed woods considerably west of the target. Two aircraft had mechanical failures, returning 16 × 500 GPs, and one aircraft was MIA; 16 × 250 GPs unaccounted for on aircraft MIA, and 2 × 250 GPs were returned through rack failures.

Moderate fairly accurate HFF from St.-Silvain area. Moderate accurate HFF from Ste. Opportune. Moderate inaccurate HFF from a four-gun position at Ouilly-le-Tesson. Weak inaccurate HFF from Mezidon, and weak to moderate accurate HFF from woods north of Mezidon; also some MG fire was encountered. Eight aircraft received Cat. A damage, one aircraft MIA, seven men MIA. One man wounded: SSgt. A. Woodby, 450th BS.

Return was a left turn to Le Merlerault to Cabourg to Brighton to Base.

Interrogation of crews began at 1930 hrs. and finished at 2026 hrs.

Mission Notes and "Flak-Bait" Crew Debrief Comments

"Flak-Bait" flew as No. 5 in the low flight, 2nd Box.

8 × 500 GPs dropped, with fair results; hit in southern part of target area.

Weak inaccurate HFF from Mezidon area.

Other Crew Comments

An aircraft thought to be an A-20 observed on ground at position U2773.

A B-26 with a wing broken off appeared to have made a good crash landing, at U2573.

MIA Information
42-95949 ER-M, "Rainbow Corner 3rd"

Flying as the No. 2 aircraft in the high flight, 1st Box, hit by flak and the left engine caught fire; aircraft pulled out of formation and the left engine was seen to come off. The aircraft went down smoking at 1827 hrs. in Allencon area, but apparently under control. Aircraft eventually crash-landed 5 miles south of Villers Bocage and set on fire by the crew.

2Lt. M. L. Bedell, pilot	evaded
2Lt. J. H. De Loach, copilot	POW
2Lt. R. C. Swart, navigator/bombardier	POW
SSgt. J. S. Harper, engineer/gunner	POW
TSgt. G. M. Wells, radio/gunner	POW
SSgt. C. D. Johnson, gunner	POW
Capt. J. F. Bell, photographer	POW (from 20th Photo Intel Det., 9th Air Force)

42-95949 ER-M, "Rainbow Corner 3rd," was lost on June 15; fortunately, all the crew survived. *Trevor J. Allen collection*

2Lt. M. L. Bedell and crew; the normal copilot did not fly on this mission. *Mike Smith, B26.com*

```
Date: June 17, 1944
Target: Bois du Homme F/D
Field Order: 9th BC F/O 377
99th CBW F/O 116
```

"Flak-Bait" Crew

1Lt. R. R. Crusey, pilot	SSgt. W. S. Allen, engineer/gunner
2Lt. N. J. Miller, copilot	SSgt. C. S. Walters, radio/gunner
SSgt. R. G. Bevers, togglier	SSgt. R. J. Buckles, gunner

Briefing started at 0515 hrs. and ended 0545 hrs.; mission delayed—new briefing started at 1715 hrs. and ended 1745 hrs.

T/off: 1846 & 1853 hrs.	Rendezvous: area cover	Landfall: 1951 & 1953 hrs.
Target: 2015 & 2017½ hrs.	Coast Out: 2025 & 2026 hrs.	Return: 2152 hrs.

Mission Narrative

Thirty-six aircraft dispatched; the 1st Box was led by Lt. Col. E. Wursten, with Capt. P. Shannon. The 2nd Box was led by Lt. Col. B. G. Willis.

Route was Base to Brighton to Cabourg to Argentan to 48.45'N, 00.45'W (Villeneuve), the IP, to the target. Allied fighters to provide area cover.

Area bombing by boxes; thirty-five aircraft attacked, dropping 89 × 500 GPs and 366 × 250 GPs from 11,500 and 11,000 ft., in clear but hazy conditions. Bombs well dispersed through western and southwestern parts of woods. One aircraft was an early return, returning 16 × 250 GPs; rack failures resulted in 2 × 250 GPs and 2 × 500 GPs being jettisoned and 5 × 500 GPs returned.

Moderate LFF at Mezidon and La Beny Bocage, but was ineffective since formation was at 11,000 ft. Moderate accurate HFF at the target, continuing for one minute. Seven aircraft received Cat. A damage.

Return was from target to 49.24'N, 01.00'W (Cartigny-l'Epinay), to Brighton to Base.

Interrogation of crews began at 2145 hrs. and finished at 2230 hrs.

Mission Notes and "Flak-Bait" Crew Debrief Comments

"Flak-Bait" flew as No. 2 aircraft in the lead flight, 2nd Box.

16 × 250 GPs in woods; no fires noticeable.

HFF moderate to accurate at target.

Other Crew Comments

At 1805 hrs., a four-engine bomber, thought to be a B-24, seen to go down in flames at U-0357; 1 chute observed.

```
Date: June 18, 1944
Target: Vignacourt Noball
Field Order: 9th BC F/O 381
99th CBW F/O 119
```

"Flak-Bait" Crew

1Lt. J. J. Farrell, pilot
F/O T. F. Moore, copilot
1Lt. O. J. Redmond, navigator/bombardier

TSgt. D. L. Tyler, engineer/gunner
SSgt. J. B. Manuel, radio/gunner
Sgt. H. Brown, gunner

Briefing started at 1800 hrs. and ended 1820 hrs.

T/off: 1926 & 1933 hrs.	Rendezvous: not recorded	Landfall: 2032 & 2035 hrs.
Target: returned from IP	Coast Out: 2130 hrs.	Return: 2218 hrs.

Mission Narrative

PFF mission. Thirty aircraft plus two PFF dispatched. The 1st Box was led by Capt. R. Foote, and the 2nd Box was by Capt. R. C. Fry.

Briefed routing was from base to rendezvous with IX FC P-47 escort at Nth Foreland to Furnes to 50.27'N, 02.59'E (Wanquetin), to target. Formation split up in clouds, resulting in many route deviations.

No attack formation encountered; cumulus-nimbus clouds 6,000 to 15,000 ft. and solid cloud at 12,200 ft. Formation returned from the IP; 218 × 500 GPs returned. Four aircraft salvoed in enemy territory when flying through a thunderstorm and in icing conditions, releasing 30 × 500 GPs; bombs fell in the vicinities of Ypres, Amiens, and Courtrai, and one unknown. One aircraft was an early return, when a bomb fell off its rack.

Three aircraft reported flak, one reported weak inaccurate from Furnes, one reported weak inaccurate HFF from Dunkirk, and another reported moderate fairly accurate HFF from Amiens and Armentieres and intense inaccurate fire from Londinieres. Two aircraft received Cat. A damage from flak near Amiens.

Briefed return was from the target, a left turn to 50.28'N, 02.39'E (Estree-Wamin), to Armentieres to Furnes. Because formation became scattered, aircraft flew back by various routes.

Interrogation of crews began at 2145 hrs. and finished at 2235 hrs.

Mission Notes and "Flak-Bait" Crew Debrief Comments

"Flak-Bait" flew as No. 2 in the high flight, 1st Box.

 8 × 500 GPs brought back; ran into clouds at Tilly, turned, and came home.

 First aircraft to land at 2116 hrs.

This was the last time that the Farrell crew flew "Flak-Bait" on a combat mission. The crew, with the exception of TSgt. D. L. Tyler, flew four more missions in June 1944 (on the twenty-first, twice on the twenty-second, and their last mission to Chartres RR Br. on the twenty-fifth). Shortly after, 1Lt. James J. Farrell, 1Lt. Owen J. Redmond, TSgt. Don L. Tyler, and SSgt. Joseph B. Manuel rotated back to the United States. Copilot F/O T. F. Moore carried on flying missions until August 6, 1944, and Sgt. Harold Brown continued flying until mid-August and later returned to the unit toward the end of 1944.

Other Crew Comments

Fourteen crews criticized PFF crews for taking the formation into clouds.

```
Date: June 22, 1944
Target: Foret d'Andaine F/D
Field Order: 9th BC F/O 389
99th CBW F/O 128
```

"Flak-Bait" Crew

1Lt. H. C. Rodgers, pilot	Pvt. V. J. Mammolito*, engineer/gunner
2Lt. R. W. Page, copilot	Pvt. O. D. Freeman*, radio/gunner
2Lt. S. G. Poss, navigator/bombardier	Pvt. A. Christopher*, gunner

* Note that all three gunners have been demoted to the rank of private, for unknown reasons, but were reinstated as sergeants once again on August 1, 1944.

Briefing started at 1815 hrs. and ended 1840 hrs.

T/off: 1945 hrs.	Rendezvous: not recorded	Landfall: 2101 hrs.
Target: 2133½ & 2125 hrs.	Coast Out: 2140 hrs.	Return: 2316 hrs.

Mission Narrative

Thirty-six aircraft dispatched; Capt. P. Shannon led the 1st Box, with Lt. Col. B. G. Willis leading the 2nd Box.

 Route was Base to St. Catherine's Point, for rendezvous with IX FC P-47 escort, to 48.38'N, 00.56'W (Le Vieux Gast), to 48.25'N, 00.49'W (Jublains), avoiding Domfront, to Ambrieres (the IP) to target.

 Bombing by spread boxes; thirty-six attacked, dropping 559 × 250 GPs from 11,500 and 10,000 ft., in clear conditions with slight haze. 1st Box made two runs and bombed last. Target well covered; however, no fires or smoke other than the bomb bursts plotted. 5 × 250 GPs returned through rack malfunction.

 Weak inaccurate HFF and LFF from Mezidon and weak inaccurate HFF from Vimont area. No damage received.

 Return was from target to Lisieux to Cabourg to Worthing to Base.

 Interrogation of crews began at 2310 hrs. and finished at 2350 hrs.

Mission Notes and "Flak-Bait" Crew Debrief Comments

"Flak-Bait" flew as No. 4 in the high flight, 2nd Box.

 16 × 250 GPs dropped; all fell in the target area.

 One 451st BS crew complained of too many bombs stacked on the hardstand, making it difficult to exit and enter.

"Flak-Bait" Crew

1Lt. J. F. Jolly, pilot
2Lt. W. G. Fort, copilot
TSgt. J. L. Campbell, togglier

Sgt. D. A. Erickson, engineer/gunner
SSgt. R. J. Sullivan, radio/gunner
Pvt. E. W. Lowary, gunner

Briefing started at 1815 hrs. and ended 1831 hrs.

T/off: 1954 & 2001 hrs.	Rendezvous: area cover	Landfall: 2105 & 2106 hrs.
Target: 2117 hrs. & no attack	Coast Out: 2126 hrs.	Return: 2236 hrs.

Mission Narrative

Thirty aircraft plus two PFF aircraft dispatched. The 1st Box was led by Capt. H. H. Herring, and the 2nd Box by 1Lt. F. E. Peters.

Route was Base to Dover to Merlimont Plage to 50.25'N, 01.20'E (Le Crotoy), the IP, to target. Allied fighters to provide area cover.

1st Box took over and bombed visually from 11,000 ft.; cloud was 2–3/10th patchy at 4,000 ft., with visibility 4–8 miles in haze. Thirteen aircraft dropped 104 × 500 GPs, but results were gross; bombs landed 5,750 ft. southwest of the target, causing no damage to the target. The PFF dropped on its own equipment, releasing 4 × 500 GPs with a possible hit to a building. The 2nd Box PFF aircraft had equipment failure, so box leader took over but suffered intercom failure; pilot thought he heard "bombs gone" so turned off the target; no release was made. Three aircraft returned early: two mechanical and one because pilot sick. A total of 140 × 500 GPs bombs returned.

Weak inaccurate HFF at target, and slight inaccurate HFF at Berck-sur-Mer. No damage received.

Return was a left turn to Berck-sur-Mer to Folkestone to Base.

Interrogation of crews began at 2230 hrs. and finished at 2305 hrs.

Mission Notes and "Flak-Bait" Crew Debrief Comments

"Flak-Bait" flew as No. 6 in the high flight, 1st Box.

8 × 500 GP; bombed on box leader; bombs went across lower part of target. The 2nd Box was right alongside.

Eight bursts of HFF, below, in target area. Four bursts of inaccurate HFF at Berck-sur-Mer.

Railroad tracks, believed at Berck-sur-Mer, under repair.

Other Crew Comments

Window dropped continuously from landfall to exit.

"Flak-Bait" Crew

2Lt. N. J. Miller, pilot
1Lt. R. R. Crusey, copilot
SSgt. R. G. Bevers, togglier

SSgt. W. S. Allen, engineer/gunner
SSgt. C. S. Walters, radio/gunner
SSgt. R. J. Buckles, gunner

Briefing started at 1615 hrs. and ended 1635 hrs.

T/off: 1733 & 1741 hrs.	Rendezvous: 1830 hrs.	Landfall: 1843 & 1842 hrs.
Target: 1857, 1859 & 1905 hrs.	Coast Out: 1909 & 1920 hrs.	Return: 1959 hrs.

Mission Narrative

Thirty-six aircraft dispatched; the 1st Box was led by Col. G. C. Nye, and the 2nd Box by Capt. R. C. Fry.

Route was Base to rendezvous with IX FC fighters at Dungeness to 6 miles south of Berck-sur-Mer to 50.20'N, 01.50'E (Somme estuary), to 50.38'N, 02.07'E (Grigny), to target.

Bombing by flights, thirty-two attacked, dropping 29 × 2,000 GPs and 136 × 500 GPs in clear conditions from 11,500 and 12,000 ft. 1st Box results were fair, gross, and poor. 2nd Box Flights 2 and 3 were gross; the first flight of the 2nd Box made three runs and dropped at 1905 hrs., but results were unobserved. No damage to the target. Two aircraft returned early, and two failed to bomb when the doors wouldn't open. 7 × 2,000 GPs and 8 × 500 GPs returned.

Weak inaccurate flak at target and weak inaccurate at Gravelines on exit. One flight, off course, flew over Dunkirk and experienced intense accurate HFF; one aircraft received Cat. A damage.

Return was a left turn to 50.50'N, 02.37'E (west of Bailleul-les-Pernes), to Gravelines to Nth Foreland to Base. Interrogation of crews began at 1955 hrs. and finished at 2035 hrs.

Mission Notes and "Flak-Bait" Crew Debrief Comments

"Flak-Bait" flew as No. 6 in the low flight, 2nd Box.

2 × 2,000 GPs released; results poor.

Weak inaccurate flak at the target, and moderate accurate HFF between Gravelines and Dunkirk.

Other Crew Comments

Window was dropped at landfall for four minutes, then again from IP to exit.

Three single-engine aircraft, believed to be enemy, seen circling Dunkirk, and two Fws seen heading out to sea on landfall.

A crew in the lead flight, 2nd Box, complained that escort left us over the target and returned with aircraft that had bombed on the first run; Why didn't they stick around while we made additional runs?

```
Date: June 25, 1944
Target: Chartres RR Br
Field Order: 9th BC F/O 395
99th CBW F/O 134
```

"Flak-Bait" Crew

2Lt. G. H. Tharp, pilot	SSgt. D. C. Mustain, engineer/gunner
1Lt. L. L. Peters, copilot	SSgt. W. J. Whitesell, radio/gunner
TSgt. D. L. Tyler, togglier	SSgt. J. G. Morgan, gunner

Briefing started at 1327 hrs. and ended 1345 hrs.

T/off: 1433 hrs.	Rendezvous: 1530 hrs.	Landfall: 1555 & 1553½ hrs.
Target: 1627 & 1629 hrs.	Coast Out: 1702 hrs.	Return: 1820 hrs.

Mission Narrative

Thirty-six aircraft dispatched; the 1st Box was led by Capt. R. H. Schmidt, and the 2nd Box by 1Lt. F. M. Remmele.

Route was Base to Hastings, for rendezvous with IX FC P-47 escort, to 49.50'N, 00.3[?]'E (vicinity of Oudalle), to 49.29'N, 00.39'E (Martainville), to 48.46'N, 00.46'E (St.-Jouin-de-Blavou), to IP to the target.

Bombing by flights, twenty-nine aircraft dropped 24 × 1,000 GPs and 92 × 1,100 GPs from 11,500 and 11,000 ft. on the primary, and five aircraft dropped 20 × 1,000 GPs on a target of opportunity, a railroad/road intersection 8½ miles east of primary, since the primary was obscured by smoke. Results 1st Box excellent,

excellent (on T of Op), and no photo coverage (this flight made two runs). 2nd Box results were poor, gross, and poor. Two aircraft, early returns, brought back 4 × 1,000 GPs and 4 × 1,100 GPs. Photo interpretation showed that one span at the western end was out completely, one bomb had cut center half in two, and several hits were on eastern approaches. Aircraft dropping on target of opportunity had a probable hit to RR viaduct and hits on road through village of Le-Gue-de-Longroi.

Moderate accurate HFF at Chartres and moderate accurate HFF on turn off target in the Maintenon area and in vicinity of Dreux A/D. Fire at Dreux more intense than at Chartres. Nineteen aircraft received Cat. A damage; one man injured: 1Lt. H. I. Lewter, pilot of the 449th BS, wounded in the hand; aircraft was flown back by the copilot.

Return was a left turn off the target to 48.35'N, 01.00'E (St.-Denis -d'Authou), to 48.46'N, 00.06'E (Colombiers), to 49.29'N, 00.39'E (La Bruyere), to 49.50'N, 00.3(?)'E (vicinity of Oudalle), to Hastings to Base.

Interrogation of crews began at 1805 hrs. and finished at 1900 hrs.

Mission Notes and "Flak-Bait" Crew Debrief Comments
"Flak-Bait" flew as No. 5 in the lead flight, 2nd Box.

4 × 1,100 GPs dropped; bombs hit short and missed target.

Cat. A damage; one hole in left wing.

Tell entire group about flak instead of just flight leaders, so we know what to expect.

Other Crew Comments
No. 6 aircraft in low flight, 2nd Box, reported that a P-47 made a perfect attack pass at this flight at same level, and that P-47 could have and perhaps should have been shot at. Such passes are dangerous.

Bomb run too long today.

Waist gunners must open window packages before throwing them.

Event: Heavy Losses on Group's 3rd Night Mission
On the night of July 7–8, the 322nd BG carried out its third night mission to attack the V-weapon head-quarters at Chateau du Ribeaucourt. "Flak-Bait" was prepared as a ground spare but was not needed, so did not fly on the mission.

Thirty-five aircraft were dispatched, with twenty-three knowing to have attacked the target. Encountering heavy night-fighter opposition, nine aircraft were MIA and another declared Cat. E in a crash landing. These were the worst losses for the

One of the aircraft lost on the group's third night mission was 41-31814 ER-F, "Bag of Bolts," seen here on a mission after June 6, 1944. *Smithsonian National Air and Space Museum, NASM 83-3806*

group since the disastrous May 17, 1943, mission. Sixty-one men were MIA, including the CO of the 451st BS, Maj. G. B. Simler, who managed to evade capture. Three men were WIA: SSgt. O. C. Brown and Sgt. F. W. Rufe from the 450th BS, and SSgt. J. K. Brandemihl of the 452nd BS, who shared the destruction of an e/a with Sgt. R. E. Johnson. Another e/a was shot down by Sgt. Locke.

Maj. Simler was succeeded by Maj. Henry C. Newcomer as CO of the 451st BS.

"Flak-Bait" Crew

1Lt. R. R. Crusey, pilot
2Lt. N. J. Miller, copilot
SSgt. R. G. Bevers, togglier

SSgt. W. S. Allen, engineer/gunner
SSgt. C. S. Walters, radio/gunner
SSgt. R. J. Buckles, gunner

Briefing started at 0330 hrs. and ended 0415 hrs.

T/off: 0505 & 0512 hrs.
Target: 0659 & 0701 hrs.

Rendezvous: area cover
Coast Out: 0707 & 0704 hrs.

Landfall: 0655 & 0657 hrs.
Return: 0900 hrs.

Mission Narrative

Mission in support of the Second Army advance on Caen.

Thirty-six aircraft dispatched; 1st Box led by Lt. Col. B. G. Willis, the 2nd Box by Capt. S. G. Rotkewicz.

Route was Base to rendezvous with 344th BG at Splasher Beacon No. 11, the 344th to lead, to Selsey Bill to St. Catherine's Point to 49.18'N, 00.15'W (St. Samson), to the target. Allied fighters to provide area cover.

Area bombing by spread boxes. Thirty-three aircraft released 651 × 260 frag bombs from 12,000 and 12,500 ft. Cloud conditions were 2–4/10th patchy medium cloud in haze. Bombs were wildly scattered, covering 1 square mile, falling about 1 mile southwest of the designated target. One aircraft had engine failure and landed at Wethersfield, and two had mechanical failures over the target. A total of 61 × 260 frags returned.

HFF, intense and accurate in the target area, following through turn off target, finally ceased at Argences. Sixteen aircraft received Cat. A damage; two men injured: SSgt. J. E. Corlew and SSgt. W. Goetz, both of 449th BS.

Return was from target to 49.07'N, 00.14'W (Vieux-Fume), to 49.12'N, 00.03'W (Bieville-Quetieville), to 49.20'N, 00.02'W (St. Jouin), to St. Catherine's Point to Base.

Interrogation of crews began at 0845 hrs. and finished at 0930 hrs.

Mission Notes and "Flak-Bait" Crew Debrief Comments

"Flak-Bait" flew as No. 2 in the lead flight, 1st Box.

20 × 260 frags dropped; crew reported good results.

A B-26 was seen to explode at the target.

Other Crew Comments

Three crews thought bombload was too heavy.

B-26 from group following peeled out of formation over Isle of Wight and headed back to England, descending, at 0615 hrs.

B-24 seen to receive direct hit and burst into flames at 0637 hrs.; two chutes observed, being fired upon by ground troops.

B-26 from group following seen to explode at 0702 hrs. (The 386th BG lost 42-96324 YA-X "Miss X" this day.)

On return to the field, formation should have carried out regular descent procedure instead of diving through openings in the cloud.

"Flak-Bait" Crew

1Lt. G. P. Jones, pilot
2Lt. H. S. Overhultz, copilot
SSgt. E. Montes de Oca, togglier

SSgt. D. C. Mustain, engineer/gunner
TSgt. W. J. Whitesell, radio/gunner
SSgt. A. J. Sosenko, gunner

Briefing started at 1400 hrs. and ended 1425 hrs.

T/off: 1531 & 1538 hrs.	Rendezvous: 1620 hrs.	Landfall: 1640 hrs.
Target: 1712 & 1714 hrs.	Coast Out: 1745 & 1746 hrs.	Return: 1854 hrs.

Mission Narrative

Thirty-six aircraft dispatched; the 1st Box was led by Lt. Col. J. B. Smith, the 2nd Box by Capt. L. E. Lunkenheimer.

Route was Base to rendezvous with IX FC P-47 escort at Dungeness to St. Valery to 49.06'N, 00.40'E (St. Germain-la-Campagne), to 48.50'N, 01.40'E (Bailleau-l'Eveque) to target.

Bombing by flights, twenty-seven attacked, dropping 108 × 1,000 GPs from 11,500 and 11,000 ft. Results for Box 1 were fair, fair, and no attack. Box 2 results were all undetermined. Overall results were thought to have been fair to good. The lead aircraft of the low flight, 1st Box, had a turret failure and could not see the escort so pulled out of formation while at Yvetot; tried to call deputy to take over, but the entire flight followed. One aircraft salvoed its load of 4 × 1,000 GPs near the river Seine after being hit by flak; the aircraft rose above the formation, but control was regained and aircraft headed back with the right engine smoking; aircraft landed at Ashford. One aircraft had a rack malfunction, and another returned early with an overheating engine. A total of 32 × 1,000 GPs returned.

Moderate accurate HFF at target and from Norville, Foret de Bretonne, and Quillebeuf. Moderate to intense accurate HFF from Yvetot and Caudebec. Twenty-one aircraft received Cat. A damage, and one Cat. AC damage. Two crewman were injured: Sgt. J. V. Cornell, 450th BS, and Sgt. W. J. Knowles, 452nd BS.

Return was a left turn and retrace route in.

Interrogation of crews began at 1845 hrs. and finished at 1930 hrs.

Mission Notes and "Flak-Bait" Crew Debrief Comments

"Flak-Bait" flew as No. 6 in the low flight, 2nd Box.

4 × 1,000 GPs dropped.

Aircraft damaged Cat. A: "some holes."

A long low ship at rest off the coast at Veules les Roses.

Moderate to intense, fairly accurate HFF at Caudebec for four minutes. Intense accurate HFF beginning at R-7048 to target and on turn off target.

Other Crew Comments

All flights too scattered today.

"Flak-Bait" Crew

1Lt. C. E. Keenan, pilot
1Lt. B. P. Burrage, copilot
TSgt. V. J. Christian, togglier

SSgt. G. G. Minter, engineer/gunner
Sgt. E. C. Schaefer, radio/gunner
SSgt. J. A. Pavesich, gunner

Briefing started at 0515 hrs. and ended 0555 hrs.; indefinite delay announced; briefing restarted at 1630 hrs. and ended 1700 hrs.

T/off: 1739 hrs. Rendezvous: 1901 hrs. Landfall: 1936 & 1932 hrs.
Target: 1956 & 1957 hrs. Coast Out: 2024 & 2025 hrs. Return: 2156 hrs.

Mission Narrative

Thirty-six aircraft dispatched; the 1st Box was led by Capt. H. H. Herring, the 2nd Box by Col. J. G. Simpson.

Route was Base to St. Catherine's Point to rendezvous with IX FC P-47 escort at 49.42'N, 01.16'W (La Grande Dune), to 49.15'N, 01.45'W (La Chasserie), to 48.33'N, 01.40'W (La Saigeais), to 48.00'N, 02.05'W (La Chapelle es Chevres), to 47.18'N, 01.51'W (Vertou), to the target.

Bombing by flights, thirty-five aircraft known to have dropped on the target, releasing 139 × 1,000 GPs and one ZG-7 leaflet bomb from 11,500 and 12,000 ft. Cloud conditions were 1–3/10th at 6,000 ft., with a break over the target. Results for Box 1 were excellent, excellent, and fair, while those for Box 2 were gross, poor, and fair, respectively. Lead flight of 1st Box bombed second out of the three flights. Although bombing was very good, no direct hits were achieved.

Intense accurate HFF in the target area for the 2nd Box, and moderate accurate for the 1st Box. One aircraft Cat. AC and eighteen aircraft Cat. A damage; two aircraft were MIA, one of which was known to have bombed the target. One aircraft, status unknown, was one of seven that landed away. Fourteen men missing.

Return was a left turn to 47.32'N, 01.10'W (Bouzille), to 48.33'N, 01.40'W (La Saigeais), to 49.15'N, 01.45'W (La Chasserie), to 49.42'N, 01.16'W (La Grande Dune), to St. Catherine's Point to Base.

Interrogation of crews began at 2200 hrs. and finished at 2245 hrs.

41-35021 SS-L, "the Sheriff Rapides Parish Louisiana," was lost on July 19, 1944. The crew pictured is that of 1Lt. U. T. Downs (*center*), who crash-landed the aircraft "Eleanor B" at Wattisham on March 26, 1944. *Trevor J. Allen collection*

Mission Notes and "Flak-Bait" Crew Debrief Comments

"Flak-Bait" flew as No. 3 aircraft in the lead flight, 1st Box.

4 × 1,000 GPs dropped; observed good results.

Moderate to intense HFF at target on bomb run, and short time after for 2–3 minutes.

After bombs away, a B-26 turned and dived to the left; leveled off for a second, then dove in and crashed just south of river at 1954 hrs.; one chute seen.

Other Crew Comments

P-47 observed to burst into flames and go straight down.

MIA Information

41-31974 ER-R, "Anonymaus"

No. 2 in low flight, 2nd Box. Smoke was observed coming from right engine; aircraft turned over on its back and fell into clouds; two chutes seen at 1955 hrs.

1Lt. J. M. Deen, pilot	KIA
1Lt. J. P. Gonet, copilot	KIA
2Lt. C. H. Sinn, navigator/bombardier	KIA
SSgt. J. E. Fox, engineer/gunner	POW
TSgt. J. F. Williams, radio/gunner	KIA
SSgt. C. I. Abady, gunner	KIA

41-35021 SS-L, "the Sheriff Rapides Parish Louisiana"

Lead aircraft of the 2nd Box, hit just after bombing at 1957 hrs.; the left engine caught fire and the aircraft banked steeply to the left, then the left wing broke off and aircraft went into a spin and crashed south of the Loire River. One chute seen; one other crew member was seen to come out, but chute not observed.

1Lt. W. E. Canfield, pilot	KIA
Col. J. G. Simpson, copilot	KIA; 322nd BG air executive officer
1Lt. H. E. Conforti, navigator/bombardier	KIA
1Lt. J. J. Burns, bombardier	KIA
SSgt. J. H. Chidester, engineer/gunner	evaded
TSgt. H. J. Hofmeister, radio/gunner	KIA
Sgt. R. V. Hehl, waist gunner	KIA; died in German hospital
SSgt. W. W. Hampton, gunner	evaded

```
Date: July 20, 1944
Target: Foret de Senonches F/D
Field Order: 9th BC F/O 438
99th CBW F/O 174
```

"Flak-Bait" Crew

1Lt. G. H. Lane, pilot	Pvt. V. J. Mammolito, engineer/gunner
2Lt. R. W. Page, copilot	Sgt. C. Fisher, radio/gunner
TSgt. V. J. Christian, togglier	Sgt. J. E. Campbell, gunner

Briefing started at 0700 hrs. and ended 0730 hrs.; mission delayed.

T/off: 1336 & 1321 hrs.	Rendezvous: 1435 & 1430 hrs.	Landfall: 1449 & 1452 hrs.
Target: 1536 & 1525 hrs.	Coast Out: 1533 & 1540 hrs.	Return: 1703 hrs.

Mission Narrative

Thirty-six aircraft dispatched; the 1st Box was led by Capt. R. H. Schmidt and the 2nd Box by Lt. Col. J. B. Smith with 1Lt. M. C. Simmons.

Briefed route was Base to rendezvous with P-47 escort at Ouistreham to Lisieux to Belleme to 48.18'N, 00.58'E (Les Mousseries), to the target. The high flight, 1st Box, and high and low flights of the 2nd Box lost the formation in weather and returned to Base from the Selsey Bill area. The 1st Box routed around Lisieux.

Briefed to bomb by flights; weather was 8–10/10th cumulus, with tops at 13,000 ft. Five aircraft from lead flight, 1st Box, dropped on the primary, releasing 152 × 100 frags and 1 × ZG-7 leaflet bomb; no photo coverage, but bombardiers thought the results were fair. The low flight, 1st Box, found heavy cloud at the primary, and after four runs they attacked Conches A/D as a casual target, dropping 168 × 100 frags at 1537 hrs.; the bombs hit in northwest corner of field on perimeter and taxi strips. Lead flight of 2nd Box made two runs but could not bomb because of weather. 12 × 100 frags were jettisoned because of rack failure. Twenty-four aircraft failed to bomb because of weather. A total of 672 × 100 frags returned.

Slight inaccurate HFF from Tricqueville, weak to moderate accurate flak from Lisieux; one aircraft Cat. A damage. One aircraft landed on a strip in France, short of fuel. The pilot, Capt. U. T. Downs, contacted higher headquarters, but message was not received by the group, and MIA telegrams were prepared. This aircraft was stranded by bad weather and suddenly appeared overhead Andrews Field some three days later.

Briefed return was a left turn to Lisieux to Ouistreham to Selsey Bill to Base.

Interrogation of crews began at 1656 hrs. and finished at 1730 hrs.

Mission Notes and "Flak-Bait" Crew Debrief Comments

"Flak-Bait" as No. 5 in low flight, 1st Box.

28 × 100 GPs dropped on airfield, don't know which one, at 1538 hrs. from 12,500 ft.

Accurate HFF from Lisieux.

Debrief form says aircraft damaged Cat. AC. Either in error or possibly not battle-related damage, since only one aircraft in formation was reported as Cat. A by flak, and that was in the lead flight, 2nd Box. "Flak-Bait" did not fly a mission again until July 26 so possibly was under some kind of repair or maintenance.

Part 3:
July 26, 1944–September 14, 1944,
Northern France Campaign

Date: July 25, 1944
Target: Foret de Senonches F/D
Field Order: 9th BC F/O 448
99th CBW F/O 184

"Flak-Bait" Crew

1Lt. G. P. Jones, pilot
2Lt. H. S. Overhultz, copilot
SSgt. E. Montes de Oca, togglier

SSgt. D. C. Mustain, engineer/gunner
TSgt. W. J. Whitesell, radio/gunner
SSgt. J. G. Morgan, gunner

Briefing started at 1730 hrs.; no end time recorded.

T/off: 1856 & 1903 hrs.	Rendezvous: 2036 hrs.	Landfall: 2036 hrs.
Target: 2100 & 2100½ hrs.	Coast Out: 2121 hrs.	Return: 2240 hrs.

Mission Narrative

Thirty-seven aircraft dispatched; the 1st Box was led by Col. E. Wursten, and the 2nd Box by Maj. D. E. Harnly.

Route was Base to St. Catherine's Point to 49.20'N, 00.00' (Gerrots), for rendezvous with IX FC fighter escort, to Breteuil (the IP) to target.

Area bombing by flights; twenty-seven attacked, dropping 752 × 100 GPs from 12,000 and 11,500 ft., through 2–4/10th patchy cloud at 7–8,000 ft. Results were good, with hits in the target area causing explosions and fires. The high flight, 1st Box, did not bomb due to pilot being injured by flak in the shoulder; aircraft crash-landed at Hendon. Three aircraft were early returns; one aircraft landed at Advanced Landing Ground A-2 on the French coast on single engine while on the route out. 56 × 100 GPs were jettisoned in Channel by two flak-damaged aircraft. A total of 200 × 100 GPs were returned, four by rack failures and 196 by aircraft failing to bomb. 28 × 100 GPs disposition unknown; aircraft crashed at Hendon and no report received.

The main formation met no opposition, but the high flight of the 1st Box became separated from the rest of the formation and got off course and received intense and accurate HFF from Pont Audemer. Five aircraft Cat. A, and one Cat. E in crash landing at Hendon; one killed, six injured.

Return was a right turn off the target and retrace route in. The high flight of the 1st Box became separated and flew off the briefed route over Pont Audemer and exited near Le Havre.

Interrogation of crews began at 2235 hrs. and finished at 2315 hrs.

The scene of destruction after 42-96282 ER-O crashed upon landing at Hendon. *USAAF*

Mission Notes and "Flak-Bait" Crew Debrief Comments

"Flak-Bait" flew as No. 5 in the lead flight, 2nd Box.

1 × 100 GP returned through rack malfunction, twenty-seven on target; saw several large explosions.

Waist gunners need field glasses for observations.

Other Crew Comments

Approximately twenty unidentified fighter-type aircraft orbiting, at approx. 1,500 ft. in vicinity of position L-6015.

An unidentified fighter was seen destroyed by Allied fighters; went down in flames at 2136 hrs.

Crews reported that escort consisted of P-47s and P-51s and not P-38s as briefed.

We had ample time to go around cloud, but entire 2nd Box went through cloud that was 2,000 ft. thick.

Category E Information

42-96282 ER-O

Pilot was 1Lt. R. T. Chambers; lead aircraft of the high flight, 1st Box, crash-landed at Hendon, after the pilot, who had been wounded in the shoulder by flak, fainted through his injuries on the final approach. One killed, six injured.

1Lt. R. T. Chambers, pilot	wounded by flak
1Lt. R. R. De Rouen, copilot	injured
2Lt. C. E. Helms, navigator	injured
2Lt. W. N. Bateman, bombardier	serious back injuries
SSgt. E. L. Kaylor, engineer/gunner	injured
TSgt. J. M. Eleazer, radio/gunner	KIA
SSgt. T. S. Cantrell, gunner	serious back injuries

Date: July 27, 1944
Target: Chartres RR Br
Field Order: 9th BC F/O 449
99th CBW F/O 185

"Flak-Bait" Crew

Lt. Jones*, pilot	engineer/gunner
copilot	radio/gunner
navigator/bombardier	gunner

* Probably 1Lt. G. P. Jones and crew, as in the previous and following mission reports.

Briefing started at 0430 hrs. and ended 0500 hrs.

T/off: 0551 hrs.	Target: no attack	Return: 0741 hrs.

Mission Narrative

Thirty-eight plus two window aircraft dispatched; the 1st Box was led by Capt. H. H. Herring, and the 2nd Box by Capt. D. W. Allen.

Route was Base to St. Catherine's Point to fighter rendezvous; formation was recalled by "Parade" two minutes before reaching the English coast, since the fighter escort was unable to take off because of the weather.

10/10th cloud with base at 2,000 ft. and tops 5,000 ft., and bulging cumulus to 10,000 ft., over the Channel.

Interrogation of crews began at 0730 hrs. and finished at 0800 hrs.

Mission Notes and "Flak-Bait" Crew Debrief Comments

"Flak-Bait" flew as No. 3 in the high flight, 1st Box.

Abortive; formation recalled. 4 × 1,000 GPs returned.

"Flak-Bait" Crew

1Lt. G. P. Jones, pilot	SSgt. D. C. Mustain, engineer/gunner
2Lt. H. S. Overhultz, copilot	TSgt. W. J. Whitesell, radio/gunner
SSgt. E. Montes de Oca, togglier	SSgt. J. G. Morgan, gunner

Briefing started at 1200 hrs. and ended 1235 hrs.

T/off: 1315 hrs.	Target: 1514 & 1513 hrs.	Return: 1708 hrs.

Mission Narrative

PFF mission; thirty aircraft plus two PFF dispatched; the 1st Box was led by Capt. H. V. Smythe, and the 2nd Box by Capt. R. H. Schmidt.

Route was Base to St. Catherine's Point to fighter rendezvous at 49.30'N, 00.10'W (Cabourg), to 49.20'N, 00.00' (Gerrots), to 48.40'N, 00.15'E (Le Grand Larrey), to target.

Thirty-one aircraft attacked; the PFF aircraft in the 1st Box was signaled off the target by ground control, so 1st Box formed up and bombed on the 2nd Box release. Results poor; no hits to the bridge; bombs hit southwest of the bridge, in a village and in fields. Tracks probably cut on the embankment 1,600 ft. southeast of the bridge. 114 × 1,000 GPs, 8 × 500 GPs, and 2 × ZG-34 leaflet bombs released. One aircraft was an early return when gunner injured hand while trying to clear a jam; 4 × 1,000 GPs returned. Weather at the target was 9–10/10th cloud, with tops at 8–9,000 ft.

No flak encountered.

Return was a left turn off the target to 49.04'N, 00.10'E (Castillon-en-Auge), to 49.20'N, 00.00' (Gerrots), to Selsey Bill to Base.

Interrogation of crews began at 1700 hrs. and finished at 1730 hrs.

Mission Notes and "Flak-Bait" Crew Debrief Comments

"Flak-Bait" flew as No. 3 in the high flight, 1st Box.

4 × 1,000 GPs on target; bridge covered by smoke; knew that bombs hit railroad tracks.

How come we were flying at 14,000 ft.?; no use in it.

"Flak-Bait" Crew

1Lt. B. P. Burrage, pilot	Sgt. J. F. Holcomb, engineer/gunner
2Lt. E. C. Pakish, copilot	SSgt. R. M. Jones, radio/gunner
2Lt. J. Carbone, navigator/bombardier	Sgt. J. F. Riffe, gunner

Briefing started at 1815 hrs. and ended 1840 hrs.

T/off: 1930 & 1937 hrs.	Rendezvous: 2055 & 2059 hrs.	Landfall: 2101 & 2101½ hrs.
Target: 2129 & 2129½ hrs.	Coast Out: 2152 hrs.	Return: 2330 hrs.

Mission Narrative

PFF mission; thirty aircraft plus two PFF dispatched; the 1st Box was led by Capt. R. W. Leonard, and the 2nd Box by 1Lt. M. C. Simmons.

Route was Base to Selsey Bill to fighter rendezvous at 49.30'W, 00.10'W (Cabourg), to 49.20'N, 00.00' (Gerrots), to 49.04'N, 00.06'E (Vieux-Pont-en-Auge), to 45.35'N, 00.10'W (Chillac), to 48.29'N, 00.02'W (Douillet), to target.

Thirty-two aircraft attacked, bombed on PFF through 8–10/10th cloud at 8,000 ft.; 820 × 100 GPs and 8 × 500 GPs on target from 13,600 and 13,000 ft.; 1st Box achieved good results; the 2nd Box results were unobserved. Bombardiers reported fires and explosions in the target area. 20 × 100 GPs returned through rack failures. PRU later revealed that bridge was still intact, although two near misses were observed on the west bank, possibly damaging rail lines, and 10–15 craters immediately northwest of target.

Weak inaccurate HFF en route and near Lisieux; formation deviated around the town. No damage received.

Return was a left turn to 49.20'N, 00.00'W (Gerrots), to Selsey Bill to Base.

Interrogation of crews began at 2315 hrs. and finished at 2404 hrs.

Mission Notes and "Flak-Bait" Crew Debrief Comments
"Flak-Bait" flew as No. 6 in the low flight, 1st Box.

28 × 100 GPs dropped; observed two large fires, about 500 yards apart, but did not observe own bombing.

Other Crew Comments
Two Me 109s seen in area of the IP; no engagements. Brown-colored Fw 190 in area of Lisieux; flew within 1,000 yds. of low flight, 1st Box, but no attack made. Three Fw 190s seen elsewhere.

Leader of 2nd Box complained that a little more discipline needed when landing; leading the 2nd Box but was last flight to land.

```
Date: July 31, 1944
Target: Foret de la Guerche F/D
Field Order: 9th BC F/O 459
99th CBW F/O 195
```

"Flak-Bait" Crew

1Lt. T. W. Piippo, pilot	SSgt. J. E. Corlew, engineer/gunner
1Lt. L. L. Peters, copilot	SSgt. M. T. Darnell Jr., radio/gunner
SSgt. H. Brown, togglier	Sgt. J. Palcich, gunner

Briefing started at 1548 hrs. and ended 1610 hrs.

T/off: 1702 hrs.	Rendezvous: not recorded	Landfall: 1850 hrs.
Target: 1912 & 1912½ hrs.	Coast Out: 1929 hrs.	Return: 2110 hrs.

Mission Narrative
Thirty-six aircraft dispatched; the 1st Box was led by Capt. H. H. Herring, and the 2nd Box by Capt. H. E. Short.

Route was base to St. Catherine's Point to 49.47'N, 01.15'W (off St. Martin-de-Varreville), to rendezvous with P-47 escort at 49.13'N, 01.39'W (St. Sauveur-Lendelin), to 48.36'N, 01.46'W (La Gennerie), to 48.00'N, 02.00'W (La Chenaye), to 47.50'N, 01.40'W (Joue-sur-Erdre), to target.

Area bombing by boxes. All attacked, dropping 1,008 × 100 GPs from 11,500 and 10,800 ft. All bombs outside target area, although some explosions larger than bomb bursts were seen. Bombs landed northwest and southwest of the designated target area.

Weak inaccurate flak at target and at La Bouexiere. Weak inaccurate from Rennes, Foret de Rennes, and Foret de Chevre. One aircraft received Cat. A damage.

Return was a left turn to 48.36'N, 01.46'W (La Gennerie), and retrace route in to St. Catherine's Point to Base.

Interrogation of crews began at 2110 hrs. and finished at 2145 hrs.

Mission Notes and "Flak-Bait" Crew Debrief Comments
"Flak-Bait" flew as No. 3 in the high flight, 1st Box.

28 × 100 GPs released. Could see heavy black smoke all the way to coast on way back.

Other Crew Comments
High flight of the 1st Box never got into formation.

Event: Col. Glenn C. Nye Returns to the US
On July 31, 1944, Col. Glenn C. Nye, group CO, was rotated back to the Z of I; he was succeeded by Lt. Col. John S. Samuel as the group commander.

```
Date: August 1, 1944
Target: Cinq-Mars RR Br
Field Order: 9th BC F/O 461
99th CBW F/O 197
```

"Flak-Bait" Crew

1Lt. J. F. Jolly, pilot	Sgt. D. A. Erickson, engineer/gunner
Brig. Gen. H. B. Thatcher, copilot	SSgt. R. J. Sullivan, radio/gunner
2Lt. T. F. Moore, navigator	Sgt. A. Christopher, gunner
TSgt. J. L. Chambers, togglier	

Briefing started at 1240 hrs. and ended 1308 hrs.

T/off: 1437 hrs.	Rendezvous: 1534 hrs.	Landfall: 1616 hrs.
Target: 1659 & 1654 hrs.	Coast Out: 1738 hrs.	Return: 1913 hrs.

Mission Narrative
F/O 196 issued to same target earlier in the day; the group was alerted but then stood down.

Thirty-six aircraft dispatched; 1st Box was led by Lt. Col. E. Wursten, and the 2nd Box by Capt. M. I. Sterngold.

Route was Base to St. Catherine's Point to rendezvous with IX FC P-38 escort at 49.19'N, 00.00'E (Gerrots), to 48.32'N, 00.32'E (Pizieux), to 47.33'N, 00.20'E (Benais), to target.

Bombing by flights, thirty-one attacked from 11,500 and 11,000 ft., dropping 62 × 2,000 GPs, for fair to good results; bombs seen to straddle the bridge, with one or two possible hits and several near misses. No. 5 aircraft in the lead flight, 1st Box, dropped 2 × 2,000 GPs 2 miles south of the target when bombardier left nose, not realizing a second run was being made. The leader of the low flight, 1st Box, had a bomb door failure so did not release, and two others did not drop because he did not release. Another aircraft had rack failure and jettisoned 2 × 2,000 GPs in the Channel. 6 × 2,000 GPs were returned. PRU shows bridge undamaged; a near miss caused possible damage to southeast approach; a concentration of bomb craters were observed northwest of the bridge.

No opposition encountered.

Return was a right turn to 48.32'N, 00.32'E (Pizieux), to 49.19'N, 00.00' (Gerrots), to St. Catherine's Point to Base.

Interrogation of crews began at 1905 hrs. and finished at 1945 hrs.

Mission Notes and "Flak-Bait" Crew Debrief Comments
"Flak-Bait" flew in the No. 4 position, low flight, 2nd Box.

Brig. Gen. Herbert B. Thatcher, CO of the 99th CBW, flew in the copilot's seat on "Flak-Bait."

2 × 2000 GPs dropped; hit to right of the target.

Saw a lone B-24 flying southeast on its own, at about 6,000 ft. and in no trouble.

Gunners briefing in room 2: no information given on temperatures, and not told where and when to use window.

"Flak-Bait" Crew

1Lt. J. F. Jolly, pilot
2Lt. T. F. Moore, copilot
TSgt. J. L. Campbell, togglier

Sgt. D. A. Erickson, engineer/gunner
SSgt. R. J. Sullivan, radio/gunner
Sgt. A. Christopher, gunner

Briefing started at 1245 hrs. and ended 1330 hrs.
T/off: 1411 hrs.   Target: 1607 hrs.   Return: 1803 hrs.

Mission Narrative

Thirty-six plus three window ships dispatched. The 1st Box was led by 1Lt. M. C. Simmons, and the 2nd Box by Maj. D. E. Harnly.

Route was Base to St. Catherine's Point to rendezvous with IX FC P-47 escort at 49.19'N, 00.00' (Gerrots), to 49.03'N, 00.11'E (La Bruyere), to 49.03'N, 00.43'E (St. Germain-la-Campagne), to target.

Bombing by flights, thirty-five attacked; window was dropped as briefed. Flights dropped in the following order: Box 1, flight 1–3–2, and Box 2 in numeric order. 140 × 1,000 GPs dropped from 12,000 and 11,100 ft.; results generally poor; low flight, Box 2: results were gross. Weather was 4–5/10th cumulus, with tops at 10,000–11,000 ft. Some hits to the rail lines, but bridges not hit. 4 × 1,000 GPs jettisoned by one aircraft that was an early return through engine trouble. PRU later showed that there were two hits to the railway tunnel, rendering that unusable, and one track received a direct hit.

Moderate accurate HFF at target and weak to moderate inaccurate HFF at Cabourg and Montfort. Fourteen aircraft received Cat. A damage; no injuries.

Return was a left turn off the target to 49.03'N, 00.11'E (La Bruyere), to 49.19'N, 00.00' (Gerrots), to St. Catherine's Point to Base.

Interrogation of crews began at 1755 hrs. and finished at 1830 hrs.

Mission Notes and "Flak-Bait" Crew Debrief Comments

"Flak-Bait" flew as No. 3 in the high flight, 2nd Box.

4 × 1,000 GPs bombs dropped: bracketed target.

Cat. A damage; one hit in horizontal stabilizer and one hole in right waist window, going through heater tube.

Observed 150–200 freight cars in M/Y at Lisieux, stationary.

Other Crew Comments

Ten to fifteen tanks observed on a highway between Bernay and Beaumont, plus ten on road between Branville to Grangues.

A dinghy spotted at about 40 miles south of St. Catherine's Point, at 1642 hrs. Two aircraft observed heading toward it.

"Flak-Bait" Crew

Capt. C. E. Davis, pilot
2Lt. G. J. Spalty, copilot
2Lt. J. F. Toscano, navigator/bombardier

SSgt. K. M. Locke, engineer/gunner
SSgt. M. T. Darnell Jr., radio/gunner
SSgt. A. J. Sosenko, gunner

Briefing started at 1900 hrs. and ended 2015 hrs.

T/off: 2157 hrs.   Target: 2347 to 2356½ hrs.   Return: 0212 hrs.

Mission Narrative

322nd BG's fourth night mission; twenty-four plus two PFF aircraft dispatched. The lead aircraft was flown by Maj. D. E. Harnly.

Route was Base to 3 miles north of Salisbury, to Cap-de-la-Hague to 48.37'N, 01.45'W (St. Georges), to 48.15'N, 00.40'W (Evron), to target. The PFF aircraft to drop two red flares at the IP and three yellow flares at the target.

Twenty-three aircraft attacked the primary from 2,500 to 4,500 ft.; cloud was 4–6/10th, with base at 5,000 ft., with a good break over the target. 643 × 100 GPs and 10 × 250 T/Is dropped; bombardiers reported good results, with hits among the T/Is in woods. One aircraft couldn't see the T/Is. A total of 29 × 100 GPs jettisoned in the Channel.

In general, LFF and HFF were received from Mayenne until exit from coast. Weak inaccurate from Fougeres and Pontorson, and intense LFF from St. Hilaire and Avranches; ships in harbor at Pontaubault and St. Malo, and moderate LFF from Domfront and Martain and weak LFF from Jersey. One aircraft reported being attacked by a night fighter one minute after entering the coast, at 2335 hrs.; the pilot made an evasive turn. Two aircraft and one PFF aircraft received Cat. A damage from flak ships. One aircraft had a compass failure and, off course, landed at Warmwell short of fuel; two of the crew bailed out over Warmwell: SSgt. J. P. Kennedy, 450th BS, broke his leg upon landing.

Return route was a left turn to 48.19'N, 00.08'W (Chaffour), to 48.37'N, 01.45'W (St. Georges), to Cap-de-la-Hague to 3 miles north of Salisbury to Base.

Interrogation of crews began at 0155 hrs. and finished at 0350 hrs.

Mission Notes and "Flak-Bait" Crew Debrief Comments

"Flak-Bait" was the second aircraft to take off.

No flak fired at this aircraft. 28 × 100 GPs dropped on the T/Is in woods, from 4,100 ft.

Cannot untie window at nite [*sic*]—especially when wearing gloves—American window preferred (the last comment was made by several crews).

> **Date: August 6, 1944**
> **Target: St.-Remi-sur-Avre RR Br**
> **Field Order: 9th BC F/O 470**
> **99th CBW F/O 205**

"Flak-Bait" Crew

1Lt. D. L. Hunter, pilot	TSgt. S. B. Marcum, engineer/gunner
1Lt. A. F. Minich, copilot	SSgt. A. I. Duncan, radio/gunner
TSgt. C. L. Zearfoss, togglier	SSgt. J. L. Smith, gunner

Briefing started at 0800 hrs. and ended 0826 hrs.

T/off: 1026 hrs.   Rendezvous: 1200 hrs.   Landfall: 1202 hrs.

Target: 1231 & 1248 hrs.   Coast Out: 1256 hrs.   Return: 1436 hrs.

Mission Narrative

Thirty-six aircraft dispatched; the 1st Box was led by Lt. Col. J. S. Samuel, and the 2nd Box by Lt. Col. F. P. Taylor.

Route was Base to St. Catherine's Point to fighter rendezvous at 49.24'N, 00.18'W (Petiville), to 49.19'N, 00.00' (Gerrots), to Bernay to 49.07'N, 01.11'E (Le Mesnil-Fuguet), to 48.57'N, 01.25'E (Thimert-Gatelles), to target. Formation was 10 miles left of the intended course on the way, in following the Eure River to Autheuil and Beuil, but was back on course between Lisieux and Bernay.

7–8/10th cloud at 10–12,000 ft. prevented bombing of the primary. The high flight, 1st Box, made four runs at the target. The high flight of the 2nd Box attacked a railway cutting/overpass at St. Thibault, ¾ miles west of Dreux. The low flight of Box 2 had an accidental release in open fields 2 miles southwest of primary, west of Les Gatines. Eleven aircraft dropping a total of 43 × 1,000 GPs and 1 × ZG-33 leaflet bomb. One aircraft jettisoned 4 × 1,000 GPs over France, when an engine was shot out, another jettisoned 4 × 1,000 GPs near the target because of a fuel shortage, and 16 × 1,000 GPs were jettisoned in the Channel. A total of 75 × 1,000 GPs and 1 × ZG-33 leaflet bomb were returned.

Flak at the target described as intense to nil. Lead flight, 1st Box, encountered intense flak and decreased until the low flight, 2nd Box, reported nil. This was taken as an indication that the heavy gun batteries are limited in the amount of ammunition that may be expended. Formation encountered weak, inaccurate flak and then weak to moderate HFF near Lisieux, and moderate accurate HFF from Trouville. Four aircraft received Cat. AC, and twenty-three aircraft received Cat. A flak damage. One man was KIA: SSgt. E. M. McCarty, 452nd BS, who had flown over sixty missions, and two were injured: SSgt. A. C. Freudenberg, 450th BS, and Maj. S. J. Past, 322nd BG Group navigator.

Return was a right turn to 49.19'N, 00.00' (Gerrots), to St. Catherine's Point to Base. A total of five aircraft landed away.

Interrogation of crews began at 1425 hrs. and finished at 1453 hrs.

Mission Notes and "Flak-Bait" Crew Debrief Comments
"Flak-Bait" flew as No. 4 in the high flight, 1st Box.

4 × 1,000 GP bombs returned; did not bomb.

Cat. A damage, a few small holes; landed at Thorney Island, short of gas.

Waist gunner and tail gunner should test guns at the same time.

```
Date: August 12, 1944
Target: Flers-Falaise Road Junctions
Field Order: 9th BC F/O 486
99th CBW F/O 220
```

"Flak-Bait" Crew

1Lt. R. M. Cooper Jr., pilot	SSgt. W. C. Upton, engineer/gunner
2Lt. R. R. Rigg, copilot	SSgt. D. N. West, radio/gunner
TSgt. P. A. Davis, togglier	SSgt. D. W. Hone, gunner

Briefing started at 1730 hrs. and ended 1740 hrs.

T/off: 1849 & 1843 hrs.	Rendezvous: area cover	Landfall: 2003 hrs.
Target: 2058 & 2040 hrs.	Coast Out: 2109 hrs.	Return: 2240 hrs.

Mission Narrative
Thirty-seven aircraft dispatched; the 1st Box was led by Lt. Col. D. D. Bentley, to attack targets in Falaise area, and the 2nd Box by Capt. A. W. Bouquet, to attack targets in the Flers area.

Route for the 1st Box was Base to Selsey Bill to Avranches to 48.28'N, 00.48'W (Grazay), to Domfront to target. Route for the 2nd Box was Base to Selsey Bill to Aura to 48.18'N, 00.22'W (Vimarce), to 48.38'N, 00.12'W (Champrousier), to target. VIII FC were to provide area cover.

Briefed to bomb by flights, but haze limited visibility to 2 miles, so no attack made. Three runs made at the target. Two aircraft could not catch the formation since they were late in having their bombs fused; bombs jettisoned. A total of 568 × 100 GPs were jettisoned; 16 × 100 GPs dropped by one aircraft, at T-8314, when they accidentally fell out of the bomb bay when doors were opened. 136 × 100 GPs returned, and 20 × 100 GPs unaccounted for in aircraft MIA.

Moderate to intense fairly accurate HFF for lead flight, 1st Box, from the Falaise area. Moderate to intense, fairly accurate HFF for lead and high flights of the 2nd Box, in the Flers area. Intense accurate HFF for the low flight, 2nd Box, in the Flers area.

Friendly fire incident: At approximately 2105 hrs., the low flight, 1st Box, failed to fly the briefed route out from the target. They were briefed to make a left turn in the Falaise area toward Bayeux. Instead they flew in a westerly direction over the Mortain area to Avranches. This flight encountered moderate to intense, accurate, and tracking antiaircraft fire 6–8 miles east of Mortain, which continued to the Avranches area.

One aircraft was MIA, two were Cat. E, one Cat. AC and ten Cat. A. Two killed, four injured, six MIA. Return for 1st Box was a left turn to Caen to Selsey Bill to Base, while for the 2nd Box was a left turn to Bayeux to Selsey Bill and Base.

Interrogation of crews began at 2215 hrs. and finished at 2300 hrs.

Mission Notes and "Flak-Bait" Crew Debrief Comments
"Flak-Bait" flew as No. 5 in the low flight, 1st Box.

Cat. A damage.
Jettisoned 20 × 100 GPs in Channel.
Inform Allied forces that we are coming.
Let's have tracer back in ammo.

Other Crew Comments
Briefing haphazard and too fast.

Aircraft like object floating on water off Isigny at 1940 hrs.
Sub sighted below surface with periscope above water, headed toward convoy at 2135 hrs.

MIA Information
41-31741 PN-N, "Winnie Dee"
Flying No. 3 in the low flight, 2nd Box, aircraft received a direct hit in the bomb bay at 2040 hrs. and caught fire immediately. Aircraft entered into a bank and peeled off to the left with the nose down; aircraft enveloped in flames, and pieces of the right wing began to break off. Aircraft exploded at approx 5,000 ft.; four chutes were reported.

1Lt. F. L. Hunt, pilot	KIA
1Lt. L. L. Peters, copilot	KIA
1Lt. M. Rafalow, navigator/bombardier	KIA
SSgt. W. F. Stark, engineer/gunner	KIA
TSgt. R. J. Morin, radio/gunner	KIA
SSgt. N. E. Thielan˙, gunner	POW

˙ Sgt. Norman E. Thielan was a part of the original crew of "Flak-Bait" and flew thirty-four missions in her; he had returned from the US after a thirty-day leave on May 18, 1944.

Category E Information
41-31894 SS-O
Pilot was Capt. M. I. Sterngold, flying No. 4 in the lead flight, 1st Box; flying on single engine and crash-landed at Strip B-11 in France and overran the strip. Crew OK.

41-31765 ER-X, "Fightin Cock"
No. 6 ship in the high flight, 2nd Box. Hydraulics and electrics were damaged; bombs were jettisoned in the Channel. Upon return, the undercarriage was pumped down, but only the nose and right main gear came down and couldn't be retracted again. Because of a wounded crewman on board, they did not want to bail the crew out, so that they could hold the wounded man during crash landing. Upon landing, the aircraft skidded into the control tower, killing the two pilots and injuring the rest of the crew; fortunately no one was injured in the tower.

2Lt. J. R. Walker, pilot	KIA
2Lt. B. Taylor, copilot	KIA
Sgt. E. Pilot, togglier	injured

"The Fightin Cock," with an unidentified crew, crashed into the control tower at Andrews Field, killing the two pilots and injuring the rest of the crew. *Trevor J. Allen collection*

Sgt. G. E. Peterson, engineer/gunner	injured
Sgt. J. B. Hill, radio/gunner	injured
Sgt. M. E. Vogt, gunner	injured

Maj. Wallace W. Kingsley, the group's engineering officer, was later awarded the Soldier's Medal for his heroism in helping to rescue the four injured crewmen. He entered the crashed aircraft and climbed on top of the wreckage for a vantage point, so as to direct the rescue work and the firefighters to prevent the fire reaching any explosive materials.

```
Date: August 13, 1944
Target: Thiberville—Lisieux Road Junctions
Field Order: 9th BC F/O 488
99th CBW F/O 221
```

"Flak-Bait" Crew

1Lt. A. F. Byrd Jr., pilot*	engineer/gunner*
copilot*	radio/gunner*
navigator/bombardier*	gunner*

* No crew manifest, so only the intended pilot's name is known.

Briefing started at 0645 hrs. and ended 0702 hrs.
T/off: 0821 hrs.   Target: 1033 to 1101 hrs.   Return: 1240 hrs.

Mission Narrative

Thirty-six aircraft dispatched; the 1st Box was led by Capt. L. J. Sebille. The 2nd Box was led by 1Lt. E. R. Bruner with Maj. D. E. Harnly.

Routing was Base to Selsey Bill to 49.20'N, 01.10'W (Montreuil), to Avranches to 48.12'N, 00.07'W (Tennie), to 48.37'N, 00.38'E (Le Ham), to 48.47'N, 00.18'E (Le Val), the IP, to the target. 11 Group RAF to provide area support.

Bombing by flights, each on a different location, twenty-seven aircraft attacked, dropping 402 × 250 GPs bombs in vicinity of the primaries, from 11,000 to 11,500 ft., but the results were generally poor. The low flight of the 1st Box made four runs and released at 1101 hrs., the results being undetermined. The high flight of 2nd Box misidentified the target and dropped 12½ miles WSW of the DMPI, near town of Livarot; bombs fell in an orchard and in fields. 111 × 250 GPs were jettisoned and 63 × 250 GPs returned.

No opposition met.

Return was from target to 49.19'N, 00.02'W (Beuvron-en-Auge), to Selsey Bill to Base.

Interrogation of crews began at 1200 hrs. and finished at 1300 hrs.

Mission Notes and "Flak-Bait" Crew Debrief Comments

"Flak-Bait" scheduled to fly as No. 2 in the high flight, 2nd Box

No takeoff: brake seal out of order.

Spare aircraft took off in the place of "Flak-Bait" but couldn't catch the formation and joined up with the wrong group; 16 × 250 GPs returned.

Category E Information

41-35263 ER-M

Pilot was 2Lt. A. M. Smith, flying in the No. 4 position of the high flight, 1st Box. Returning short of gas when the controls locked up, aircraft was abandoned between Maldon and Tollesbury and crashed near Witham; crew safe.

```
Date: August 13, 1944
Target: Peronne RR Br
Field Order: 9th BC F/O 489
99th CBW F/O 222
```

"Flak-Bait" Crew

1Lt. B. P. Burrage, pilot
2Lt. E. C. Pakish, copilot
2Lt. J. Carbone, navigator/bombardier

Sgt. J. F. Holcomb, engineer/gunner
SSgt. G. F. Van Meter, radio/gunner
Sgt. J. E. Campbell, gunner

Briefing started at 1615 hrs. and ended 1640 hrs.

T/off: 1749 hrs.	Rendezvous: not recorded	Landfall: 1900 hrs.
Target: 1939 & 1940 hrs.	Coast Out: 2005 hrs.	Return: 2105 hrs.

Mission Narrative

Thirty-six aircraft dispatched; the 1st Box was led by Capt. H. H. Herring, the 2nd Box by Capt. R. W. Leonard.

Route was Base to Selsey Bill to rendezvous with RAF Spitfires at 49.50'N, 00.32'E (Sandouville), to 49.43'N, 01.13'E (Bonsecours), to 49.28'N, 01.30'E (Vatteville), to 49.35'N, 02.05'E (Berneuil-en-Bray), to 49.25'N, 02.50'E (Creil), to 49.35'N, 03.00'E (Pierrefonds), to target.

Bombing by flights, thirty-six attacked, bombing in the following order, with respective results. Box 1, low flight, excellent; Box 1, lead flight, excellent; Box 2, low flight, good; Box 1, high flight, poor; Box 2, lead flight, fair; and Box 2, high flight, excellent. 142 × 1,000 GPs dropped in clear conditions. Bridge completely covered with bursts. 2 × 1,000 GPs returned through rack failures.

No flak encountered.

Return was a left turn to 50.16'N, 02.30'E (Hem-Hardinval), to 50.28'N, 02.55'E (Avesnes-le-Comte), to Furness to the Naze to Base.

Interrogation of crews began at 2100 hrs. and finished at 2150 hrs.

Mission Notes and "Flak-Bait" Crew Debrief Comments

"Flak-Bait" flew as No. 3 in the lead flight, 1st Box.

4 × 1,000 GPs released; observed good results.

Two trains observed at Lens.

Other Crew Comments

Three Me 109s flew beneath the formation between Crevecoeur and Compeigne; no attack.

Allied fighter, possibly a P-51, seen to crash-land in a field at 1910 hrs.

```
Date: August 16, 1944
Target: Nassandres Hwy Br, 1st Box
Le Bourg Hwy Br, 2nd Box
Field Order: 9th BC F/O 500
99th CBW F/O 229
```

"Flak-Bait" Crew

1Lt. G. K. Eubank, pilot
2Lt. N. J. Miller, copilot
Sgt. H. Brown, togglier

SSgt. S. J. Nicoletti, engineer/gunner
Sgt. J. A. Smith, radio/gunner
Sgt. M. B. Schmidt, gunner

Briefing started at 1645 hrs.; no end time recorded.

T/off: 1805 hrs.
Target: 1940 & 1941 hrs.

Rendezvous: area cover
Coast Out: 1955 hrs.

Landfall: 1926 hrs.
Return: 2145 hrs.

Mission Narrative

PFF mission; thirty-one plus two PFF aircraft dispatched. The 1st Box was led by Capt. J. M. Bennett, and the 2nd Box by Capt. M. I. Sterngold.

Route was Base to Selsey Bill to 49.05'N, 00.05'W (Coconville), to target. IX TAC to provide area cover.

Bombing on PFF from 12,000 ft. and 12,700 ft., in clear conditions but with thick haze. Box 1, attacking Nassandres, had poor results, with hits in a good concentration 1,545 ft. east of DMPI, landing in the northern end of the village on a road intersection. Box 2, attacking Le Bourg, achieved good results, with bombs landing 360 ft. south of the target, on houses and industrial buildings and a road intersection. Fifteen aircraft dropped on each target, releasing 112 × 1,000 GPs and 8 × 500 GPs in total. Three aircraft experienced engine problems, one jettisoned 4 × 1,000 GPs, and the other two returned 8 × 1,000 GPs.

Moderate HFF from Cormeilles area: accurate for the 1st Box, inaccurate for the 2nd Box; thought to have been mobile guns covering withdrawing troops; no flak at the target. Two aircraft received Cat. AC damage, and nine Cat. A damage. One aircraft was Cat. E in a crash landing at Ford; three killed, three injured. One other person was KIA: SSgt. F. H. Keeley, 452nd BS; the aircraft made an emergency landing at Hurn.

"The 49ers" crashed at Ford Aerodrome on the south coast of England. *Smithsonian National Air and Space Museum, NASM 77-7326*

Briefed return was a right turn to 49.19'N, 00.02'W (Beuvron-en-Auge), but the formation flew to the north of the briefed route, close to Cormeilles and Blangy, before correcting to the west and exiting the coast close to Auberville, then to Selsey Bill to Base.

Interrogation of crews began at 2123 hrs. and finished at 2200 hrs.

Mission Notes and "Flak-Bait" Crew Debrief Comments

"Flak-Bait" was scheduled to fly as No. 2 in the low flight, 1st Box, but bombed from the No. 5 position.

4 × 1,000 GPs dropped on PFF; well concentrated but did not see target.

Cat. AC damage: hydraulic system shot out, right engine caught fire on landing, used air bottle.

Category E Information
42-107749 PN-N, "the 49ers"

Crashed at Ford due to flak damage; aircraft was on single engine with the landing gear partially down, which collapsed upon landing, resulting in the aircraft crashing through a dispersal, hitting three Bowsers and a Spitfire (s/n PL401, 331st Squadron).

2Lt. R. J. Moths, pilot	KIA
2Lt. J. H. Thomas, copilot	serious injuries
2Lt. C. R. Lock, navigator/bombardier	KIA
SSgt. J. Hastings, engineer/gunner	serious injuries
SSgt. L. E. Parker, radio/gunner	serious injuries; died in the hospital three days later
Pvt. E. Lowary, gunner	KIA

(The enlisted men on the crew had all flown on "Flak-Bait," Pvt. Lowary twice.)

Date: August 25, 1944
Target: Brest "B" Gun Position
Field Order: 9th BC F/O 511
99th CBW F/O 239

"Flak-Bait" Crew

1Lt. R. M. Cooper Jr., pilot	SSgt. R. J. Keating, engineer/gunner
2Lt. J. S. Avooski, copilot	SSgt. D. N. West, radio/gunner
TSgt. R. G. Bevers, togglier	SSgt. D. W. Hone, gunner

Briefing started at 1230 hrs. and ended 1255 hrs.

T/off: 1340 hrs.	Rendezvous: area cover	Landfall: 1546 hrs.
Target: 1550 hrs.	Coast Out: 1607 hrs.	Return: 1806 hrs.

Mission Narrative

Thirty-six aircraft dispatched; the 1st Box was led by Capt. H. E. Short, and the 2nd Box by Capt. M. I. Sterngold.

Route was Base to Portland Bill to 48.28'N, 04.46'W (Lanveoc), to target. RAF Spitfires provided area cover.

Bombing by flights, with 5–6/10th cloud, tops 5–6,000 ft., made it difficult for the flight leaders and bombardiers to pick out the target. Eighteen aircraft attacked; Box 1 lead flight and high flight and the Box 2 lead flight were the only flights to drop. 496 × 100 GPs released from 10,500 to 11,500 ft.; two crews reported good to fair results. One aircraft had 2 × 100 GPs fall out when the bomb bay doors were opened; another aircraft, from the lead flight, 2nd Box, dropped 6 miles northwest of the target. One aircraft lost the formation and returned early. A total of 510 × 100 GPs were returned by seventeen aircraft aborting because of the weather, and one aircraft that lost the formation. A 391st BG ship joined the formation and flew as No. 3 in the high flight, 2nd Box.

Slight inaccurate HFF over the target; no damage received.

Return was a left turn off the target to 48.21'N, 03.55'W (Motreff), to Portland Bill to Base.

Interrogation of crews began at 1745 hrs. and finished at 1830 hrs.

Mission Notes and "Flak-Bait" Crew Debrief Comments

"Flak-Bait" flew as No. 2 in the low flight, 1st Box.

28 × 100 GPs returned; leader did not drop.

Too much talking over Command channel; can't contact crew members over interphone.

Other Crew Comments

B-24 or B-17 observed ditched at 49.32'N, 03.44'W (west of Guernsey); no dinghy seen.

P-47s observed dive-bombing a docked freighter; missed by 500 yds.

Three dinghies seen, all empty.

Between 1600 and 1615 hrs., a B-26 flew alongside between Box 1 and Box 2, with no distinguishing markings visible, north of Les Sept Isles.

Leader of low flight, 1st Box, stated that no turns over 45 degrees should be made when turning from IP to the target.

```
Date: August 26, 1944
Target: Fournival-Bois de Mont F/D
Field Order: 9th BC F/O 512
99th CBW F/O 240
```

"Flak-Bait" Crew

1Lt. G. P. Jones, pilot
2Lt. H. S. Overhultz, copilot
TSgt. E. Montes de Oca, togglier

SSgt. D. C. Mustain, engineer/gunner
TSgt. W. J. Whitesell, radio/gunner
Sgt. R. J. Tonelli, gunner

Briefing started at 0815 hrs. and ended 0915 hrs.

T/off: 1100 & 1107 hrs.	Rendezvous: 1200 & 1158 hrs.	Landfall: 1200 & 1158 hrs.
Target: 1234 hrs.	Coast Out: 1256 & 1259 hrs.	Return: 1413 hrs.

Mission Narrative

Thirty-six aircraft dispatched; the 1st Box was led by Capt. R. W. Leonard, and the 2nd Box by 1Lt. W. G. Fort.

Route was Base to Clacton to Furnes, for rendezvous with RAF 11 Group Spitfires, to 49.45'N, 03.00'E (St.-Crepin-aux-Bois), to 49.35'N, 02.55'E (Sacy-le-Grand), to target.

Area bombing by flights, all thirty-six attacked, dropping 984 × 100 GPs on the primary, in hazy conditions; one aircraft carried 20 × 100 GPs but with a twelve-hour-delay fuse. Most bombs were outside the designated target area, cutting railroad lines in at least five places and causing one large explosion; high flight, Box 2, put most of their bombs within the designated target area. Crews reported fair to good results. 16 × 100 GPs were returned due to rack malfunctions.

Moderate accurate HFF from the IP in the Boyon area; weak to moderate, generally accurate HFF on route out from Serqueux, St. Saens, Bellencombre, Mesnil, Neufchatel, and Longueville. None at the target itself. Ten aircraft received Cat. A damage.

Briefed return was a right turn to 49.37'N, 02.05'E (Berneuil-en-Bray), to 49.27'N, 01.36'E (Cuverville), to 49.43'N, 01.13'E (Bonnsecours), to St. Valery to Selsey Bill to Base, but route flown was to east of briefed route over Serqueux, Neufchatel, and La Longueville, then left around Dieppe, to exit coast between St. Valery and Dieppe.

Interrogation of crews began at 1417 hrs. and finished at 1510 hrs.

Mission Notes and "Flak-Bait" Crew Debrief Comments

"Flak-Bait" flew as No. 6 in the high flight, 2nd Box.

28 × 100 GPs dropped; hits seen on south side of road; saw big fire: heavy black smoke.

Area flooded inland east of Dunkirk to Ostend.

Several convoys seen on roads northeast of Bethune and near Coxyde.

"Flak-Bait" Crew

Capt. C. E. Davis, pilot

2Lt. G. J. Spalty, copilot

2Lt. J. F. Toscano, navigator/bombardier

SSgt. K. M. Locke, engineer/gunner

SSgt. J. H. Urbanovsky, radio/gunner

SSgt. A. J. Sosenko, gunner

Briefing started at 1900 hrs.; no end time recorded.

T/off: 2058 hrs.   Target: 2203½ to 2207 hrs.   Return: 2314 hrs.

Mission Narrative

322nd BG's fifth, and last, night mission; twenty aircraft plus three PFF dispatched.

Routing was Base to Splasher Beacon No. 11 to 49.42'N, 00.36'E (Berville-sur-Mer), to target.

Nineteen aircraft dropped 238 × 100 GPs and 64 × 500 M17IBs, from 4,500 to 7,000 ft. The three PFF aircraft dropped T/Is only. PFF to drop red T/Is at the IP and two yellow and one green T/I at the target. The target was a fuel dump on either side of the road. Crews reported good to excellent results, with many large fires observed. One aircraft had a rack failure and returned 28 × 100 GPs; a further 14 × 100 GPs were returned for reasons unknown.

Some crews reported weak inaccurate HFF and LFF in the target area, no searchlights. No damage received.

Return was a right turn off the target to Splasher Beacon No. 11, to Base. Thirteen aircraft landed at Holmsley South, two at Ford, and one at Latham [sic] (this is how it is presented in the records, but it was more likely to have been Lasham).

No interrogation times recorded.

Mission Notes and "Flak-Bait" Crew Debrief Comments

"Flak-Bait" No. 3 in the third flight to take off.

28 × 100 GPs carried, but further details unknown since aircraft diverted upon return.

"Flak-Bait" Crew

2Lt. R. L. Hall, pilot

2Lt. R. E. O'Rourke, copilot

2Lt. S. Block, navigator/bombardier

Sgt. R. E. Rotman, engineer/gunner

Sgt. E. W. Riggs, radio/gunner

Sgt. J. Barrier, gunner

Briefing started at 1700 hrs. and ended 1714 hrs.

T/off: 1820 & 1827 hrs.   Rendezvous: 1844 hrs.   Landfall: 1915 hrs.

Target: 1957 & 2000 hrs.   Coast Out: 2030 & 2038 hrs.   Return: 2129 hrs.

Mission Narrative

Thirty-seven aircraft dispatched; the 1st Box was led by Lt. Col. B. G. Willis, and the 2nd Box by 1Lt. W. A. Taylor.

Route was Base to Clacton to Furnes, for rendezvous with RAF 11 Group Spitfires, to 49.45'N, 03.00'E (St. Crepin-aux-Bois), to 49.15'N, 03.14'E (Vaux Parfond), to 49.14'N, 02.53'E (Orry-la-Ville), to target.

Area bombing by flights, thirty-five aircraft dropped 967 × 100 GPs from 11,500 to 11,000 ft., through 3–5/10th thin stratus with tops at 5–6,000 ft. Results were good for all flights except the low flight, Box 2, whose results were poor to fair. Two aircraft were early return through engine and propeller problems, one of which landed at Great Dunmow. A total of 68 × 100 GPs returned. 1 × 100 GP jettisoned through rack failure.

Moderate accurate HFF at Lens and weak inaccurate HFF from Nieuport. Four aircraft received Cat. A damage, all in the Lens area.

Return was from target to 49.45'N, 03.00.'E (St. Crepin-aux-Bois), to 50.33'N, 02.50'E (Penin), to Furnes to Clacton to Base.

Interrogation of crews began at 2135 hrs. and finished at 2215 hrs.

Mission Notes and "Flak-Bait" Crew Debrief Comments
"Flak-Bait" flew as No. 5 in the high flight, 1st Box.

23 × 100 GPs dropped, and 5 × 100 GPs returned, rack malfunction: released too slow, personnel failure. HFF in Furnes area going in; fired at low flight.

Event: Liberated Airmen Return to Squadron
On September 5, 1944, 1Lt. Wolff, TSgt. Mertes, SSgt. Greer, and SSgt. Butterfield returned to the 449th BS, having been shot down several months earlier and hiding in occupied France prior to being liberated by Allied armies. On September 10, they began their journey home to the United States.

```
Date: September 6, 1944
Target: Brest S/P
Field Order: 9th BC F/O 532
99th CBW F/O 257
```

"Flak-Bait" Crew

2Lt. W. J. Frank, pilot	Sgt. A. R. Heredia, engineer/gunner
2Lt. J. H. Donahue, copilot	Sgt. J. P. Saladino, radio/gunner
2Lt. W. G. Leffler, navigator/bombardier	Sgt. W. R. Fry, gunner

Briefing started at 0615 hrs. and ended 0637 hrs.

T/off: 0753 & 0747 hrs.	Rendezvous: none scheduled	Landfall: 0941 & 0940 hrs.
Target: 1004 & 0955 hrs.	Coast Out: 1002 hrs.	Return: 1147 hrs.

Mission Narrative
Thirty-six aircraft dispatched; the 1st Box was led by Maj. D. E. Harnly, and the 2nd Box by 1Lt. A. E. Prestridge.

Route was Base to Portland Bill to 48.40'N, 03.55'W (Plourac'h), to 48.17'N, 04.12'W (woods near Cast), to target.

Bombing by flights, thirty-six aircraft attacked, dropping a total of 282 × 500 GPs bombs from 11,500 to 11,000 ft.; visibility was reduced by smoke in the target area, and cloud was nil to 2/10th patchy cumulus, with tops at 6,000 ft. Results were not observed, but interpretation had them as Box 1: poor, good, and fair, and Box 2: excellent, fair, and PNB: bombardier misidentified target; bombs fell in a good concentration on a road intersection 770 ft. from the DMPI. 6 × 500 GPs returned due to an intervalometer problem.

No flak encountered.

Return was a right turn off the target to Selsey Bill to Base.

Interrogation of crews began at 1150 hrs. and finished at 1227 hrs.

Mission Notes and "Flak-Bait" Crew Debrief Comments
"Flak-Bait" flew as No. 5 in the lead flight, 1st Box.

8 × 500 GPs dropped; observed good results.

Other Crew Comments
Several crews complained about issue of British candy, since was poor grade and not tasting good.

Transportation poor; trucks not at hardstands to pick up crews.

"Flak-Bait" Crew

2Lt. J. S. Avooski, pilot
2Lt. H. C. Bryant, copilot
TSgt. J. L. Campbell, togglier

Sgt. W. F. Carter Jr., engineer/gunner
Sgt. L. D. Case, radio/gunner
Sgt. V. Alvarado, gunner

Briefing started at 1430 hrs.; no end time recorded.
T/off: 1530 & 1537 hrs.   Target: 1757 & 1750 hrs.   Return: 1953 hrs.

Mission Narrative

Thirty-six aircraft dispatched; the 1st Box was led by Capt. R. W. Leonard, and the 2nd Box by Capt. H. M. Posson.

Route was Base to Portland Bill to 48.40'N, 04.58'W (lake east of Kersquivit), to 48.24'N, 04.58'W (Kerguille), to target.

Bombing by flights, thirty-six aircraft attacked, dropping 287 × 500 GPs from 3,500 and 2,500 ft. Results for Box 1 were fair, poor, and unobserved, and for Box 2 they were poor, gross, and fair, respectively. No damage to either target. 10/10th multilayered cloud with poor visibility over the city due to smoke. 1 × 500 GP returned; bomb shackle installed incorrectly.

Weak, generally inaccurate LFF from the target area; two crews reported tracer fire from a hospital building 200 yards west of the target. Two aircraft received Cat. A damage.

Return was a left off the target to Portland Bill to Base.

Interrogation of crews began at 1945 hrs. and finished at 2050 hrs.

Mission Notes and "Flak-Bait" Crew Debrief Comments

"Flak-Bait" flew as No. 6 in the low flight, 2nd Box.

8 × 500 GPs on target; fell in area with leader's bombs.

Light flak near target.

Other Crew Comments

In weather like this, wouldn't it be better to fly at 6,000 ft instead of 11,000 ft.?; we had to drop 8,000 ft. in a short distance.

Bombing too low; felt concussion of own bombs.

"Flak-Bait" Crew

2Lt. R. L. Hall, pilot
2Lt. R. E. O'Rourke, copilot
2Lt. S. Block, navigator/bombardier

Sgt. A. E. Rotman, engineer/gunner
Sgt. E. W. Riggs, radio/gunner
Sgt. J. Barrier, gunner

Briefing started at 0649 hrs. and ended 0710 hrs.
T/off: 0800 hrs.   Rendezvous: area cover   Landfall: 0856 hrs.
Target: 1003 hrs.   Coast Out: 1113 hrs.   Return: 1203 hrs.

Mission Narrative

Thirty-six aircraft dispatched; the 1st Box was led by 1Lt. E. R. Bruner with Lt. Col. B. G. Willis, and the 2nd Box by Capt. J. M. Bennett and Capt. P. Shannon.

Route was Base to Clacton to Nth Foreland to Gravelines to 48.32'E, 05.43'E (Orquevaux), to target. IX TAC to provide area support.

Attack was at the request of Gen. Patton, whose advance had been held up with heavy troop concentrations in the area. Thirty-four attacked by flights. Area bombing, but all the bombs were outside designated target area in woods. 886 × 100 GPs dropped from 11,500 and 11,000 ft., in clear conditions but with haze. Two aircraft failed to bomb: one when the bombardier failed to turn the intervalometer on, and another had bombs hang up and jettisoned 28 × 100 GPs in channel. In total, 94 × 100 GPs returned.

No opposition met.

Return was a left turn to Gravelines to Nth Foreland to Base.

Interrogation of crews began at 1200 hrs. and finished at 1225 hrs.

Mission Notes and "Flak-Bait" Crew Debrief Comments

No takeoff; reason not given.

Was due to fly in the No. 6 position in the high flight, 1st Box. Bombload was 28 × 100 GPs. Spare aircraft filled in.

```
Date: September 11, 1944
Target: Metz Strongpoints
Field Order: 9th BC F/O 542
99th CBW F/O 265
```

"Flak-Bait" Crew

2Lt. H. C. Bozarth, pilot	SSgt. W. L. Johnston, engineer/gunner
1Lt. D. B. Barker, copilot	SSgt. M. T. Darnell Jr., radio/gunner
TSgt. H. L. Gray, togglier	Sgt. R. L. Bassler, gunner

Briefing started at 0730 hrs. and ended 0750 hrs.

T/off: 0850 hrs.	Rendezvous: area cover	Landfall: 0944 hrs.
Target: 1055 & 1056 hrs.	Coast Out: not recorded	Return: 1315 hrs.

Mission Narrative

Thirty-six aircraft dispatched; the 1st Box was led by Col. E. Wursten, and the 2nd Box by Lt. Col. D. D. Bentley.

Route was Base to Nth Foreland to Gravelines to 48.46'N, 06.07'E (Vroncourt), the IP, to the target. XIX TAC to provide P-51 area cover.

Targets were gun emplacements at Verny and Orny. Bombing was by flights; thirty-three aircraft dropped 131 × 1,000 GPs from 11,500 and 11,000 ft. in CAVU conditions. Results for Box 1 were fair, excellent (after two runs: released at 1107 hrs.), and excellent. Box 2 results were PNB for all flights; the lead and high flights misidentified the targets, and the low flight hit a Box 1 target. Three aircraft failed to bomb; one was an early return, one couldn't see the leader's release, and another was forced out of formation after another aircraft received a flak hit. A total of 13 × 1,000 GPs returned.

Flak was moderate inaccurate for the 1st Box but moderate accurate for the 2nd Box while on the bomb run and over the target area, and at Metz town. Six aircraft Cat. A, three aircraft Cat. AC, and one Cat. E in crash landing at Base; one man injured in parachute landing. One of the Cat. AC aircraft overran the runway upon landing because the brakes were out. Another of the Cat. AC aircraft (41-31757 PN-G, "We Dood It") was hit by flak between IP and target and jettisoned bombs; left engine caught fire and feathered prop; tried to stay in formation but had to pull out. Was last seen heading west under control and was heard calling for landing instructions at 1100 hrs. Aircraft landed at A-69 Laon-Athies. Repairs took six days to complete.

Return was a left turn off the target and retrace route in.

Interrogation of crews began at 1250 hrs. and finished at 1325 hrs.

41-31757 PN-G, "We Dood It," landed at A-69 Laon-Athies after flak set the left engine on fire. *Trevor J. Allen collection*

Mission Notes and "Flak-Bait" Crew Debrief Comments

"Flak-Bait" flew as No. 6 in the low flight, 2nd Box.

Cat. A damage; four small holes.

4 × 1,000 GPs dropped near target area.

Aircraft 757-G last seen flying west under control; no fire seen (later reported as having landed at A-69 Laon-Athies).

Category E Information
41-31915 PN-J, "Sin Twister"

Pilot was 2Lt. R. W. Page, flying No. 3 in the low flight, 2nd Box. Aircraft was hit by flak on the bomb run; bombs salvoed in the Metz area and returned on single engine. Found that the nosewheel would not lower, and made a crash landing. SSgt. H. W. Burgoyne, toggler, and SSgt. R. J. Sullivan, the radio/gunner, bailed out over base and were slightly injured in parachute landing, 449th BS.

```
Date: September 12, 1944
Target: Scheid-Siegfried Line Strongpoints
Field Order: 9th BC F/O 545
99th CBW F/O 267
```

"Flak-Bait" Crew

2Lt. J. S. Avooski, pilot	Sgt. W. F. Carter Jr., engineer/gunner
2Lt. H. C. Bryant, copilot	Sgt. L. D. Case, radio/gunner
TSgt. J. L. Campbell, toggler	Sgt. V. Alvarado, gunner

Briefing started at 0700 hrs. and ended 0715 hrs.

T/off: 0805 hrs.	Rendezvous: area cover	Landfall: 0904 hrs.
Target: 1004½ & 1000 hrs.	Coast Out: 1046 hrs.	Return: 1142 hrs.

Mission Narrative

The group's first mission over Germany itself.

Thirty-six aircraft dispatched; the 1st Box was led by Lt. Col. J. B. Smith, and the 2nd Box by 1Lt. W. G. Fort.

Route was Base to Clacton to Ostend to 50.09'N, 06.20'E (Irrhausen), to target. IX FC to provide P-47 area cover.

Area bombing, by flights from 11,500 and 11,000 ft. in clear conditions but with thick haze. Twenty-nine aircraft attacked, dropping 111 × 1,000 GPs on or near target for fair to good results. High flight, 1st Box, did not attack; intercom and PDI were out in the lead aircraft; made three runs at the target. One aircraft of this flight had an accidental release 4 miles north of the target, dropping 4 × 1,000 GPs. One aircraft returned early when a crew member forgot his parachute harness. 29 × 1,000 GPs returned by seven aircraft failing to bomb, and one that had 1 × 1,000 GP hang up.

One crew reported six bursts of weak inaccurate of HFF just before bombs away. No damage received.

Return was a left turn off the target and retrace route in.

Interrogation of crews began at 1145 hrs. and finished at 1215 hrs.

Mission Notes and "Flak-Bait" Crew Debrief Comments

"137th Mission" marked on debrief form.

"Flak-Bait" flew as No. 2 aircraft in lead flight, 2nd Box.

4 × 1,000 GPs dropped; bombs hit in tank traps.

B-26 seen on ground at location J-5573 at 1045 hrs.; appears to have made crash landing, with deep furrows in ground.

Other Crew Comments

Three crews from the 449th BS complained that trucks to crew rooms very slow; too frequently occurs.

Debrief forms were annotated with reports on aircraft with high numbers of missions

41-31773 PN-O, "Flak-Bait"	137th mission	
41-31919 DR-N, "Peasapis"	126th mission	aircraft Cat. E on December 25, 1944
41-34847 SS-K, "Idiots Delight"	117th mission	was an early return on this mission?
Aircraft retired after 151 missions		
41-18272 PN-D, "Murder Inc."	114th mission	Cat. E on December 25, 1944
41-31777 ER-C, "Zombie III"	114th mission	S. war with 162 missions
41-31744 PN-M, "Hanks Yanks"	113th mission	S. war
41-31824 ER-U, "Pete's Avenger"	108th mission	S. war

> **Date: September 14, 1944**
> **Target: Brest area Strongpoints**
> **Field Order: 9th BC F/O 550**
> **99th CBW F/O 270**

"Flak-Bait" Crew

2Lt. W. J. Frank, pilot
2Lt. J. H. Donahue, copilot
2Lt. W. G. Leffler, navigator/bombardier

Sgt. A. R. Heredia, engineer/gunner
Sgt. J. P. Saladino, radio/gunner
Sgt. W. R. Fry, gunner

Briefing started at 1230 hrs. and ended 1250 hrs.

T/off: 1335 & 1342 hrs.   Target: 1555 hrs.: 1st Box   Return: 1825 hrs.
                                                               1625, 1635 & 1612½ hrs.: 2nd Box

Mission Narrative

Thirty-six aircraft dispatched; the 1st Box was led by Capt. H. V. Smythe, to attack the Heavy AA Battery at Brest-Ile-Longue. The 2nd Box was led by Capt. W. A. Taylor and briefed to attack Kerveneuse Fort.

Route was Base to Portland Bill to 48.24'N, 04.57'W (off Pointe de Dinan), the IP, to targets.

Bombing by flights; weather encountered by the 1st Box was 6–8/10th, tops 5–6,000 ft., while the 2nd Box had 9–10/10th with base at 1,000 ft. Eighteen aircraft from the 1st Box dropped 72 × 1,000 GP from 10,000 ft.; results were good, poor, and fair, respectively. Sixteen aircraft from the 2nd Box dropped 62 × 1,000 GP from 2–3,000 ft. Lead flight made three runs, the high flight four runs, and the low flight two runs. The high flight achieved excellent results, while the results for the other flights were unobserved. Two aircraft failed to bomb: one because it was out of formation at the time, and the other because the bombardier failed to see the leader's drop because of a cloud bank. Two aircraft had one bomb hang up. A total of 10 × 1,000 GPs were returned.

Weak fairly accurate LFF and MG fire from a blockhouse; altitude at time 3,000 ft. One aircraft Cat. A damage.

Return was a left turn to Portland Bill to Base.

Interrogation of crews began at 1755 hrs. and finished at 1845 hrs.

Mission Notes and "Flak-Bait" Crew Debrief Comments

"Flak-Bait" flew as No. 2 in the lead flight, 1st Box.

4 × 1,000 GPs dropped, for good results.

Event: More Evaders Return

In September, three other crew members returned to the squadron, having evaded capture and later being liberated by Allied armies. SSgt. Brogle returned on September 15, and SSgt. Coon and SSgt. Dumais returned two days later. They all began their journey to the United States later in the month.

Event: 9th Bomber Command Redesignation

On September 16, 1944, 9th Bomber Command was redesignated as the 9th Bombardment Division.

Date: September 27, 1944
Target: Foret de Parroy T/C
Field Order: 9th BD F/O 570
99th CBW F/O 289

"Flak-Bait" Crew

2Lt. W. J. Frank, pilot
2Lt. J. H. Donahue, copilot
2Lt. W. G. Leffler, navigator/bombardier

Sgt. A. R. Heredia, engineer/gunner
Sgt. J. P. Saladino, radio/gunner
Sgt. W. R. Fry, gunner

Briefing started at 0730 hrs. and ended 0800 hrs.

T/off: 0845 hrs.   Target: 1104 hrs.   Return: 1323 hrs.

Mission Narrative

Thirty-six aircraft dispatched; the 1st Box was led by Capt. M. I. Sterngold, and the 2nd Box by Capt. H. V. Smythe.

Route was Base to Gravelines to 48.22'N, 06.38'E (Domevre-sur-Aviere), to 48.27'N, 06.45'E (Girmont), the IP, to target. XIX TAC to provide area cover.

Mission abortive; one aircraft returned early with a gas leak, and thirty-five because of 10/10th cloud cover. Formation returned after making two runs at the target. 648 × 260 M81 frags returned.

One aircraft reported weak inaccurate HFF, 3 miles east of Dunkirk.

Return was a left turn to Gravelines and Base.

Interrogation of crews began at 1330 hrs. and finished at 1350 hrs.

Mission Notes and "Flak-Bait" Crew Debrief Comments

"Flak-Bait" flew as No. 6 in the lead flight, 2nd Box.

Bombload was 18 × 260 M81 frags; bombs returned.

Other Crew Comments

A lone Fw 190 observed flying at 18,000 ft. over the target.

Six aircraft landed away to refuel.

This was the 322nd BG's last mission from Andrews Field.

Event: 322nd BG Moves to ALG A-61 Beauvais-Tille

Following the invasion and the Allies' advance across France, the distance to potential targets became ever greater, and it was inevitable that a move to be closer to the battle lines would be necessary.

The B-26 units of the 98th CBW had moved to bases in the south of England from late July 1944, prior to beginning their move to the Continent. The four groups of the 99th CBW stayed in Essex and moved directly to bases in France in mid-September 1944.

For the 322nd BG the process of moving to their new home at A-61 Beauvais-Tille began on September 19, with the departure from Andrews Field of the reconnaissance echelon, by motor convoy. They would prepare the base for the arrival of the group, erecting tents to accommodate the living quarters, mess halls, and necessary operational sections.

An advance party left on September 21, and the rear echelon left on September 23, some by motor convoy, while others were ferried over in the group's aircraft.

On September 29, the air echelon moved into A-61, with some of the ground personnel and equipment traveling by C-47 aircraft.

The rear echelon, traveling by motor convoy, did not arrive at Beauvais-Tille until October 6, 1944.

Date: October 2, 1944
Target: Herbach Area C Strongpoint
Field Order: 9th BD F/O 578

"Flak-Bait" Crew

2Lt. J. L. Nichols, pilot	Sgt. G. Rodridgues, engineer/gunner
2Lt. S. A. Norstrom, copilot	Sgt. H. L. Reinig, radio/gunner
2Lt. J. B. Vandermay, navigator/bombardier	Sgt. F. B. Rice, gunner

Briefing started at 0645 hrs. and ended 0715 hrs.
T/off: 0815 hrs.   Target: 0954 & 1022½ hrs.   Return: 1129 hrs.

Mission Narrative

The group's first mission performed from A-61 Beauvais-Tille.

Thirty-six aircraft dispatched; the 1st Box was led by Col. D. D. Bentley, and the 2nd Box by Col. J. S. Samuel.

Route was Base to Charleroi to 51.45'N, 05.42'E (Eindhoven), to 51.13'N, 06.05'E (Posterholt), to target. IX TAC to provide area cover.

Bombing by flights, only the lead flight, 2nd Box, actually released; five aircraft dropped 20 × 1,000 GPs from 11,000 ft. on the fourth run at the target but misidentified the AP and released on buildings 1½ miles north of the target. 8–10/10th stratocumulus prevented the remainder from attacking; the lead flight of the 1st Box made two runs. 124 × 1,000 GPs returned.

Moderate accurate HFF was encountered; it is thought the gunners had a break in the clouds and had an opportunity to engage the lead flight, 2nd Box, while on the third and fourth runs. Five aircraft received Cat. A damage. One man slightly injured by flak: SSgt. A. W. Marti, 451st BS.

Return was a left turn off the target to Base.

Interrogation of crews began at 1100 hrs. and finished at 1200 hrs.

Mission Notes and "Flak-Bait" Crew Debrief Comments

"Flak-Bait" flew as No. 5 in the lead flight, 1st Box.

4 × 1,000 GPs returned.

Date: October 14, 1944
Target: Konz-Karthaus RR Br
Field Order: 9th BD F/O 596
99th CBW F/O 308

"Flak-Bait" Crew

2Lt. H. D. Hurlbut, pilot	SSgt. R. L. Robinson, engineer/gunner
2Lt. S. J. Price, copilot	Cpl. T. H. Templeton, radio/gunner
2Lt. F. E. Ennis, navigator/bombardier	Cpl. J. A. Peters, gunner

Briefing started at 0645 hrs. and ended 0720 hrs.
T/off: 0900 hrs.   Target: 1012½ & 1013 hrs.   Return: 1125 hrs.

Mission Narrative

Thirty-six aircraft dispatched; the 1st Box was led by Lt. Col. D. D. Bentley, and the 2nd Box by 1Lt. E. R. Bruner.

Route was Base to Luxembourg to northeast of Saarburg, to target.

All aircraft abortive; target overcast, 10/10th low cloud at 5–6,000 ft. 144 × 1,000 GPs returned.

One aircraft damaged by a 0.50 shell, ejected by preceding aircraft while circling to land.

Return was to retrace route in.

No interrogation times recorded.

Mission Notes and "Flak-Bait" Crew Debrief Comments

"Flak-Bait" flew as No. 5 in the high flight, 2nd Box.

4 × 1,000 GPs returned.

Other Crew Comments

Several crews reported vertical vapor trails breaking through the overcast between the IP and target; undecided whether they were rockets or vapor trails of jet aircraft.

Weather Difficulties

Following this abortive mission to attack this important railroad bridge across the Moselle River, the target was briefed on thirteen consecutive occasions, only to be scrubbed because of poor weather. The group finally attacked the target on October 29, although "Flak-Bait" did not take part in that mission.

Event: 322nd Bomb Group Awarded the Distinguished Unit Citation

On October 28, 1944, the group learned that they had been awarded the Distinguished Unit Citation, per General Order No. 254, Headquarters, 9th Air Force.

The citation read in part, "For outstanding performance of duty in action in the European Theater of Operations from May 14, 1943 to July 24, 1944."

```
Date: October 30, 1944
Target: Trier-Pfalzel RR Br
Field Order: 9th BD F/O 613
99th CBW F/O 329
```

"Flak-Bait" Crew

2Lt. E. B. Fitch, pilot
F/O C. A. Luke, copilot
2Lt. F. I. Clark, navigator/bombardier

SSgt. S. J. Box, engineer/gunner
Sgt. H. A. Wall, radio/gunner
Sgt. J. F. Riffe, gunner

Briefing started at 0635 hrs.; no end time recorded.
T/off: 0820 hrs.   Target: no attack   Return: 1015 hrs.

Mission Narrative

Thirty-six aircraft dispatched; the 1st Box was led by Col. J. S. Samuel, and the 2nd Box by Capt. G. M. Allen.

Formation recalled by 9th BD before entering enemy territory; turned back at 0925 hrs., in vicinity of Bouillon. 144 × 1,000 GPs returned. 10/10th cloud at 4–5,000 ft.

Interrogation of crews began at 1020 hrs. and finished at 1040 hrs.

Mission Notes and "Flak-Bait" Crew Debrief Comments

"Flak-Bait" flew as No. 2 in the lead flight, 1st Box.

4 × 1,000 GPs returned.

"Flak-Bait" Crew

2Lt. E. B. Fitch, pilot	SSgt. S. J. Box, engineer/gunner
F/O C. A. Luke, copilot	Sgt. H. A. Wall, radio/gunner
2Lt. F. I. Clark, navigator/bombardier	Sgt. J. F. Riffe, gunner

Briefing started at 1115 hrs. and ended 1145 hrs.

T/off: 1343 hrs.   Target: 1505 & 1508 hrs.   Return: 1630 hrs.

Mission Narrative

PFF mission. Thirty aircraft plus two PFF dispatched; 1st Box was led by Col. J. S. Samuel, and the 2nd Box by 1Lt. W. V. Humphreys.

Route was Base to Hollange (the IP) to the target. XXIX TAC to provide area cover.

Thirty-one aircraft attacked on PFF equipment, dropping 111 × 1,000 GPs and 8 × 500 GPs from 13,250 and 12,700 ft. Box 1 results were poor, landing in a loose pattern 1,960 ft. west of the DMPI; one hit to the rail line. Box 2 achieved excellent results, centered on the DMPI, with at least two direct hits on the bridge. A total of 9 × 1,000 GPs were returned due to mechanical and rack failures.

Weak to moderate, fairly accurate HFF over the target area. Eight aircraft received Cat. A damage.

Return was a right turn to north of Saarburg to Mersch to Base.

Interrogation of crews began at 1630 hrs. and finished at 1700 hrs.

Mission Notes and "Flak-Bait" Crew Debrief Comments

"Flak-Bait" flew as No. 2 in the lead flight, 1st Box.

2 × 1,000 GPs released, but intervalometer did not run out; stopped at fifteen seconds. 2 × 1,000 GPs brought back.

Moderate inaccurate HFF at target.

Other Crew Comments

Suggest that F and G models should not be used as lead aircraft: cannot tell whether all or any bombs have released. (The later B-26F and G models featured a 3½-inch increase in wing incidence; this resulted in the aircraft flying in a slightly nose-down attitude compared to the earlier B and C models.)

"Flak-Bait" Crew

2Lt. H. J. Bye, pilot	Sgt. T. H. Olinger, engineer/gunner
2Lt. M. F. Lewonowski, copilot	Sgt. A. Taylor, radio/gunner
2Lt. R. L. La Chapelle, navigator/bombardier	Sgt. W. R. Narramore, gunner

No briefing or interrogation timings recorded.

T/off: 0915 hrs.   Target: 1115 to 1130 hrs.   Return: 1340 hrs.

Mission Narrative

Fifty-four aircraft dispatched in three boxes. The 1st Box was led by Col. J. S. Samuel, the 2nd Box by Lt. Col. F. P. Taylor, and the 3rd Box by Capt. J. A. Swindle.

Route was Base to rendezvous with XXIX TAC fighter escort at Z-4976, to Luneville to Lutzelhouse to Ingwiller to Wissembourg to target.

Formation encountered 10/10th cloud, tops at 10,000–12,000 ft., with severe icing. 1st Box turned back southeast of Metz at 1105 hrs. because of the weather. Twenty-six aircraft attacked five casual targets, releasing 105 × 1,000 GPs as follows: Box 2, lead flight, dropped on a road junction south of Strasbourg for fair results. High flight aimed at a road bridge north of Strasbourg for fair results, and the low flight dropped on a bridge over the Rhine near Landau, with a good concentration and probable hits. Box 3, lead flight, did not drop; high flight released on an undetermined target; and the low flight released on a dam on the Rhine near Rheinsfelden; bombs fell 2,000 ft. to the left of the dam.

Four aircraft jettisoned a total of 16 × 1,000 GPs: one on Arbonne bombing range after having a flak hit, one salvoed "safe" after aircraft iced up, location unknown, one salvoed 8 miles east of Bitchie, with engine problems, and one salvoed "safe" near Sons. Three aircraft were early returns: One because the undercarriage was raised too soon on takeoff and bent the props; aircraft landed again on single engine. One had engine trouble, and one because it had iced up; a total of 83 × 1,000 GPs returned. 12 × 1,000 GPs unaccounted for in missing and crash-landed aircraft.

1st and 3rd Boxes experienced moderate accurate HFF 8–10 miles west of the IP (Wissembourg), which continued to that town. Nine aircraft received Cat. A damage. Five aircraft were Cat. E and one Cat. AC in crash and forced landings; one man injured in a crash landing. Two aircraft MIA. Twelve crew MIA.

Briefed return was a left turn and retrace route in.

Mission Notes and "Flak-Bait" Crew Debrief Comments

"Flak-Bait" flew as No. 5 in the high flight, 1st Box.

Returned 4 × 1,000 GPs due to weather. Heavy inaccurate HFF near IP for thirty seconds.

More time needed between briefing and takeoff.

Other Crew Comments

Many crews questioned the wisdom of continuing the mission in such bad weather conditions, and stated that some were flying as high as 14,000 ft. without oxygen. Many aircraft became scattered because of the weather conditions.

MIA Information

43-34187 SS-F, "Little Audrey"

Flying as No. 3 in the lead flight, Box 3, hit by flak and was last seen in a spin at 8,000 ft., 8–10 miles west of Wissembourg. Six chutes observed; one chute hit the tail of another aircraft on the way down. Ground fire was observed shooting at other crew members.

2Lt. J. A. Corley, pilot	POW
2Lt. G. D. McLaughlin, copilot	KIA; killed by ground fire
2Lt. P. Sachs, navigator/bombardier	KIA; shot by SS troops after capture
Sgt. C. J. Green, engineer/gunner	KIA
Sgt. M. M. Mandell, radio/gunner	KIA
Sgt. D. D. Jackson, gunner	KIA

43-34146 DR-U

No. 5 in the low flight, 1st Box; crashed in friendly territory, southwest of Nancy; last seen peeling out of formation under control and disappeared into clouds; formation was encountering severe icing conditions at that time.

Capt. R. R. Hall, pilot	KIA (previously had done a tour in the Pacific)
2Lt. G. C. Rosenow, copilot	KIA
1Lt. B. Lipsky, navigator/bombardier	KIA

SSgt. P. M. Steele, engineer/gunner   KIA
SSgt. R. L. Surratt, radio/gunner   KIA
SSgt. R. W. Ryan, gunner   KIA

1Lt J. A. Corley, *center front*, with his crew, was the only crewman to survive when "Little Audrey" was shot down. *Mike Smith, B26.com*

43-34146 DR-U, which crashed in friendly territory after encountering severe icing conditions; sadly, none of the crew survived. *Mike Smith, B26.com*

Five aircraft Category E in crash landings in bad weather and short of fuel

41-34762 SS-G, "Lights Out" (formerly "Sarah E"); pilot was 1Lt. H. D. Allen. Crash-landed in a pasture near St. Ouen, out of fuel; four of crew bailed out, crew safe.

42-107587 DR-R; pilot was 1Lt. G. H. Dexter. Aircraft on single engine and iced up; crash-landed at Verbiesles, near Chaumont-en-Bassigny; one man injured.

42-107849 ER-B, "Abie's Irish Rose"; pilot was 2Lt. G. T. Behnke. Crash-landed in an open field near Ferrier. Pilot injured.

43-34157 DR-C; pilot was 2Lt. D. L. Frank. Crash-landed 15 miles east of Dijon.

43-34160 SS-V; pilot was 1Lt. J. L. Miller. Crash-landed at Gy, 40 miles ENE of Dijon, out of fuel.

In addition, aircraft 43-34135 SS-W; pilot was 2Lt. T. E. Mattax. Landed on a road between Til-Chatel and Lux, out of fuel, with Cat. AC damage; this aircraft was subsequently written off.

"Abie's Irish Rose" crash-landed in a field near Ferrier, injuring the pilot, 2Lt. G. T. Behnke. *Trevor J. Allen collection*

"Flak-Bait" Crew

2Lt. H. J. Bye, pilot
2Lt. M. F. Lewonowski, copilot
2Lt. R. L. La Chapelle, navigator/bombardier

Sgt. T. H. Olinger, engineer/gunner
Sgt. A. Taylor, radio/gunner
Sgt. W. R. Narramore, gunner

Briefing started at 0745 hrs. and ended 0825 hrs.
T/off: 1055 hrs.   Target: 1235½ & 1236 hrs.   Return: 1412 hrs.

Mission Narrative

Thirty-six aircraft dispatched; the 1st Box was led by Col. J. S. Samuel, and the 2nd Box by Maj. J. C. Ruse.

Route was Base to rendezvous with XII TAC fighters at Z-5075 to Neufchatel to Remiremont to west of Oberhergheim to target.

Thirty-one aircraft attacked, dropping 123 × 1,000 GP from 11,500 and 11,000 ft., with no low cloud. Results for Box 1 were excellent, unsatisfactory, and no attack: the flight leader had a rack malfunction; results for Box 2 were all excellent. 21 × 1,000 GPs were returned.

Moderate fairly accurate HFF in the target area and through turn off target. Eleven aircraft received Cat. A damage.

Return was a left turn and retrace route in.

Interrogation of crews began at 1420 hrs. and finished at 1500 hrs.

Mission Notes and "Flak-Bait" Crew Debrief Comments

"Flak-Bait" flew as No. 2 in the high flight, 2nd Box.

4 × 1,000 GPs on target; hit pontoon bridge to left of target; believed that bridge hit but did not fall.

Heavy inaccurate HFF at target for forty seconds. Flak guns on either end of bridge: approx. eight guns.

Saw flashes, seemingly a mirror signal, from near Remiremont on way back.

"Flak-Bait" Crew

1Lt. K. W. Goldacker, pilot
2Lt. T. H. Felker, copilot
2Lt. W. L. Hoenshel, navigator/bombardier

Sgt. J. Foorman, engineer/gunner
SSgt. C. C. Hendrix, radio/gunner
Sgt. J. A. Circelli, gunner

No briefing or interrogation timings recorded.
T/off: 1000 hrs.   Target: 1119 & 1120 hrs.   Return: 1257 hrs.

Mission Narrative

PFF mission. Thirty plus two window and two PFF aircraft off. The 1st Box was led by Capt. C. L. Anderson, and the 2nd Box by Maj. L. J. Sebille.

Route was Base to Bilsen to Eschweiler to target. IX TAC to provide area cover.

Area bombing; thirty-two aircraft attacked visually, releasing 462 × 250 GPs, 2 × 1,000 GPs, and 3 × 500 GPs on the target. 18 × 250 GPs and 1 × 500 GP returned due to rack malfunctions. Most bombs were in the target area.

Moderate fairly accurate HFF from the target area; one aircraft received Cat. AC and six aircraft Cat. A damage. Return was a right turn off the target to Base.

Mission Notes and "Flak-Bait" Crew Debrief Comments
"Flak-Bait" flew as No. 5 in the high flight, 1st Box.
    16 × 250 GPs dropped.
    Moderate inaccurate HFF on run and turn off target.

Other Crew Comments
Message from PFF: Group did not notify PFF ship of intention to take over lead to allow ample time for PFF ship to form on group.

```
Date: November 26, 1944
Target: Bergzabern Warehouse Area
Field Order: 9th BD F/O 645
99th CBW F/O 362
```

"Flak-Bait" Crew
2Lt. W. C. Cornwall, pilot   Sgt. T. W. Gatzounas, engineer/gunner
2Lt. C. W. Honhold, copilot   Sgt. R. H. Pacey, radio/gunner
2Lt. G. F. Meily, navigator/bombardier   Sgt. E. M. Little, gunner

Briefing started at 0608 hrs. and ended 0630 hrs.
T/off: 0825 hrs.   Target: 1011 & 1012 hrs.   Return: 1145 hrs.

Mission Narrative
PFF mission. Thirty plus three window and two PFF aircraft dispatched. The 1st Box was led by Lt. Col. D. D. Bentley, and the 2nd Box by Maj. L. A. Tenold.

Route was Base to Nancy to Maizieres to Steinbourg to IP to target. Formation deviated from course almost immediately due to rain squalls, PFF took lead before reaching the waiting point, in an attempt to reach the target at time scheduled; however, arrived too late to drop on equipment. XXIX TAC to provide area cover.

No attack due to PFF failure; 10/10th cloud with tops of 7–8,000 ft. High flight, Box 1, lost formation in clouds; flew over the target area but cloud prevented bombing. One aircraft from high flight, Box 2, lost formation before reaching the IP and returned early. A total of 496 × 250 GPs were returned.

Briefed return was from target to Steinbourg and retrace.

Interrogation of crews began at 1145 hrs. and finished at 1215 hrs.

Mission Notes and "Flak-Bait" Crew Debrief Comments
"Flak-Bait" flew as No. 6 in the low flight, 1st Box.
    16 × 250 GPs returned.

Other Crew Comments
Leader of Box 1 asked PFF for a second run but was told no because of equipment failure.

"Flak-Bait" Crew

2Lt. W. C. Cornwall, pilot
2Lt. C. W. Honhold, copilot
2Lt. G. F. Meily, navigator/bombardier

Sgt. R. H. Pacey, engineer/gunner
Sgt. T. W. Gatzounas, radio/gunner
Sgt. E. M. Little, gunner

No briefing held, since the target was the same as the morning mission.
T/off: 1440 hrs   Target: 1627 & 1628 hrs.   Return: 1810 hrs.

Mission Narrative

PFF mission. Thirty-one plus three window and two PFF aircraft dispatched. The 1st Box was led by Lt. Col. D. D. Bentley, and the 2nd Box by Maj. L. A. Tenold.

Route was Base to Nancy to Maizieres to Steinbourg to IP to target. XXIX TAC to provide area cover.

5/10th patchy stratocumulus encountered at the target tops, 5–6,000 ft.; twenty-eight aircraft released 431 × 250 GPs, from 14,000 and 13,000 ft., on the primary, for fair to good results. 49 × 250 GPs were returned due to rack failures, and one aircraft because bomb bay doors would not open in time. 16 × 250 GPs lost in aircraft with Cat. E damage; a spare filled in.

Weak to inaccurate HFF between the IP and target; two rocket trails reaching 20,000 ft. seen in area of flak. No flak damage received. One aircraft Cat. E; crashed on takeoff; crew safe.

Crew of aircraft flying No. 4 position in the low flight, 1st Box, reported four Me 109s engaging in area of target, low at three o'clock and then around to five o'clock before coming up and in; did not see e/a fire. Turret and waist gunners fired at 1,000 yds.; no effect seen, and e/a broke off attack.

Return was a left turn from target and retrace.

Interrogation of crews began at 1815 hrs. and finished at 1900 hrs.

Mission Notes and "Flak-Bait" Crew Debrief Comments

"Flak-Bait" flew as No. 6 in the low flight, 1st Box.

Cat. A damage: bomb struck bomb bay door.
16 × 250 GPs released.
Weak inaccurate flak encountered at 1610 hrs.

Author's note: At some point in "Flak-Bait's" career, the left-hand bomb bay doors were replaced, possibly as a result of the damage on this day. These replacement doors were of the later design with the open ends, as fitted to later production models so as to reduce drag (it appears that these were introduced from the B-26B-45-MA models on the Baltimore production line; the B-26C models, produced at Omaha, apparently did not feature this modification); however, the right-hand doors, with the closed-off ends, were retained, which may have resulted in an element of asymmetric drag when the doors were opened.

Other Crew Comments

Window aircraft flew at same altitude; window came directly into the formation.

Many gunners do not open waist windows, and some turrets do not have gunners at the helm.

Category E Information
43-34444 SS-S

Pilot was 2Lt. D. R. Conley; No. 6 ship in the high flight, 2nd Box, had a runaway propeller on takeoff and crashed. The bombload exploded. Crew safe.

"Flak-Bait" Crew

1Lt. R. L. Hall, pilot
2Lt. R. E. O'Rourke, copilot
1Lt. J. F. Toscano, navigator/bombardier

SSgt. A. E. Rotman, engineer/gunner
Sgt. E. W. Riggs, radio/gunner
Sgt. J. Barrier, gunner

Briefing started at 0715 hrs. and ended 0755 hrs.
T/off: 0920 hrs.   Target: 1056½ & 1057 hrs.   Return: 1200 hrs.

Mission Narrative

PFF mission. Thirty plus one spare, three window, and two PFF aircraft dispatched. The 1st Box was led by Maj. J. C. Ruse, and the 2nd Box by Lt. Col. D. D. Bentley.

Route was Base to K-5433 to target. IX TAC to provide area cover.

Thirty-two attacked by boxes, on PFF equipment through 10/10th cloud, from 13,500 and 13,000 ft. 114 × 1,000 GPs and 8 × 500 GPs released. 6 × 1,000 GPs returned due to rack failures; spare returned 4 × 1,000 GPs.

No flak encountered.

Return route was a right turn to Zingsheim to Stadkyll to St.-Vith to La Roche to Fumay to Base. Interrogation of crews began at 1215 hrs.; no end time recorded.

Mission Notes and "Flak-Bait" Crew Debrief Comments

"Flak-Bait" flew as No. 2 in the lead flight, 1st Box.

2 × 1,000 GPs dropped, and 2 × 1,000 GPs returned due to rack malfunction.

"Flak-Bait" Crew

1Lt. H. C. Bozarth, pilot
1Lt. S. V. N. Best, copilot
Sgt. T. B. Gee, toggler

SSgt. W. L. Johnston, engineer/gunner
TSgt. S. P. Smith, radio/gunner
Sgt. R. L. Bassler, gunner

Briefing started at 0715 hrs. and ended 0800 hrs.
T/off: 0920 hrs.   Target: 1100 hrs.   Return: 1210 hrs.

Mission Narrative

Mission to attack defenses on the Siegfried Line in support of Gen. Patton's 3rd Army.

PFF mission; thirty-three plus three window and one PFF aircraft dispatched. The 1st Box was led by Col. J. S. Samuel, and the 2nd Box by Maj. G. H. Watson.

Route was Base to Arlon to Luxembourg (the IP) to target. XIX TAC to provide area cover.

10/10th cloud with tops at 6,000 ft.; bombed on PFF. Thirty-three aircraft released 494 × 500 GPs and 4 × 500 GPs from 12,300 and 11,800 ft. Results unobserved. One aircraft was an early return and jettisoned 16 × 250 GPs, (thirteen "safe" and three "armed") near Oignies, in friendly territory, due to a loss of power. 18 × 250 GPs returned due to rack failures.

No opposition encountered.

Return was a right turn off target to Base.
No interrogation times recorded.

Mission Notes and "Flak-Bait" Crew Debrief Comments
"Flak-Bait" flew as No. 2, low flight in the 1st Box.
9 × 250 GPs on target and 7 × 250 GPs salvoed after 2–3 seconds delay due to rack malfunction, in area of target.

Other Crew Comments
Sixty-five missions too much!

```
Date: December 2, 1944
Target: Saarlautern D/A
Field Order: 9th BD F/O 653
99th CBW F/O 370
```

"Flak-Bait" Crew
2Lt. W. C. Cornwall, pilot   Sgt. T. W. Gatzounas, engineer/gunner
2Lt. C. W. Honhold, copilot   SSgt. R. E. Richardson, radio/gunner
2Lt. G. F. Meily, navigator/bombardier   Sgt. E. M. Little, gunner

Briefing started at 0715 hrs. and ended 0750 hrs.
T/off: 0925 hrs.   Target: 1101½ hrs.   Return: 1226 hrs.

Mission Narrative
PFF mission. Thirty-three plus three window and one PFF aircraft dispatched. 1st Box was led by Capt. H. E. Short, and the 2nd Box by Capt. E. R. Bruner.
Route was Base to P-6122 to P-9317 to target. XIX TAC to provide area cover.
Only the 1st Box attacked, with fifteen aircraft dropping 255 × 250 GPs through 3–5/10th cloud at 3–5,000 ft. Bombardier misidentified the target, and bombs fell 900 yards SSE of the target in town of Ensdorf, landing in a good concentration in houses and among slit trenches and foxholes. 2nd Box did not drop, PFF did not attack, and box leader had no time to bomb visually, believing that another group was following behind. Three aircraft in the low flight, 1st Box, did not release since leader did not drop. One aircraft was an early return due to an oil pump failure. A total of 273 × 250 GPs were returned.
Weak to moderate, inaccurate HFF at the target. Four aircraft received Cat. A damage, and one was Cat. E, all in the lead flight, 2nd Box.
Return was a right turn to Metz to Base.
No interrogation times recorded.

Mission Notes and "Flak-Bait" Crew Debrief Comments
"Flak-Bait" flew as No. 3 in the high flight, 2nd Box.
16 × 250 GPs returned.
Weak inaccurate HFF on bomb run and over target.

Other Crew Comments
Repair holes in the perimeter track.

Category E Information
43-34459 PN-F
Pilot was 2Lt. L. V. McDugald. No. 3 in the lead flight, 2nd Box, hit by flak over target area; observed with one engine knocked out; left formation heading toward our lines under control; crew bailed out over friendly territory; two injured by Plexiglas shards: 2Lt. C. A. Luke, copilot, and Sgt. S. J. Box, engineer/gunner.

"Flak-Bait" Crew

1Lt. H. C. Bozarth, pilot

1Lt. S. V. N. Best, copilot

Sgt. T. B. Gee, togglier

SSgt. W. L. Johnston, engineer/gunner

TSgt. M. Darnell Jr., radio/gunner

Sgt. R. L. Bassler, gunner

Briefing started at 0730 hrs. and ended 0750 hrs.

T/off: 0927 hrs.   Target: 1111½ & 1112 hrs.   Return: 1241 hrs.

Mission Narrative

Mission to attack tank and gun emplacements near Duppenweiler on the Siegfried Line.

PFF mission. Thirty-three plus three window and one PFF aircraft dispatched. 1st Box was led by Capt. W. G. Fort, and the 2nd Box led by Maj. G. H. Watson.

Route was Base to Luxembourg to target. IX and XIX TAC to provide area cover.

Dropped on PFF through 10/10th cloud; thirty-two aircraft released 486 × 250 GPs and 4 × 500 GPs; results unobserved. Two did not bomb: one had a rack malfunction, and another failed to see leader drop because screen was frosted over. 42 × 250 GPs returned.

No opposition met.

Return was a right turn to Metz to Base.

Interrogation of crews began at 1250 hrs. and finished at 1300 hrs.

Mission Notes and "Flak-Bait" Crew Debrief Comments

"Flak-Bait" flew as No. 2 in the high flight, 1st Box.

16 × 250 GPs dropped; results unobserved.

Other Crew Comments

Report from one of the window aircraft. At 1107 hours, a silver-colored aircraft was seen at 20,000 ft. (reported elsewhere as a Messerschmitt Me 163); it made a wide, slightly climbing turn in front of the formation. Plane was emitting a bluish smoke trail, intermittently, lasting about five seconds, cutting out for same, then beginning again. Aircraft disappeared into glare of the sun.

"Flak-Bait" Crew

2Lt. W. C. Cornwall, pilot

2Lt. C. W. Honhold, copilot

2Lt. G. F. Meily, navigator/bombardier

Sgt. T. W. Gatzounas, engineer/gunner

SSgt. R. H. Pacey, radio/gunner

Sgt. E. M. Little, gunner

Briefing started at 1215 hrs. and ended 1255 hrs.

T/off: 1425 hrs.   Target: 1606 hrs.   Return: 1759 hrs.

Mission Narrative

PFF mission. Thirty-four plus three window and one PFF aircraft dispatched. The 1st Box was led by 1Lt. A. E. Prestridge, and the 2nd Box by 1Lt. J. H. McCarty.

"Pin Up Girl" being recovered after the landing mishap. *Trevor J. Allen collection*

The tail section of "Pin Up Girl" is recovered; note olive-drab-colored rudder. *Trevor J. Allen collection*

Route was Base to Longuyon to Thionville (IP) to target. XXIX TAC to provide area cover.

10/10th cloud with tops at 8,000 ft. encountered; thirty-three aircraft released 486 × 250 GPs and 4 × 500 GPs from 12,600 and 12,000 ft.; two aircraft returned early, one because of oil pressure and another because a crew member was burned when a flare went off in the cockpit: SSgt. L. C. Warfield, 452nd BS. A total of 58 × 250 GPs were returned.

Weak inaccurate HFF from Merzig area; no damage received. One aircraft Cat. E damage in crash landing; 1 man injured.

Return was a left turn to Merzig to Thionville and retrace.

No interrogation times recorded.

Mission Notes and "Flak-Bait" Crew Debrief Comments

"Flak-Bait" flew as No. 3 in the low flight, 2nd Box.

6 × 250 GPs on target; ten hung up and returned.

Other Crew Comments

Flight leader, low flight, 1st Box, commented that P-47s made passes at formation, coming in closer than we would like.

Category E Information
42-107722 DR-W, "Pin Up Girl"

Pilot was 1Lt. K. L. Van Slyke; No. 6 in high flight, 2nd Box, had left gear collapse on landing; tail gunner SSgt. H. Rosenbaum, 452nd BS, received back injuries.

```
Date: December 10, 1944
Target: Birkesdorf D/A
Field Order: 9th BD F/O 664
99th CBW F/O 384
```

"Flak-Bait" Crew

2Lt. W. C. Cornwall, pilot
2Lt. C. W. Honhold, copilot
2Lt. G. F. Meily, navigator/bombardier

Sgt. T. W. Gatzounas, engineer/gunner
SSgt. R. H. Pacey, radio/gunner
Sgt. E. M. Little, gunner

Briefing started at 0630 hrs. and ended 0710 hrs.; at 0745 hrs., a two-hour delay was announced.

T/off: 1040 hrs.　　　　　Target: 1222 & 1226 hrs.　　　　　Return: 1324 hrs.

Mission Narrative

PFF mission; thirty plus three window and two PFF aircraft dispatched. 1st Box was led by Lt. Col. D. D. Bentley, and the 2nd Box by Lt. Col. B. G. Willis.

Route was Base to Givet to St. Trond to Maastricht to target. XXIX TAC to provide area cover.

PFF aircraft did not bomb; area bombing by flights. Twenty aircraft attacked, dropping 319 × 250 GPs. Weather was 5–7/10th cloud. Bombing was generally scattered and mostly outside the target area, anything from ½ mile to 7¼ miles from the designated target. Three aircraft of the high flight, 1st Box, pulled out of formation to test guns and were out of position; the 1st Box then turned across them, and they were unable to catch the formation again. The leader of the high flight, 2nd Box, was hit by flak and forced out of formation; rest of flight did not bomb because leader did not drop. A total of 161 × 250 GPs and 8 × 500 GPs (by the PFF aircraft) were returned.

Moderate accurate HFF from Duren area. Thirteen aircraft received Cat. A damage.

Return was a right turn to Aachen to Base.

The high flight of the 2nd Box, consisting of four aircraft, landed at B-58 (Brussels/Melsbroek); the flight leader's aircraft had an instrument failure, and he flew to the north to avoid a weather front and landed to get weather information.

No interrogation times recorded.

Mission Notes and "Flak-Bait" Crew Debrief Comments

"Flak-Bait" flew as No. 3 in the high flight, 2nd Box.

Cat. A damage; five flak holes.

PFF did not drop; flight made two runs but could not pick out target; couldn't make a third run because of group following. Flight leader hit by flak and forced out of formation. 16 × 250 GPs returned.

Moderate accurate HFF at target on first run, following on turn off.

```
Date: December 13, 1944
Target: Wollseifen D/A
Field Order: 9th BD F/O 668
99th CBW F/O 388
```

"Flak-Bait" Crew

1Lt. R. L. Hall, pilot

2Lt. R. E. O'Rourke, copilot

1Lt. J. F. Toscano, navigator/bombardier

SSgt. A. E. Rotman, engineer/gunner

Sgt. E. W. Riggs, radio/gunner

Sgt. J. Barrier, gunner

Briefing started at 0700 hrs. and ended 0745 hrs.

T/off: 1030 hrs.　　　　　Target: 1235½ hrs.　　　　　Return: 1419 hrs.

Mission Narrative

PFF mission. Thirty-three plus three window and one aircraft dispatched. The 1st Box was led by Col. J. S. Samuel, and the 2nd Box by Lt. Col. H. E. Newcomer.

Route was from Base to Ettelbruck to IP, east of Waxweiler, to Schleiden to target. PFF aircraft had equipment failure at primary, so formation turned right to attack Eurskirchen on GEE. XXIX TAC to provide area cover.

10/10th cloud with tops at 8–9,000 ft. All aircraft bombed on the 1st Box leader, who bombed on GEE equipment after the PFF equipment had failed, PFF say drop was between Zulpich and Euskirchen; thirty-two aircraft released 245 × 500 GPs from 12,700 and 12,000 ft., the PFF aircraft dropped with the group's aircraft. One aircraft could not get the bomb bay doors to open, and another left formation before the IP and landed at B-17 (Caen-Carpiquet) with a bad engine and low on gas. A total of 29 × 500 GPs were returned.

No opposition met.

Formation turned left off target to K-9338 and then to Base.

No interrogation times recorded.

Mission Notes and "Flak-Bait" Crew Debrief Comments

"Flak-Bait" flew as No. 3 in the low flight, 2nd Box.

8 × 500 GPs dropped on leader; results unobserved.

Other Crew Comments

PFF aircraft got in way of the high flight, 2nd Box, and nearly dropped bombs on it. It also disrupted the low flight: broke up the entire flight.

```
Date: December 15, 1944
Target: Wollseifen D/A
Field Order: 9th BD F/O 671
99th CBW F/O 390
```

"Flak-Bait" Crew

1Lt. M. F. Dombroski, pilot	SSgt. J. S. Rowell, engineer/gunner
2Lt. C. W. Thomas, copilot	SSgt. W. M. Ek, radio/gunner
TSgt. G. D. Tesnow, togglier	SSgt. Gosudra, gunner

Briefing started at 0845 hrs. and ended 0915 hrs.

T/off: 1045 hrs.   Target: 1227 hrs.   Return: 1323 hrs.

Mission Narrative

PFF mission. Thirty-three plus three window and one PFF aircraft dispatched. 1st Box was led by Maj. G. H. Watson, and the 2nd Box by Capt. H. E. Short.

Route was from Base to Ettelbruck to the IP, east of Waxweiler, to Schleiden to target. XXIX TAC to provide area cover.

Formation dropped on PFF through 10/10th cloud from 12,800 ft. Thirty-three aircraft released 494 × 250 GPss and 4 × 500 GPs; results were unobserved. One aircraft was an early return after being hit by shell casings from an aircraft ahead firing the package guns; aircraft jettisoned 16 × 250 GPs on Arbonne range. 18 × 250 GPs returned due to rack failures.

No opposition met.

Return was a left turn to K-9338 to Base.

No interrogation times recorded.

Mission Notes and "Flak-Bait" Crew Debrief Comments

"Flak-Bait" flew as one of the window ships.

No flak; used all of the window.

Other Comments

Thirty-two aircraft diverted to A-68 (Juvincourt); the window aircraft (including "Flak-Bait") returned to Base.

Date: December 18, 1944
Target: Dreiborn D/V
Field Order: 9th BD F/O 674
99th CBW F/O 393

"Flak-Bait" Crew

1Lt. K. W. Goldacker, pilot	Sgt. J. Foorman, engineer/gunner
2Lt. T. H. Felker, copilot	SSgt. C. C. Hendrix, radio/gunner
2Lt. W. L. Hoenshel, navigator/bombardier	Sgt. J. A. Circelli, gunner

Briefing started at 0630 hrs. and no end time recorded. Mission scrubbed at 1005 hrs., and group placed on standby. At 1030 hrs., orders came through to set up the same mission with a takeoff of at 1505 hrs.

T/off: 1455 hrs.   Target: 1634 hrs.   Return: 1823 hrs.

Mission Narrative

An attack on defenses of the Siegfried Line near Dreiborn.

PFF mission; thirty-four plus three window and one PFF aircraft off. The 1st Box led by Capt. J. M. Bennett, and the 2nd Box by Capt. W. G. Fort.

Because of the urgency of the situation on the ground, the aircraft took off among snowstorms and from an ice-packed runway.

Route was Base to Dinkirch to L-0865 (the IP) to target. XXIX TAC to provide area support.

Thirty-two aircraft attacked on PFF through 9–10/10th cloud from 12 × 500 GPs, releasing 489 × 250 GPs and 4 × 500 GPs on "other" target. A GEE fix indicated it was near the town of Olef, 5 miles east of the primary. The interphone on the PFF ship from the special-equipment operator to the pilot was out, and the navigator had to talk the pilot on course and through bomb run; as a result, at bombs away the PFF ship was to the right of briefed course. Three aircraft were early return due to mechanical failures, and one window ship because a gunner was ill. 55 × 250 GPs were returned.

No damage received.

Return was a left turn to Stolberg to Base.

No interrogation times recorded.

Mission Notes and "Flak-Bait" Crew Debrief Comments

"Flak-Bait" flew as No. 3 in the lead flight, 2nd Box.

16 × 250 GPs dropped; target unidentified.

Observed flare bursting below formation 6 miles north of target.

Briefing Note

It is brought to your attention that all of the crews are to be appraised [sic] of the seriousness of the situation existing in the target area front. The enemy breakthrough has created a serious threat to our organization in this sector, and the crews should be made fully conscious of the importance of this mission.

Message to be read to crews at briefing

"The enemy today achieved a 6-mile breakthrough on our front. When you consider that we have made no progress on this front for one month, the critical situation created by this breakthrough is apparent. Our targets today are selected with the view not only of stopping further breakthroughs but of preventing the enemy exploiting the breakthrough achieved. It is of prime importance that these targets are bombed. Every expedient will be used to hit these targets; if necessary you will bomb from minimum altitude." —Anderson.

Event: New CO for the 449th BS

On December 18, 1944, Lt. Col. Benjamin G. Willis was released from his assignment as CO of the 449th BS and transferred to the 127th Replacement Battalion on the first leg on his journey home at the completion of his tour. He was succeeded by Maj. John C. Ruse.

```
Date: December 24, 1944
Target: Konz-Karthaus RR Br
Field Order: 9th BD F/O 680
99th CBW F/O 400
```

"Flak-Bait" Crew

1Lt. W. C. George, pilot	Sgt. S. J. Nicoletti, engineer/gunner
2Lt. E. C. Pakish, copilot	SSgt. J. A. Smith, radio/gunner
TSgt. H. Brown, toggler	SSgt. M. B. Schmidt, gunner

Briefing started at 0900 hrs. and ended 1000 hrs.
T/off: 1125 hrs.   Target: 1318 (P) & 1316 (Cas) hrs.   Return: 1415 hrs.

Mission Narrative

Thirty-five aircraft dispatched. Lt. Col. H. C. Newcomer led the 1st Box, and Capt. L. W. Rice the 2nd Box.

Route was Base to U-4597 for rendezvous with IX TAC fighters, to Longuyon to Luxembourg (the IP) to target.

Bombing by flights from 11,500 and 11,000 ft. Results were as follows: Box 1, lead flight—excellent; high flight—no attack, interphone out; and low flight—PNB, misidentified target, the bombs landing in a good concentration in the town of Grevenmacher. Box 2 results were excellent, excellent, and superior, respectively, with an excellent concentration on the DMPI covering the bridge. Twenty-three aircraft dropped 99 × 1,000 GPs on the primary; four dropped 14 × 1,000 GPs on Grevenmacher. Two aircraft were early return due to mechanical problems, and six failed to bomb. A total of 37 × 1,000 GPs returned.

Weak inaccurate HFF experienced in the target area. No damage received.

Return was a right turn toward Saarburg to Luxembourg to Base.

No interrogation times recorded.

Mission Notes and "Flak-Bait" Crew Debrief Comments

"Flak-Bait" flew as No. 2 in the low flight, 1st Box.

4 × 1,000 GPs dropped on leader, who misidentified target; results poor.

Too much chatter on the radio: giving away too much information.

Other Crew Comments

Lead aircraft contacted "Parade" since fighters not visible at the IP; advised to go in. Friendly fighters did turn up and escorted us in.

Several crews reported jet aircraft trails.

Someone was transmitting from the time of takeoff to target and back.

Briefing Note

Because of major fighter opposition the day before (December 23) and the loss of thirty-five B-26s, most of which fell to enemy fighter attack, with many others written off due to battle damage (the 322nd BG was fortunate in that it did not lose any aircraft this day), the following message was read out at the following morning's briefing:

Yesterday was a rough day for you. It was a rougher day for the enemy. He lost 187 planes: 233 tracked vehicles and motor transport; thirteen locomotives; two bridges destroyed; nine marshaling yards disrupted. He gained no ground. Further, your courageous work in spite of adverse visibility, intense flak, and savage fighter attacks has raised the morale of our ground forces immensely. The enemy cannot stand many more days like yesterday. I thank you for your sacrifices and your gallant fighting. Today and every day weather permits, you must make more sacrifices and do more gallant fighting. This must continue until the Hun is smashed. If it does not continue, France, Belgium, and Holland will again be under Nazi domination: Our fields will be overrun; our cause will be lost; past sacrifices will have been in vain. I know your courage and I know your [sic] are equal to the task. I salute you all.
Signed: Anderson.

In addition, the following message was received from 9th BD:

Until further notice, no group is authorized to proceed on mission unless fighter rendezvous is made. If an ordered fighter rendezvous is not made, operations will be abandoned and this headquarters so notified by VHF Channel B.

```
Date: December 25, 1944
Target: Bitburg Crossroads
Field Order: 9th BD F/O 682
99th CBW F/O 401
```

"Flak-Bait" Crew

1Lt. W. C. George, pilot
2Lt. E. C. Pakish, copilot
TSgt. H. Brown, togglier

Sgt. S. J. Nicoletti, engineer/gunner
SSgt. J. A. Smith, radio/gunner
SSgt. M. B. Schmidt, gunner

Briefing started at 0710 hrs. and ended 0740 hrs.
T/off: 0909 hrs.   Target: 1039 to 1042 hrs.   Return: 1140 hrs.

Mission Narrative

Thirty-seven aircraft dispatched; the 1st Box was led by Lt. Col. D. Bentley, and the 2nd Box by Capt. W. G. Fort.
Route was Base to rendezvous with 2nd TAF fighters to Longuyon to Luxembourg (the IP) to target.
Area bombing by flights, thirty-six aircraft attacked in CAVU conditions; the flights bombed in the following order: 4, 1, 6, 5, 3, and 2. All flights achieved good concentrations, and all hit in the town of Bitburg, with results either excellent or superior for all flights. 523 × 250 GPs and 4 × 1,000 GPs dropped on target. One aircraft jettisoned 16 × 250 GPs in Channel after flak hit, and crash-landed. 6 × 250 GPs were returned through rack failures.
Flak was generally moderate accurate HFF from the IP to the target and turn off target and on the return route. Fifteen aircraft received Cat. A damage, two Cat. AC, and two Cat. E. Three persons injured: 1Lt. J. Carbone, and SSgt. A. W. Mensen of the 449th BS, and SSgt. I. A. Pearson of the 452nd BS.
Return was a right turn to Wolsfeld to Luxembourg to Base.
Interrogation of crews began at 1135 hrs. and finished at 1230 hrs.

Mission Notes and "Flak-Bait" Crew Debrief Comments

"Flak-Bait" flew as No. 5 in the lead flight, 2nd Box.

No damage.

16 × 250 GPs dropped; hit on crossroads.

Other Crew Comments

One Fw 190 approached aircraft 43-34307 PN-S, "Miss 28th Seabee" (lead aircraft of the 2nd Box), which was on single engine and being protected by another B-26 from this group. E/a may have fired 3–4 rounds of 20 mm; gunners did not fire. (Aircraft damaged Cat. AC, and the radio/gunner, SSgt. A. W. Mensen, received leg wounds from flak.)

An Fw 190 was observed being engaged by P-47s on the turn off the target.

Category E Information
41-31919 DR-N, "Peasapis"

Pilot was 1Lt. A. M. Samuelson, flying in the No. 3 position of the lead flight, 1st Box. Hit by flak between IP and target; hydraulic system shot out; bombs jettisoned safe in the Channel. One man wounded: SSgt. I. A. Pearson, 452nd BS. Crash-landed at base.

"Peasapis" crash-landed at A-61 Beauvais-Tille on Christmas Day 1944. *Trevor J. Allen collection*

"Clarks Little Pill" was another Christmas Day loss, having been abandoned over friendly territory while on its 155th mission; SSgt. W. H. Ensminger was killed when his parachute failed to open. *Trevor J. Allen collection*

41-34959 SS-Q, "Clarks Little Pill"

Pilot was 1Lt. M. A. Neher, flying No. 6 position in low flight, 1st Box. Having bombed the target, the aircraft was hit by flak and the right engine caught fire, when about 1 or 2 miles west of Bitburg. Aircraft was seen to crash at position P-881432 in friendly territory; three chutes were observed. Five of the crew escaped uninjured, but SSgt. W. H. Ensminger was reported as missing; it was later determined that his parachute had failed to open. Aircraft was on its 155th mission.

41-18272 PN-D, "Murder Inc."

Pilot was 1Lt. C. W. Thomas, flying in the No. 5 in the high flight, 2nd Box; crashed upon landing at A-61 Beauvais-Tille; no further details known; crew safe.

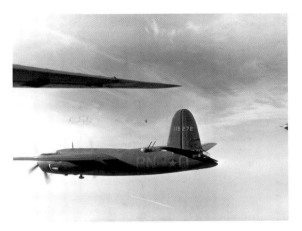

Also written off this day was veteran ship "Murder Inc." *Roger A. Freeman collection*

"Murder Inc." in flight on one of the group's early missions in the summer of 1943. *USAAF*

Event: Christmas Celebrations

Because of the serious situation for the ground forces in Ardennes area, there was no Christmas stand-down, and missions continued unabated. Two missions were flown on Christmas Day, but the cooks did put on a Christmas meal in the interval between the missions.

```
Date: December 25, 1944
Target: Taben Hwy Br
Field Order: 9th BD F/O 683
99th CBW F/O 402
```

"Flak-Bait" Crew

1Lt. W. C. George, pilot
2Lt. E. C. Pakish, copilot
TSgt. H. Brown, togglier

Sgt. S. J. Nicoletti, engineer/gunner
SSgt. J. A. Smith, radio/gunner
SSgt. M. B. Schmidt, gunner

Briefing started at 1233 hrs. and ended 1240 hrs.
T/off: 1400 hrs.   Target: 1532 to 1544 & 1549 (Cas) hrs.   Return: 1647 hrs.

Mission Narrative

Thirty aircraft dispatched; the 1st Box was led by Maj. J. C. Ruse, and the 2nd Box by Maj. L. A. Tenold.

Route was Base to rendezvous with IX TAC escort at U-2866 to Sierck (the IP) to target.

Although conditions were CAVU, smoke from the previous group's attack (391st BG) obscured the target; twenty-four aircraft attacked the primary, from 11,500 and 11,000 ft., dropping 94 × 1,000 GPs. Six aircraft attacked a casual target, dropping 24 × 1,000 GPs. Results as follows: Box 1, lead flight, made two runs but could not pick out target because of smoke, so attacked a casual target, a road and rail junction at Rheinfeld; bombs hit 1,500 ft. northwest of selected target. High flight made one run at primary, but bombs fell 1,650 ft. southwest of selected target. The low flight made two runs, but the results were undetermined. The 2nd Box: both flights achieved excellent results, having made two runs each. 2 × 1,000 GPs were returned.

Leader of 2nd Box reported weak inaccurate flak at the target. No damage received.

Return was a left turn to Sierck and retrace.

Interrogation of crews began at 1705 hrs. and finished at 1740 hrs.

Mission Notes and "Flak-Bait" Crew Debrief Comments

"Flak-Bait" flew as No. 2 in the high flight, 1st Box.

4 × 1,000 GPs dropped; results unobserved since bridge obscured by smoke.

Other Crew Comments

Crews commented that P-51s came in directly at the formation; this seemed poor policy since gunners were ready to fire. Otherwise they did a good job of escort.

```
Date: December 26, 1944
Target: Bad Munster RR Br
Field Order: 9th BD F/O 684
99th CBW F/O 403
```

"Flak-Bait" Crew

1Lt. H. C. Bozarth, pilot
1Lt. S. V. N. Best, copilot
Sgt. T. B. Gee, togglier

SSgt. W. L. Johnston, engineer/gunner
TSgt. M. Darnell Jr., radio/gunner
Sgt. R. L. Bassler, gunner

No briefing times recorded; mission delayed by one hour at 0945 hrs. and then by another thirty minutes.
T/off: 1145 hrs.　　　　　Target: 1350 to 1403 (P) hrs.　　　Return: 1534 hrs.
　　　　　　　　　　　1409 (Cas 1) & 1416 (Cas 2) hrs.

Mission Narrative

Thirty-six aircraft dispatched. The 1st Box was led by Lt. Col. J. B. Smith, and the 2nd Box by Capt. H. E. Short.

Route was Base to rendezvous with XIX TAC fighters at U-8658 to Reichshoffen to Lambrecht to Mannheim (the IP) to target.

Although conditions were CAVU, smoke from the preceding 391st BG attack hindered target identification. Twenty-four attacked in the vicinity of the primary, dropping 96 × 1,000 GPs, most with unsatisfactory results. The low flight, Box 1, achieved excellent results, with hits on town and across railroad station, after two runs. Because of the poor visibility, two flights selected casual targets. Box 2, high flight, dropped 24 × 1,000 GPs on a factory southwest of Eisenberg at 1409 hrs., and the high flight, Box 1, dropped 24 × 1,000 GPs on an overpass northeast of Kaiserlautern at 1416 hrs., having made two runs at the primary, although results on each were poor.

An indication of the terrible conditions at A-61 Beauvais-Tille during the severe winter of 1944–45. This is part of the 452nd BS dispersal area. Pity the poor ground crews who had to work outside in these conditions. *Trevor J. Allen collection*

B-26s taxi for takeoff in the snow at A-61. *Smithsonian National Air and Space Museum, NASM 9A12284*

Moderate inaccurate HFF from Kaiserlautern and Diffenbach areas. No damage received.
Return was a left turn off the target and retrace route in.
Interrogation of crews began at 1600 hrs. and finished at 1645 hrs.

Mission Notes and "Flak-Bait" Crew Debrief Comments
"Flak-Bait" flew as No. 2 in the low flight, 1st Box.
Made two runs; 4 × 1,000 GPs dropped; results believed to be good.
More evasive action, not so much straight and level.

Other Crew Comments
Leader of the 2nd Box reported two jets in the target area.

```
Date: January 5, 1945
Target: Gouvy Comm Cen
Field Order: 9th BD F/O 698
99th CBW F/O 415
```

"Flak-Bait" Crew

2Lt. T. H. Felker, pilot	SSgt. W. L. Johnston, engineer/gunner
1Lt. S. V. N. Best, copilot	TSgt. M. Darnell Jr., radio/gunner
Sgt. T. B. Gee, togglier	Sgt. R. L. Bassler, gunner

Briefing started at 1130 hrs. and ended 1150 hrs.
T/off: 1340 hrs.   Target: 1526 & 1526½ hrs.   Return: 1656 hrs.

Mission Narrative
PFF mission. Thirty-three plus two window and one PFF aircraft dispatched. 1st Box was led by Maj. G. H. Watson, and the 2nd Box by Capt. C. L. Anderson.

Routing was Base to St. Trond to K-6134 (the IP) to target. 2nd TAF to provide area support.

4–6/10th cloud with tops at 5,000 ft. encountered; bombed on PFF equipment from 13,000 and 12,600 ft. Thirty-one aircraft attacked, dropping 234 × 500 GPs bombs for excellent results, with over 50% of all bombs within 1,000 ft. of the DMPI. Two aircraft did not drop, since they could not see the PFF drop because of glare from the sun. A total of 26 × 500 GPs returned; 8 × 500 GPs on Cat. E aircraft unaccounted for.

Moderate to intense accurate HFF from Vielsalm to the target area. Slightly more accurate for the 1st Box. Twenty-four aircraft Cat. A, including the PFF aircraft, and one aircraft Cat. E.

Return was a right turn to K-3808 to Base.

No interrogation times recorded.

Mission Notes and "Flak-Bait" Crew Debrief Comments
"Flak-Bait" flew as No. 5 in the high flight, 2nd Box.
8 × 500 GPs dropped; results unobserved.
Cat. A: a few holes.

Other Crew Comments
Several crews reported approximately four e/a about a mile away from the formation as it turned off target; no attacks made.

Crew of aircraft 43-34145 ER-R, the lead aircraft of the low flight, 1st Box, piloted by 1Lt. R. E. Ferguson, praised the efforts of their tail gunner, SSgt. T. A. Morgan. Although dazed when his turret was almost knocked out, he used good judgment with the tools he had on hand, along with some bomb safety wire to repair the elevator cables to enable the aircraft to return home safely.

449th BS crews want better weather reconnaissance and briefings.

Category E Information
44-67815 PN-D
Pilot was 1Lt. H. J. Bye. No. 2 in the high flight, 2nd Box. Hit by flak over the target and last seen with the right engine feathered and descending under control; three chutes observed at 1534 hrs. before the aircraft entered the cloud base. Aircraft crashed near the town of Barvaux, Belgium, in friendly territory.

1Lt. H. J. Bye, pilot	parachuted
2Lt. M. F. Lewonowski, copilot	parachuted
Cpl. B. N. Foss, togglier	parachuted
Sgt. T. H. Olinger, engineer/gunner	KIA
Sgt. A. Taylor, radio/gunner	KIA
Sgt. W. R. Narramore, gunner	KIA

> **Date: January 14, 1945**
> **Target: Landau-Thaleischweiler RR Br**
> **Field Order: 9th BD F/O 707**
> **99th CBW F/O 424**

"Flak-Bait" Crew

1Lt. H. C. Bozarth, pilot	SSgt. W. L. Johnston, engineer/gunner
1Lt. S. V. N. Best, copilot	TSgt. M. Darnell Jr., radio/gunner
Sgt. T. B. Gee, togglier	Sgt. R. L. Bassler, gunner

Briefing started at 0815 hrs. and ended 0840 hrs.; mission delayed by 1 hour at 0940 hrs.

T/off: 1110 hrs.	Target: 1335 to 1352 hrs.	Return: 1459 hrs.
	1342 (Cas 1), 1353 (Cas 2) hrs.	

Mission Narrative
Thirty-six aircraft dispatched; the 1st Box was led by Maj. L. A. Tenold, and the 2nd Box by Capt. C. L. Anderson.

Route was Base to rendezvous with XIX TAC escort at U-7735 to Q-8131 to target.

Bombing by flights; in clear but hazy conditions the snow on the ground made target identification difficult; thirty-five aircraft attacked, releasing a total of 137 × 1,000 GPs; one aircraft failed to bomb due to rack failure, returning 4 × 1,000 GPs, and 3 × 1,000 GPs were returned because of other rack failures.

Box 1, lead flight: PNB; attacked a junction at Dahn, 1 mile southeast of target, dropping 24 × 1,000 GPs, with hits on a much-used highway; flight made two runs. The high flight dropped 24 × 1,000 GPs on the primary, for good results, with 40% of bombs within DMPI after three runs. The low flight made three runs, but bombardier failed to pick up target, so dropped on the high flight's release; 24 × 1,000 GPs dropped, results unsatisfactory, with 20% of bombs within 1,000 ft. of DMPI, with some hits to rail lines.

Box 2, lead flight: PNB; made two runs and dropped 24 × 1,000 GPs on Schonau, 13½ miles southwest of primary. The high flight: PNB; dropped 21 × 1,000 GPs in an excellent concentration ½ mile from Albersweiler, 5 miles east of primary after two runs (casual 1). The low flight: PNB; made three runs; 20 × 1,000 GP bombs landed in an excellent concentration 1 mile northwest of Bitchie (casual 2); bombardier could not identify primary because of snow.

The 1st Box did not experience any flak; the 2nd Box reported moderate inaccurate from Pirmasens, moderate accurate from Dambach, and weak inaccurate from Ketterichoff and from Fischbach. Six aircraft received Cat. A damage.

Briefed return was a left turn off the target and retrace the route in, although the 2nd Box took a route farther to the east and nearer to Pirmasens and Bitchie to attack casual targets before picking up the briefed return route.

Interrogation of crews began at 1512 hrs.; no end time recorded.

Mission Notes and "Flak-Bait" Crew Debrief Comments

"Flak-Bait" flew as No. 5 in the lead flight, 2nd Box.

Made two runs, with 4 × 1,000 GPs dropped; results unobserved, possibly in the water.

Rocket observed going straight up to 20,000 ft. some distance from the aircraft, 3–4 miles southeast of the target.

44-67879 PN-Q, "Lil Murf," flew her first mission on January 14, 1945, and is seen here over a snow-covered landscape. *Smithsonian National Air and Space Museum, NASM 00068349*

```
Date: January 16, 1945
Target: Bullay RR Br
Field Order: 9th BD F/O 709
99th CBW F/O 426
```

"Flak-Bait" Crew

1Lt. C. W. Thomas, pilot	Sgt. W. H. Myers, engineer/gunner
Capt. H. K. Levy, copilot	Sgt. A. J. Villasenor, radio/gunner
F/O J. Facok, navigator/bombardier	Sgt. D. H. Summerville, gunner

Briefing started at 0902 hrs. and ended 0915 hrs.

T/off: 1110 hrs.　　　　　Target: 1320 to 1326 hrs.　　　　　Return: 1435 hrs.

Mission Narrative

PFF mission. Thirty plus three window and two PFF aircraft dispatched. The 1st Box was led by Lt. Col. D. D. Bentley, and the 2nd Box by Capt. A. W. Smith.

Route was Base to rendezvous with XIX TAC fighter escort at U-7735 to Q-9437 to M-2916 to L-8930 (the IP) to target.

Twenty-one aircraft attacked the primary, dropping 40 × 2,000 GPs and 4 × 500 GPs from 12,800 and 13,500 ft. Results as follows. Box 1, lead flight: superior with one probable direct hit. High flight: excellent with hits to approach and on tunnel entrance. Low flight: undetermined; bombs fell in the smoke of the other bombs, after two runs. 2nd Box, lead flight: no attack; leader could not open bomb bay doors. High flight: no attack; bombardier unable to synchronize and unable to make a second run due to other groups in the area, Low flight: excellent. A total of 20 × 2,000 GPs were returned. 4 × 500 GPs were returned by the PFF aircraft of the 2nd Box, since the leader did not make contact with the PFF ship, so PFF did not take over; PFF reported that conditions were clearly visual.

Weak inaccurate HFF from Trier. Two aircraft Cat. A from flak, one aircraft Cat. AC due to a flat tire, and one aircraft Cat. E when undercarriage collapsed on landing.

Return was a left turn to L-3955 to L-3618 to P-8414 to Base.

Interrogation of crews began at 1500 hrs. and finished at 1545 hrs.

Mission Notes and "Flak-Bait" Crew Debrief Comments

"Flak-Bait" flew as one of the window ships.

Window aircraft; made three runs at target. HFF fairly weak in target area.

Category E Information
42-95977 ER-P

Pilot was 1Lt. J. R. Thomas; gear collapsed upon landing, Cat. E.

In addition, aircraft 42-96277 DR-Z "The Cuban Holiday," with pilot 2Lt. O. J. Cox, slid on snow upon landing and burst a tire; one gear ripped off, and damage to the tail. Initially declared as Cat. AC but subsequently written off.

"Flak-Bait" Crew

1Lt. H. C. Bozarth, pilot
2Lt. H. K. Megson, copilot
F/O O. D. Fields, navigator/bombardier

Sgt. H. T. Neidenberg, engineer/gunner
Sgt. W. M. Washer, radio/gunner
Sgt. H. M. Szewczak, gunner

Briefing started at 1112 hrs. and ended 1130 hrs.
T/off: 1230 hrs.   Target: 1406 to 1421 hrs.   Return: 1523 hrs.

Mission Narrative

Thirty-seven aircraft off; the 1st Box was led by Maj. J. C. Ruse, and the 2nd Box by Capt. A. W. Smith with Lt. Col. D. D. Bentley.

Route was Base to J-9611 to Malmedy (the IP) to target. 2nd TAF to provide area cover.

Bombing by flights; weather was clear with 3/10th cloud at 6,000 ft. Results as follows. Box 1, lead flight: excellent, after one run. High flight: PNB, misidentified target; bombs fell 1 mile west of the target, after one run. Low flight: no attack; leader's doors wouldn't open on the first run; they opened on the second run but closed immediately again. Box 2, lead flight: excellent; three runs made. High flight: unsatisfactory, bombs scattered; pilot did not hear bombardier say follow PDI, made one run. Low flight: PNB, misidentified target; bombs fell ½ mile east of Kall, after two runs. Twenty-seven aircraft dropped 210 × 500 GPs. One aircraft was an early return due to engine failure. A total of 78 × 500 GPs returned, and 8 × 500 GPs were lost in the aircraft, Cat. E.

Weak inaccurate HFF in target area, increasing to moderate accurate for flights making second and third runs. Moderate accurate HFF from Wahlen encountered by the low flight, 1st Box, on turn off target. Eight aircraft received Cat. A damage, one aircraft Cat. E; two killed, one injured.

Return was a left turn and retrace route in.

No interrogation times recorded.

Mission Notes and "Flak-Bait" Crew Debrief Comments

"Flak-Bait" flew as No. 2 in the lead flight, 1st Box.

8 × 500 GPs dropped; believed to be good results.

Inaccurate HFF at target.

Category E Information

42-96266 SS-L

Pilot was 1Lt. J. L. Moore; No. 5 aircraft in low flight, 2nd Box; radioed he was losing oil pressure, and aircraft was icing up. Crew bailed out and the aircraft crashed 7 miles southwest of Peronne.

Two persons were killed: the pilot, 1Lt. J. L. Moore, whose parachute did not open, and the radio/gunner, TSgt. Henderson. The engineer, SSgt. C. Bosic, broke a leg upon landing; all from the 451st BS.

January 28, 1945: Mission Scrub

On January 28, 1945, "Flak-Bait" was due to be part of a formation to attack Remagen RR bridge, piloted by 2Lt. T. H. Felker and crew, and was scheduled to fly in the No. 5 position of the high flight, 2nd Box.

The crews were briefed at 0830 hrs., but this was followed by two delays of thirty minutes each, and then, at 1140 hrs., the entire 2nd Box was scrubbed from the mission.

The 1st Box, consisting of fifteen aircraft plus three window and one PFF aircraft, was dispatched at 1245 hrs. and attacked at 1456 hrs., with fifteen aircraft dropping a total of $27 \times 2,000$ GPs and 4×500 GP bombs; one aircraft was a late takeoff and couldn't catch the formation, returning $2 \times 2,000$ GPs. Results were reported as fair to good, and no aircraft were damaged.

Date: January 29, 1945
Target: Kall Comm Cen
Field Order: 9th BD F/O 724
99th CBW F/O 440

"Flak-Bait" Crew

1Lt. T. H. Felker, pilot

1Lt. H. C. Bryant, copilot

TSgt. G. D. Tesnow, togglier

SSgt. J. S. Rowell, engineer/gunner

Sgt. F. R. Gonzales, radio/gunner

SSgt. C. N. Stearns, gunner

Briefing started at 0815 hrs. and ended 0920 hrs.

T/off: 1015 hrs.   Target: 1205 hrs.   Return: 1330 hrs.

Mission Narrative

PFF mission. Thirty-three plus three window and one PFF aircraft dispatched. The 1st Box was led by Maj. J. C. Ruse, and the 2nd Box by Lt. Col. D. D. Bentley.

Route was Base to Hannut to K-7228 (the IP) to target. XIX TAC to provide area cover.

Area bombing on PFF through 10/10th cloud; thirty-four aircraft dropped 522×250 GPs and 4×500 GPs from 12,700 and 11,700 ft. 6×250 GPs were returned through rack failures. Bombs for 1st Box fell in a good concentration on an intersection in the middle of the town, with possible hits to a road bridge over the river. Those for the 2nd Box hit in the target area, but the pattern was rather scattered, falling on roads and buildings in the southern part of the town and across railroad lines east of the town.

No flak encountered. One crewman, SSgt. A. E. Duvall, 449th BS, the turret gunner on Maj. Ruse's aircraft, was injured when his aircraft was hit by the spinner from a bomb released by another aircraft. All of the turret glass was knocked out; aircraft Cat. AC.

Return was a right turn to Malmedy to Base.

No interrogation times recorded.

Mission Notes and "Flak-Bait" Crew Debrief Comments

"Flak-Bait" flew as No. 5 in the high flight, 1st Box.

16×250 GPs dropped on PFF; 10/10th cloud.

"Flak-Bait" Crew

1Lt. F. M. Wise, pilot

2Lt. D. E. Bredell, copilot

TSgt. H. W. Burgoyne, togglier

Sgt. J. G. Urbonavichuis, engineer/gunner

Sgt. J. W. Linton, radio/gunner

Sgt. R. J. Tonelli, gunner

Briefing started at 0800 hrs. and ended 0840 hrs.

T/off: 1025 hrs.   Target: 1210 to 1228 hrs.   Return: 1401 hrs.

Mission Narrative

PFF mission; thirty-three plus three window and one PFF aircraft dispatched. The 1st Box was led by Capt. L. W. Rice, and the 2nd Box by Capt. C. L. Anderson.

Route was Base to rendezvous with XIX TAC escort at P-8414 to L-3820 to L-3548 to L-4260 to L-6559 (the IP) to target.

PFF did not receive the release signal on the first run, so flights bombed visually from 10,500 to 13,750 ft. Results were mostly unknown due to a lack of photo coverage but were believed to be fair, with the majority of hits just over the target. All flights made three runs except the lead flight, Box 2, which made four runs, and the low flight, 2nd Box, which dropped on their second run, for excellent results. Thirty-one aircraft dropped 62 × 2,000 GPs and 4 × 500 GPs. One aircraft had a toggle switch malfunction at primary, so released 2 × 2,000 GPs on a railroad line near the Rhine as a casual target. One aircraft had rack malfunction and returned 2 × 2,000 GPs.

Moderate accurate HFF encountered at Boppard on the first run, continuing until 4 miles from the target, probably from two flak barges that were known to be there. Moderate accurate HFF from the Trier area. Fifteen aircraft received Cat. A damage, and one Cat. AC.

Return was a wide right turn and retrace route in.

No interrogation times recorded.

Mission Notes and "Flak-Bait" Crew Debrief Comments

"Flak-Bait" flew as No. 2 in the high flight, 2nd Box.

Three runs made; dropped 2 × 2,000 GPs; hit in town.

Cat. A damage; one flak hole.

Other Crew Comments

Route was too close to Trier.

PFF ship criticized poor formation flying, and that they tried to take the lead but the group would not follow. Took over at the bomb line.

Event: A-61 Beauvais-Tille closed for repairs

Conditions at A-61 had always been challenging, with most of the facilities having been destroyed by Allied bombing.

With the harsh winter of 1944–45, the thaw in January 1945 turned the temporary repairs to the runway to something resembling a mush, the chalklike materials used in the repairs having given way when it had absorbed the water.

Col. John S. Samuel, the group CO, was told by the engineers that repairs would take some two months to complete. This was unacceptable, so Col. Samuel closed the airfield on February 3, 1945, and mobilized every available person in the group to carry out the repairs themselves, working day and night.

Some 1,175 tons of rock were used to help fill in the 105 holes in the runway; these were anything from 3 to 40 ft. in diameter and up to 6 ft. in depth. Every available truck was commandeered to help carry the materials.

After four days of hard work, the repairs were completed on the evening of February 7, and the group was operational again the next day, with a mission to Horrem Town.

```
Date: February 8, 1945
Target: Horrem Town
Field Order: 9th BD F/O 738
99th CBW F/O 451
```

"Flak-Bait" Crew

1Lt. H. C. Bozarth, pilot
1Lt. S. V. N. Best, copilot
Sgt. T. B. Gee, togglier

SSgt. W. L. Johnston, engineer/gunner
TSgt. M. Darnell Jr., radio/gunner
Sgt. R. L. Bassler, gunner

Briefing started at 0545 hrs. and ended 0630 hrs.
T/off: 1120 hrs.   Target: 1258½ (P) & 1255 (S) hrs.   Return: 1452 hrs.

Mission Narrative
PFF mission. Forty-four plus five window and three PFF aircraft dispatched in three boxes. 1st Box was to be led by Lt. Col. D. D. Bentley, who aborted on the taxi strip, so Capt. J. H. McCarty took over. The 2nd Box was led by Capt. G. H. Lane, and the 3rd Box by Maj. L. J. Sebille.

Route was Base to K-2050 to K-6972 (the IP) to target. Ground counter battery fire was to be coordinated with the approach of the formation.

Area bombing, the PFF ship in the 1st Box had equipment failure, the lead and high flights did not bomb, and the low flight bombed with Box 3 on GEE, with the bombs landing in fields 2 miles southeast of Zulpich (secondary target). Box 2 attacked the primary, with fifteen aircraft dropping 204 × 250 GPs and 4 × 500 GPs on PFF; bombs fell 3½ miles east of Horrem and 1 mile west of Frechen on an active factory and across rail tracks. Box 3 dropped on GEE, after the PFF had equipment failure, with sixteen aircraft dropping 244 × 250 GPs (includes those of the low flight, Box 1) and the bombs landing in a good pattern 1½ miles southeast of Zulpich, the briefed GEE target. Bombs fell on farm buildings and a highway. A total of 256 × 250 GPs were brought back; this was made up of 14 × 250 GPs by two aircraft that had a rack failure while attacking the secondary, 18 × 250 GPs by aircraft with other rack failures while attacking the primary, and 190 × 250 GPs by abortive aircraft, which includes one aircraft that was a late takeoff and could not catch the formation. In addition, one of the PFF aircraft returned 4 × 500 GP bombs.

All three boxes encountered moderate accurate HFF from Erkelenz and the IP area; the 1st Box turned around in this area. From the IP to the target, HFF ranged from moderate to weak and was generally inaccurate. Flak continued through turn off target into Duren area. Box 3, which continued to Zulpich, experienced weak to moderate inaccurate HFF. Three aircraft received Cat. AC damage, and seventeen Cat. A damage.

Briefed return was a left turn off the target to K-9647 to P-2983 to Base.
Interrogation of crews began at 1430 hrs. and finished at 1550 hrs.

Mission Notes and "Flak-Bait" Crew Debrief Comments
"Flak-Bait" was No. 3 in the lead flight, 2nd Box.
16 × 250 GPs dropped on Zulpich.
Moderate inaccurate on bomb run and over target; no damage received.

Date: February 13, 1945
Target: Iserlohn M/T Depot Area B
Field Order: 9th BD F/O 746
99th CBW F/O 456

"Flak-Bait" Crew

1Lt. E. C. Schnatz, pilot

Capt. H. K. Levy, copilot

F/O J. Facok, navigator/bombardier

Sgt. W. H. Myers, engineer/gunner

Sgt. A. J. Villasenor, radio/gunner

Sgt. D. H. Summerville, gunner

Briefing started at 0620 hrs. and ended 0640 hrs.

T/off: 0920 hrs. Target: 1121½ & 1210 (Cas) hrs. Return: 1322 hrs.

Mission Narrative

PFF mission. Thirty-three plus three window and one PFF aircraft dispatched. The 1st Box was to be led by Maj. P. Shannon, but this aircraft had an instrument failure and returned early; Capt. J. H. McCarty took over the lead. The 2nd Box was led by Maj. J. C. Ruse.

Briefed route was Base to rendezvous with IX TAC fighters at P-8413 to Nastatten to Plettenberg (the IP) to target.

Bombed on PFF; thirty-four aircraft dropped 255 × 500 GPs from 12,880 ft.; cloud was 10/10th at 7,000 ft. One window aircraft dropped 28 × 100 GPs at position Q-420920 when it was unable to obtain a GEE fix at the primary; the other two window aircraft were not ready when leader dropped, so returned 56 × 100 GP bombs. One aircraft salvoed 2 × 500 GPs after the turn off target 7 miles west of Iserlohn, when they failed to release at the primary. Formation leader had instrument failure and returned shortly after takeoff, returning 8 × 500 GPs, and 3 × 500 GPs were returned by another aircraft with rack failure.

Weak inaccurate HFF experienced from Nastatten, Nassau, and Limburg; no damage received.

Briefed return was a left turn to Ostrich and then retrace. PFF reported that the group was 25 miles east of briefed course on route out near the bomb line.

Interrogation of crews began at 1320 hrs. and finished at 1340 hrs.

Mission Notes and "Flak-Bait" Crew Debrief Comments

"Flak-Bait" flew as No. 5 in the lead flight, 2nd Box.

8 × 500 GPs dropped on PFF through 10/10th cloud.

HFF on way in at Nastatten radar flak; ten bursts but inaccurate.

Saw what appeared to be four P-38s; thought we were to have P-47s or P-51s.

Other Crew Comments

Box leaders should not argue among themselves on air.

Window ships not out in front of formation.

Too much chatter aircraft to aircraft, coming off the target and on return.

Date: February 14, 1945
Target: Kevelaer Comm Cen
Field Order: 9th BD F/O 747
99th CBW F/O 457

"Flak-Bait" Crew

1Lt. H. C. Bozarth, pilot

1Lt. S. V. N. Best, copilot

Sgt. T. B. Gee, togglier

SSgt. W. L. Johnston, engineer/gunner

TSgt. M. Darnell Jr., radio/gunner

Sgt. R. L. Bassler, gunner

Briefing started at 0615 hrs. and ended 0650 hrs.

T/off: 0905 hrs.   Target: 1035 to 1121½ hrs.   Return: 1220 hrs.

Mission Narrative

Thirty-six aircraft dispatched; the 1st Box was led by Maj. J. C. Ruse, and the 2nd Box by Capt. A. W. Smith.

Route was Base to Helmond (the IP) to target. High flight, 2nd Box, got lost and carried on to the Xanten and Wesel area before turning back. No fighter support scheduled.

Twenty-six aircraft attacked, by flights, from 10,300 to 11,750 ft., dropping a total of 50 × 2,000 GPs in the vicinity of the primary. Results as follows. Box 1, lead flight: PNB; could not identify target; excellent pattern fell 3¾ miles northwest of primary after two runs. High flight: PNB; could not identify target; bombs fell 3 miles northwest of primary after three runs; the bombs from these two flights landed near Weese. The results of the low flight, Box 1, were unsatisfactory; bombs were scattered 4,800 ft. southwest of DMPI. The results of Box 2, lead and low flights, were excellent; the high flight became lost and did not attack. 22 × 2,000 GPs returned by four aircraft that could not get the bomb bay to doors open, and six aircraft because leader did not drop.

Weak inaccurate flak at target, increased to moderate fairly accurate on the flights making second and third runs. One flight became lost and encountered intense accurate flak in Xanten and Wesel areas. Two aircraft received Cat. AC damage, and seven Cat. A damage.

Return was a right turn and retrace.

Interrogation of crews began at 1220 hrs. and finished at 1400 hrs.

Mission Notes and "Flak-Bait" Crew Debrief Comments

"Flak-Bait" flew as No. 3 in the high flight, 1st Box.

2 × 2,000 GPs dropped; bombs hit to right of town across railroad.

Weak inaccurate HFF at Kevelaer; no damage received.

> **Date: February 14, 1945**
> **Target: Rees Comm Cen**
> **Field Order: 9th BD F/O 748**
> **99th CBW F/O 458**

"Flak-Bait" Crew

1Lt. J. B. Lynch, pilot   SSgt. L. G. Thorworth, engineer/gunner
2Lt. D. E. Straight, copilot   Sgt. O. S. Stephenson, radio/gunner
2Lt. R. R. Reiman, navigator/bombardier   Sgt. C. S. Bixler, gunner

Briefing started at 1245 hrs. and ended 1310 hrs. New target announced; briefing restarted at 1330 hrs. and ended 1350 hrs.

T/off: 1455 hrs.   Target: no attack   Return: 1800 hrs.

Mission Narrative

Thirty-four aircraft dispatched. The 1st Box was to be led by Lt. Col. D. D. Bentley, but he could not take off, so 1Lt. R. E. Ferguson took over the lead. The 2nd Box was led by Capt. A. R. Pfleger.

Route was Base to Mook (the IP) to target. A fighter sweep was to precede this operation.

No attack; 10/10th cloud starting in the Eindhoven area; unable to bomb on GEE because of jamming. Formation turned around in the area of Wissel at 1628 hrs. Box 1 went down to 8,000 ft. but ran into multilayered cloud. Box 2 tried to go under but was advised by Command not to do so. 272 × 500 GPs bombs returned.

Flak was encountered as the formation made turn two minutes before the target. Moderate inaccurate HFF from Wissel area and Emmerich and Elten areas throughout the turn. 2nd Box encountered intense inaccurate HFF from the Cleve area. No damage received. One aircraft received Cat. AC damage when it ran off the runway on landing; one aircraft sustained Cat. E damage when it crash-landed 10 miles from Base through mechanical difficulties, with three crewmen injured.

Return was a left turn off the target and retrace.

Interrogation of crews began at 1800 hrs. and finished at 1835 hrs.

Mission Notes and "Flak-Bait" Crew Debrief Comments

"Flak-Bait" flew as No. 3 in the low flight, 2nd Box.

8 × 500 GPs brought back.

Weak very inaccurate HFF in target area; continued for 2–3 minutes.

Category E Information

42-107578 PN-W

Pilot was 2Lt. J. L. Cunzeman, flying the No. 6 position in the low flight, 2nd Box. The fuel pressure on the right engine went down, the prop governor was out, and aircraft was unable to maintain airspeed. Aircraft crash-landed 10 miles north of Base, at Maisoncelle-St. Pierre. Three injured: Sgt. J. A. Gardner and Sgt. R. Denczak, but the third crew man is not identified in records (possibly TSgt. M. T. Darnell); all 449th BS.

```
Date: February 15, 1945
Target: Sinzig RR Br
Field Order: 9th BD F/O 749
99th CBW F/O 459
```

"Flak-Bait" Crew

1Lt. H. J. Bye, pilot

2Lt. M. F. Lewonowski, copilot

Sgt. B. N. Foss, togglier

TSgt. D. E. Walton, engineer/gunner

Sgt. W. M. Washer, radio/gunner

SSgt. E. W. Wortman, gunner

Briefing started at 0730 hrs. and ended 0800 hrs.

T/off: 1425 hrs.   Target: 1615 to 1634 hrs.   Return: 1758 hrs.

Mission Narrative

Thirty-four plus three window ships dispatched. The 1st Box was led by Lt. Col. D. D. Bentley, and the 2nd Box by Capt. G. H. Lane.

Route was Base to P-8413 to L-3820 to L-3955 to L-4882 (the IP) to target. Allied fighters to provide area support.

Twenty-one aircraft attacked the primary, releasing 40 × 2,000 GPs for fair to good results; ten aircraft dropped 19 × 2,000 GPs on three casual targets. Lead flight, 1st Box, consisting of four aircraft, could not synchronize and went round for a second run, but sight not working due to a personnel error; was going to hand over to deputy but saw that another group (391st BG) was approaching, so bombed Eller RR bridge (casual 1) for excellent results. Low flight, 2nd Box, consisting of five aircraft, bombed town of Honningen (casual 2) for good results, after a flak hit to the nose prevented release on first run at the primary, and bombardier could not pick out target on the second run. The three window aircraft saw the target too late to set up bombsight, so dropped 21 × 500 GPs on the edge of Bremm town (casual 3), 25 miles southwest of Sinzig, for fair results. Three aircraft had one bomb hang up, two jettisoned over enemy territory, one jettisoned over the Channel, and another released early after leader had taken a flak hit, thinking he had released, dropping 2 × 2,000 GPs on the edge of Sinzig. One aircraft returned 2 × 2,000 GPs, and one window ship had 3 × 500 GPs hang up, which were returned.

Moderate accurate to intense accurate HFF on second run at target; weak inaccurate HFF also reported from Weidenbach. Four aircraft Cat. AC damage, ten aircraft Cat. A, and one aircraft MIA.

Return was a right turn off the target and retrace.

Interrogation of crews began at 1820 hrs. and finished at 1900 hrs.

Mission Notes and "Flak-Bait" Crew Debrief Comments

"Flak-Bait" flew as No. 6 in the high flight, 2nd Box.

2 × 2,000 GPs dropped; results good; hits at immediate target; one run made.

HFF encountered at the target; no damage received.

MIA Information

44-67907 DR-M

No. 3 in the low flight, 2nd Box. Lost to flak on the second run at 1628 hrs.; aircraft began to lag behind, with the right engine smoking and with occasional shots of flame coming out. Aircraft started to dive and went into a spin and was seen to crash and explode near Sinzig; four chutes seen.

450th BS crew

2Lt. F. D. Barzilauskas, pilot	POW
2Lt. D. G. Newstrand, copilot	POW
1Lt. A. W. Morris, navigator/bombardier	POW
Sgt. M. C. Martin, engineer/gunner	POW
Sgt. R. L. Singer, radio/gunner	POW
Sgt. E. P. Lankston Jr., gunner	KIA

```
Date: February 16, 1945
Target: Rees Comm Cen
Field Order: 9th BD F/O 750
99th CBW F/O 460
```

"Flak-Bait" Crew

450th BS crew

2Lt. W. E. Stanley, pilot	Sgt. F. E. Smith engineer/gunner
2Lt. J. M. Corbitt, copilot	Sgt. P. Wohl, radio/gunner
2Lt. W. C. Lane, navigator/bombardier	Sgt. W. T. Snyder, gunner

Briefing started at 0630 hrs. and ended 0715 hrs.

T/off: 1125 hrs.   Target: 1214 & 1223 hrs.   Return: 1335 hrs.

Mission Narrative

PFF mission; thirty aircraft plus two window and two PFF aircraft dispatched; the 1st Box was led by Maj. P. Shannon, and the 2nd Box by Maj. L. J. Sebille.

Route was Base to Eindhoven to Batenburg to target. 2nd TAF to provide area cover.

Area bombing, thirty-one aircraft dropped 120 × 500 M17 IBs and 120 × 500 GPs on the primary; weather was thick haze to 5,000 ft., with visibility about 3 miles. The two window aircraft dropped 16 × 500 GPs on Wesel, one of which observed a huge explosion. Box 1 bombed on PFF on the first run; the bombs fell in a scattered pattern outside the target area. Box 2 bombed by flights, each making two runs; lead flight results undetermined, since they fell into smoke, but crews thought they achieved excellent results. High flight: no coverage, but new fires were observed north of the target area. The low flight's bombs fell beyond the designated target area, when leader had an accidental release of one bomb behind the PFF ship, and the rest of the flight released on this drop. The lead aircraft of this flight went around again, alone, to drop the seven remaining bombs, saying results were good. PFF aircraft for 2nd Box returned 4 × 500 GPs after group took over two minutes before the target, and so left formation.

Box 1 encountered weak inaccurate HFF in immediate target area. Box 2 experienced moderate accurate HFF from Goch, Xanten, and Emmerich. One aircraft Cat. AC and ten Cat. A damage: includes the PFF ship from the 2nd Box.

Return was a right turn off the target to Esch to Eindhoven to Base.

Interrogation of crews began at 1415 hrs. and finished at 1515 hrs.

Mission Notes and "Flak-Bait" Crew Debrief Comments

"Flak-Bait" flew as No. 3 in the high flight, 2nd Box.

8 × 500 M17 IBs dropped; excellent results.

Cat. A damage; a few small flak holes. Moderate fairly accurate HFF at target.

```
Date: February 18, 1945
Target: Dottesfeld RR Br
Field Order: 9th BD F/O 752
99th CBW F/O 462
```

"Flak-Bait" Crew

2Lt. H. K. Megson, pilot	Sgt. H. T. Neidenberg, engineer/gunner
2Lt. W. J. Poplack, copilot	Sgt. W. M. Washer, radio/gunner
F/O O. D. Fields, navigator/bombardier	Sgt. H. M. Szewczak, gunner

Briefing started at 0815 hrs. and ended 0835 hrs.

T/off: 1350 hrs.　　　　Target: 1551 & 1552 hrs. (P)　　　Return: 1715 hrs.
　　　　　　　　　　　　1603 (Casual) hrs.

Mission Narrative

PFF mission. Thirty-three plus three window and one PFF aircraft dispatched. The 1st Box was led by Maj. J. C. Ruse, and the 2nd Box was led by Capt. A. R. Pfleger.

Route was Base to P-8413 to L-3821 to Great Littgen to Boos (the IP) to target. IX TAC to provide area cover.

Formation encountered 10/10th multilayered cloud. Box 1, lead and high flights, and all of Box 2 dropped on the PFF, twenty-five aircraft dropping 94 × 1,000 GPs and 4 × 500 GPs from 13,500 and 11,750 ft.; results unobserved. One aircraft ("Flak-Bait") dropped 1 × 1,000 GP nine minutes after the target, near Nassau, after it had hung up at the target. The low flight, 1st Box, was in cloud and not in position at the time of release, so dropped 24 × 1,000 GPs on Burgen, using GEE. The window aircraft did not release; clouds were too high, preventing them from getting to their target at Simmern. The No. 6 aircraft of the low flight, 2nd Box, could not catch the formation so contacted "Ripsaw," who guided them over enemy territory and told them when to release their load of 4 × 1,000 GPs; location was unknown. One aircraft returned early when it iced up, and another had fuel pressure low so returned from the Reinsfeld area, returning 4 × 1,000 GPs each. Window aircraft returned 12 × 1,000 GPs, and one other 1,000 GP hung up.

Weak to moderate inaccurate HFF encountered near Laacher Lake. One flight became separated and encountered weak to moderate accurate HFF at Boppard; fired through 10/10th cloud. Four aircraft received Cat. A damage.

Return was a right turn to Freilingen to Nastatten to Senheim to Great Littgen to Base. The low flight, Box 1, became separated and returned alone, deviating from the briefed return route.

Interrogation of crews began at 1745 hrs. and finished at 1815 hrs.

Mission Notes and "Flak-Bait" Crew Debrief Comments

"Flak-Bait" flew as No. 6 in the high flight, 1st Box.

Dropped 3 × 1,000 GPs bombs on primary on PFF; 1 × 1,000 GP hung up and fell through bomb bay doors, damaging them; fell near Nassau nine minutes after the target.

Weak inaccurate HFF at the IP.

Other Crew Comments

PFF reported that the group followed very well through adverse weather conditions.

"Flak-Bait" Crew

1Lt. W. C. Cornwall, pilot
2Lt. C. W. Honhold, copilot
2Lt. G. F. Meily, navigator/bombardier

TSgt. T. W. Gatzounas, engineer/gunner
Sgt. R. H. Pacey, radio/gunner
Sgt. E. M. Little, gunner

Briefing started at 1015 hrs. and ended 1050 hrs.
T/off: 1330 hrs.   Target: 1544 & 1551 (w) hrs.   Return: 1711 hrs.

Mission Narrative

PFF mission. Thirty-three plus three window and one PFF aircraft dispatched. The 1st Box was led by Capt. J. H. McCarty, and the 2nd Box by Capt. G. H. Lane.

Route was Base to Great Littgen to P-6004 to Zissen to Honningen to target. IX TAC to provide area cover.

Encountered 8–10/10th cloud, with tops at 8–9,000 ft. between the IP and the target, so attacked on PFF. Thirty-four aircraft attacked, including one window aircraft that could not get ahead of the formation and dropped with the low flight, 2nd Box. 132 × 1,000 GPs and 4 × 500 GPs dropped on the primary from 12,500 and 12,700 ft.; results unobserved. Two window aircraft found GEE equipment jammed at their briefed target of Nastatten, so bombed Kisselbach as a casual target, releasing 8 × 1,000 GPs from 10,600 ft. at 1551 hrs. One aircraft had one bomb hang up at target, so jettisoned in enemy territory, and 3 × 1,000 GPs were returned.

1st Box encountered weak inaccurate HFF from Honningen area; the 2nd Box encountered weak inaccurate HFF from Laacher. The window aircraft reported weak inaccurate HFF coming from the Zissen area, and weak inaccurate LFF when crossing front lines of east of Luxembourg. No damage received.

Return was a right turn to Freilingen to Nastatten to Senheim to Great Littgen to Base.

Interrogation of crews began at 1720 hrs. and finished at 1750 hrs.

Mission Notes and "Flak-Bait" Crew Debrief Comments

"Flak-Bait" scheduled to fly as No. 5 in the high flight, 2nd Box, but moved up to the No. 2 position in the flight (the aircraft that was due to fly No. 2 position joined the low flight of the 1st Box).

4 × 1,000 GPs dropped; results unobserved.

As the 322nd entered enemy territory, they observed another group coming out, about 5 miles to the north, which appeared to be getting heavy flak fire.

Other Crew Comments

PFF complained that group was not formed up in time over the field, but commented that formation flying was excellent.

The group noted that the PFF flew too much evasive action and did not smooth out soon enough.

"Flak-Bait" Crew

Capt. H. K. Levy, pilot
2Lt. L. L. Pisel, copilot
F/O J. Facok, navigator/bombardier

Sgt. W. H. Myers, engineer/gunner
Sgt. A. J. Villasenor, radio/gunner
Sgt. D. H. Summerville, gunner

Briefing started at 0705 hrs. and ended 0815 hrs.; at 1005 hrs. a 90-minute delay announced.
T/off: not recorded   Target: 1401 hrs.   Return: 1511 hrs.

Mission Narrative

Seventeen aircraft dispatched, to rendezvous with a flight of six aircraft from the 344th BG; formation was led by Capt. A. R. Pfleger.

Route was Base to Cambrai, to rendezvous with the 344th BG flight at 6,000 ft., to Eindhoven to Helmond to Goch (the IP) to target. 2nd TAF to provide area cover.

Bombing by flights, each on a different road junction, a total of twenty-three aircraft dropped 92 × 1,000 GPs (the seventeen aircraft of the 322nd BG dropped 68 × 1,000 GPs), from 11,250 to 11,700 ft. in CAVU conditions. One aircraft from the 344th BG did not bomb. The three flights from the 322nd BG achieved superior, excellent, and excellent results, respectively. The results for the flight from the 344th BG were unsatisfactory with bombs 1,710 ft. southeast of DMPI, the bomb run being too short.

Formation encountered moderate accurate HFF from the IP that continued until the target, with the intensity increasing as target was approached, and on the return trip. Three aircraft from the 322nd BG received Cat. A damage (four aircraft from the 344th BG also received Cat. A damage, with one crewman wounded).

Return was a right turn and retrace route in.

Interrogation of crews began at 1734 hrs. and finished at 1750 hrs.

Mission Notes and "Flak-Bait" Crew Debrief Comments

"Flak-Bait" flew as No. 5 in the low flight.

4 × 1,000 GPs dropped; observed good results.

Weak inaccurate HFF from bomb line to target; no damage.

Other Crew Comments

Friendly fighters should not make pass at our formation; passes made in Brussels area.

Two Me 109s observed in the target area at 14–15,000 ft.; another single-engine aircraft seen while group was on the bomb run at 1400 hrs.

At 1355 hrs., observed a B-26 from another group hit by flak and went into a steep dive, out of control.

Date: February 22, 1945
Target: Butzbach M/Ys
Field Order: Operation "Clarion" #46

"Flak-Bait" Crew

2Lt. E. C. Pakish, pilot
2Lt. S. A. Norstrom, copilot
TSgt. G. D. Tesnow, togglier

SSgt. S. J. Nicoletti, engineer/gunner
SSgt. J. A. Smith, radio/gunner
SSgt. M. B. Schmidt, gunner

Briefing started at 0650 hrs. and ended 0735 hrs.
T/off: 1125 to 1148 hrs.   Target: 1328 to 1346 hrs.   Return: 1511 to 1538 hrs.

Mission Narrative

Operation Clarion, which had been planned since December 1944, was aimed at seriously disrupting the enemy's transportation and communications infrastructure, with all groups dispatched against rail and road centers, and, unusually, some of the bombers were briefed to descend to low altitude and strafe any targets of opportunity.

Fifty-three aircraft dispatched in three boxes. The 1st Box was led by Col. J. S. Samuel, the 2nd Box by Lt. Col. J. B. Smith, and the 3rd Box by Capt. J. H. McCarty.

Routing was from base to Luxembourg to Reinsfeld to Wittlich to Cochem; details from this point on are not entirely clear, but the formation split at a point between Koblenz and Wiesbaden to their individual targets; the 1st and 2nd Boxes went on to Schmitten (the IP), where they divided up to their individual targets and then returned via the same route. Details of fighter support not known.

Weather was CAVU but with haze at all targets.

Box 1: Freidburg "34" roundhouse and flyover; eighteen aircraft dispatched and sixteen attacked, dropping 20 × 1,000 GPs and 96 × 500 GPs, the 1st flight on the roundhouse and the rest on the flyover. Results excellent, excellent, and unsatisfactory; haze hindered bombing. No damage received. One aircraft, with a loss of power, returned early with 4 × 1,000 GPs.

Box 2: Lang Gons "48" tracks and bridge; twelve aircraft dispatched and eleven attacked, dropping 88 × 500 GPs, for superior results. Weak inaccurate HFF encountered on the bomb run, moderate accurate LFF on the strafing run, and weak inaccurate HFF over Trier on the way out. One aircraft was an early return with the throttle sticking; 8 × 500 GPs returned. One aircraft Cat. AC, three aircraft Cat. A, and one aircraft MIA.

Butzbach "46" M/Y; six aircraft dispatched and all released, dropping 48 × 500 GPs with excellent results. Moderate accurate HFF encountered from the Wiesbaden area, weak accurate LFF encountered from 2 miles south of Butzbach and into the town on the strafing run, and weak inaccurate HFF from Bad Neuhem. One aircraft Cat. A damage.

Box 3: Niederhausen "51" platform and flyover; twelve aircraft dispatched, with one flight on the platform and one on the flyover. All attacked, dropping 96 × 500 GP for superior results.

Montabaur bridge "10"; five aircraft dispatched and all attacked, dropping 36 × 500 GPs, having made three runs at the target. Results were unsatisfactory due to haze. Weak accurate LFF was encountered on the strafing run. One aircraft Cat. AC and three Cat. A. One aircraft crashed on takeoff: one killed, six injured, Cat. E.

Interrogation of crews began at 1520 hrs. and finished at 1745 hrs.

Mission Notes and "Flak-Bait" Crew Debrief Comments

"Flak-Bait" flew as No. 5 in the low flight, 2nd Box, to attack Butzbach "46."

8 × 500 GPs dropped from 7,500 ft. Fair results; hit short of the target.

No flak at target, light flak on deck only.

Cat. A damage; landed at A-68, Juvincourt, at 1510 hrs. (While the records show only Cat. A damage, it is probable that the damage was more severe, since repairs took some time to complete.)

Train observed going into town of Lich, approximately twenty cars in length.

Other Crew Comments

B-26 not built for strafing and not planned enough; did not come down low enough.

MIA Information

42-107745 ER-O, "Mrs. Mac"

Lead aircraft of the 2nd Box. Hit by LFF after bombs away, while on strafing run at 300 ft. Both engines were on fire; aircraft was seen to turn as if to make a crash landing but dug left wing in and crashed and exploded at Pohl Gons.

Lt. Col. J. B. Smith, pilot	KIA; 450th BS CO (replaced by Maj. John L. Egan)
1Lt. J. B. Mossman, copilot	KIA
Capt. G. H. Thiebault, navigator/bombardier	KIA
1Lt. D. H. Dorr, bombardier	KIA
SSgt. W. L. Jennings, engineer/gunner	KIA
TSgt. L. F. Rehmi, radio/gunner	KIA
SSgt. J. R. Callahan, gunner	KIA
SSgt. J. R. Logan, gunner	KIA

Category E Information

43-34433 PN-P

Lead aircraft of the low flight, 3rd Box. Crashed off the end of the runway on takeoff and exploded several minutes later; one killed and six injured.

Capt. E. R. Bruner, pilot	injured
2Lt. F. M. Kelly, copilot	injured

1Lt. I. Pincus, navigator	injured
Capt. R. H. Buk, bombardier	KIA; group bombardier
SSgt. A. E. Duvall, radio/gunner	injured
TSgt. N. A. Chapman, engineer/gunner	injured
SSgt. W. J. Hess, gunner	injured

The blast from this aircraft also destroyed a parked B-26 42-107739, assigned to the 391st BG.

The tragic aftermath of the takeoff accident involving aircraft 43-34433 PN-P as she burns and explodes off the end of the runway. *Mike Smith, B26.com*

Date: March 9, 1945
Target: Wiesbaden Stores Depot
Field Order: 9th BD F/O 782
99th CBW F/O 486

"Flak-Bait" Crew

1Lt. H. C. Bozarth, pilot	TSgt. W. L. Johnston, engineer/gunner
1Lt. S. V. N. Best, copilot	TSgt. M. T. Darnell Jr., radio/gunner
Sgt. T. B. Gee, togglier	Sgt. R. L. Bassler, gunner

Briefing started at 0700 hrs. and ended 0715 hrs.

| T/off: 0950 hrs. | Target: 1217½ & 1218 hrs. | Return: 1356 hrs. |
| | 1230 hrs. (w) | |

Mission Narrative

PFF mission. Thirty plus three window and two PFF aircraft dispatched. The 1st Box was led by Maj. J. C. Ruse, and the 2nd Box by 1Lt. R. L. Beeson.

Route was Base to 49.57'N, 05.00'E (Yoncq), to Bastogne to Kyllburg to Nastatten to Westerburg to 50.47'N, 08.23'E (west of Kirschhofen), to Grunberg to 50.27'N, 08.48'E (east of Schmitten), the IP, to target. 8th FC to provide area cover.

Thirty-one aircraft attacked on PFF through 10/10th cloud, dropping 464 × 250 GPs and 8 × 500 GP bombs from 10,500 ft.; results were unobserved. The three window ships dropped on their primary at Simmern, on GEE, dropping 48 × 250 GPs. One aircraft was an early return when the left gun misfired in the top turret and damaged the vertical stabilizer; 16 × 250 GPs returned.

Moderate to intense inaccurate HFF at the target, continuing for two minutes; this seemed to be from the edge of Wiesbaden, with most bursting in the window cloud. Weak to moderate inaccurate HFF also encountered from Giessen. One aircraft received Cat. A damage.

Return was a right turn to Nastatten to Kyllburg and retrace.

Interrogation of crews began at 1345 hrs. and finished at 1445 hrs.

Mission Notes and "Flak-Bait" Crew Debrief Comments

"Flak-Bait" flew as one of the window ships.

16 × 250 GPs dropped on GEE; flak shooting at the window and the window aircraft; flak at the target was generally trailing.

> **Date: March 10, 1945**
> **Target: Erndtebruck M/Y**
> **Field Order: 9th BD F/O 783**
> **99th CBW F/O 487**

"Flak-Bait" Crew

2Lt. J. H. Alderson, pilot
1Lt. M. F. Lewonowski, copilot
F/O T. R. Lee, navigator/bombardier

Sgt. J. W. Bradley, engineer/gunner
Sgt. W. A. Markley, radio/gunner
Sgt. J. A. Keating, gunner

Briefing started at 0930 hrs. and ended 0955 hrs.
T/off: 1236 hrs.   Target: 1438½ & 1439½ hrs.   Return: 1603 hrs.

Mission Narrative

PFF mission. Thirty plus two PFF aircraft dispatched. The 1st Box was led by Lt. Col. D. D. Bentley, and the 2nd Box by 1Lt. A. P. Lee.

Briefed route was Base to rendezvous with XXIX TAC fighter escort at K-7905 to Sinzig to Dreisbach to target.

Thirty-two aircraft dropped on the PFF, releasing 240 × 500 GPs and 8 × 500 IBs; results were unobserved. Weather was 10/10th cloud with tops at 6,500–7,000 ft.

No flak or damage received.

Return was a left turn to Sinzig, to Malmedy and retrace route in.

Interrogation of crews began at 1630 hrs. and finished at 1700 hrs.

Mission Notes and "Flak-Bait" Crew Debrief Comments

"Flak-Bait" flew as No. 6 in the low flight, 2nd Box.

8 × 500 GPs dropped; results unobserved.

Other Crew Comments

Fighters did not catch formation until after the turn off target.

PFF commented that the group's formation was superior.

> **Date: March 11, 1945**
> **Target: Ettinghausen A/F**
> **Field Order: 9th BD F/O 785**
> **99th CBW F/O 488**

"Flak-Bait" Crew

1Lt. H. C. Bozarth, pilot
2Lt. S. J. Price, copilot
Sgt. T. B. Gee, togglier

TSgt. W. L. Johnston, engineer/gunner
TSgt. M. T. Darnell Jr., radio/gunner
Sgt. R. L. Bassler, gunner

Briefing started at 0730 hrs. and ended 0755 hrs.
T/off: 1010 hrs.   Target: 1228 & 1229 hrs.   Return: 1405 hrs.
                          1232 hrs. (w)

Mission Narrative

PFF mission. Thirty plus three window and two PFF aircraft dispatched. The 1st Box was led by Maj. J. L. Egan, and the 2nd Box by Capt. J. L. Lane.

Route was Base to rendezvous with XXIX TAC fighters at P-5658, to Sinzig to Hachenburg to Berleburg to Bromkirchen to Laubach to target.

Thirty-two aircraft dropped 245 × 500 GPs on the primary, from 12,450 and 13,100 ft., through 10/10th cloud with the tops at 5,000 ft. The three window ships dropped 24 × 500 GPs on Butzbach on ETA, since GEE was jammed. One aircraft had a gas leak so returned early with 8 × 500 GPs; a further 3 × 500 GPs were returned through rack failures.

No flak encountered.

Return was a right turn to Butzbach to Westerburg to P-6516 and retrace.

Interrogation of crews began at 1420 hrs. and finished at 1450 hrs.

Mission Notes and "Flak-Bait" Crew Debrief Comments

"Flak-Bait" flew as No. 2 in the lead flight, 2nd Box.

8 × 500 GPs dropped on PFF ship.

How about some transportation from ships? (five crews from the 449th BS made this comment).

Other Crew Comments

PFF stated that the group formation was excellent and that the window ships were good.

```
Date: March 14, 1945
Target: Niederscheld RR Br
Field Order: 9th BD F/O 791
99th CBW F/O 495
```

"Flak-Bait" Crew

1Lt. H. C. Bozarth, pilot

1Lt. S. V. N. Best, copilot

Sgt. T. B. Gee, togglier

TSgt. W. L. Johnston, engineer/gunner

TSgt. M. T. Darnell Jr., radio/gunner

Sgt. R. L. Bassler, gunner

Briefing started at 0830 hrs. and ended 0900 hrs.

T/off: 1300 & 1320 hrs.   Target: 1450 to 1452 hrs., 1st Box   Return: 1619 & 1657 hrs.
1513, 1514 & 1524 hrs., 2nd Box

Mission Narrative

Forty-eight aircraft dispatched in two boxes of twenty-four aircraft each in four flights. The 1st Box was led by Lt. Col. D. D. Bentley, and the 2nd Box by Maj. J. C. Ruse; the 2nd Box trailed the 1st Box by twenty minutes.

Route was Base to rendezvous with XXIX TAC fighter escort at Arlon to Cochem to Nastatten to Hachenburg to 50.47'N, 08.00'E (south of Dornburg), the IP, to the target.

Forty-seven aircraft attacked by flights in CAVU conditions, dropping 94 × 2,000 GPs from 11,000 and 10,000 ft. Lead flight, 1st Box, achieved superior results; all the other flights achieved excellent results. The lead flight, 2nd Box, made two runs. One aircraft had an engine cut out and jettisoned 2 × 2,000 GPs "safe" at Mougen, in friendly territory; this aircraft landed at A-68 (Juvincourt) on single engine.

Weak accurate HFF experienced by the 2nd Box from Nastatten, Nassau, and Bendorf. No flak encountered by the 1st Box. One aircraft received Cat. AC damage and one MIA. One crewman was injured: Sgt. J. F. Myers, 450th BS, along with six MIA.

Return was a right turn to Laacher Lake to Base.

Interrogation of crews began at 1635 hrs. and finished at 1715 hrs.

Mission Notes and "Flak-Bait" Crew Debrief Comments

"Flak-Bait" flew as No. 2 in the lead flight, 1st Box.

2 × 2,000 GPs dropped; observed good results. Target area covered with smoke.

Twenty-three freight cars observed in yard at Hachenburg, and sixteen railroad cars in a siding at the IP.

Flak observed three minutes from the IP but not experienced.

MIA Information
44-68100 ER-W

Flying No. 6 position in the low flight, 2nd Box. Hit by flak in the cockpit area and seen to crash and explode 1 mile southeast of Bonfeld; one chute was reported from the waist position.

2Lt. J. W. Logue, pilot	KIA
2Lt. R. C. Patrick Jr., copilot	RTD
F/O M. E. Donaldson, navigator/bombardier	KIA
Sgt. R. B. Munson Jr., engineer/gunner	KIA
Sgt. D. E. Marshall, radio/gunner	KIA
Sgt. D. V. Rosfeld, gunner	KIA

```
Date: March 15, 1945
Target: Neunkirchen Comm Cen
Field Order: 9th BD F/O 794
99th CBW F/O 496
```

"Flak-Bait" Crew

1Lt. H. C. Bozarth, pilot
1Lt. S. V. N. Best, copilot
Sgt. T. B. Gee, togglier

TSgt. W. L. Johnston, engineer/gunner
Sgt. J. S. Devine, radio/gunner
Sgt. R. L. Bassler, gunner

Briefing started at 1000 hrs. and ended 1030 hrs.

T/off: 1245 hrs.   Target: 1421, 1431 & 1432 hrs.   Return: 1552 hrs.

Mission Narrative

Forty-two aircraft dispatched; the 1st Box was led by Capt. A. R. Pfleger, and the 2nd Box, made up of four flights, was led by Capt. J. L. Lane.

Route was Base to Dienkirch to the troop line to L-5409 (the IP) to target. XXIX TAC to provide area cover.

Forty-two aircraft attacked, in clear conditions but with haze, dropping 334 × 500 M17 IBs (set to air-burst at 5,000 ft.) from 11,000 to 12,500 ft., for superior and excellent results; many fires were seen. Lead and high flights of the 1st Box made two runs; the rest dropped on their first run. 2 × 500 M17s returned through rack failure.

Weak inaccurate LFF reaching 8,000 ft. at the target. No damage received.

Return was a right turn and retrace route in.

Interrogation of crews began at 1620 hrs. and finished at 1645 hrs.

41-32010, originally coded PN-L but recoded as PN-C by July 23, 1944, flew her last mission on March 15, 1945; the aircraft was declared as salvaged in June 1945. *Smithsonian National Air and Space Museum, NASM 00068361*

Mission Notes and "Flak-Bait" Crew Debrief Comments

"Flak-Bait" flew as No. 2 in the lead flight, 2nd Box.

8 × 500 M17 IBs dropped; observed good results.

```
Date: March 16, 1945
Target: Niederscheld RR Br
Field Order: 9th BD F/O 796
99th CBW F/O 497
```

"Flak-Bait" Crew

1Lt. W. C. Cornwall, pilot	SSgt. T. W. Gatzounas, engineer/gunner
2Lt. C. W. Honhold, copilot	SSgt. R. H. Pacey, radio/gunner
2Lt. G. F. Meily, navigator/bombardier	Sgt. M. Kushmer, gunner

Briefing started at 0900 hrs.; no end time recorded.

T/off: 1240 hrs.   Target: 1446, 1457, 1525 & 1533 (c) hrs.   Return: 1635 hrs.

Mission Narrative

Twenty-four aircraft dispatched in four flights, led by Maj. J. C. Ruse.

Route was Base to Bastogne to Bremm to Nastatten to 50.44'N, 07.47'E (Neuwied), to 50.43'N, 07.58'E (Bendorf), to target. XXIX TAC to provide area cover.

Cloud 5/10th with tops at 8–9,000 ft. and thick haze made target observation very difficult. Bombing by flights. Eighteen aircraft attacked the primary, dropping 36 × 2,000 GPs. Flight 1 dropped after two runs, at 1446 hrs. The results were unsatisfactory; bombardier misidentified the target and attacked a bridge ¾ mile northwest of Biedenkopf, which was 16 miles northeast of the DMPI. Flight 2: no attack due to cloud cover; made four runs at the target. Flight 3 dropped at 1457 hrs. after three runs; results were undetermined. The 4th flight dropped at 1525 hrs., after three runs, with excellent results. One aircraft dropped 2 × 2,000 GPs on a casual target at Hachenburg at 1533 hrs., after the bomb bay doors would not open at the IP. Two aircraft accidentally released 4 × 2,000 GPs on southern end of Niederscheld. Four aircraft returned 8 × 2,000 GPs, one because of a mechanical failure and three because the leader did not drop.

Weak inaccurate HFF from Wissen and Hachenburg. Three aircraft received Cat. A damage.

Return was a left turn off the target to 50.44'N, 07.47'E (Neuweid), and retrace route in.

Interrogation of crews began at 1700 hrs. and finished at 1745 hrs.

Mission Notes and "Flak-Bait" Crew Debrief Comments

"Flak-Bait" flew as No. 5 in Flight 2 (high flight).

No attack; 2 × 2,000 GPs returned; made five runs ([*sic*] mission report says four runs were made).

Inaccurate HFF encountered at IP.

```
Date: March 17, 1945
Target: Neustadt M/Y
Field Order: 9th BD F/O 798
99th CBW F/O 498
```

"Flak-Bait" Crew

1Lt. H. C. Bozarth, pilot	TSgt. W. L. Johnston, engineer/gunner
1Lt. S. V. N. Best, copilot	TSgt. M. Darnell Jr., radio/gunner
SSgt. T. B. Gee, togglier	SSgt. R. L. Bassler, gunner

Briefing started at 0745 hrs. and ended 0800 hrs.

T/off: 1020 hrs.   Target: 1209½ & 1217 hrs. (w)   Return: 1340 hrs.

Mission Narrative

PFF mission. Thirty-four plus three window and one PFF aircraft dispatched. The 1st Box was led by 1Lt. R. L. Beeson, with Capt. L. W. Rice. The 2nd Box was led by Capt. W. G. Fort.

Route was Base to 49.57'N, 05.00'E (Yoncq), to Bastogne to Bremm to Kirchberg to 49.50'N, 07.46'E (Matzenbach), the IP, to the target. No fighter cover scheduled.

Bombing on PFF, thirty-four aircraft dropped 268 × 500 GPs on the primary, from 12,500 and 13,000 ft. through 10/10th cloud with tops at 9,000 ft. The three window aircraft dropped 24 × 500 GPs on their briefed target at Landau on ETA, after a GEE failure. One aircraft returned early due to a fuel leak; 8 × 500 GPs returned.

Return was a right turn to Wingen to Metz to Base.

Interrogation of crews began at 1400 hrs. and finished at 1445 hrs.

Mission Notes and "Flak-Bait" Crew Debrief Comments

"Flak-Bait" flew as No. 5 in the low flight, 2nd Box.

8 × 500 GPs dropped on PFF.

Saw balloon and fired at it, with many hits, but balloon did not go down.

```
Date: March 18, 1945
Target: Wetzlar M/Y
Field Order: 9th BD F/O 801
99th CBW F/O 500
```

"Flak-Bait" Crew

1Lt. H. C. Bozarth, pilot	TSgt. W. L. Johnston, engineer/gunner
1Lt. S. V. N. Best, copilot	TSgt. M. Darnell Jr., radio/gunner
SSgt. T. B. Gee togglier	SSgt. R. L. Bassler, gunner

Briefing started at 0545 hrs. and ended 0615 hrs.

T/off: 0840 hrs.   Target: 1028½ & 1029 hrs.   Return: 1203 hrs.

Mission Narrative

PFF mission; thirty-six aircraft plus one PFF dispatched. Col. J. S. Samuel led the 1st Box, and Capt. J. L. Lane the 2nd Box.

Route was Base to 49.57'N, 05.00'E (Yoncq), to St. Vith to Laacher Lake to 53.41'N, 07.41'E (east of Ihlow), the IP, to target. IX and XXIX TAC to provide area cover.

7/10th cloud with tops at 6–7,000 ft. with thick haze. Bombed on PFF, but results unsatisfactory; formation was flying through clouds and could not fly close formation; therefore bombing pattern was scattered. Thirty-two aircraft dropped 251 × 500 GPs on the primary, from 12,500 and 13,000 ft. One aircraft was an early return with engine trouble, 8 × 500 GPs returned, and 1 × 500 GP was returned through a rack failure.

Flak was slight but accurate for the lead flight, 1st Box, and inaccurate for the remaining flights. Weak inaccurate HFF was also encountered during the turn off the target. Three aircraft were Cat. E, all in the low flight, 1st Box, after they collided during the form-up; eighteen killed, one injured. The disposition of the bombs on these aircraft (24 × 500 GPs) is undetermined: some exploded, and others to be disposed of by demolition squad.

43-34409 SS-M, one of the three aircraft lost in the terrible collision while forming up on March 18, 1945. *Trevor J. Allen collection*

Return was a right turn to 50.38'N, 07.38'E (Plaidt), to Laacher Lake to Base.
Interrogation of crews began at 1220 hrs. and finished at 1345 hrs.

Mission Notes and "Flak-Bait" Crew Debrief Comments

"Flak-Bait" flew as No. 2 in the lead flight, 2nd Box.
    8 × 500 GPs dropped, for good results.
    Three bursts of inaccurate HFF on way out, 4 miles north of Neuwied.

Category E Information

Three aircraft in the low flight, 1st Box, collided during the formation form-up. The No. 6 aircraft collided with the lead ship, and the debris brought down the No. 4 aircraft. The aircraft came down approximately 2 miles northwest of Beauvais; eighteen killed, one injured, all from the 451st BS.

43-34409 SS-M   Lead aircraft
1Lt. A. Cordes, pilot   injured; thrown clear in collision and managed
                                                         to open parachute

2Lt. R. L. Rice, copilot	KIA
Capt. G. A. Snokleburg, navigator	KIA
2Lt. W. M. Myers, bombardier	KIA
SSgt. J. L. Callaway, engineer/gunner	KIA
TSgt. T. B. Colley, radio/gunner	KIA
SSgt. J. E. Fox, gunner	KIA

43-34155 SS-J   No. 4 aircraft

1Lt. L. E. Barton, pilot	KIA
2Lt. E. U. Moffitt, copilot	KIA
2Lt. J. W. Regmund, navigator/bombardier	KIA
Sgt. J. W. Templeton, engineer/gunner	KIA
Sgt. M. Escamilla, radio/gunner	KIA
Sgt. T. Lamb, gunner	KIA

43-34422 SS-G   No. 6 aircraft

2Lt. J. A. Shettles, pilot	KIA
2Lt. L. F. Watson, copilot	KIA
2Lt. V. Kaston, navigator/bombardier	KIA
Sgt. J. F. Pratt, engineer/gunner	KIA
Sgt. F. W. Wittig, radio/gunner	KIA
Sgt. J. J. Jelly, gunner	KIA

```
Date: March 18, 1945
Target: Bad Durkeim Comm Cen
Field Order: 9th BD F/O 802
99th CBW F/O 501
```

"Flak-Bait" Crew

2Lt. R. H. Pederson, pilot	Sgt. B. K. Packer, engineer/gunner
2Lt. L. C. Stewart, copilot	Sgt. K. K. Korell, radio/gunner
SSgt. T. B. Gee, toggler	Sgt. R. N. Cannon, gunner

Briefing started at 1215 hrs. and ended 1245 hrs.
T/off: 1500 hrs.   Target: 1641 hrs.   Return: 1815 hrs.

Mission Narrative

PFF mission. Thirty-three plus three window and two PFF aircraft dispatched. Lt. Col. D. D. Bentley led the 1st Box, and Lt. Col. H. C. Newcomer the 2nd Box.

Route was Base to L-5971 to Bremm to Stromberg to 49.56'N, 07.45'E (Bedesbach), the IP, to the target. XIX TAC to provide area cover.

10/10th cloud with tops at 6–7,000 ft. was encountered; bombed on PFF. Thirty-five aircraft dropped 868 × 100 GPs and 8 × 500 GPs on the primary, from 12,500 and 11,800 ft. The window aircraft had their GEE equipment jammed, so returned with 84 × 100 GPs bombs.

No opposition met.

Return was a right turn to 49.40'N, 08.00'E (south of Weidenthal), to Bremm to Base.

Interrogation of crews began at 1840 hrs. and finished at 1900 hrs.

Mission Notes and "Flak-Bait" Crew Debrief Comments

"Flak-Bait" flew as No. 4 in the lead flight, 1st Box.

28 × 100 GPs dropped; results unobserved.

Other Crew Comments

PFF crews report that group formation was excellent and that the window ships were good.

> **Date: March 19, 1945**
> **Target: Nieder-Marsberg RR Br**
> **Field Order: 9th BD F/O 803**
> **99th CBW F/O 502**

"Flak-Bait" Crew

2Lt. H. Shudinis, pilot
2Lt. J. H. Carter, copilot
2Lt. J. J. Keenan, navigator/bombardier

Sgt. H. E. Shemoney, engineer/gunner
Sgt. J. Wiygul, radio/gunner
Sgt. M. T. Rimmer, gunner

Briefing started at 0717 hrs.; no end time recorded.
T/off: 1035 hrs.   Target: 1224 hrs.   Return: 1433 hrs.

Mission Narrative

Twenty-four aircraft dispatched in four flights, led by Capt. A. R. Pfleger.

Route was Base to 49.15'N, 05.00'E (east of Le Claon), to rendezvous with 2nd TAF fighters at Vielsalm to Laacher Lake to Hachenburg to the IP to the target. Group to fire green flares at the fighter rendezvous.

Bombing by flights, twenty-three aircraft attacked in CAVU conditions, releasing 45 × 2,000 GPs on the primary, from 11,250 to 12,000 ft. 1 × 2,000 GP jettisoned just north of Nuttlar after it had hung up on the primary. Results for 1st and 2nd flights were superior, with the 3rd and 4th flights being excellent. One aircraft dropped 2 × 2,000 GPs, following a flak hit, 20 miles southwest of the primary.

Moderate very accurate HFF in areas southwest of Hachenburg; twelve aircraft received Cat. A damage. One man injured, 2Lt. C. L. Collier, and one man KIA, Sgt. E. Neely, both from the 451st BS.

Return was a left turn to Hachenburg to Laacher Lake to Base.

The group dispatched another formation of twelve ships that was briefed to attack the Volkmarsen RR bridge, joining thirteen aircraft from the 344th BG, who were to lead. These aircraft dropped 24 × 2,000 GPs for excellent results. This formation encountered moderate accurate HFF in area of Hachenburg, but no damage was received.

Interrogation of crews began at 1445 hrs. and finished at 1520 hrs.

Mission Notes and "Flak-Bait" Crew Debrief Comments

"Flak-Bait" flew as No. 3 in the fourth flight.

   2 × 2,000 GPs dropped; missed bridge, hit approach.

   Moderate accurate HFF at Hachenburg.

   M/Y at target was active, and M/Y at Hachenburg was quite full of cars.

```
Date: March 21, 1945
Target: Stadtlohn Comm Cen
Field Order: 9th BD F/O 807
99th CBW F/O 506
```

"Flak-Bait" Crew
451st BS crew

1Lt. T. G. Laster, pilot	SSgt. J. F. McKeever, engineer/gunner
2Lt. E. H. Schroder, copilot	SSgt. R. Saldato, radio/gunner
2Lt. C. M. Ford, navigator/bombardier	SSgt. K. M. Meyer, gunner

Briefing started at 1200 hrs.; no end time recorded.

T/off: 1500 hrs.   Target: 1652 to 1705 hrs.   Return: 1832 hrs.

Mission Narrative

Thirty-six aircraft dispatched; the 1st Box was led by Col. J. S. Samuel, and the 2nd Box by 1Lt. A. P. Lee.

   Route was Base to 50.20'N, 04.13'E (west of Hestrud), to Goch to Grenlo (the IP) to the target. 2nd TAF to provide area cover.

   Conditions clear but with a lot of battle smoke. Bombing by flights, thirty-five aircraft attacked the primary, dropping 280 × 500 IBs. Results as follows. Box 1, lead flight: superior; made two runs. High flight: excellent after one run, and low flight: excellent after one run. Box 2, lead flight: superior; made one run. High flight: superior; made two runs. The low flight was undetermined due to a camera failure, although the crews reported seeing good results; flight made three runs. One aircraft, on single engine, dropped 8 × 500 IBs at Verseveld, 6 miles northeast of the bomb line.

   Weak inaccurate HFF at the target; moderate flak was encountered at the bomb line both on the route in and out. Moderate accurate HFF at Emmerich, but to the north of Emmerich it was nil to weak and inaccurate. It was felt that bombing with air burst fuses was effective in countering flak. On way out, flak was encountered south of Winterswijk. One aircraft suffered Cat. AC damage, and twelve aircraft had Cat. A.

   Return was a right turn to Grenlo to Goch to Base.

   Interrogation of crews began at 1840 hrs. and finished at 1900 hrs.

Mission Notes and "Flak-Bait" Crew Debrief Comments

"Flak-Bait" flew as No. 5 in the high flight, 1st Box.

   8 × 500 IBs for good results.

   No damage received. Flak from Rees/Emmerich area. Evasive action was effective.

Other Crew Comments

Col. Samuel reported that another group was on same course as we were (we were on course as briefed): plenty of confusion in target area.

CHAPTER 9

Part 7:
March 22, 1945–April 24, 1945,
Central Europe Campaign

Date: March 22, 1945
Target: Sudlohn Comm Cen
Field Order: 9th BD F/O 808
99th CBW F/O 507

"Flak-Bait" Crew

2Lt. H. Shudinis, pilot	Sgt. P. R. Roberts, engineer/gunner
F/O J. E. Dibert, copilot	Sgt. A. E. Varley, radio/gunner
F/O A. G. Sakharoff, navigator/bombardier	Sgt. G. E. Vasco, gunner

Briefing started at 0500 hrs. and ended 0545 hrs.
T/off: 0725 hrs.   Target: 0941½ to 0947 hrs.   Return: 1119 hrs.

Mission Narrative

Thirty-six aircraft dispatched; the 1st Box was led by Maj. J. C. Ruse, and the 2nd Box by Capt. R. L. Beeson.

Route was Base to rendezvous with 2nd TAF fighters; group to fire a green flare at the rendezvous (although crews report that the fighters were not seen), to 50.20'N, 04.13'E (west of Hestrud), to Kevelaar to 51.47'N, 05.42'E (Eindhoven), to 52.08'N, 05.35'E (Maarn), to 52.20'N, 06.01'E (Apeldoorn), to Neuenhaus to Ochtrup (the IP) to target.

Thirty-four aircraft dropped 946 × 100 GPs on or near the primary, in CAVU conditions, from 10,900 to 12,500 ft. Bombing by flights; the results were as follows:

Box 1: lead flight: excellent; high flight: misidentified primary and bombed Stadthein, 4 miles northeast of the target, for excellent results; low flight misidentified target and bombed Stadlohn for excellent results, after two runs.

Box 2: lead flight: excellent; high flight: excellent after two runs; and low flight: unsatisfactory, with bombs dropped 1,150 ft. southeast of DMPI in fields and across some buildings. One aircraft from the low flight had 5 × 100 GPs accidentally fall out of aircraft when the bomb bay doors opened two minutes before the target, and another aircraft released 28 × 100 GPs on this release. 1 × 100 GP returned through rack failure. Disposition of bombs on MIA aircraft unknown.

Intense, inaccurate HFF from Markluiden; weak to moderate, inaccurate HFF from Olst; weak accurate HFF from Rees; and moderate accurate HFF from Emmerich. High flight, 2nd Box, deviated from briefed route and came in range of the Arnhem defenses; moderate accurate HFF experienced, one aircraft MIA. Four other aircraft received Cat. A damage.

Return was a right turn to 51.50'N, 06.33'E (Geldern), to Goch to Base. The high flight, 2nd Box, continued straight on after the target and flew into the Arnhem area.

Interrogation of crews began at 1130 hrs. and finished at 1200 hrs.

Mission Notes and "Flak-Bait" Crew Debrief Comments

"Flak-Bait" flew as No. 2 in the lead flight, 1st Box.

28 × 100 GPs dropped; good hits observed in center of town.

Other Crew Comments

Lead of the low flight, Box 1, reported that a group of A-26s twice crossed course of this group and flew under the formation on the bomb run.

MIA Information

44-67870 ER-J

Flying in the No. 5 position of the high flight, 1st Box. Flight was off course; aircraft was hit by flak in the area of Arnhem and seen to explode and disintegrate in the air, 2 miles east of the Rhine River; 3–4 chutes observed.

449th BS crew

2Lt. H. K. Megson, pilot	POW
2Lt. W. J. Poplack, copilot	POW
Sgt. B. N. Foss, togglier	KIA
Sgt. H. T. Neidenberg, engineer/gunner	POW
Sgt. W. M. Washer Jr., radio/gunner	POW
Sgt. H. M. Szewczak, gunner	KIA

(all had flown on "Flak-Bait," most two or three times)

```
Date: March 22, 1945
Target: Sudlohn Comm Cen
Field Order: 9th BD F/O 809
99th CBW F/O 508
```

"Flak-Bait" Crew

1Lt. F. R. Shaffer, pilot	Sgt. R. C. Mixon, engineer/gunner
2Lt. N. D. Rockefeller, copilot	Sgt. W. J. Bajorek, radio/gunner
2Lt. J. T. Fitzwilliam, navigator/bombardier	Sgt. V. R. Griffin, gunner

Briefing started at 1200 hrs. and ended 1230 hrs.

T/off: 1400 hrs.   Target: 1556 to 1641 hrs.   Return: 1743 hrs.

Mission Narrative

Thirty-six aircraft dispatched; the 1st Box was led by Lt. Col. D. D. Bentley, and the 2nd Box by Lt. Col. H. C. Newcomer.

Route was Base to rendezvous with 2nd TAF fighters at E-4318; group to fire a red flare at the rendezvous point, to E-5957 to E-5396 to Z-8422 to Neede (the IP) to target.

No cloud, but conditions very hazy. Bombing by flights. Results were as follows:

Box 1, lead flight, after two runs at the primary attacked Stadlohn, as did the high flight after one run; eleven aircraft released 275 × 150 GPs. The low flight attacked Enschede after one run at the primary, six aircraft dropping 149 × 150 GPs.

Box 2, lead and high flights attacked the primary; twelve aircraft dropped 150 × 150 GPs and 164 × 100 GPs; both flights made three runs. The low flight attacked Ahaus after one run at the primary, dropping 150 × 150 GPs.

All results were categorized as superior except low flight, 2nd Box, which were excellent. One aircraft returned early with a fuel leak, returning 26 × 150 GPs.

No flak at the target; moderate accurate HFF from Enschede and Hengelo Airfield area, accurate for altitude. Flights that did not bomb primary circled in the area of Hengelo Airfield. Ten aircraft received Cat. A damage.

Return was a left turn off the target and retrace.

Interrogation of crews began at 1755 hrs. and finished at 1830 hrs.

Mission Notes and "Flak-Bait" Crew Debrief Comments

"Flak-Bait" flew as No. 3 in the low flight, 1st Box.

25 × 150 GPs dropped; believed we bombed Enschede with good results.

Very hazy visibility 2–3 miles.

Moderate inaccurate HFF following on turn off target and lasted thirty seconds. Flak came from Enschede; seemed to be aimed at another formation after thirty seconds.

```
Date: March 23, 1945
Target: Dinslaken Comm Cen
Field Order: 9th BD F/O 811
99th CBW F/O 509
```

"Flak-Bait" Crew

1Lt. R. L. Hall, pilot
2Lt. M. F. Lewonowski, copilot
2Lt. C. Brown Jr., navigator/bombardier

SSgt. A. E. Rotman, engineer/gunner
SSgt. E. W. Riggs, radio/gunner
SSgt. J. Barrier, gunner

Briefing started at 0600 hrs. and ended 0645 hrs.

T/off: 0830 hrs.   Target: 1012, 1019 & 1035 hrs.   Return: 1150 hrs.

Mission Narrative

Forty aircraft dispatched; the 1st Box was led by Capt. A. R. Pfleger, and the 2nd Box, made up of four flights, by Col. J. S. Samuel.

Route was Base to Chievres to 50.20'N, 04.13'E (Hestrud), to Weert to Kempen (the IP) to target. 2nd TAF to provide area cover.

Nil cloud but with smoke and haze. Bombing by flights. Thirty-four aircraft attacked the primary, dropping 952 × 100 GP bombs; this includes the No. 4 aircraft of the high flight, 2nd Box, which became separated and joined the 391st BG formation and bombed with them. Results were mainly undetermined, although crews reported seeing good results. Most flights made two or three runs on the target. The 4th flight of the 2nd Box misidentified the target and dropped on Lohberg; results were excellent on the AMPI. In the high flight, 2nd Box, having made two runs at the primary, the leader's PDI went out so handed lead over to deputy, who accidentally clutched in the sight and dropped early; these five aircraft released 140 × 100 GPs on Orsoy, in friendly territory. The No. 4 aircraft in the lead flight, 1st Box, was an early return, with an engine cutting out and losing power, so jettisoned 28 × 100 GPs "safe" in woods 4 miles south of Epinoy in French territory and landed at A-72 (Peronne).

Flak was more intense for the 322nd BG than the rest of formations attacking. The 1st Box encountered moderate fairly accurate HFF on the bomb run and turn off target. On the second and third runs the flak was even more accurate. The 2nd Box encountered only weak inaccurate fire. One aircraft received Cat. AC damage, and eleven aircraft Cat. A damage.

Return was a left turn from the target to Kempen to Weert to Base.

Interrogation of crews began at 1200 hrs. and finished at 1320 hrs.

Mission Notes and "Flak-Bait" Crew Debrief Comments

"Flak-Bait" flew as No. 3 in the lead flight, 2nd Box.

28 × 100 GPs dropped; results unobserved; made two runs.

Weak inaccurate HFF at target just after bombs away. Also LFF going over bomb line. No damage received.

"Flak-Bait" Crew

1Lt. R. L. Hall, pilot
2Lt. S. A. Norstrom, copilot
2Lt. C. Brown Jr., navigator/bombardier

SSgt. A. E. Rotman, engineer/gunner
SSgt. E. W. Riggs, radio/gunner
SSgt. J. Barrier, gunner

Briefing started at 1215 hrs. and ended 1250 hrs.
T/off: 1420 hrs.   Target: 1555 to 1618½ hrs.   Return: 1717 hrs.

Mission Narrative

Thirty-nine aircraft dispatched; the 1st Box was led by Capt. J. L. Lane, and the 2nd Box, consisting of four flights, by Capt. W. G. Fort.

Route was Base to Kempen (the IP) to target. XXIX TAC to provide area cover.

Weather was CAVU with haze; bombing by flights, thirty-seven aircraft dropped 716 × 100 frags and 24 × 100 GPs on the primary from 11,750 to 13,250 ft. Results as follows:

Box 1: lead and high flights made one run and dropped with superior results. The low flight made four runs, but the results were undetermined; bombs fell into the smoke, but results thought to be excellent.

Box 2: lead flight leader had accidental release and deputy dropped on him on first run, releasing 40 × 100 frags in friendly territory. Leader continued run and instructed flight to drop on a flare; flare did not go off, but flight dropped on a radio call from the leader; bombs thought to be just over the target. High and low flights dropped on the first run, for superior results, while the fourth flight made three runs; results were un-determined, but bombs are thought to have fallen 300 ft. northwest of DMPI.

Weak inaccurate HFF at the target area and turn off the target for all flights. One aircraft Cat. A from flak, while nine others were damaged by falling bombs from aircraft ahead: four Cat. AC, four Cat. A, and one Cat. E. One man injured by broken Plexiglas: SSgt. T. E. Blanchard, 451st BS, and one man injured in parachute jump: 2Lt. E. W. Hardy, 451st BS.

Return was a left turn and retrace.

Interrogation of crews began at 1740 hrs. and finished at 1820 hrs.

Mission Notes and "Flak-Bait" Crew Debrief Comments

"Flak-Bait" flew as No. 5 in the lead flight, 1st Box.

20 × M1 A1 frags dropped, for good results.

Plane observed to crash on the edge of woods, at 51.33'N, 06.34'E (vicinity of Grefrath), 1603 hrs.; five chutes seen.

Other Crew Comments

Much criticism over the use of the frag bombs: seventeen crews complained. Bombs open up too soon: fuses too short. If used, stack flights up, not down.

Category E Information
44-68088 SS-P

Pilot was 1Lt. P. C. Gerhard, with Lt. Col. H. C. Newcomer as copilot. No. 4 aircraft in low flight, 2nd Box, hit in the left engine by a bomb falling from preceding aircraft. Left engine caught on fire; aircraft was held under control and crew bailed out from 7,000 ft. All are believed to have landed in friendly territory. Bombardier 2Lt. E. W. Hardy, 451st BS, was slightly injured in the jump. Aircraft came down in the British Second Army Sector, west of the Rhine.

"Flak-Bait" Crew

1Lt. K. W. Goldacker, pilot
2Lt. C. Skoubes, copilot
SSgt. E. L. Arceneaux, togglier

SSgt. J. Foorman, engineer/gunner
TSgt. C. C. Hendrix, radio/gunner
SSgt. J. A. Circelli, gunner

Briefing started at 0345 hrs. and ended 0420 hrs.
T/off: 0635 hrs.   Target: 0834 hrs.   Return: 0957 hrs.

Mission Narrative

Mission was in support of the 21st Army offensive on the Rhine crossing.

PFF mission. Thirty-eight plus three window and one PFF aircraft dispatched. The 1st Box was led by Capt. J. H. McCarty, and the 2nd Box by Lt. Col. F. P. Taylor.

Route was Base to 50.20'N, 04.13'E (Hestrud), to Grave to 52.07'N, 05.37'E (Maarn), to 52.21'N, 06.60'E (Kerspel Goor), to 52.22'N, 06.23'E (Epse), to 52.10'N, 06.19'E (River Ijssel near Cortenoever), the IP, to the target. Allied fighters to provide area support.

Weather was CAVU but with haze; thirty-three aircraft dropped on PFF, releasing 636 × 260 frags and 4 × 500 GPs from 12,500 and 12,200 ft., for fair results; 30% of the bombs fell within 1,000 ft. of DMPI in a good concentration.

A special flight of six aircraft joined a flight from the 344th BG, who led, to attack two flak positions at Zutphen en route (three aircraft on each); 108 × 260 frags were dropped. Bombardiers could not pick out the positions, so dropped on ETA; results unsatisfactory and undetermined.

Nil flak was encountered by the main formation, the special flight 1st element encountered moderate accurate flak, and the 2nd element encountered weak inaccurate flak; one aircraft Cat. A damage.

Return was a right turn to Grave and Base.

Interrogation of crews began at 0950 hrs. and finished at 1000 hrs.

Mission Notes and "Flak-Bait" Crew Debrief Comments

"Flak-Bait" flew as No. 2 in the low flight, 2nd Box.

18 × 260 M81 frags dropped (one of two aircraft to have a load of eighteen bombs; the rest had a load of twenty).

Weak inaccurate flak just over target.

Saw C-47 and gliders and a convoy of vehicles: was called in.

"Flak-Bait" Crew
452nd BS crew

1Lt. H. E. Holland, pilot
2Lt. A. J. Hillsamer, copilot
[none listed] navigator/bombardier

SSgt. C. B. Waganer, engineer/gunner
Sgt. V. Marcella, radio/gunner
Sgt. R. M. Fragoso, gunner

Briefing started at 0600 hrs. and ended 0650 hrs.
T/off: 0905 hrs.   Target: 1109 to 1201 hrs.   Return: 1320 hrs.

Mission Narrative

Thirty-seven aircraft dispatched; the 1st Box was led by Maj. J. C. Ruse, and the 2nd Box by Capt. R. L. Beeson.

Route was Base to Cochem to St. Goar to 50.19'N, 07.55'E (Kratzenburg), to 50.31'N 07.56'E (Rhine River near Koblenz), the IP, to the target. No fighter support was scheduled.

Nil cloud below the formation, but bombardiers had difficulty picking out the target. Bombing by flights, seventeen aircraft dropped 66 × 1,000 GPs on the primary, and fifteen dropped 60 × 1,000 GPs on three casual targets, while a flak suppression flight of three aircraft dropped 54 × 260 frag bombs. 18 × 1,000 GPs were returned. Details and results as follows:

Box 1, lead flight: five runs on primary; five aircraft dropped 22 × 1,000 GPs at 1201 hrs., but results were unsatisfactory due to a late release because of an intervalometer problem. One aircraft returned 2 × 1,000 GPs because of a rack failure.

Box 1, high flight: after three runs at the primary, four aircraft dropped 16 × 1,000 GPs on Mundersbach at 1150 hrs. as a casual target; results thought to be good. One aircraft was an early return through a loss of power, and one was abortive because of weather after the aircraft iced up. 8 × 1,000 GPs returned.

Box 1, low flight: after two runs at primary, five aircraft dropped 20 × 1,000 GPs on Altenkirchen M/Y at 1152 hrs. as a casual target, for superior results. One aircraft had a fire in the VHF set on the bomb run so did not release; 4 × 1,000 GPs returned.

Box 2, lead flight: six aircraft dropped 24 × 1,000 GPs on primary at 1119 hrs., but results were unsatisfactory; after an accidental release while lining up on the target, bombs dropped near the town of Raubach, 6½ miles southeast of the DMPI.

Box 2, high flight: after one run at the primary, six aircraft released 24 × 1,000 GPs on rail lines at Seelbach at 1127 hrs. as a casual target, for excellent results.

Box 2, low flight: five aircraft dropped 20 × 1,000 GPs on the primary at 1144 hrs., on the first run, for excellent results. One aircraft was abortive after it iced up; 4 × 1,000 GPs returned.

Flak suppression flight: three aircraft were briefed to bomb flak positions on the route at Limburg two minutes before the main formation. They released 54 × 260 frags, but the results were unsatisfactory, landing 900 ft. west of probable flak position after two runs.

All flights encountered moderate, accurate HFF on the turn off the target on second to fifth runs. While making the extra runs, moderate accurate fire was encountered from Mudenbach, Herschbach, and Hachenburg; this fire increased to intense accurate on the third and fourth runs but decreased to moderate accurate again on the fifth run. Flak suppression flight encountered weak, accurate HFF at Nastatten. Two aircraft received Cat. AC and eleven aircraft Cat. A damage.

Return was a left turn to Laacher Lake and Base.

Interrogation of crews began at 1300 hrs. and finished at 1400 hrs.

Mission Notes and "Flak-Bait" Crew Debrief Comments

"Flak-Bait" briefed as No. 6 in high flight, 2nd Box, but moved up to the No. 3 position.

4 × 1,000 GPs dropped, for good results.

Damage: 10 to 12 small holes.

HFF very accurate; made a right turn on second run.

Other Crew Comments

Leader could have gone around tops rather than through them.

2nd Box leader requests oxygen—flying at 19,000 ft.—crew reactions were sluggish.

Formation made too many 360-degree turns in trying to get up through clouds.

Event: 322nd BG moves to A-89 Le Culot, Belgium

With the continued advance into Germany a further move was required; this time the group moved to ALG A-89 Le Culot, Belgium. The squadrons of the group staggered their move: the 449th and 452nd BS moved between March 30 and April 1, 1945, and the 450th and 451st BS moved between April 5 and 8, 1945.

The conditions at A-89 Le Culot were an improvement over those at A-61, with the runways in better conditions and a number of buildings still intact.

The 322nd flew its first mission from Le Culot on April 4, 1945, with a mission to the oil depot at Erbach.

```
Date: April 8, 1945
Target: Celle M/Y
Field Order: 9th BD F/O 840
99th CBW F/O 534
```

"Flak-Bait" Crew

1Lt. W. Langer, pilot
1Lt. J. E. Smith, copilot
SSgt. J. D. Privette, togglier

SSgt. G. D. Mitchell, engineer/gunner
TSgt. E. F. Smith, radio/gunner
SSgt. B. H. Scales, gunner

Briefing started at 0500 hrs. and ended 0600 hrs. Delay of 8½ hours; briefing started again at 1500 hrs. and finished at 1525 hrs.

T/off: 1605 hrs.   Target: 1811 to 1812 hrs.   Return: 1936 hrs.

Mission Narrative

Fifty-two aircraft dispatched in three boxes. The 1st Box was led by Col. J. S. Samuel, the 2nd Box by 1Lt. L. E. Goss, and the 3rd Box by Maj. J. L. Egan.

Routing was Base to Tilburg to Eindhoven to Goch to Warendorf to Nienburg to Bergen (the IP) to target. IX TAC to provide escort; 322nd to fire yellow flares at the fighter rendezvous.

Fifty-two aircraft dropped 208 × 1,000 GPs on the primary in CAVU conditions, bombing by flights from 10,150 down to 8,150 ft. Lead flight, 1st Box, could not pick out the briefed sidings so chose a M/Y to the south, which had lots of cars in it, and achieved superior results on SMPI. All other flights scored either superior or excellent results.

Moderate tracking HFF encountered from two batteries near Nienburg, the 1st Box being tracked and was accurate for altitude. 3rd Box reported only weak inaccurate HFF over this point. Six aircraft received Cat. A damage.

Return was from target to Peine to Hildesheim to Weidenbruck to Goch to Base.

Interrogation of crews began at 1955 hrs. and finished at 2040 hrs.

Mission Notes and "Flak-Bait" Crew Debrief Comments

"Flak-Bait" flew as No. 2 in the high flight, 1st Box.

4 × 1,000 GPs dropped; good results observed; oil fires and flames, and when 15 miles from target, saw what appeared to be an explosion.

Moderate inaccurate HFF from Nienburg: tracking.

Observed barracks in woods west of Celle, with vehicles, parallel to road.

43-34154, "Esky," seen here with her 450th BS ground crew, where she was originally coded ER-D. Transferred into the 449th BS after having suffered an accident on January 21, 1945, flying her first mission with the 449th as PN-L on April 8, 1945. *Peter Dole*

Other Crew Comments
Three Me 163s sighted just past the target, flying north at 6,000 ft.; no approaches made.

```
Date: April 9, 1945
Target: Naumburg Ord Depot
Field Order: 9th BD F/O 841
99th CBW F/O 536
```

"Flak-Bait" Crew
1Lt. W. Langer, pilot
1Lt. J. E. Smith, copilot
2Lt. W. E. Hugelman, navigator/bombardier

SSgt. G. D. Mitchell, engineer/gunner
TSgt. E. F. Smith, radio/gunner
SSgt. B. H. Scales, gunner

Briefing started at 0551 hrs. and ended 0605 hrs. Two delays announced: first of one hour and then of three hours.

T/off: 1305 hrs.   Target: 1548 to 1559 hrs.   Return: 1718 hrs.

Mission Narrative
Fifty-two aircraft dispatched in three boxes. The 1st Box was led by Capt. J. H. McCarty, the 2nd Box by Capt. A. P. Lee, and the 3rd Box by Capt. A. R. Pfleger.

Route was Base to Zulpich to Hillesheim to Giessen, for rendezvous with XXIX TAC fighter escort—the 322nd to fire yellow flares at the rendezvous—to Neustadt to Isenberg (the IP) to target.

6/10th cloud, tops 4–5,000 ft., with a large patch of cloud over the target and thick haze, making target acquisition difficult. Bombing by flights from heights of 10,550 down to 8,300 ft. as follows:

All of Box 1 and the lead flight of Box 3 dropped on or in vicinity of primary, after three runs. Clouds on run forced some bombardiers to synchronize on eastern end of target; results for Box 1 were superior, while those for lead flight, Box 3, could not be determined because of smoke from preceding bombs. Twenty-four aircraft attacked, dropping 64 × 1,000 GPs and 64 × 500 GPs.

All of Box 2 and the high and low flights of Box 3 bombed Naumburg town as a casual target, because cloud prevented bombardiers from picking up the primary, with all flights making either three or four runs at the target. A total of twenty-eight aircraft dropped 42 × 1,000 GPs and 136 × 500 GPs; all flights achieved superior results on AMPI except low flight, Box 3, whose results were excellent.

2 × 1,000 GPs returned through rack failures.

No flak encountered.

Return was a left turn to J-2890 to Sinzig to Base.

Interrogation of crews began at 1745 hrs. and finished at 1830 hrs.

Mission Notes and "Flak-Bait" Crew Debrief Comments
"Flak-Bait" flew as No. 6 in the low flight, 2nd Box.

4 × 1,000 GPs dropped; hit center of town.

Many rail cars at Hemsdorf, in sidings, and streams of motor cars seen at Neustadt and Rudelstadt.

```
Date: April 10, 1945
Target: Eger RR Br
Field Order: 9th BD F/O 844
99th CBW F/O 539
```

"Flak-Bait" Crew
1Lt. E. C. Pakish, pilot
2Lt. S. A. Norstrom, copilot
F/O G. L. Rorke, navigator/bombardier

TSgt. W. L. Johnston, engineer/gunner
Sgt. J. S. Devine, radio/gunner
SSgt. R. L. Bassler, gunner

Briefing started at 0515 hrs. and ended 0545 hrs.; mission subject to three delays

T/off: 1505 hrs. Target: 1723 to 1725 hrs. Return: 1905 hrs.

Mission Narrative

Twenty-two aircraft dispatched in four flights, led by Col. H. C. Newcomer.

Route was Base to rendezvous with XXIX TAC fighters at M-6741 to N-6821 to O-4030 to P-2054 to target.

Bombing by flights, sixteen aircraft attacked, dropping 31 × 2,000 GPs. Results were superior, excellent, and excellent for the first three flights. One aircraft had bomb selection switches off so jettisoned on Eger M/Y, dropping 2 × 2,000 GPs for undetermined results. The fourth flight did not bomb, due to smoke and haze from the previous flights bombs obscuring the target. The bombardier on "Flak-Bait," flying in the fourth flight, dropped 2 × 2,000 GPs in error when bomb bay doors were closed; location unknown. No second runs were made since the formation leader called for the flights to stay together, since e/a had been reported in the area. Formation leader got suspicious when the fighters, believed to be the escort, did not respond to his challenge. One aircraft (42-107689 PN-U, "Ginger II") crash-landed damaged upon landing at Y-51 Vogelsang; crew safe, aircraft jettisoned 2 × 2,000 GPs bombs, and the aircraft was returned to service by April 19, 1945. A total of 9 × 2,000 GPs were returned.

No flak encountered.

Return was a left turn to N-6780 to Base.

Interrogation of crews began at 1922 hrs. and finished at 2000 hrs.

Mission Notes and "Flak-Bait" Crew Debrief Comments

"Flak-Bait" flew as No. 2 in the fourth flight.

Flight failed to drop. Bombardier dropped 2 × 2,000 GPs in error when copilot called for bomb bay doors to be closed; results unobserved.

Other Crew Comments

"Why am I up at 5:00 a.m. for afternoon briefing?"

When mission is delayed a long time, a new weather briefing should be held.

When calling, fighters' exact position should not be given (complaint made by several crews).

42-107689 PN-U, "Ginger II," was involved in a landing accident at Y-51 Vogelsang on April 10, 1945, but was returned to service on the nineteenth of the month. *Randy Wells*

Date: April 11, 1945
Target: Aschersleben M/Y
Field Order: 9th BD F/O 845
99th CBW F/O 540

"Flak-Bait" Crew

1Lt. W. Langer, pilot
1Lt. J. E. Smith, copilot
Sgt. C. S. Bixler, togglier

SSgt. G. D. Mitchell, engineer/gunner
TSgt. E. F. Smith, radio/gunner
Sgt. B. H. Scales, gunner

Briefing started at 0730 hrs. and ended 0800 hrs.

T/off: 1000 hrs. Target: 1207½ to 1233 hrs. Return: 1357 hrs.

Mission Narrative

Forty-four aircraft dispatched, in three boxes. The 1st Box was led by Lt. Col. D. D. Bentley, the 2nd Box by Capt. R. Behr, and the 3rd Box by 1Lt. L. E. Goss; the 3rd Box was made up of two flights of four aircraft.

Route was Base to Zulpich to Hillesheim to rendezvous with XXIX TAC fighters at Giessen; group to fire yellow flares at the rendezvous point, to 51.41'N, 10.58'E (Bleicherode), the IP, to the target.

No cloud but hazy conditions. Bombing by flights. Thirty-five aircraft dropped on or in the vicinity of the primary, releasing 208 × 500 GPs. A further 68 × 500 GPs were jettisoned or dropped in the area of the primary. Three aircraft dropped 24 × 500 GPs on some barracks at Ousten, as a casual target. 44 × 500 GP2 were returned. 8 × 500 GPs unaccounted for in aircraft MIA.

Box 1 results were superior, excellent, and unsatisfactory: the low flight leader's aircraft had mechanical failure and accidentally released four bombs; the rest of flight dropped on him. Bombs fell 7½ miles WSW of the target area, on a road junction. Flight made four runs to try to drop remainder of bombs.

Box 2, lead flight, made three runs but could not pick out the target due to smoke and haze so picked out a barracks at Ousten 6½ miles northeast of target as a casual target; results superior: three aircraft dropped 24 × 500 GPs. High flight was unsatisfactory; made two runs but bombardier could not pick out the target until fifteen seconds from release, so was not synchronized properly; bombs fell 4,000 ft. south of the target, covering houses and roads. Low flight: no attack; made three runs at the primary and tried two runs at the secondary but had a PDI failure; bombs returned. One aircraft was an early return with engine trouble, returning 8 × 500 GPs.

Box 3, which was made up of two flights of four aircraft each, achieved excellent and superior results.

No flak encountered in the target area. The low flight, 2nd Box, got off course due to the number of bomb runs, and evasive action being taken. This flight drifted into the southern portion of the Ruhr, near Marburg, which was north of the briefed route, and received weak accurate LFF, which lasted for thirty seconds; the flight was flying at 4–5,000 ft. and was approximately 5 miles north of Bonn. One aircraft was MIA.

Return was a right turn and retrace the route in.

Interrogation of crews began at 1408 hrs. and finished at 1450 hrs.

Mission Notes and "Flak-Bait" Crew Debrief Comments
"Flak-Bait" flew as No. 2 in the high flight, 1st Box.

Made one run; dropped 8 × 500 GPs, for good results.

Haze but no cloud.

MIA Information
42-96030 ER-P (formerly coded 4T-B with the 585th BS 394th BG)
No. 4 aircraft in the low flight, 2nd Box. Flight was off course and drifted into southern part of the Ruhr near Marburg. Hit in left engine by LFF, 5 miles south of Bonn. A fire started between the fuselage and the right nacelle, and the aircraft went into a shallow dive and crashed. Ground forces report that aircraft crashed at F-478483, on the east side of the Rhine. One killed and four wounded. The pilot, 2Lt. J. T. Hopkins, was uninjured and was made a POW. Due to the fact that the Germans had no medical facilities, a momentary local truce was arranged, and ground forces evacuated the wounded by boat to friendly territory. Injured transferred to 124th Evac Hospital. (*Author's note*: While listed as MIA this aircraft was officially declared Cat E).

2Lt. J. T. Hopkins Jr., pilot	POW
2Lt. J. E. Lidicker Jr., copilot	injured
2Lt. D. M. Wolberg, navigator/bombardier	injured
Sgt. A. Samar, engineer/gunner	injured
Sgt. W. J. Dwyer, radio/gunner	KIA
SSgt. E. J. Koker Jr., gunner	injured

Date: April 11, 1945
Target: Kothen M/Y
Field Order: 9th BD F/O 846
99th CBW F/O 541

"Flak-Bait" Crew
1Lt. W. Langer, pilot	SSgt. G. D. Mitchell, engineer/gunner
1Lt. J. E. Smith, copilot	TSgt. E. F. Smith, radio/gunner
2Lt. R. H. Figueroa, navigator/bombardier	Sgt. B. H. Scales, gunner

Briefing started at 1315 hrs. and ended 1350 hrs.

T/off: 1605 hrs.   Target: 1809, 1810 & 1815 hrs.   Return: 1949 hrs.

Mission Narrative

Thirty-six aircraft dispatched; the 1st Box was led by Capt. A. R. Pfleger, and the 2nd Box by Capt. R. E. Ferguson.

Route was Base to Zulpich to Hillesheim to Koblenz to rendezvous with IX TAC fighters at 50.51'N, 08.49'E (Huttenberg), to Sandersleben (the IP) to the target.

Thirty-six aircraft attacked by flights, dropping 288 × 500 M17 IBs, fused to open at 5,000 ft., in clear conditions but with thick haze. Bombing was made from 10,500, 11,000, and 12,300 ft. Results from Box 1, lead flight, were superior, but the remaining flights were all undetermined due to the type of bombs used and smoke; all are thought to have been excellent; the high flight of the 2nd Box made two runs.

No flak encountered.

Return was a right turn off the target to Sandersleben and retrace route in.

Interrogation of crews began at 2010 hrs. and finished at 2100 hrs.

Mission Notes and "Flak-Bait" Crew Debrief Comments

"Flak-Bait" flew as No. 3 in the low flight, 2nd Box.

8 × 500 IBs dropped; bombs hit in M/Y; many explosions observed.

Other Crew Comments

Very good fighter escort.

Capt. Pfleger complained that there was too much radio chatter.

Crews in the 2nd Box reported large explosions at the target, with smoke rising to over 10,000 ft.

> **Date: April 12, 1945**
> **Target: Kempten Ord Dep**
> **Field Order: 9th BD F/O 847**
> **99th CBW F/O 542**

"Flak-Bait" Crew

1Lt. E. C. Pakish, pilot

2Lt. S. A. Norstrom, copilot

F/O G. L. Rorke, navigator/bombardier

TSgt. L. V. Mead, engineer/gunner

TSgt. J. Smith, radio/gunner

SSgt. M. B. Schmidt, gunner

Briefing started at 0600 hrs. and ended 0630 hrs.

T/off: 0850 hrs.   Target: 1112 & 1121 hrs.   Return: 1302 hrs.

Mission Narrative

Forty aircraft dispatched; the 1st Box was led by Maj. J. L. Egan, and the 2nd Box, made up of four flights, by Capt. W. G. Fort.

Route was Base to 49.44'N, 06.37'E (Sierck-les-Bains), to 49.58'N, 07.00'E (Braunshausen), to rendezvous with 8th FC escort at Mannheim, 322nd to fire yellow flares, to 48.37'N, 10.32'E (Ichenhausen), to Kaufbeuren (the IP) to target.

10/10th multilayered cloud with tops at 7,000 ft. encountered. Bombing by flights, thirty-two aircraft attacked, dropping 255 × 500 GPs from 5,500 to 7,650 ft. Results were as follows:

Box 1, lead flight: superior results with a "zero" circular error, in an excellent pattern. High flight was too close to the lead on the approach so selected buildings 3,000 ft. south of DMPI; results superior on SMPI. Low flight results were superior on the DMPI, again with a "zero" circular error. One aircraft from the lead flight was an early return because of engine trouble, and another, from the high flight, lost the formation and turned back from enemy territory just before the IP. 16 × 500 GPs returned.

Results from Box 2, lead flight, excellent on DMPI, with all but one or two bombs within 1,000 ft. high flight; no attack made; encountered haze and rain with poor visibility; flight went down to 4,000 ft. and tried on the secondary target, but the same conditions were encountered; 48 × 500 GPs returned. Low flight missed the DMPI but synchronized on a building in the same area; excellent results achieved on SMPI. The fourth flight achieved excellent results on the DMPI. One aircraft from the lead flight returned 1 × 500 GP through a rack failure.

Lead flight of 1st Box experienced inaccurate LFF from a road west of the target. Moderate inaccurate HFF was encountered by the low flight, 1st Box, in the vicinity of Blaubeuren.

Return was a right turn to Biberach to Gappingen to Helibronn to Mannheim to Base.

Interrogation of crews began at 1300 hrs.; no end time recorded.

Mission Notes and "Flak-Bait" Crew Debrief Comments
"Flak-Bait" flew as No. 3 in the high flight, 2nd Box.

8 × 500 GPs returned; flight leader did not bomb due to weather.

"198th mission."

Briefing Note
At briefing, crews cautioned to be careful and not to drop bombs on Switzerland, whose border was close to the target.

Other Crew Comments
Group leader praised all crews who flew through the weather and did a good job of bombing.
Very good fighter escort.

```
Date: April 15, 1945
Target: Ulm M/Y
Field Order: 9th BD F/O 852
99th CBW F/O 546
```

"Flak-Bait" Crew
1Lt. E. C. Pakish, pilot
2Lt. S. A. Norstrom, copilot
2Lt. R. H. Figueroa, navigator/bombardier

Sgt. R. C. Mixon, engineer/gunner
TSgt. J. Smith, radio/gunner
SSgt. M. B. Schmidt, gunner

Briefing started at 0900 hrs. and ended 0930 hrs.
T/off: 1155 hrs.   Target: 1401 & 1402 hrs.   Return: 1550 hrs.

Mission Narrative
PFF mission. Thirty plus two PFF aircraft dispatched. The 1st Box was led by Lt. Col. E. Wursten, and the 2nd Box by Capt. R. Behr.

Route was Base to 49.44'N, 06.37'E (Rustroff), to Roussy to Barr, for rendezvous with 8th FC fighters, the 322nd to fire Green flares at the rendezvous, to Triberg to Blumenfeld to 48.12'N, 09.13'E (Sigmaringen), the IP, to the target.

Bombed on PFF; weather was 10/10th cloud with tops at 11–12,000 ft. All thirty-two aircraft attacked, dropping 59 × 2,000 GPs and 8 × 500 GPs, from 13,150 and 12,540 ft. Results were undetermined. 1 × 2,000 GPs returned due to a rack failure,

452nd BS aircraft of the high flight, 1st Box, on the mission to Ulm. The camouflaged aircraft in the No. 6 position, 41-31847 DR-D, "Jolly Roger" (formerly with the 1st PFF Squadron), has had one 2,000 lb. GP hang up, which was returned to base. The bomb that did release can be seen passing the No. 5 aircraft DR-A. *Trevor J. Allen collection*

No flak encountered.

Return was a right turn to Laupheim to Blumenfeld to 48.08'N, 08.11'E (Simonswald), to Barr to Base.

Interrogation of crews began at 1620 hrs. and finished at 1700 hrs.

Mission Notes and "Flak-Bait" Crew Debrief Comments

"Flak-Bait" flew as No. 2 in the low flight, 2nd Box.

2 × 2,000 GPs dropped on PFF, through 10/10th cloud.

Fighters not seen (other crews reported excellent fighter escort).

Other Crew Comments

PFF reported group formation was good.

Group leader reported that the fighter escort was excellent.

Two crews complained of no food before the mission; breakfast at 0700 and nothing until evening meal.

```
Date: April 17, 1945
Target: Magdeburg D/A
Field Order: 9th BD F/O 855
99th CBW F/O 549
```

"Flak-Bait" Crew

Capt. W. G. Fort, pilot	TSgt. K. M. Locke, engineer/gunner
Col. J. S. Samuel, copilot	TSgt. C. Fisher, radio/gunner
1Lt. W. D. Brearley, bombardier	TSgt. W. J. Hess, gunner
1Lt. A. D. Perkins, navigator	war correspondent O. C. Hutton, passenger

Briefing started at 0800 hrs. and ended 0820 hrs.

T/off: 1100 hrs.   Target: 1256 to 1258 hrs.   Return: 1443 hrs.

Mission Narrative

200th mission.

All eleven 9th BD groups attacked this target with twenty-minute intervals; the 322nd was the seventh group to attack.

Thirty-six aircraft dispatched. The 1st Box was to be led by Capt. W. G. Fort in "Flak-Bait." The 2nd Box was led by Capt. J. H. McCarty. "Flak-Bait" was to be the lead aircraft, but she had a PDI problem so was dropped to the No. 4 position in the flight, and 1Lt. J. H. Alderson took over the lead of the flight. This flight then changed places with the high flight, led by 1Lt. J. S. Avooski, who then led the formation.

Route was Base to Aachen to Blankenheim to Konigswinter to Leopoldshall to Barby (the IP) to target. XXIX TAC to provide area cover.

One small patch of cloud on the first part of the run; otherwise clear but with haze. Smoke and haze made target identification difficult. Thirty-four aircraft attacked by flights, dropping 67 × 2,000 GPs from 12,750 to 11,750 ft.

Results as per the revised formation layout, with "Flak-Bait" now a part of the high flight.

Box 1, lead flight: unsatisfactory; bombardier misidentified DMPI due to haze and smoke; all bombs fell 1,000 ft. beyond SMPI, covering some dock facilities and storage buildings. High flight was excellent on SMPI, since haze and smoke prevented sighting on DMPI; bombs hit a crossing point of six roads and buildings and into a park. Low flight was superior on SMPI; smoke and haze caused bombardier to misidentify the DMPI. Bombs hit on a main bridge and on a road and buildings adjoining.

Box 2 was superior, superior, and excellent, respectively, on the DMPI. Two aircraft had bomb bay door failures and returned 4 × 2,000 GPs, and another aircraft had a bomb that had hung up, which fell through the doors "safe" upon landing (42-107664 PN-A, "Je Reviens," and "Slug"; pilot was 1Lt. J. H. Alderson).

No flak encountered.

Return was a left turn to Konigswinter to Base.

Interrogation of crews began at 1500 hrs. and finished at 1545 hrs.

Mission Notes and "Flak-Bait" Crew Debrief Comments

"Flak-Bait" was to be the formation lead aircraft but had a PDI problem so dropped to the No. 4 position within the flight, and 1Lt. J. H. Alderson took over the lead of the flight. This flight then changed places with the high flight, led by 1Lt. J. S. Avooski, who then led of formation. The passenger on board "Flak-Bait" for this momentous flight was war correspondent Oram C. "Bud" Hutton, a staff writer for *Stars & Stripes*.

2 × 2,000 GPs dropped; results unobserved.

Haze and smoke around target. Up-sun (visibility) was bad all the way from Rhine up.

42-107664 PN-A, "Je Reviens," and "Slug" had a bomb hang up that fell through the bomb bay doors upon landing. This aircraft was displayed under the Eiffel Tower in an exhibition in the summer of 1945. *Mike Smith, B26.com*

Briefing Note

During briefing, crews cautioned not to drop early or late, since Allied troops were within 1,500 yards of the target. Cerise and yellow panels will be laid to mark the forward troop line.

The 449th BS records have the following entry regarding "Flak-Bait." Taken from a P.R.O. release:

Story on "Flak-Bait"

When the Ninth Air Force Marauder "Flak-Bait" (a/c 773-O) recently led the "Annihilators" Marauder Group in a bombing attack against the German town of Magdeburg (17 April '45), it became the first allied bomber in the European Theater of Operations to complete 200 missions against Nazi targets in Western Europe.

"Flak-Bait" flew its first mission on August 16, 1943 (1), in an attack on Beaumont-le-Roger Airdrome in France. On this mission five Focke-Wulfe's [*sic*] attacked the formation, but "Flak-Bait" was untouched.

Since that day, this veteran bomber has compiled an impressive record. It has dropped over 375,000 pounds of bombs in 31 attacks against V-1 launching sites, 5 against Nazi ship-yards and E-Boat pens, 35 against Nazi airfields, 45 against communications centers, including railway yards, 15 against fuel dumps, 31 against bridges, 8 against gun emplacements and 20 against defended towns.

The bomber participated on one night mission (2), went out twice on D-Day (3) and later participated in attacks in which allied tactical air power blasted enemy resistance in the path of our ground troops. Among these were Brest, the Falaise Gap and the Siegfried line, and later the German counter-attack in the Belgian Bulge.

"Flak-Bait's" 200th mission, against Magdeburg, marks the climax of the tactical air offensive. A sizeable German force had been holding out in the town, the first organized resistance since the Allied breakthrough toward Berlin.

Once considered mechanically unfit for combat, "Flak-Bait" has sustained so much battle damage that every bit of moveable surface has had to be changed, yet in all 200 missions only one combat man (4), a bombardier, was slightly wounded. More than 300 metal patches conceal the 1,000-odd flak holes it has received. Its electrical system was shot out twice, and its hydraulic system once. But "Flak-Bait" never has failed to touch down safely after a mission, even though it has made two single-engine landings, once with one of its engines burning.

One of the bomber[']s original engines racked up 616 hours before requiring a change. Only three other engine changes have been necessary since that time.

"Flak-Bait" has made over 500 take-offs and landings, many of which were made on a bomb-blasted runway in France on an airdrome which "Flak-Bait" itself had previously attacked.

The Marauder has consumed 157,850 gallons of gasoline and has travelled 177,460 miles, or equivalent to more than six times around the World. It has flown over 1,300 individual sorties.

According to Captain William G. Fort, who piloted the ship on its record-breaking 200th mission, "Flak-Bait" is faster today than at any time during her 21 months of combat service. Capt. Fort has flown on 65 missions. Colonel J. S. Samuel, Commanding Officer of the "Annihilators," flew as Co-pilot. Colonel Samuel, who has chalked up 71 missions and wears the Distinguished Flying Cross and the Silver Star, comments that "200 missions are a lot for any ship, but 'Flak-Bait' carries her age well."

Author's note: Wartime is never a time for accurate research, and this release does carry a few inaccuracies, as indicated: (1) "Flak-Bait's" first mission was to Le Trait shipyards on August 4, 1943; Beaumont-le-Roger was the aircraft's second mission on August 16, 1943. (2) She participated in three of the group's five night missions. (3) She flew on all three D-day missions that the 322nd BG flew that day. (4) Two crewmen were wounded while flying in "Flak-Bait": 1Lt. James J. Farrell, the original pilot, on September 6, 1943, and 1Lt. Owen Redmond, the original bombardier, on April 11, 1944; fortunately, both were only minor wounds.

```
Date: April 24, 1945
Target: Schroben Hausen POL Dep
Field Order: 9th BD F/O 871
99th CBW F/O 560
```

"Flak-Bait" Crew

1Lt. W. Langer, pilot
1Lt. J. E. Smith, copilot
Sgt. J. Baker, togglier

SSgt. G. D. Mitchell, engineer/gunner
TSgt. E. F. Smith, radio/gunner
Sgt. B. H. Scales, gunner

Briefing started at 0803 hrs. and ended 0830 hrs.
T/off: 1330 hrs.   Target: 1537 hrs.   Return: 1730 hrs.

Mission Narrative

PFF mission. Thirty plus three window and two PFF aircraft dispatched. The 1st Box was led by Lt. Col. H. C. Newcomer, and the 2nd Box by Capt. J. L. Lane.

Route was Base to Trier to 49.58'N, 07.00'E (Braunshausen), to rendezvous with IX TAC escort at Ludwigshafen to 49.02'N, 11.22'E (Titting), to 48.56'N, 11.45'E (woods west of Eutenhofen), the IP, to the target.

Cloud was 10/10th with tops at 8,000 ft.; thirty-one aircraft attacked on PFF, releasing 236 × 500 M17 IBs from 13,450 and 12,000 ft.; results were unobserved. The 2nd Box PFF ship had an equipment failure, so they bombed on the 1st Box release. One aircraft had an engine cut out on the bomb run and jettisoned 8 × 50 M17 IBs near the target; later the engine came back on again. One aircraft landed immediately after takeoff after one engine cut out on takeoff; 8 × 500 M17 IBs returned. 4 × 500 M17 IBs returned by one aircraft with rack failure.

A few bursts of weak inaccurate HFF from Ingoldstadt area, fired at the window aircraft only. No damage received.

Return was a right turn to Heilbronn to Base.

Interrogation of crews began at 1730 hrs. and finished at 1755 hrs.

Mission Notes and "Flak-Bait" Crew Debrief Comments

"Flak-Bait" flew as No. 2 in the high flight, 2nd Box.
    8 × 500 IBs dropped through 10/10th cloud.

Other Crew Comments

Two Me 262s, in trail, approached the window flight at 1540 hrs., just as the formation made the turn off the target; one approached from twelve o'clock and passed under the formation without attacking and departed to the southeast at 12,000 ft., and the second broke away before coming into range.

PFF reported that the group formation was good but the window ships were poor.

Group leader stated that bombs were released by the PFF just as the formation was in a turn; the run-up to that time had been smooth.

Having taken part in the mission to Schroben-Hausen on April 24, 1945, the group continued to be alerted for missions, only to be stood down as the rapidly advancing ground troops overran potential targets, so while it wasn't known at that time, the war was over for the men of the 322nd Bomb Group.

After the cessation of hostilities, on May 8, 1945, the men of the 322nd eagerly awaited news as to what the future held for them. Some were eager to get to the Pacific and fight the Japanese forces, but the vast majority simply wanted to get home and restart their lives and careers as civilians.

Toward the end of May, news came through that the 322nd Bomb Group would be a part of the postwar occupational forces, news that was greeted with mixed emotions by the men of the group. However, a few days later this was amended, and it was announced that they would be assigned to disarmament duties, with personnel assigned to carry out inspections and disassembly of military establishments and factories.

During this period there was much movement of personnel between units of the 9th Air Force; a return to the Zone of the Interior (mainland US) was based on a points system, and a score of over 100 would be sufficient for a person to be rotated. Combat personnel gained points for the number of missions flown, as well as the length of time served overseas, while for the ground personnel it was just based on the amount of time served overseas, which made it more difficult for them to accrue the sufficient amount of points to qualify for an early return.

At the end of May 1945, most of the aircrews were transferred to the 394th Bomb Group, which was at that time based at Y-55 Venlo in Holland, while each squadron retained two crews at A-89 Le Culot to assist in the ferrying of the group's B-26 aircraft to storage sites in Germany. The majority ended up at R-54 Landsberg, near Munich, where they would eventually

Aerial view of Landsberg Airfield, with B-26 Marauders lined up ready for scrapping at the war's end. *USAAF*

Awaiting their fate, the nearer aircraft are from the 322nd BG, including 44-68163 SS-L; 43-34342 ER-W (formerly PN-G), "Lil Maggie"; 43-34154 PN-N, "Esky"; and 44-67839 DR-H. Farther back is 44-67875, "Early Morning Scrub," of the 1st PFF, and 43-34371 PN-X, "Belle of Bayou." *Trevor J. Allen collection*

be destroyed; the USAAF no longer had a need for the Martin B-26 Marauder, since the Douglas A-26 Invader had already begun replacing the type, starting in December 1944, and had the war continued, all of the B-26 units would have been reequipped. Indeed, shortly before VE-day, some ground personnel of the 322nd BG had already been sent on conversion courses as an introduction to the type.

In June 1945, the 322nd Bomb Group headquarters relocated to Y-86 Fritzlar, and the individual squadrons were dispersed to different locations to carry out their inspection duties. The 449th Bomb Squadron eventually established itself at Y-91 Hanau/Langendiebach, with personnel rotating to the Marburg area to carry

With 4 pounds of TNT, the aircraft were blown up, and the resulting wreckage was taken away and used to help revitalize German industry. *Author's collection*

out inspections of potential military sites and factories to ensure the disarmament program was enforced.

Records of personnel movements and transfers are not extensive during this period; the only mention of the ground crew transfers for anyone associated with "Flak-Bait" shows that Pvt. George Sangregorio, mechanic on "Flak-Bait," was transferred to the P-47-equipped 367th Fighter Group on July 5, 1945. This group was located at Y-74 Frankfurt/Eschborn and later in that month began the process of returning to the Zone of the Interior.

On July 12, 1945, Col. John S. Samuel, the 322nd Bomb Group CO, was transferred to the 391st Bomb Group, at Vitry-en-Artois, in France, and Maj. John L. Egan, formerly CO of the 450th Bomb Squadron, took over command. The 322nd Bomb Group completed its tasks on disarmament duties on September 5, 1945, and the group, by then a shadow of its former self, began its preparations for a return to the US, where they were formally disbanded at Camp Kilmer, on December 15, 1945. At this point, Maj. Egan transferred to the 394th Bomb Group, then based at R-6 Kitzingen, near Wurzburg, Germany, as the group operations officer under the CO there, Col. Gove C. Celio Jr., who was formerly a squadron commander of the 452nd BS.

The 394th Bomb Group began conversion to the Douglas A-26 Invader in the first week of September 1945 and moved to R-6 Kitzingen the following week; they were destined to be the last of the Ninth Air

Force's bomb groups to remain in Europe, the unit finally being deactivated on February 15, 1946, and returned to the US, although this was in unit number only, without aircraft or personnel.

It was the head of the USAAF, Gen. Henry "Hap" Arnold, who requested that certain significant airframes be saved for preservation, and "Flak-Bait," with her notoriety as the only USAAF bomber to fly more than 200 combat missions in the ETO, escaped the fate of so many of her brethren; in fact, of all the B-26 Marauders to see combat in the Mediterranean and European theaters of combat with the USAAF, she is the sole survivor.

The actual movements of "Flak-Bait" during this period are not recorded; there are reports of her being stored at R-77 Gablingen in the summer of 1945. Fortunately, details of her last flight are recorded in an article in the B-26 Marauder Historical Society's *Marauder Thunder Newsletter* of April 1993. In this article, Maj. Egan relates how he, along with copilot Capt. Norman Schloesser, ferried "Flak-Bait" from Kitzingen to an air depot at Oberpfaffenhofen, west of Munich, on March 18, 1946, with a logged flight time of fifty-five minutes. In the article he explains that there were some safety concerns, since the aircraft had not flown for some six months (which may tie in with an approximate date of September 1945 for her arrival at Kitzingen), so a high-speed run was performed down the runway to check out some of the aircraft systems prior to the actual takeoff.

It was at Oberpfaffenhofen that "Flak-Bait" was disassembled, ready for shipment to the US by ship. The crew chief overseeing this operation was Sgt. A. Aymond, along with assistant Cpl. G. Bunch and a team of seven others, their names being recorded on the right-hand nosewheel door.

Lt. Col. John Egan, the last man to pilot "Flak-Bait" when she was ferried to Oberpfaffenhofen for onward shipment to the US. *Trevor J. Allen collection*

A time frame for this work or details of her actual shipment are not known, but scratched into the entrance door to the bomb bay is "RER 7/25/46 Oberpfaffenhofen, GR," which indicates she was still there in late July 1946. The AFLC record card picks up her return to the US with an entry on December 7, 1946, when she is recorded as being with the 4119th Base Unit at Brookley Field, Mobile, Alabama. Mobile is a deepwater port on the Gulf of Mexico, so she probably arrived by ship at this port, shortly before that date. From Brookley, the final entry on her AFLC card shows her as being at Orchard Place, Park Ridge, Illinois, under "Class 32" on December 21, 1946, probably having been shipped by train.

"Class 32" was the status that aircraft were placed under when they were reserved for museum or display purposes. For "Flak-Bait," her homecoming was not greeted with any fanfare, and, with the hostilities over, there was no requirement for any kind of publicity or bond-raising tours or the like.

Many of the airframes earmarked for preservation were initially stored at Orchard Place, but due to the needs for rapid expansion of the USAF (as the USAAF was renamed on September 18, 1947) as a result of the Korean conflict, the space was required for other purposes.

Transferred to the Smithsonian Institute in 1949, she, along with other airframes then in storage, was transported by rail to the Paul E. Garber facility, at Silver Hill, Maryland. With the vast collection of artifacts that the Smithsonian holds, space was always at a premium, and for many of the airframes this would preclude them from being displayed. Eventually the nose section of "Flak-Bait" was displayed in the NASM Building on the Mall in Washington, DC, and was placed at the entrance to Gallery 205, the World War II hall, when that opened in 1976.

At some point while the plane was on display, McDonald T. Darnell Jr., who, as a tech sergeant, had flown as the radio operator / gunner on "Hank" Bozarth's crew and logged fifteen missions on "Flak-Bait," donated his A-2 jacket to the NASM, this being placed over the radio operator's seat.

A major step forward in the fortunes of the NASM was an extremely large donation, in 1979, from Steven F. Udvar-Hazy, cofounder of the International Lease Finance Corporation, which allowed for the construction of an annex, covering some 760,000 sq. ft. of space, that bears his name. This was constructed alongside the airport at Washington Dulles, Chantilly, Virginia, and allowed for many of the airframes held in store to go on public display. This annex opened in December 2003.

A further step forward was a donation from Airbus America Inc. for the construction and opening of the Mary Baker Engen Restoration Hangar. This facility was opened in 2010 and greatly enhanced the NASM's abilities in restoring some of the airframes. This building includes a public gallery allowing for visitors to view some of the work taking place within.

Depending on an individual's own preferences, there are many choices as to which airframes should be worked on and in what order they should be moved to the restoration hangar. "Flak-Bait" was high on many people's lists, and her time finally came in the summer of 2014.

The nose section was carefully removed from Gallery 205 and arrived at the Mary Baker Engen facility on June 19, 2014, to be joined shortly thereafter by the rest of the airframe from Silver Hill.

There is no doubt that the passage of time has seen some deterioration to the airframe, but what the NASM has is a unique time capsule, with everything remaining exactly as it was after the plane's final flight in March 1946.

The story of the restoration process is deserving of its own detailed account; suffice to say that this will result in the most original restoration ever accomplished. No components, no matter how small, are being replaced unless it is absolutely necessary. Some of the interior padding and insulation have rotted away, and these will need replacing, but all the original metal fixings will be incorporated.

The restoration team, under the curator of American military aviation, Jeremy Kinney, consists of team leader Pat Robinson, along with museum specialist Chris Moore and conservators Lauren Horelick and Malcolm Collum, all of whom are working at conserving this unique airframe in as near an original condition as is possible, the latter two concentrating on the paintwork and researching ways to stabilize it from further deterioration, borrowing processes normally seen in the restoration of valuable pieces of art.

Even the original fabric from the control surfaces is being preserved. The structures are being covered in Ceconite, and then the original is meticulously overlaid onto this, with any resultant gaps being carefully blended in.

During the restoration process, a number of interesting discoveries have been made on the airframe. On the internal bulkheads were pasted several paper clock faces; these are believed to have been used so that crew members could call out the relevant positions of approaching enemy aircraft.

When the rear fuselage flooring was removed, among the residue of mud and dirt there were many spent wooden matches and cigarette butts (smoking having been allowed on USAAF aircraft at the pilot's discretion), no doubt offering some slight relief from the stress of flying combat missions. Also in this area were four spent 0.50 shell casings, of 1942 manufacture, that had probably been fired from the waist position at some point in time. In the area along the seam between the bomb bay doors, among the dirt and grime that had accumulated there, they found examples of Wrigley's gum wrappers, remnants of chaff shavings, and bomb tags.

When the wooden flooring under the radio operators seat was lifted, a previously undiscovered piece of German flak was found to be buried within it. Although it will not be visible once the aircraft is on display, it has been decided to leave the piece in situ to preserve the total accuracy of the airframe—a tangible reminder of the very many flak hits that she took (some sources say that she took as many as 1,000 hits by flak fragments or e/a damage) in the course of her remarkable combat career.

When the nose section was placed on display in the Mall, the upper and lower surfaces were painted in olive drab and gray to clean up the appearance of the aircraft. The upper surface paint has been carefully removed, revealing the original weathered appearance, but the gray lower surfaces have not been attended to at the time of writing and may present more of a challenge in ensuring that the original bomb symbols are not compromised in any way.

The restoration and preservation work is expected to last until until late 2025 or early 2026; to many this may seem an inordinate amount of time, but this process is not simply a case of bolting her back together, but of inspecting every component and analyzing the flaking and chipped paintwork and finding a way of stabilizing it for the future, and ensuring that any corrosion that is found is treated, thereby ensuring her preservation for future generations to admire and enjoy and to find ways to ensure that any remedial work retains a battle-weary and aged appearance, so as to blend in with the rest of the airframe.

Camouflage Paint

When the aircraft that was to become "Flak-Bait" left the production line, she was finished in the standard Dark Olive Drab upper surfaces and Neutral Gray undersurfaces. Along the fuselage the division was a continuous wavy line, while on the engine nacelles this was a straight line following the curvature of the top of the undercarriage doors, and across the lower cowling panels. The only thing that actually identified her from the many hundreds of other B-26s that had both preceded her and would follow was the 12" high serial number, 131773, painted on the fin and rudder in Identification Yellow, 2½" above the central rudder hinge.

National Insignia and Tactical Markings

The national insignia used at this time was known as the Type 2 and lacked the red central disk in the star of the earlier version. On the fuselage this consisted of a 30" blue disk, containing the five-pointed star in white, positioned 15" behind the lower fuselage hatch, the center of the star lining up with the leading edge of the tailplane. On the upper port wing and lower starboard wing, there was a larger version, of 40" diameter, centered 8'10½" from the wingtip.

It was in this rather nondescript scheme that she arrived in the UK and was assigned to the 449th Bomb Squadron, as part of the 322nd Bomb Group, based at AAF Station No. 485, Andrews Field.

Normally, USAAF units adopted a plane in group number, as an individual identifier; however, those units assigned to the VIII Air Force, and later the Ninth Air Force, adopted the British system of a two-letter code that would identify the squadron to which the aircraft was assigned; this was positioned ahead of the fuselage national insignia and an individual aircraft letter that would be positioned aft of the national insignia.

The four squadrons of the 322nd BG were assigned squadron codes as follows: the 449th, PN; 450th, ER;

451st, SS; and 452nd, DR. These codes were painted in Medium Gray on camouflaged aircraft and in Black on later natural-metal aircraft. "Flak-Bait" was given the individual letter of O and thus became PN-O. By measuring those applied to "Flak-Bait," these were 40" high and 28" wide, with a stroke width of 5½".

It seems that the first B-26 groups assigned to the VIII Air Force had the white stars of the national insignia toned down and were overpainted in a light gray. Aircraft of both the 322nd and 323rd Groups can be seen with such toned-down insignia, "Flak-Bait" being one of them.

Changes to the national insignia were introduced on June 29, 1943; these called for a rectangular bar to be added to each side of the national insignia, and the length was to be half the width of the star itself and one-quarter of the depth of the star and then surrounded by a red border, officially one-sixteenth of the diameter of the star. In such a style it became known as the Type 3 National Insignia. However this was not acted on immediately, and some 322nd BG aircraft entered combat still sporting the original Type 2 insignia.

Because the squadron codes and individual aircraft letters had already been applied to the aircraft, the rearmost bar to the star impinged over the individual letter, which was positioned under the tailplane; such was the case with "Flak-Bait." Later groups joining the 8th and 9th Air Forces and replacement aircraft had their fuselage star and bar moved forward to allow space for the individual aircraft letter. Late in the war, "Flak-Bait" had her squadron codes overpainted in white, this time with the white passing over the bar of the national insignia.

It was soon established that the red border to the national insignia did not stand out clearly enough, so a further change, effective starting on September 17, 1943, called for the border to be overpainted in blue. By observing those on "Flak-Bait," it is clear that this was hand-painted, and because this blue paint was fresher it gave the appearance of a darker border surrounding the star and bar. In this guise it was known as the Type 4 National Insignia. Again, by measuring those on the airframe itself, it appears that the bars were 14" in width (instead of the stipulated 15") and that the border was 1½" around the star and 2" wide around the bars. On the wings the borders were 3" wide.

Group Markings

During the summer of 1943, and with four B-26 groups based in proximity within the county of Essex, they were experiencing problems during the formation join-up process, with aircraft joining the wrong formations and flying with them to their target.

The solution was the adoption of distinctive tail markings to help identify the different groups' aircraft in flight. These began to be applied starting in early November 1943, shortly after the groups had been transferred to the newly established 9th Air Force. The 322nd BG, being the oldest group in the UK, was distinctive in that it did not have any group markings applied to the tails of their aircraft. The 1st PFF Squadron (P), which was later established at Andrews Field, followed suit and had no distinguishing tail markings. The other three groups adopted a 30" wide band across the fin and rudder above the serial number: the 323rd had a white band, the 386th a yellow band, and the 387th yellow and black diagonal stripes. Later, from early 1944 onward, four more groups began to arrive at bases in Essex, and they adopted the following markings: the 344th and 391st had a white and yellow triangle, respectively, while the 394th and 397th adopted a diagonal stripe, 18" wide, up the entire fin and rudder, in white and yellow, respectively.

Nose Art and Individual Markings

Once the Farrell crew had become aware that 41-31773 PN-O would be their regular plane, the crew members had their names applied next to their regular crew positions; these were painted in yellow and positioned as follows:

> Jim "Boss" Farrell, under the pilot's window
> "Tarheel" Tom Moore, under the copilot's window
> O. J. "Red" Redmond, diagonally on left side of nose, by bombardier's position
> J. B. "Polock" Manuel, under the radio compartment window
> "Flackhappy" Thielan, under the top turret on the left fuselage side
> Tim Tyler, under the rear turret Plexiglas on the left side

On many aircraft, once the original crew had rotated home and new crews were assigned, they would overpaint the original names with their own and sometimes even rename the aircraft itself, but in the case of "Flak-Bait," this did not occur.

In addition, the crew chief had his name painted on the nosewheel door, and later, at the time of the 200th mission, the entire ground crew's names were added in white:

> TSgt. Charles F. Thompson, crew chief (painted in black), and marked as "rotated" (in white)

At the time of 200th mission, below the name of TSgt. Charles F. Thompson the following names were added as follows, painted in white:

> SSgt. C. G. Goodrich, crew chief
> Cpl. Dave Rich, assistant
> PFC Geo Sangregorio, mechanic
> PFC James Ryan, armorer

In addition, on the right-hand nosewheel door the names Sgt. C. Goodrich and Sgt. J. Connelly were painted in yellow; the role of the latter person is not confirmed but he may have been an assistant crew chief at some point. This right-hand door was appended with the names of the disassembly crew, painted in white as follows:

> *Disassembly crew*
> Sgt. A. Aymond, crew chief
> Sgt. R. Cook
> Cpl. G. Bunch, asst. crew chief
> Cpl. R. Olsen
> Cpl. C. Strelz
> PFC E. Mills
> PFC C. Mongillo
> PFC E. Stokley
> PFC R. Bunqcayao

The center disk of the nosewheel was painted with a yellow star with white and blue circles radiating outward, and where they crossed over the star they were painted in red.

Nose Art

In addition to having their names applied next to their crew positions, the Farrell crew began thinking of a suitable nickname and nose art to be applied to "their" ship. It was the pilot, Jim Farrell, who suggested the name "Flak-Bait," the inspiration having come from his brother's nickname for the family dog, which he had called "Flea-Bait"; the change to "Flak-Bait" seemed most appropriate, and the crew agreed.

The nose art was painted on the left-hand side of the nose by Sgt. Ted Simonaitis, assistant crew chief on the aircraft "Sit 'N' Git," following a sketch given to him by Jim Farrell, which showed an exploding flak burst with the name blazoned across in red and yellow. Among these red, white, and yellow streaks, in the right lower portion, can be seen his name in small white letters.

Mission Symbols

Just as fighter pilots recorded their kill markings on their aircraft, a bomber's score was usually marked by the painting of a bomb symbol for each mission completed, generally applied by the ground crews who looked after the aircraft.

The official way of recording an accredited sortie was that if the aircraft had entered enemy airspace or had met with enemy opposition, then a mission credit would be awarded and would count as part of a combat tour; mechanical aborts and early returns would not count. After the invasion the criterion would be if the aircraft had crossed the bomb line.

Because of the sheer number of missions that many B-26 Marauders logged, the bomb symbols were not necessarily applied in a regimented left-to-right, top-to-bottom manner, with existing lines of mission symbols being extended both to the left and right to squeeze them in, and such was the case with "Flak-Bait," certainly on the top row of bomb symbols.

For the record, the nose of "Flak-Bait" displays 199 bomb symbols, plus the larger bomb marked with the figure "200"; in addition, below the first row of bombs is a swastika to mark the enemy fighter shot down by TSgt. D. L. Tyler on October 24, 1943. Alongside that are six duck symbols; these were applied to represent diversionary or decoy missions. "Flak-Bait" flew on only one of the official diversionary sweeps, on July 27, 1943, so the other five are hard to determine as to exactly what missions they were applied for, but they probably signify some of the missions that were weather recalls.

Initially, these duck symbols were painted below the second line of missions, but as the number of missions flown built up, they were repainted alongside the swastika marking, below the first row of bombs.

The original bomb symbols were painted in yellow and were probably begun just below the pilot's name. Eventually this top row was extended both to the left and to the right to reach a figure of fifty mission symbols, but not until after the second row of bomb symbols was being used. Photographs showing "Flak-Bait" with 123 bomb symbols, plus the six decoy missions, appear to be of a lighter color, but by the time she had reached 137 bomb symbols, they appear to be of a darker color, so presumably they were overpainted in the red we see today. This would indicate a time period between late July and early September 1944.

Initially, every fifth bomb symbol had a darker-painted fin on the bomb symbol, but once these symbols had been repainted in red, the fin of each fifth bomb was painted white.

The final layout would show a top row of fifty bomb symbols, a second row showing the swastika and six decoy symbols, and then two further rows of fifty missions each, followed by a row of twenty-nine bomb symbols that ends at the top package gun housing and a final row of twenty bombs, to make the total of 199. The large 200-bomb symbol (marked "200 missions") was initially painted on card and attached higher on the fuselage for publicity shots, before being painted lower on the fuselage in the position we see today, with the figure of "200" superimposed on it. The final (201st) bomb symbol seems never to have been applied.

In fact, a study of the actual missions performed by "Flak-Bait" reveals that, in fact, she may have completed 202 missions, but that is down to the interpretation of each mission report. A handwritten note on the debriefing form for September 12, 1944, states that it was the 137th mission and if correct (a review of the actual missions performed can be made to tally with this total but, as stated, it is all down to interpretation) and a mission count from this date forward does seem to point to the fact that she may have reached a total of 202 missions. The answer may lie with the six decoy mission symbols applied to the nose as only the first diversionary sweep can accurately be accounted for and the extra mission may have been applied as a decoy, but they were all applied before June 1, 1944, so the true answer will never be known today. What is not in doubt is that all the official publicity was for the 200th mission was on April 17, 1945, and only one more mission was completed after that date so 201 has to remain the formally recognized total.

In addition the 132nd bomb symbol, as we see it today, is painted black and represents one of the three night missions that "Flak-Bait" had taken part in. The 322nd BG flew a total of five night missions and was the only B-26-equipped group within 9th Bomber Command to carry out these type of missions during the summer of 1944.

D-day Stripes

For the D-day landings, it was felt necessary to adorn all Allied aircraft with distinctive tactical markings to help aid identification by antiaircraft gunners. This was adopted by all single- and twin-engine aircraft and those four-engined Halifax and Stirling bombers engaged in glider-towing operations.

These stripes would comprise alternating black and white stripes (three white and two black) painted around the rear fuselage and on both upper and lower surfaces of the wings. On the B-26 Marauder, these were specified to be 24" wide on the rear fuselage, to the rear of the wing, and 20" wide on the wings outside the engine nacelles. Because these were hastily applied by hand, some variations did occur (on the actual airframe, these are 22" wide on the wings, while those on the fuselage are too faint to be measured).

In the 322nd BG the original and early replacement aircraft, which did not have their fuselage national insignia moved forward, resulted in the D-day stripes completely encircling the fuselage, bordering the gray-colored squadron codes and the forward part of the star and bar.

In late July 1944, it was felt that these identification stripes were no longer required on the upper surfaces, and they were gradually removed, seemingly by the use of fuel-coated rags. Initially this was down the fuselage sides to the midpoint of the fuselage codes and, later still, was further extended to below the squadron code letters. The D-day stripes under the lower fuselage and wing undersurfaces remained, although gradually they became very weathered and faded, as can be witnessed on the airframe today.

The nose section of "Flak-Bait" was installed in Gallery 203 at the NASM in 1976, being admired by many thousands of visitors. Over the years, the many hands that had rested on the airframe resulted in the paint wearing away, causing a preservation problem for the staff today. After twenty-eight years she was finally moved to the Udvar-Hazy Center at Dulles for a full restoration. *Author's collection*

Pictured on June 22, 1993, McDonald Darnell Jr., *on the left*, with Sherman V. N. Best, pose in front of the fuselage section of "Flak-Bait," with McDonald Darnell's original A-2 jacket placed on the radio operator's seat. *Smithsonian National Air and Space Museum, NASM 9A12311*

McDonald Darnell Jr.'s A-2 jacket, showing "Flak-Bait" art and mission symbols. *Photo by Mark Avino, Smithsonian National Air and Space Museum, NASM 99-41162*

View from the public gallery across the Mary Engen Restoration Hangar, showing all the components of "Flak-Bait." *Author's collection*

The cockpit section of "Flak-Bait," showing the worn state of the olive drab on the upper fuselage. When placed on display in the Mall, this area had been overpainted, this paint having now been meticulously removed to reveal the original weathered finish. *Author's collection*

The nose section, showing the bare-metal areas where the paint has been worn away by the many thousands of hands that had touched her while on display. The work of the restoration team is challenged in finding ways to blend this back in, without leaving obvious signs of respraying. *Author's collection*

The original project number, possibly 92113R, oversprayed and replaced with the number 92096R. *Author's collection*

The model number, amended from B-26B-25-MA, altered to B-26B-26-MA to reflect the modification state of the aircraft. These modifications were made at the Martin Omaha Plant in Nebraska in early May 1943. *Author's collection*

The "Flak-Bait" artwork was applied by Sgt. Ted Simonaitis; his name can be seen at the lower right, just above the 200th bomb symbol. *Author's collection*

Each of the original crew members had his name applied adjacent to their position; these were never overpainted by later crews. First of all, the pilot, Jim "Boss" Farrell. *Author's collection*

Copilot Tom "Tarheel" Moore. *Author's collection*

The bombardier had his name painted on the left hand side of the nose as O. J. "Red" Redmond. *Author's collection*

Radio operator J. B. "Polock" Manuel's name as it appeared under the left-hand window, adjacent to his position. *Author's collection*

Below the middle upper turret on the left-hand side of the fuselage is "Flackhappy" Thielan; note the misspelling of the word "flak." *Author's collection*

On the left-hand side of the tail turret position is painted Tim Tyler's name. *Author's collection*

T/Sgt. C.F. THOMPSON
Crew Chief - ROTATED
S/SGT. C.G. GOODRICH - Crewchief
CPL. DAVE RICH - Assistant
PFC. GEO. SANGREGORIO - Mechanic
PFC. JAMES RYAN - Armorer

The left-hand nosewheel door, showing the ground crew names; those in white were applied shortly before the 200th mission. *Author's collection*

Disassembly Crew
Oberpfaffenhofen: Ger.

Sgt. A. Aymond Crew Chief
Sgt. R. Cook
Cpl. G. Bunch Asst. C. Chief
Cpl. R. Olsen
Cpl. C. Streiz
Pfc. E. Mills   Pfc. R. Bunqcayao
Pfc. C. Monqillo
Pfc. E. Stokley

On the right-hand nosewheel door, the names of the crew that dismantled the airframe at Oberpfaffenhofen in the summer of 1946 were added. *Author's collection*

On the forward part of the right-hand nosewheel door, the names of crew chief Sgt. C. Goodrich and Sgt. J. Connelly were applied. Sgt. Connelly's role in maintaining "Flak-Bait" is not known. *Author's collection*

Detail view of the area around the radio operator's position, showing some of the many flak patches on the airframe; these were finished in primer and not oversprayed with olive drab. Also the 132nd bomb symbol in black, representing one of the night missions completed by "Flak-Bait," even though night missions had finished by this time in her career. *Author's collection*

Upper view of the left-hand wing, showing the extreme wear on the paint surfaces and further flak patches. Also of note is the darker edge to the national insignia. *Author's collection*

Undersurface of the right wing, again showing the extreme weathering of the paintwork and the remains of the D-day stripes. *Author's collection*

The rear fuselage and tail turret area, showing the individual code letter "O," with the original gray paint showing through; late in the war this was overpainted white, which has mostly weathered away. The pointed structures in the foreground are the rear sections of the nacelles. *Author's collection*

Close-up of the individual code letter "O" on the right-hand side of the fuselage; note that when this was overpainted in white toward the end of the war that it passed over the star and bar. *Author's collection*

The rear sections of the engine nacelles; note the exhaust staining. *Author's collection*

Waist gun position and fuselage star and bar; note how the red that originally surrounded the insignia can be seen showing through the overpainted blue, which superseded it in late 1943, in some places. *Author's collection*

Left and right views of the tail section, respectively, showing the 449th BS code of PN. The B-26 was of modular construction, with the fuselage built in three sections and joined together in final assembly. *Author's collection*

The fuselage center section, incorporating the bomb bays. *Author's collection*

Close-up of the left-hand side of the nose, showing the distinctive flak patches; compare with the black-and-white photo of the same area. *Author's collection*

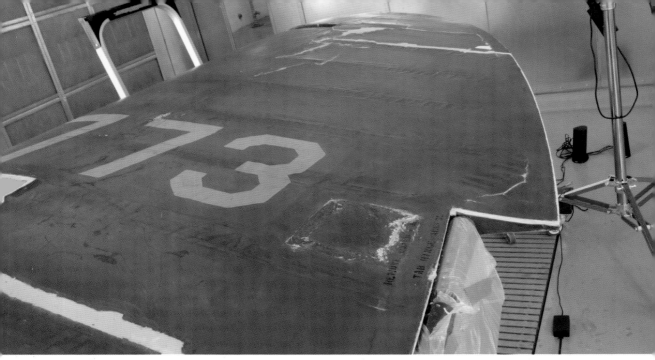

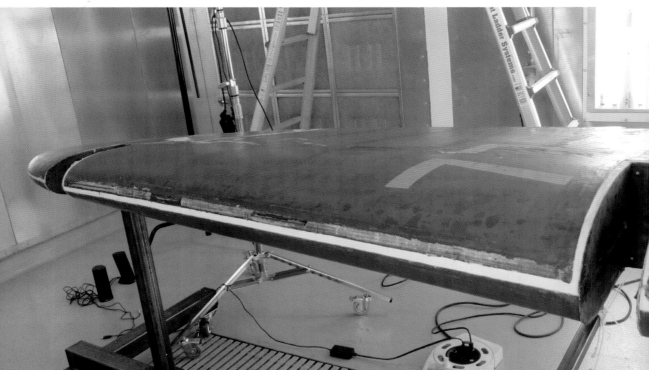

The rudder undergoing restoration; the original structure has been overlaid with new fabric, to which the original fabric, showing the last three digits of the serial number, 773, is overlaid. The difficult part will be to blend in the gaps at the edges in a way that will not show. *Author's collection*

One of the wingtips, showing a tear in the skin that will need repair. *Author's collection*

Close-up of the wingtip formation lights; these were added as a field modification, a fiddly task for the electricians, and were not universally fitted. *Author's collection*

The right-hand and left-hand bomb bay doors as fitted to "Flak-Bait" late in the war; note how the left-hand one is of the later design, with the open ends to reduce drag; one wonders if there was a slight element of asymmetric drag when these were opened. *Author's collection*

Wing leading-edge sections, showing a landing light. Note the patch repair where the deicing equipment had been deleted and holes covered up. *Author's collection*

The Pratt & Whitney R2800 engines were completely stripped and rebuilt during the restoration and are now ready for when she is reassembled. *Author's collection*

One of the side package gun housings in storage, showing the front section painted black; these were repainted in the fall of 1944. *Author's collection*

The main undercarriage legs await their turn for overhaul. *Author's collection*

The nosewheel and leg awaiting restoration; the tire is badly split and will be replaced. *Author's collection*

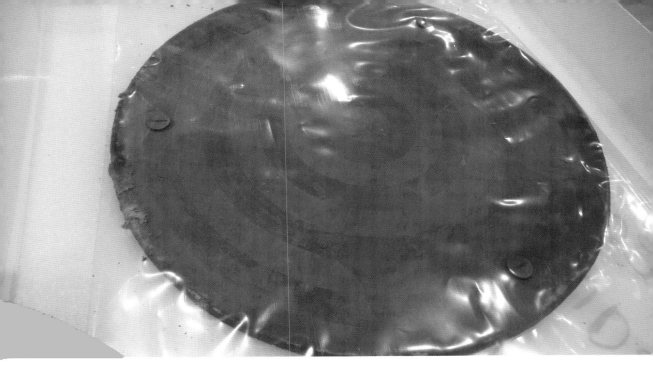

The nosewheel center disk, showing the star and rings; the paintwork is in a delicate state and will need careful handling and restoration. *Author's collection*

The Martin 250CE upper turret, showing the Glenn L. Martin Company motif on the armor plating; behind are the inner flaps. *Author's collection*

While much of the interior is stripped out for conservation purposes, the instrument panel is complete. *Author's collection*

Close-up of the instrument panel, showing the radio call placard bearing the aircraft's serial number, 131773. *Author's collection*

The stripped-out radio operator's station. *Author's collection*

Opposite the radio operator was the navigator's position; again, this has been stripped out for preservation purposes. *Author's collection*

FLUORESCENT SPARE LAMPS

KEEP BRAKE AIR BOTTLE FILLED TO 1200 P.S.I.

Close-up view of the radio operator's table, showing the radio call placard with the aircraft's serial number, 131773. *Author's collection*

Above the navigator's position is the card clock face, three of which were found in the fuselage, which helped crew members call out relative positions of approaching enemy aircraft or other items of interest. *Author's collection*

View into the main bomb bay area, looking aft. *Author's collection*

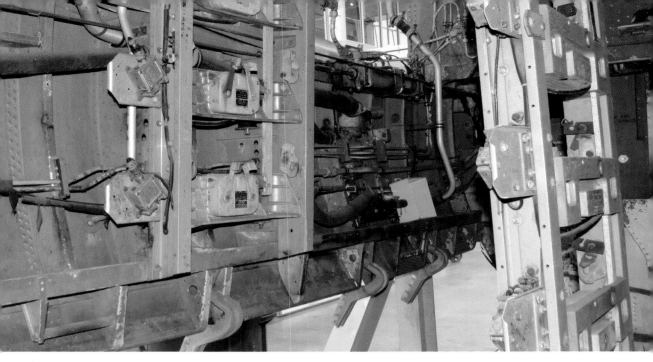

The side wall of the fuselage in the bomb bay area, showing the bomb station mechanisms and the hinges for the bomb bay doors. *Author's collection*

The rear bomb bay area, looking forward to the main bomb bay. The rear bomb bay was not utilized in the ETO, and on the B-26B-25-MA model, of which "Flak-Bait" was the first produced, the operating mechanisms and racks were not installed. *Author's collection*

The stripped-out rear fuselage area, looking back to the tail turret position. *Author's collection*

Jeremy Kinney (*left*), of the NASM's Aeronautics Department, points out details on the rear fuselage to Sherman V. N. Best, former copilot on "Flak-Bait." Sadly, Sherman Best has passed away since the time the photograph was taken. *Thomas Farrell*

NAME	POSITION	MISSION DATE(S)	NOTES
1Lt. John H. Alderson	pilot	3/10/45	
1Lt. Donald W. Allen	copilot (later capt.)	12/22/43	
SSgt. William S. Allen	engineer/gunner	4/10/44, 4/10/44 (2), 6/17/44, 6/24/44, 7/18/44	
Sgt. Vincente Alvarado	tail gunner	9/6/44 (2), 9/12/44	
SSgt. Edwin L. Arceneaux	togglier	3/24/45	
2Lt. John S. Avooski	copilot & pilot	8/25/44, 9/6/44 (2), 9/12/44	
1Lt. George B. Backes	pilot	2/8/44 (sp)	
Sgt. W. J. Bajorek	radio/gunner	3/22/45 (2)	
Sgt. J. Baker	togglier	4/24/45	
2Lt. William A. Barbour	navigator/ bombardier	3/7/44, 3/8/44, 3/26/44, 4/18/44	
1Lt. Douglas B. Barker	copilot & pilot	4/8/44, 5/4/44, 5/7/44, 5/7/44 (2), 5/8/44, 5/27/44, 9/11/44	
Sgt. Jack Barrier	tail gunner (later ssgt.)	8/28/44, 9/10/44 (NTO), 11/30/44, 12/13/44, 3/23/45, 3/23/45 (2)	
Sgt Russell L. Bassler	tail gunner (later ssgt.)	9/11/44, 12/1/44, 12/5/44, 12/26/44, 1/5/45, 1/14/45, 2/8/45, 2/14/45, 3/9/45, 3/11/45, 3/14/45, 3/15/45, 3/17/45, 3/18/45, 4/10/45	
SSgt. Raymond G. Baum	radio/gunner (later t/sgt.)	1/21/44, 2/13/44 (ER),	(POW 5/27/44)
2Lt. Emmerson I. Baughman	navigator/bombar- dier (later 1lt.)	1/21/44, 2/13/44 (ER), 2/24/44, 5/8/44 (2)	
1Lt. Kenneth L. Bayles	pilot (later capt.)	11/7/43	(MIA 7/8/44 night)
2Lt. Burton T. Belleson	copilot	2/13/44 (ER)	
SSgt. Richard P. Bender	radio/gunner	9/22/43, 9/23/43, 2/25/44 (2)	
SSgt. Bernard O. Benoit	radio/gunner	11/19/43	
2Lt. Sherman V. N. Best	copilot & pilot (later 1lt.)	6/15/44 (2), 12/1/44, 12/5/44, 12/26/44, 1/5/45, 1/14/45, 2/8/45, 2/14/45, 3/9/45, 3/14/45, 3/15/45, 3/17/45, 3/18/45	

NAME	POSITION	MISSION DATE(S)	NOTES
SSgt. Robert G. Bevers	togglier (later tsgt.)	6/17/44, 6/24/44, 7/18/44, 8/25/44	
Sgt. Clarence S. Bixler	tail gunner & togglier (later ssgt.)	2/14/45 (2), 4/11/45	
2Lt. Samuel Block	navigator/ bombardier	8/28/44, 9/10/44 (NTO)	
2Lt. Stanley S. Bolesta	navigator/ bombardier	9/5/43	(MIA 11/5/43; evaded but captured 2/26/44)
SSgt. Stanley J. Box	engineer/gunner	5/27/44 (2), 10/30/44, 11/2/44	
2Lt. Henry C. Bozarth	copilot & pilot (later 1lt.)	6/6/44 (3), 9/11/44, 12/1/44, 12/5/44, 12/26/44, 1/14/45, 1/22/45, 2/8/45, 2/14/45, 3/9/45, 3/11/45, 3/14/45, 3/15/45, 3/17/45, 3/18/45	
Sgt. J. W. Bradley	engineer/gunner	3/10/45	
2Lt. Richard W. Bradley	copilot	7/27/43, 8/4/43	
TSgt. Austin W. Bradshaw	radio/gunner	5/20/44 (2)	(MIA 7/8/44 night)
2Lt. William D. Brearley	navigator/bombardier (later 1lt.)	5/27/44 (2), 4/17/45	
2Lt. Donald E. Bredell	copilot	2/2/45	
2Lt. Kenneth A. Brower	navigator/ bombardier	2/20/44, 2/21/44, 2/22/44, 2/25/44	(MIA 7/8/44 night)
2Lt. Clarence Brown Jr.	navigator/ bombardier	3/23/45, 3/23/45 (2)	
Sgt. Harold Brown	tail gunner & togglier (later ssgt. & tsgt.)	5/27/44 (2), 5/29/44), 5/30/44, 6/4/44, 6/5/44, 6/6/44, 6/7/44, 6/18/44, 7/31/44, 8/16/44, 12/24/44, 12/25/44, 12/25/44 (2)	
2Lt. Evan R. Bruner	pilot	11/19/43	
2Lt. Henry C. Bryant	copilot (later 1lt.)	9/6/44 (2), 9/12/44, 1/29/45	
SSgt. Robert J. Buckles	tail gunner	4/10/44, 4/10/44 (2), 6/17/44, 6/24/44, 7/18/44	
Sgt. Hurburt W. Burgoyne	tail gunner & togglier (later tsgt.)	6/15/44 (2), 2/2/45	
2Lt. Beverley P. Burrage	copilot & pilot (later 1lt.)	2/20/44, 2/21/44, 2/22/44, 2/25/44, 3/7/44, 3/8/44, 3/20/44, 3/23/44, 3/26/44, 4/18/44, 4/19/44, 4/20/44, 5/28/44 (2), 6/1/44, 6/2/44, 7/19/44, 7/28/44 (2), 8/13/44(2)	
Sgt. Orval F. Burton	passenger	1/4/44, 1/4/44 (2)	
2Lt. Harold J. Bye	pilot (later 1lt.)	11/9/44, 11/18/44, 2/15/45	
1Lt. Andrew F. Byrd Jr.	pilot & copilot	5/6/44, 5/12/44, 5/12/44 (2), 8/13/44 (NTO)	
2Lt. Robert G. Caldwell	navigator/ bombardier	9/22/43, 9/23/43, 11/3/43, 2/25/44 (2)	

NAME	POSITION	MISSION DATE(S)	NOTES
Sgt. John. E. Campbell	tail gunner (later ssgt.)	7/20/44, 8/13/44 (2)	
SSgt. James L. Campbell	togglier (later tsgt.)	4/21/44, 5/6/44, 5/12/44, 5/12/44 (2), 5/28/44, 2/6/44, 6/23/44, 8/1/44, 8/3/44, 9/6/44 (2), 9/12/44	
Sgt. Raymond N. Cannon	tail gunner	3/18/45 (2)	
2Lt. John Carbone	navigator/bombardier	7/28/44 (2), 8/13/44 (2)	(WIA 12/25/44)
2Lt. John H. Carter	copilot	3/19/45	
Sgt. William F. Carter Jr.	engineer/gunner	9/6/44 (2), 9/12/44	
Sgt. Leo D. Case	radio/gunner	9/6/44 (2), 9/12/44	
TSgt. J. L. Chambers	togglier	8/1/44	
2Lt. Stephen M. Chase	copilot (later 1lt.)	11/7/43, 1/21/44, 2/13/44 (ER), 2/24/44, 5/8/44 (2)	
SSgt. Virgil J. Christian	engineer/gunner & togglier (later tsgt.)	9/22/43, 9/23/43, 7/19/44, 7/20/44	
Sgt Albert Christopher	tail gunner (to pvt., 6/44; to ssgt., 8/1/44)	2/20/44, 2/21/44, 2/22/44, 2/25/44, 3/7/44, 3/8/44, 3/20/44, 3/23/44, 3/26/44, 4/18/44, 4/19/44, 4/20/44, 5/15/44, 5/20/44 (2), 5/21/44, 6/10/44, 6/13–14/44 (night), 6/22/44 (2), 8/1/44, 8/3/44	
Sgt. Joseph A. Circelli	tail gunner	11/19/44, 12/18/44, 3/24/45	
2Lt. Frank I. Clark	navigator/bombardier	10/30/44, 11/2/44	
TSgt. Walter E. Clark Jr.	radio/gunner	3/15/44	
Sgt. Charles W. Coon	engineer/gunner (later ssgt.)	5/28/44 (2)	(MIA 7/8/44 night; evaded, return by 9/17/44)
1Lt. Robert M. Cooper Jr.	copilot & pilot	5/6/44, 5/12/44, 5/12/44 (2), 8/12/44, 8/25/44	
2Lt. James M. Corbitt	copilot	(450th BS) 2/16/45	
SSgt. James E. Corlew	engineer/gunner	3/25/44, 5/9/44, 5/11/44, 5/24/44, 6/6/44 (2), 6/13/44	(WIA 8/18/44)
2Lt. Woodie C. Cornwall	pilot (later 1lt.)	11/26/44, 11/26/44 (2), 12/2/44, 12/9/44, 12/10/44, 2/19/45, 3/16/45	
TSgt. H. D. Coulson	engineer/gunner	1/7/44	
2Lt. Robert R. Crusey	copilot & pilot (later 1lt.)	11/19/43, 4/10/44, 4/10/44 (2), 6/17/44, 6/24/44, 7/18/44	
SSgt. Henry T. Cunningham	tail gunner	9/5/43	(POW 11/5/43)

NAME	POSITION	MISSION DATE(S)	NOTES
SSgt. McDonald T. Darnell Jr.	radio/gunner (later tsgt.)	6/15/44 (2), 7/31/44, 8/4–5/44 (night), 9/11/44, 12/5/44, 12/26/44, 1/5/45, 1/14/45, 2/8/45, 2/14/45, 3/9/45, 3/11/45, 3/14/45, 3/17/45, 3/18/45	
Capt. Carl E. Davis	pilot	3/17/44, 8/4–5/44 (night), 8/26/44 (night)	
SSgt. Paschal A. Davis	tail gunner & togglier (later tsgt.)	5/6/44, 5/12/44, 5/12/44 (2), 6/10/44, 8/12/44	
Sgt. J. S. Devine	radio/gunner	3/15/45, 4/10/45	
F/O Jess E. Dibert	copilot	3/22/45	
1Lt. Joseph C. Dick	navigator/bombardier	12/22/43	(bailed out over France, 5/27/44)
Sgt. J. Docca	engineer/gunner	(452nd BS) 2/15/44	
2Lt. Marion F. Dombrowski	copilot & pilot (later 1lt.)	5/8/44 (2), 12/15/44	
2Lt. Joseph H. Donahue	copilot	9/6/44, 9/14/44, 9/27/44	
2Lt. W. F. Dreyer	copilot	10/3/43	
SSgt. Clyde T. Duke	tail gunner	2/8/44 (sp)	
Sgt. Theodore J. Dumais	tail gunner (later ssgt.)	5/28/44 (2)	(MIA 7/8/44 night; evaded, return by 9/17/44)
SSgt. Argel I. Duncan	radio/gunner	3/17/44, 8/6/44	
Capt. Joe O. Eaton	observer (387th BG)	5/11/44	
Capt. J. P. Eckenrode	observer (449th BS ordnance officer)	2/21/44, 2/22/44	
TSgt. Fred T. Ehrgood	engineer/gunner	5/20/44, 5/22/44, 5/26/44, 6/15/44	
TSgt. Sol Einbinder	radio/gunner	2/15/44	
SSgt. Warren M. Ek	radio/gunner	12/15/44	
SSgt. Malcolm D. Enlow	engineer/gunner	12/24/43, 2/8/44 (sp)	
2Lt. Francis E. Ennis	navigator/bombardier	10/14/44	
Sgt. Douglas A. Erickson	engineer/gunner	6/23/44, 8/1/44, 8/3/44	
1Lt. Graydon K. Eubank	pilot & copilot	4/21/44, 5/9/44 (2), 5/10/44, 5/13/44, 8/16/44	
TSgt. Walter H. Evans	engineer/gunner	1911//43	
F/O J. Facok	navigator/bombardier	1/16/45, 2/13/45, 2/21/45	

NAME	POSITION	MISSION DATE(S)	NOTES
1Lt. James J. Farrell	pilot	7/27/43, 8/16/43, 8/19/43, 9/2/43, 9/4/43, 9/6/43 (WIA), 9/9/43, 9/11/43, 9/16/43, 9/24/43, 10/2/43, 10/3/43, 10/22/43, 10/24/43, 11/3/43, 11/5/43, 11/10/43, 11/11/43, 11/23/43, 11/29/43, 12/4/43, 12/5/43, 12/20/43, 12/21/43, 12/30/43, 12/31/43, 1/4/44, 1/4/44 (2), 1/14/44, 1/23/44, 1/24/44, 1/29/44, 2/3/44, 4/11/44, 5/29/44, 5/30/44, 6/4/44, 6/6/44, 6/7/44, 6/18/44	
2Lt. Thomas H. Felker	copilot & pilot (later 1lt.)	11/19/44, 12/18/44, 1/5/45, 1/29/45 (KIA 2/10/45)	
SSgt. Joseph G. Ferrell	engineer/gunner	(451st BS) 2/24/44	
F/O Omar D. Fields	navigator/ bombardier	1/22/45, 2/18/45	
2Lt. Robert H. Figueroa	navigator/ bombardier	4/11/45 (2), 4/15/45	
Sgt. Cecil Fisher	radio/gunner (later tsgt.)	7/20/44, 4/17/45	
2Lt. Edward B. Fitch	pilot	10/30/44, 11/2/44	
2Lt. John T. Fitzwilliam	navigator/ bombardier	3/22/45 (2)	
2Lt. Robert W. Fletcher	navigator/ bombardier	9/25/43, 9/27/43, 10/8/43, 10/18/43, 12/24/43, 1/7/44, 6/6/44 (3)	
Sgt. John Foorman	engineer/gunner	11/19/44, 12/18/44, 3/24/45	
2Lt. C. M. Ford	navigator/ bombardier	(451st BS) 3/21/45	
2Lt. Clyttis A. Forrester	copilot	9/25/43, 9/27/43, 10/8/43, 10/18/43, 12/24/43, 1/7/44	(transferred to 495th BS, 344th BG; KIA 5/28/44)
2Lt. William G. Fort	pilot & copilot (later 1lt. and capt.)	5/27/44 (2), 6/15/44 (2), 6/23/44, 4/17/45	
Sgt. Benson N. Foss	togglier	2/15/45	(KIA 3/22/45)
1Lt. Chilton M. Foster	copilot	2/15/44, 5/27/44 (2)	
Sgt. R. M. Fragoso	tail gunner	(452nd BS) 3/25/45	
2Lt. Walter J. Frank	pilot	9/6/44, 9/14/44, 9/27/44	
TSgt. Oran D. Freeman	radio/gunner (to pvt., 6/44; to sgt., 8/1/44)	2/20/44, 2/21/44, 2/22/44, 2/25/44, 3/7/44, 3/8/44, 3/20/44, 3/23/44, 3/26/44, 4/18/44, 4/19/44, 4/20/44, 5/15/44, 6/10/44, 6/13–14/44 (night), 6/22/44 (2)	
Sgt. William R. Fry	tail gunner	9/6/44, 9/14/44, 9/27/44	
Sgt. Theodore W. Gatzounas	engineer/gunner (later tsgt.)	11/26/44, 11/26/44 (2), 12/2/44, 12/9/44, 12/10/44, 2/19/45, 3/16/45	(WIA 2/23/45)

NAME	POSITION	MISSION DATE(S)	NOTES
Sgt. Thomas B. Gee	togglier	12/1/44, 12/5/44, 12/26/44, 1/5/45, 1/14/45, 2/8/45, 2/14/45, 3/9/45, 3/11/45, 3/14/45, 3/15/45, 3/17/45, 3/18/45, 3/18/45 (2)	
2Lt. Charles J. Gemmell	copilot	12/1/43	
1Lt. William C. George	pilot	12/24/44, 12/25/44, 12/25/44 (2)	
SSgt. Emmett W. Gibson	tail gunner	11/19/43	
SSgt. George N. Gibson	tail gunner	(451st BS) 2/24/44	
2Lt. Robert P. Gilmore	navigator/ bombardier	11/19/43	(transferred to 495th BS / 344th BG; KIA 5/28/44)
SSgt. William Goetz Jr.	radio/gunner	3/25/44, 5/9/44, 5/11/44, 5/21/44, 5/24/44, 6/6/44 (2), 6/8/44, 6/13/44	(WIA 8/18/44)
2Lt. George S. Goldstein	navigator/ bombardier	11/11/43	
1Lt. Kenneth W. Goldacker	pilot	11/19/44, 12/18/44, 3/24/45	
Sgt. Frank R. Gonzales	radio/gunner	1/29/45	
2Lt. Ernest W. Goodwin	pilot (later 1lt.)	9/22/43, 9/23/43, 2/25/44 (2)	
SSgt. Gosudra	tail gunner	12/15/44	
TSgt. Harry L. Gray	togglier	4/20/44, 5/15/44, 9/11/44	
2Lt. William F. Green	copilot & pilot (later 1lt.)	12/5/43, 5/4/44, 5/7/44, 5/7/44 (2), 5/20/44, 5/22/44, 5/26/44, 6/15/44	
SSgt. Wayne M. Greer	engineer/gunner	12/1/43	(MIA 1/14/44, evaded, return by 9/5/44)
Sgt. V. R. Griffin	tail gunner	3/22/45	
1Lt. William F. Groman	copilot	(452nd BS) 2/15/44	
F/O Ernest O. Grubb	copilot	9/5/43	(MIA 11/5/43, evaded, return by 3/2/44)
SSgt. George W. Gueterman	togglier (later tsgt.)	4/8/44, 4/10/44, 4/19/44, 5/4/44, 5/7/44, 5/7/44 (2), 5/8/44, 5/10/44, 5/13/44, 5/20/44, 5/27/44, 6/15/44	
SSgt. William T. Guyette	engineer/gunner	1/21/44, 2/13/44 (ER), 5/8/44 (2)	
SSgt. Orville Hahn	tail gunner	5/20/44, 5/22/44, 5/26/44, 6/15/44	
2Lt. Robert L. Hall	copilot & pilot (later 1lt.)	8/28/44, 9/10/44 (NTO), 11/30/44, 12/13/44, 3/23/45, 3/23/45 (2)	
F/O Jack L. Hancock	copilot	2/8/44 (sp)	

NAME	POSITION	MISSION DATE(S)	NOTES
Sgt. John L. Harding Jr.	tail gunner	12/30/43, 12/31/43, 1/4/44, 1/4/44, 4/8/44, 5/4/44, 5/7/44, 5/7/44(2), 5/8/44, 5/27/44	
Sgt. Jesse O. Hartsell	tail gunner	1/21/44, 2/13/44 (ER), 5/8/44 (2)	
Sgt. Jack Hastings	radio/gunner	6/5/44	(injured in crash at Ford 8/16/44)
SSgt. Carl C. Hendrix	radio/gunner (later tsgt.)	11/19/44, 12/18/44, 3/24/45	
Sgt. Anthony R. Heredia	engineer/gunner (later ssgt.)	9/6/44, 9/14/44, 9/27/44	
TSgt. William J. Hess	tail gunner	4/17/45	
Sgt. Curtis B. Hill	tail gunner	2/5/44, 2/6/44, 2/9/44, 2/10/44, 2/11/44, 2/24/44	(POW 4/21/44)
2Lt. A. J. Hillsamer	copilot	(452nd BS) 3/25/45	
2Lt. Wendell L. Hoenshel	navigator/ bombardier	11/19/44, 12/18/44	
Sgt. Joe F. Holcomb	engineer/gunner	7/28/44 (2), 8/13/44 (2)	
1Lt. H. E. Holland	pilot	(452nd BS) 3/25/45	
SSgt. S. R. Holliday	engineer/gunner	4/8/43	
1Lt. Larry L. Holmes	pilot	(452nd BS) 2/15/44	(KIA 6/13/44)
Sgt. David W. Hone	tail gunner (later ssgt.)	6/12/44, 8/12/44, 8/25/44	
2Lt. Charles W. Honhold	copilot	11/26/44, 11/26/44 (2), 12/2/44, 12/9/44, 12/10/44, 2/19/45, 3/16/45	
1Lt. Harry C. Huber	navigator/ bombardier	2/8/44 (sp)	
2Lt. William E. Hugelman	navigator/ bombardier	4/9/45	
F/O T. Hunt	copilot	6/6/44	
2Lt. Donald L. Hunter	copilot & pilot	3/17/44, 5/28/44, 8/6/44	
2Lt. Harold D. Hurlbut	pilot	10/14/44	
W/C Oram C. "Bud" Hutton	passenger on 200th	4/17/45	(war correspondent, writer for Stars & Stripes)
1Lt. Dan Isgrig	pilot	12/1/43	
SSgt. William L. Johnston	engineer/gunner (later tsgt.)	9/11/44, 12/1/44, 12/5/44, 12/26/44, 1/5/45, 1/14/45, 2/8/45, 2/14/45, 3/9/45, 3/11/45, 3/14/45, 3/15/45, 3/17/45, 3/18/45, 4/10/45	
1Lt. James F. Jolly	pilot	6/23/44, 8/1/44, 8/3/44	
1Lt. Claude B. Jones	pilot	(451st BS) 2/24/44 (2)	
2Lt. Glendon P. Jones	pilot (later 1lt.)	3/25/44 (sp), 5/24/44, 6/13/44, 7/18/44 (2), 7/26/44, 7/27/44 (ab), 7/28/44, 8/26/44	
SSgt. Robert M. Jones	radio/gunner	7/28/44 (2)	

NAME	POSITION	MISSION DATE(S)	NOTES
SSgt. Wilfred S. Jones	engineer/gunner	2/15/44	
1Lt. Wilton L. Juneau	navigator/ bombardier	8/4/43, 4/8/44	
2Lt. Leo Karlinsky	bombardier	6/7/44	
Sgt. James A. Keating	tail gunner	3/10/45	
Sgt. Raymond J. Keating	engineer/gunner (later ssgt.)	2/25/44 (2), 5/4/44, 6/12/44, 8/25/44	
1Lt. Charles E. Keenan	copilot & pilot	5/28/44, 7/19/44	
2Lt. Joseph J. Keenan	navigator/ bombardier	3/19/45	
TSgt. Anthony M. Kondrasky	engineer/gunner	12/22/43	
Sgt. Keith K. Korell	radio/gunner	3/18/45 (2)	
SSgt. Steve Krykla	tail gunner	3/15/44	(MIA 6/13/44; returned to UK)
Sgt. John L. Kuhl	engineer/gunner	1/14/44	(MIA 6/13/44; returned to UK)
Sgt. Martin Kushmer	tail gunner	3/16/45	
2Lt. Ray L. La Chapelle	navigator/ bombardier	11/9/44, 11/18/44	
SSgt. William K. Lahm	radio/gunner	9/5/43	(POW 11/3/43)
2Lt. George H. Lane	copilot & pilot (later 1lt.)	3/15/44, 7/20/44	
2Lt. William C. Lane	navigator/ bombardier	(450th BS) 2/16/45	
1Lt. Warren Langer	pilot	4/8/45, 4/9/45, 4/11/45, 4/11/45 (2), 4/24/45	
1Lt. Tom G. Laster	pilot	(451st BS) 3/21/45	
F/O T. R. Lee	navigator/ bombardier	3/10/45	
2Lt. Walter G. Leffler	navigator/ bombardier	9/6/44, 9/14/44, 9/27/44	
Sgt. C. Leja	radio/gunner	(452nd BS) 2/15/44	
Capt. Harold K. Levy	copilot	1/16/45, 2/13/45, 2/21/45	
2Lt. Mathew F. Lewonowski	copilot (later 1lt.)	11/9/44, 11/18/44, 2/15/45, 3/10/45, 3/23/45	
1Lt. Harleth I. Lewter	pilot & copilot	3/15/44, 5/27/44	
2Lt. Vaun N. Liniger	pilot	9/25/43, 9/27/43, 10/8/43, 10/18/43, 12/24/43, 1/7/44, 6/6/44 (3)	
Sgt. John W. Linton Sr.	radio/gunner	2/2/45	
Sgt. Emmitt M. Little	tail gunner	11/26/44, 11/26/44 (2), 12/2/44, 12/9/44, 12/10/44, 2/19/45	(WIA 2/23/45)
SSgt. Kenneth M. Locke	engineer/gunner (later tsgt.)	5/7/44, 5/7/44 (2), 5/28/44, 6/15/44 (2), 8/4–5/44 (night), 8/26/44 (night), 4/17/45	

NAME	POSITION	MISSION DATE(S)	NOTES
TSgt. William Lopatin	radio/gunner	2/8/44 (sp)	
SSgt. Eddie W. Lowary	tail gunner	8/4/43, 6/23/44 (reduced to private on 2/6/44, when it was discovered he had not completed gunnery training; taken off combat status; reinstated at a later date)	(WIA 7/19/44) (KIA 8/16/44)
F/O Claude A. Luke	copilot (later 2lt.)	10/30/44, 11/2/44	
1Lt. John B. Lynch	pilot	2/14/45 (2)	
SSgt. J. F. McKeever	engineer/gunner	(451st BS) 3/21/45	
SSgt. Paul E. McManes	radio/gunner	2/5/44, 2/6/44, 2/9/44, 2/10/44, 2/11/44, 2/24/44	(POW 4/21/44)
2Lt. George L. McMillan	navigator/ bombardier	11/10/43	
SSgt. Edward V. McWilliams	radio/gunner	12/22/43	(KIA 5/27/44)
Sgt. Ellis C. Malone	radio/gunner	5/8/44 (2), 5/22/44, 5/26/44, 5/28/44 (2)	
SSgt. Vincent J. Mammolito	engineer/gunner (to pvt., 6/44; to sgt., 8/1/44)	2/20/44, 2/21/44, 2/22/44, 2/25/44, 3/7/44, 3/20/44, 3/23/44, 3/26/44, 4/18/44, 4/19/44, 4/20/44, 5/15/44, 5/20/44 (2), 5/21/44, 6/8/44, 6/10/44, 6/13–14/44 (night), 6/22/44 (2), 7/20/44	
SSgt. Joseph B. Manuel	radio/gunner	7/27/43, 8/16/43, 8/19/43, 9/2/43, 9/4/43, 9/6/43, 9/9/43, 9/11/43, 9/16/43, 9/24/43, 10/2/43, 10/3/43, 10/22/43, 10/24/43, 11/3/43, 11/5/43, 11/10/43, 11/11/43, 11/13/43, 11/29/43, 12/4/43, 12/5/43, 12/20/43, 12/21/43, 12/30/43, 12/31/43, 1/4/44, 1/4/44 (2), 1/14/44, 1/23/44, 1/24/44, 1/29/44, 2/3/44, 4/11/44, 5/29/44, 5/30/44, 6/4/44, 6/6/44, 6/7/44, 6/18/44	
Sgt. V. Marcella	radio/gunner	(452nd BS) 3/25/45	
SSgt. Stanford B. Marcum	engineer/gunner (later tsgt.)	3/17/44, 8/6/44	
Sgt. W. A. Markley	radio/gunner	3/10/45	
1Lt. Joseph T. Masters	copilot	(451st BS) 2/24/44	
TSgt. Linford V. Mead	engineer/gunner	4/12/45	
2Lt. Harry K. Megson	copilot & pilot	1/22/45, 2/18/45	(POW 3/22/45)
2Lt. George F. Meily	navigator/ bombardier	11/26/44, 11/26/44 (2), 12/2/44, 12/9/44, 12/10/44, 2/19/45, 3/16/45	
TSgt. Daniel J. Mertes	radio/gunner	12/1/43	(MIA 1/14/44; evaded; returned 9/44)
Sgt. Kenneth M. Meyer	tail gunner	(451st BS) 3/21/45	

NAME	POSITION	MISSION DATE(S)	NOTES
F/O William E. Mildren	pilot	9/5/43	(POW 11/5/43)
2Lt. Norman J. Miller	copilot & pilot	6/17/44, 6/24/44, 7/18/44, 8/16/44	
SSgt. D. F. Milligan	radio/gunner	8/4/43	
2Lt. Allen F. Minich	copilot (later 1lt.)	4/10/44, 5/8/44, 8/6/44	
Sgt. Gordon G. Minter	engineer/gunner (later ssgt.)	4/21/44, 5/9/44 (2), 5/10/44, 5/13/44, 7/19/44	
SSgt. John L. Misarko	togglier	3/20/44, 3/23/44	(POW 4/21/44)
SSgt. Gerald D. Mitchell	engineer/gunner	4/8/45, 4/9/45, 4/11/45, 4/11/45 (2), 4/24/45	
SSgt. James B. Mitchell	tail gunner & togglier	9/25/43, 9/27/43, 10/8/43, 10/18/43, 12/24/43, 1/7/44, 4/10/44 (2), 4/19/44 (2)	(MIA 5/19/44)
Sgt. R. C. Mixon	engineer/gunner	3/22/45 (2), 4/15/45	
2Lt. Richard E. Moninger	copilot & pilot	9/24/43, 1/14/44, 2/15/44	(MIA 6/13/44; returned to UK)
TSgt. Edward Montes de Oca	togglier	5/9/44 (2), (MIA 6/13/44; returned to UK), 7/18/44 (2), 7/26/44, 7/28/44, 8/26/44	
F/O Thomas F. Moore	copilot (later 2lt.)	8/16/43, 8/19/43, 9/2/43, 9/4/43, 9/6/43, 9/16/43, 10/22/43, 10/24/43, 11/3/43, 11/5/43, 11/10/43, 11/11/43, 11/23/43, 11/29/43, 12/4/43, 12/20/43, 12/21/43, 12/30/43, 12/31/43, 1/23/44, 1/24/44, 1/29/44, 2/3/44, 4/11/44, 5/11/44, 5/29/44, 5/30/44, 6/4/44, 6/7/44, 6/18/44, 8/1/44, 8/3/44	
SSgt. Wilbur L. Moore	engineer/gunner	1/23/44, 1/24/44, 2/5/44, 2/6/44, 2/9/44, 2/10/44, 2/11/44, 2/24/44	(POW 4/21/44)
SSgt. James G. Morgan	tail gunner	4/19/44 (2), 6/1/44, 6/2/44, 6/25/44, 7/26/44, 7/28/44	
SSgt. John O. Mullen	engineer/gunner	9/25/43, 9/27/43, 10/8/43, 10/18/43, 6/6/44 (3)	
1Lt. Robert R. Murray	copilot & pilot	4/21/44, 5/9/44 (2), 5/10/44, 5/13/44	
SSgt. Durland C. Mustain	engineer/gunner	4/8/44, 4/19/44 (2), 6/1/44, 6/2/44, 6/25/44, 7/18/44 (2), 7/26/44, 7/28/44, 8/26/44	
Sgt. W. H. Myers	engineer/gunner	1/16/45, 2/13/45, 2/21/45	
Sgt. William R. Narramore	tail gunner	11/9/44, 11/18/44	(KIA 1/5/45)
Sgt. Howard T. Neidenberg	engineer/gunner	1/22/45, 2/18/45	(POW 3/22/45)
2Lt. James L. Nichols	pilot	10/2/44	
SSgt. Stephen J. Nicoletti	engineer/gunner	8/16/44, 12/24/44, 12/25/44, 12/25/44 (2), 2/22/45	
2Lt. Svenn A. Norstrom	copilot	10/2/44, 2/22/45, 3/23/45 (2), 4/10/45, 4/12/45, 4/15/45	

NAME	POSITION	MISSION DATE(S)	NOTES
2Lt. Terrance J. O'Neill	navigator/bombardier (later 1lt.)	6/13/44	
2Lt. Robert E. O'Rourke	copilot	8/28/44, 9/10/44 (NTO), 11/30/44, 12/13/44	
Sgt. Thurman H. Olinger	engineer/gunner	11/9/44, 11/18/44	(KIA 1/5/45)
SSgt. Karl A. Ottocrans	tail gunner	2/15/44	
2Lt. Herbert S. Overhultz	copilot	7/18/44 (2), 7/26/44, 7/28/44, 8/26/44	
Sgt. Russell H. Pacey	radio/gunner (later ssgt.)	11/26/44, 11/26/44 (2), 12/9/44, 12/10/44, 2/19/45, 3/16/45	
Sgt. Bruce K. Packer	engineer/gunner	3/18/45 (2)	
2Lt. Richard W. Page	copilot	6/5/44, 6/6/44 (2), 6/8/44, 6/10/44, 6/13–14/44 (night), 6/22/44 (2), 7/20/44	
2Lt. Edwin C. Pakish	copilot & pilot (later 1lt.)	7/28/44 (2), 8/13/44 (2), 12/24/44, 12/25/44, 12/25/44 (2), 2/22/45, 4/10/45, 4/12/45	
Sgt. John Palcich	tail gunner	3/25/44, 5/9/44, 5/11/44, 5/24/44, 6/13/44	
2Lt. Douglas A. Palmer	copilot & pilot (later 1lt.)	10/2/43, 5/20/44 (2), 5/21/44, 6/13/44	
1Lt. Robert E. Palmer	navigator/ bombardier	2/5/44, 2/6/44, 2/15/44	(WIA 4/11/44)
1Lt. John Papastergiou	navigator/ bombardier	11/7/43	
Sgt. Lawrence E. Parker	engineer/gunner	6/5/44	(injured in crash at Ford 8/16/44; died 3 days later)
SSgt. James A. Pavesich	tail gunner	4/21/44, 5/9/44 (2), 5/10/44, 5/13/44, 7/19/44	
2Lt. Robert H. Pederson	pilot	3/18/45 (2)	
2Lt. Arthur D. Perkins	navigator (later 1lt.)	5/29/44, 6/4/44, 4/17/45	
Cpl. James A. Peters	tail gunner	10/14/44	
2Lt. Lyle L. Peters	copilot	4/19/44 (2), 6/2/44, 6/25/44, 7/31/44	(MIA 8/12/44)
1Lt. Toivo W. Piippo	copilot	3/25/44, 5/9/44, 5/11/44, 5/24/44, 7/31/44	
2Lt. Leo L. Pisel	copilot	2/21/45	
2Lt. William J. Poplack	copilot	2/18/45	
2Lt. Sydney G. Poss	navigator/ bombardier	6/22/44 (2)	
2Lt. Reuben E. Potratz	navigator/ bombardier	(451st BS) 2/24/44	

NAME	POSITION	MISSION DATE(S)	NOTES
2Lt. Stanley J. Price	copilot	10/14/44, 3/11/45	
SSgt. John D. Privette	togglier	4/8/45	
2Lt. Owen J. Redmond Jr.	navigator/bombardier (later 1lt.)	7/27/43, 8/16/43, 8/19/43, 9/2/43, 9/4/43, 9/6/43, 9/16/43, 9/24/43, 10/2/43, 10/3/43, 10/22/43, 11/5/43, 11/23/43, 11/29/43, 12/4/43, 12/5/43, 12/20/43, 12/21/43, 12/30/43, 12/31/43, 1/4/44, 1/4/44 (2), 1/14/44, 1/23/44, 1/24/44, 1/29/44, 2/3/44, 4/11/44 (WIA), 5/29/44, 5/29/44, 5/30/44, 6/4/44, 6/6/44, 6/7/44, 6/18/44	
2Lt. Kenneth W. Reed	pilot	12/22/43, 4/5/44	
2Lt. Robert R. Reiman	navigator/bombardier	2/14/45 (2)	
Sgt. Harold. L. Reinig	radio/gunner	10/2/44	
Sgt. Thomas E. Renfroe	radio/gunner	(451st BS) 2/24/44	
Sgt. Frank B. Rice	tail gunner	10/2/44	
1Lt. Cay H. Richardson	navigator/bombardier	10/24/43, 12/1/43	
SSgt. Russell E. Richardson	radio/gunner (later tsgt.)	5/27/44 (2), 12/2/44	(KIA 12/12/44)
Sgt. Joseph F. Riffe	tail gunner	7/28/44 (2), 10/30/44, 11/2/44	
2Lt. Richard R. Rigg	copilot	5/9/44, 5/15/44, 6/12/44, 8/12/44	
Sgt. Earl W. Riggs	radio/gunner	8/28/44, 9/10/44 (NTO), 11/30/44, 12/13/44, 3/23/45, 3/23/45 (2)	
SSgt. Kenneth M. Rimer	engineer/gunner (later tsgt.)	9/5/43	(POW 11/5/43)
Sgt. M. T. Rimmer	tail gunner	3/19/45	
F/O Thomas H. Rivenbark	copilot & pilot	1/4/44, 2/5/44, 2/6/44, 2/9/44, 2/10/44, 2/11/44, 2/24/44	(POW 4/21/44)
Sgt. P. R. Roberts	engineer/gunner	3/22/45	
SSgt. Robert L. Robinson	engineer/gunner	10/14/44	
2Lt. N. D. Rockefeller	copilot	3/22/45 (2)	
2Lt. Horace C. Rodgers	copilot & pilot	2/20/44, 2/21/44, 2/22/44, 2/25/44, 3/7/44, 3/8/44, 3/20/44, 3/23/44, 3/26/44, 4/18/44, 4/19/44, 4/20/44, 5/15/44, 5/20/44 (2), 5/21/44, 5/28/44 (2), 6/1/44, 5/6/44, 6/6/44 (2), 8/6/44, 10/6/44, 6/13–14/44 (night), 6/22/44 (2)	
Sgt. George Rodridgues	engineer/gunner	10/2/44	
2Lt. Ralph W. Rodriquez	navigator/bombardier	3/25/44, 5/9/44, 5/11/44, 5/24/44	

NAME	POSITION	MISSION DATE(S)	NOTES
2Lt. Robert L. Roland	navigator/ bombardier	(452nd BS) 2/15/44	(KIA 3/25/44)
F/O George L. Rorke	navigator/ bombardier	4/10/45, 4/12/45	
1Lt. Prentice E. Ross	navigator/ bombardier	2/9/44, 2/10/44, 2/11/44	
Sgt. Albert E. Rotman	engineer/gunner (later ssgt.)	8/28/44, 9/10/44 (NTO), 11/30/44, 12/13/44, 3/23/45, 3/23/45 (2)	
SSgt. James S. Rowell	engineer/gunner	12/15/44, 1/29/45	
SSgt. Paul Saffron	radio/gunner	11/7/43	
F/O Albert G. Sakharoff	navigator/ bombardier	3/22/45	
SSgt. Rosco Saldato	radio/gunner	(451st BS) 3/21/45	
Sgt. Joseph P. Saladino	radio/gunner	9/6/44, 9/14/44, 9/27/44	
Col. John S. Samuel	copilot on 200th	4/17/45	(322nd BG CO)
SSgt. Walter B. Satterfield	tail gunner	12/1/43	(MIA 1/14/44; returned to UK 8/1944)
SSgt. Bert H. Scales	tail gunner	4/8/45, 4/9/45, 4/11/45, 4/11/45 (2), 4/24/45	
Sgt. Edward C. Schaefer	radio/gunner	4/21/44, 5/9/44 (2), 5/10/44, 5/13/44, 7/19/44	
Sgt. Mitchell B. Schmidt	tail gunner (later ssgt.)	8/16/44, 12/24/44, 12/25/44, 12/25/44 (2), 2/22/45, 4/12/45, 4/15/45	
1Lt. Eugene C. Schnatz	pilot	2/13/45	
2Lt. Melvin R. Schultz	navigator/ bombardier	5/22/44, 5/26/44	
2Lt. E. H. Schroder	copilot	(451st BS) 3/21/45	
1Lt. Frederick R. Shaffer	pilot	3/22/45 (2)	
Sgt. Ralph E. Shemoney	engineer/gunner	3/19/45	
2Lt. Henry Shudinis	pilot	3/19/45, 3/22/45	
2Lt. Chris Skoubes	copilot	3/24/45	
TSgt. Chester M. Smajenski	engineer/gunner	11/7/43	
TSgt. Eldon F. Smith	radio/gunner	4/8/45, 4/9/45, 4/11/45, 4/11/45 (2), 4/24/45	
Sgt. Fred E. Smith	engineer/gunner	(450th BS) 2/16/45	
Sgt. John A. M. Smith	radio/gunner (later ssgt.)	8/16/44, 12/24/44, 12/25/44, 12/25/44 (2), 2/22/45	
TSgt. J. Smith	radio/gunner	4/12/45, 4/15/45	
1Lt. James E. Smith	copilot	4/8/45, 4/9/45, 4/11/45, 4/11/45 (2), 4/24/45	

NAME	POSITION	MISSION DATE(S)	NOTES
SSgt. Jasper L. Smith	tail gunner	3/17/44, 5/28/44, 8/6/44	
SSgt. Silas P. Smith	engineer/radio & tail gunner (later tsgt.)	4/8/44, 5/4/44, 5/7/44, 5/7/44 (2), 5/8/44, 5/27/44, 12/1/44	
1Lt. Howard V. Smythe	pilot (later capt.)	8/4/43	
Sgt. Walter T. Snyder	tail gunner	(450th BS) 2/16/45	
Sgt. Anthony J. Sosenko	tail gunner (later ssgt.)	9/22/43, 9/23/43, 2/25/44 (2), 7/18/44 (2), 8/4–5/44 (night), 8/26/44 (night)	
2Lt. Gordon J. Spalty	copilot	8/4–5/44 (night), 8/26/44 (night)	
2Lt. William E. Stanley	pilot	(450th BS) 2/16/45	
2Lt. L. E. Stanford	copilot	1/21/44	
SSgt. Charles N. Stearns	tail gunner	1/29/45	(KIA: parachute failed to open, 2/10/45)
Sgt. Oscar S. Stephenson	radio/gunner	2/14/45 (2)	
2Lt. Lewis C. Stewart	copilot	3/18/45 (2)	
SSgt. Robert F. Stickney	radio/gunner	9/25/43, 9/27/43, 10/8/43, 10/18/43, 12/24/43, 1/7/44, 6/6/44 (3)	
Sgt. Bob D. Stoddard	tail gunner	12/22/43, 6/6/44	
2Lt. Galend E. Stone	copilot	2/5/44, 2/6/44, 2/9/44, 2/10/44, 2/11/44	(POW 4/21/44)
2Lt. Danely E. Straight	copilot	2/14/45 (2)	
SSgt. Roger J. Sullivan	radio/gunner	6/23/44, 8/1/44, 8/3/44	
Sgt. D. H. Summerville	tail gunner	1/16/45, 2/13/45, 2/21/45	
Sgt. Harold M. Szewczak	tail gunner	1/22/45, 2/18/45	(KIA 3/22/45)
Sgt. Archie Taylor	radio/gunner	11/9/44, 11/18/44	(KIA 1/5/45)
Cpl. Terry H. Templeton	radio/gunner	10/14/44	
TSgt. George D. Tesnow	togglier	12/15/44, 1/29/45, 2/22/45	
F/O Gordon H. Tharp	copilot & pilot (later 2lt.)	4/10/44 (2), 4/19/44 (2), 6/25/44	
Brig. Gen. Herbert B. Thatcher	copilot	8/1/44	(99th CBW CO)

NAME	POSITION	MISSION DATE(S)	NOTES
SSgt. Norman E. Thielan	tail gunner	7/27/43, 8/16/43, 8/19/43, 9/2/43, 9/4/43, 9/6/43, 9/9/43, 9/11/43, 9/16/43, 9/24/43, 10/2/43, 10/3/43, 10/22/43, 10/24/43, 11/3/43, 11/5/43, 11/10/43, 11/11/43, 11/23/43, 11/29/43, 12/4/43, 12/5/43, 12/20/43, 12/21/43, 12/30/43, 12/31/43, 1/4/44, 1/4/44 (2), 1/14/44, 1/23/44, 1/24/44, 1/29/44, 2/3/44, 4/11/44 (to USA on 30-day leave 5/13/44)	(POW 8/12/44)
2Lt. Charles W. Thomas	copilot & pilot (later 1lt.)	12/15/44, 1/16/45	
SSgt. Louis G. Thorworth	engineer/gunner	2/14/45 (2)	
Sgt. Raymond J. Tonelli	tail gunner	8/26/44, 2/2/45	
2Lt. James F. Toscano	navigator/bombardier (later 1lt.)	6/15/44 (2), 8/4–5/44 (night), 8/26/44 (night), 11/30/44, 12/13/44	
TSgt. Donald L. Tyler	engineer/gunner & togglier	7/27/43, 8/16/43, 8/19/43, 9/2/43, 9/4/43, 9/6/43, 9/9/43, 9/11/43, 9/16/43, 9/24/43, 10/2/43, 10/3/43, 10/22/43, 10/24/43, 11/3/43, 11/5/43, 11/10/43, 11/11/43, 11/23/43, 11/29/43, 12/4/43, 12/5/43, 12/20/43, 12/21/43, 12/30/43, 12/31/43, 1/4/44, 1/4/44 (2), 1/29/44, 2/3/44, 4/11/44, 5/29/44, 5/30/44, 6/4/44, 6/6/44, 6/7/44, 6/18/44, 6/25/44	
SSgt. William C. Upton	engineer/gunner & togglier	3/8/44, 3/15/44, 5/8/44, 5/27/44, 8/12/44	
SSgt. Joe H. Urbanovsky	radio/gunner	6/15/44, 8/26/44 (night)	
Sgt. Joseph G. Urbonavichuis	engineer/gunner	2/2/45	
2Lt. John B. Vandermay	navigator/bombardier	10/2/44	
SSgt. George F. Van Meter	radio/gunner	5/6/44, 5/12/44, 5/12/44 (2), 5/20/44, 5/28/44, 8/13/44 (2)	
Sgt. Alvin E. Varley	radio/gunner	3/22/45	
Sgt. George E. Vasco	tail gunner	3/22/45	
1Lt. William F. Vaughan	navigator/bombardier	5/20/44 (2), 5/21/44, 5/28/44 (2), 6/1/44, 6/4/44, 6/6/44 (2), 6/8/44, 6/10/44, 6/13–14/44 (night)	
Sgt. James W. Venable	tail gunner	(452nd BS) 2/15/44	
Sgt. A. J. Villasenor	radio/gunner	1/16/45, 2/13/45, 2/21/45	
SSgt. C. B. Waganer	engineer/gunner	(452nd BS) 3/25/45	

NAME	POSITION	MISSION DATE(S)	NOTES
1Lt. Willard A. Wagener	copilot & pilot	5/20/44, 5/22/44, 5/26/44, 6/15/44	
SSgt. Hardy A. Wall	radio/gunner	10/30/44, 11/2/44	
Sgt. Charles S. Walters	radio/gunner & engineer/gunner (later ssgt.)	4/10/44, 4/10/44 (2), 6/17/44, 6/24/44, 7/18/44	
TSgt. Dean E. Walton	engineer/gunner	2/15/45	
Sgt. Willis M. Washer	radio/gunner	1/22/45, 2/15/45, 2/18/45	(POW 3/22/45)
SSgt. David N. West	radio/gunner	6/12/44, 8/12/44, 8/25/44	
SSgt. William J. Whitesell	radio/gunner (later tsgt.)	4/19/44, 6/1/44, 6/2/44, 6/25/44, 7/18/44 (2), 7/26/44, 7/28/44, 8/26/44	
SSgt. Elmo M. Winstead	engineer/gunner	5/6/44, 5/12/44, 5/12/44 (2)	
1Lt. Frederick M. Wise	pilot	2/2/45	
Sgt. J. Wiygul	radio/gunner	3/19/45	
Sgt. Paul Wohl	radio/gunner	(450th BS) 2/16/45	
SSgt. Emmett W. Wortman	tail gunner	2/15/45	
SSgt. Israel C. Wynn	tail gunner	11/7/43	
SSgt. Emery H. Young	engineer/gunner	3/15/44	
2Lt. Leo U. Yount	copilot & pilot (later 1lt.)	9/22/43, 9/23/43, 2/25/44 (2), 6/12/44	
TSgt. Carl L. Zearfoss	togglier	3/17/44, 8/6/44	(WIA 4/11/44)

Notes: (2) = p.m. mission; (3) = 3rd mission of day; (ab) = abortive mission; (ER) = early return; (night) = night mission; (NTO) = no takeoff; (sp) = spare aircraft

On October 18 and 21, 1943, both of which were abortive missions, no crew rosters are available. On the July 27, 1944, abortive mission, only the pilot's name, 1Lt. Jones (either C. B. or G. P.; probably the latter), is known, and on August 13, 1944, a NTO, only the pilot's name, 1Lt. Byrd, is known.

APPENDIX 3

1Lt. James J. Farrell: A Biography

Distinguished Flying Cross, Purple Heart
Air Medal with four bronze Oak Leaf Clusters
American Theater Service Medal
European–Africa–Middle East Service Medal with two Oak Leaf Clusters
World War Victory Medal and Honorable Service Lapel Button

1Lt. James J. Farrell.
Thomas Farrell

1Lt. James J. Farrell in late 1943,
at Andrews Field. *Thomas Farrell*

One name that is synonymous with the aircraft "Flak-Bait" is that of 1Lt. James J Farrell, her original combat pilot, and the person who suggested the nickname for the aircraft. He also came up with the artwork design that was given to Sgt. Ted Simonaitis for application to the aircraft.

James Farrell was born on August 22, 1921, in Manhattan, New York, the sixth of eight children born to George and Margaret Farrell (née McGlochlin). James excelled at school, particularly in American and European history, initially studying at Flushing High School and eventually graduating from the prestigious Stuyvesant High School in New York City, and he had enrolled at New York University when the attack on Pearl Harbor occurred.

Like many of his generation, James had a keen interest in aviation and had intended to join the Army Air Corps after finishing college. In addition to his studies, James acquired a job with American Airlines, working evenings in their Maintenance Dispatch Office at La Guardia Airport, and worked with them from 1939 until the time of his enlistment.

Following the attack at Pearl Harbor, James, along with his best friend, Ray Noble, volunteered for the Army with the hope of entering pilot training (Ray eventually graduated as a bombardier and flew with the 447th BG on B-17s prior to retraining as a pilot and eventually becoming a flight instructor). His actual induction was on January 19, 1942, at Mitchel Field, situated at Hempstead Plains on Long Island, where he was allocated the aviation cadet serial number 12052535. His place of residence at the that time was in the Flushing area of Queens, New York.

Following induction, James went to Maxwell Field, Alabama, for preflight pilot training. This would last eight weeks and included a series of aptitude and fitness tests. Following satisfactory completion of this phase, James went to Carlston Field, Arcadia, Florida, to undertake primary training on the PT-17 aircraft. Primary training was an introduction to basic flying and handling skills.

Each phase of the flying-training program would last eight weeks, and anyone not making the grade could be washed out at any time during the process.

Following completion of primary training, James was posted to Gunter Field, Alabama, for basic training. This would be conducted on the more advanced Vultee BT-13 Valiant aircraft. This phase of training would introduce pupils to more-complex flying activities, including navigation, formation flying, and night flying. It was during this process that pupils would be assessed for either single-engine or multiengine training. The next stage of his training was advanced training, this time conducted at Columbus Field, Mississippi. It was here that he was introduced to twin-engine aircraft, checking out on the Curtiss Wright AT-9 Jeep and the Beech AT-10 Wichita aircraft, the former being somewhat tricky to fly and considered ideal for pilots who would eventually fly the B-26 Marauder or P-38 Lightning.

James satisfactorily completed his pilot training and graduated as part of Class 42J, whereupon he was commissioned as a second lieutenant on November 10, 1942. At this point his serial number was changed to 0-793751 to indicate his officer status.

The final stage of his journey to a combat unit was transition training onto the B-26 Marauder. This was conducted at Barksdale Field, Louisiana, where he joined the 335th Bomb Group, this unit acting as a replacement training unit for the type. Here he would first train to fly and handle the B-26 and then be assigned his crew, which would then work up together, ready for a combat assignment.

According to the interview with James Farrell in the September 1978 edition of *Airpower* magazine, once the crew had completed their training they were sent overseas direct from Barksdale Field, as part of a small formation of aircraft, via the southern ferry route. Departure from the mainland was made from Morrison Field, West Palm Beach, Florida, routing via Puerto Rico, British Guiana, Belem, and Natal in Brazil, and out across the Atlantic to Ascension Island, then to Liberia, Senegal, Marrakesh, and Port Lyautey in Morocco, and finally to England, where the entry terminal, for aircraft flying the southern route was set up at St. Mawgan, Cornwall. His service records show that he departed the US on May 2, 1943, with the arrival in the ETO given as May 27, 1943. From here the crews were led to Rougham Airfield, Suffolk, which was the home to the 322nd Bomb Group at this time. Upon arrival, the Farrell crew was assigned to the 449th Bomb Squadron.

James Farrell (who by now had been promoted to first lieutenant) and his crew flew their first mission, a diversionary sweep on July 27, 1943, in "Flak-Bait," and from this date through to February 3, 1944, the Farrell crew flew her on thirty-three occasions, with three other missions flown in other aircraft (on September 8, 1943; December 1, 1943; and December 13, 1943). Other crews flew "Flak-Bait" on sixteen other occasions during this period.

From February 4, 1944, until April 11, 1944, 1Lt. Farrell and his crew were not scheduled on any missions with the 322nd BG; sadly, there is no reason recorded in the official records to account for this ten-week gap, so the reason remains unclear.

The crew flew their next mission on April 11, 1944, to the marshaling yards at Montignes-sur Sambre, again flying "Flak-Bait." From this point to the end of his combat tour, in late June 1944, they flew her on only six missions; a further eighteen missions were flown in other aircraft. This was mainly due to the fact that the crew were now primarily flying as a lead crew, initially as deputy lead, (flying the No. 4 position in a flight), and later as lead of a flight or box. For this they tended to fly other aircraft, probably equipped with updated or newer navigation equipment.

James Farrell, and several of his crew, flew their last combat mission with the 322nd BG on June 25, 1944, to the railroad bridge at Chartres, leading the high flight of the 2nd Box. The 449th BS records for June 1944 are missing from the archives, so his departure from the squadron is not recorded, but normally personnel would be transferred to a replacement depot awaiting their return to the US. 1Lt. James Farrell's personnel records show that he departed England on July 25, 1944, arriving back in the US on August 1, 1944.

Upon return, and after a period of leave, 1Lt. James Farrell joined Air Transport Command (ATC), initially flying the Douglas C-47 and ferrying troops and cargo. At some point he was posted to Homestead Field, Florida, for four weeks of transition training on four-engine types, followed by six weeks at Charleston, South Carolina, and was eventually checked out on the Douglas C-54 and Consolidated C-87 types. At some point, exact timing not known, he made four trips to Europe with the ATC, each totaling ten days in duration. Later he flew from the West Coast, making a trip to the Asia-Pacific theater, arriving on August 22, 1945, and departing again on September 13, 1945.

1Lt. James Farrell's last posting was with the 1504th AAFBU, at McClelland Field, California, and it was from here that he was demobilized on December 29, 1945.

Returning to civilian life, he rejoined American Airlines, this time as a pilot. It was a time of expansion in civil air transport, and it was during this time period with American Airlines that James would meet his future wife, Dorothy Tomasick, who was raised in Hazelton, Pennsylvania. Dorothy also worked with American Airlines, as a flight attendant based at Los Angeles, California. The couple first met at Midway Airport, Chicago, Illinois, when their respective crews were snowed in and were accommodated in the same hotel.

James and Dorothy were married on September 25, 1949, at Queens, New York, and eventually had three children (Thomas, Lynn, and Nancy) together.

Dorothy Tomasick (*second from left*), later Mrs. Farrell. She worked as a flight attendant for American Airlines and was chosen to feature on one of the airline's advertising posters, which is seen on the wall behind. *Thomas Farrell*

James Farrell as a pilot with American Airlines. *Thomas Farrell*

Around 1950 or 1951, James left American to join the General Electric Company, which was establishing its Corporate Aviation Division, and spent the next thirty-five years flying for them, initially on types such as the Beech 18, Douglas 23, Douglas DC-3, and Convair 340. Later, with the introduction of corporate jets into the fleet, he would go on to fly the Dassault Fan Jet Falcon and the Grumman Gulfstream series of aircraft out of Westchester County Airport, 30 miles north of New York City, until the time of his retirement.

Fondly remembered by his friends and colleagues, and noted for his gentle wit and humor, James had a passion for playing golf, and some remarked that his golf clubs would be the first thing placed onto the aircraft, and he would play at courses throughout the country when the opportunities arose.

Sadly, James Farrell, who was by then residing at Greenwich, Fairfield County, Connecticut, passed away on January 24, 1997, after a long battle with lymphoma, and was interred in St. Mary's Cemetery in Greenwich.

Jim Farrell pays a visit to the NASM shortly after the nose section of "Flak-Bait" was put on display. *Smithsonian National Air and Space Museum, NASM 76-19263*

by Edwin Carl Pakish

The mission I'll never forget was on February 22, 1945. The sergeant from CQ came into our tent very early in the morning and woke me up. He told me to get ready for the day's mission. I told him that he must have had the wrong guy because I wasn't scheduled to fly that day. "You are now," he said.

After getting dressed, washed, and breakfast, I went to the briefing room. The briefing officer told us that the mission this day would be a very special one known as Operation Clarion. It would be an all-out attack on transportation facilities all over Germany by planes from the 8th and 9th Air Forces from England and France and also the 12th Air Force from Italy.

This mission would be a "maximum effort" by our groups, so instead of the normal thirty-six planes, there would be fifty-four planes going out today. And instead of all of the planes bombing one target, which was the usual procedure, the nine flights in the group would be divided and bomb five different targets. The flight I was in would bomb the marshaling yard at Butzbach. The bombing altitude would be at 8,000 feet instead of the usual 12,000. And here was the kicker: after bombing, we were to peel off and descend to ground level and strafe the target with our package guns. We were all in a state of shock when we heard that; I and all of the others there remembered the infamous B-26 mission to Ijmuiden, where all the planes were lost on that low-level mission.

The briefing was very thorough and explicit. We were told where the heavy antiaircraft guns were located and where the light guns were thought to be. And after we did the strafing, we were to bank 45 degrees to a forest where there [weren't] guns, and it should be safe to pull up and climb back to a comfortable altitude. That forest was the only safe area to climb.

After the briefing, I went back to my tent and I couldn't help but think of the Ijmuiden mission. I sat down and wrote my mother a "goodbye" letter, which I gave to a buddy in my tent to mail in case I did not return. This was to be my forty-fourth mission, and

I was to pilot #773 PN-O, which was "Flak-Bait," and this was its 175th mission. I was to fly #5 in the third flight in the 2nd Box.

We took off around 11:30 a.m. and were to be over [the] target at 13:42 in the afternoon. The flight to Butzbach was uneventful. I called the bombardier-navigator to be sure to watch for that forest, so that we could climb up to altitude. We test-fired all of the guns. I tested the four package guns and all was OK.

We got to the IP point at 13:37 and made the bomb run at Butzbach. We dropped the bombs at 8,000 feet and then put the throttles full forward as we peeled off, one at a time, and descended in a circle as fast as we could. We completed the circle at low level and were to strafe anything in front of us in the marshaling yard, which was mostly boxcars. As I started to approach the yard at low level, I started to get some light cannon flak. I could see the sides of some of the boxcars falling, and on the car floor were Germans with either cannons or machine guns getting ready to fire on us.

After strafing the boxcars, I passed the marshaling yard and made the 45-degree turn to the right, where the forest was to be. I called the bombardier-navigator, and he said he had no idea where the forest was, and said what I'll never forget: "[I don't] know where we're at." Holy cow; what do I do now? At [that] level I couldn't see any other planes. I called the gunners in the back, and they couldn't see any planes anywhere. Should I start to climb? If there were antiaircraft guns around, we would be dead ducks. I decided to stay at low level with the engines wide open in order to get out of Germany as soon as possible.

It must have been 130 miles to the front line, which at that time was the Rhine River. We headed west, close [to the] ground as possible. Occasionally, we would get some light flak, and I would shoot at anything that might look like it had some military value. We'd see people in the villages that we were flying over. We could see them running for shelter or jumping off their bikes and diving down on the street. I saw a building that could have been a sawmill or factory, and fired at it. One of the package guns jammed in the "on" position, and it continued to fire until it ran out of ammunition. We were over a large wooded area and just a few feet above the trees. In front of us I could see a large clearing; it must have been a large farm, and the wooded area continued on the left. When we got to the clearing, I dropped down lower to the ground. All of a sudden there was a lot of flak coming from the woods at the left. There were machine guns and light cannons. It was very intense. Throughout this whole clearing, which must have been a mile or a mile and a half long, we were fired upon. They must have been waiting for us. There was a loud bang and the plane shuddered, the nose [went down] and [the] left wing went up, and I quickly leveled it. There were more woods in front of us, so I pulled up over the trees and the firing stopped. I still had the engines wide open.

After about forty minutes or so, we finally got to the Rhine River, which like I said was the front line. Once over the river, I pulled up and climbed 3,000 or 4,000 feet in order to try to find out where we were at. The bombardier-navigator checked some of the landmarks in the area by the river and determined where we were at, and gave me a compass heading to get back to the base. I cut back on the throttle to cruising speed and headed for our base. Shortly after that, the flight engineer said we were getting low on fuel and didn't think we had enough to get back home, which was about 150 miles away. We used a lot of fuel, of course, since we had the engines wide open for such a long time.

I called the emergency channel on the radio and told them we were low on fuel and didn't know if we could make it back to base. I was directed to go to a P-47 fighter strip [sic] ("Flak-Bait" landed at A-68 Juvincourt, which was home to the A-20-equipped 410th BG at this time) that was close to the front line. We found the strip, and I called the tower for landing instructions. We made the approach and lowered the flaps and landing gear, and on the final approach the tower called and said it didn't look like our landing gear was all the way down, and not to land but to make a pass by the tower for a better look. I gave full throttle and pulled up and flew past the tower. The wheels didn't look like they were down, I was told. I circled around and the copilot pushed and pulled the landing-gear lever. We made another pass by the tower, and they thought it looked OK now.

Just in case the gear didn't hold up, I had the crew take crash-landing position, and we circled around and got into the final approach. I touched down and the gear did not collapse. Of course I was relieved, and I pressed down on the brake pedals to put on the brakes and nothing happened. Both the copilot and I pumped the brake pedals and got very little brakes, very little indeed, and not enough to stop on the strip. We went down and off the end of the runway. We went into the dirt and finally stopped in a small ditch.

We all got out of the plane, and an ambulance, jeep, and a truck came down the runway toward us. I walked around the plane to see what damage there was. There was about a 4-inch hole in the left landing-gear strut. I was surprised that the gear didn't collapse on landing. And there was an 8-inch hole in the vertical fin. Beside that, there were many, many flak holes. I quit counting after seventy-five holes, when the jeep pulled up, and some of the base officers come [came] to us. I dug out two pieces of flak shrapnel, which I still have among my souvenirs.

We stayed at the P-47 [sic] strip overnight and were driven back to the home base the next day. I learned later that an engine, a landing gear, and the hydraulic system had to be replaced before the plane was able to be returned to our home base. So that was "Flak-Bait's" 175th mission, and one mission I'll never forget.

This story was originally published on the website of Clydedwillis.tripod.com; it does include a number of missing items and text, and these have been corrected or added by the author in brackets, along with editorial corrections.

by Svenn A. Norstrom

I also took part in that low-level strafing effort on that date. The 449th BS was one of two flights that were briefed to take part in this low-level effort. Our target was the Lang Gons RR tracks and bridge, which we attacked from 10,000 ft. with excellent results. Immediately after releasing our bombload, we peeled off in groups of three and went down on the deck and strafed the Butzbach marshaling yards, a railway station at Friedberg, and a factory at Bad Nauheim.

Ed Pakish was our first pilot, I flew copilot, and George Tesnow was our bombardier. Our enlisted crew were Steve Nicoletti, John A. Smith, and Mitchell Schmidt. Our aircraft assignment was number 773-O (good old "Flak-Bait"). We were the number 3 aircraft on the strafing run, and we were drawing considerable ground fire. In fact, we had the impression that there were some antiaircraft 88s situated on high ground that were firing at us down in the valleys.

Fortunately we did not receive any serious damage; at least none that we were aware of at the time. The number 1 and number 2 aircraft were rapidly outdistancing us, and even with maximum power, old "Flak-Bait" couldn't keep up. Ultimately we were all alone, not another B-26 in sight. Since we were drawing so much ground fire, we remained on the deck until we were across the Rhine River and into friendly territory.

Upon returning to normal altitude and heading for home, we realized that due to the high fuel consumption during our low-level flight, we did not have adequate fuel to reach our base at Beauvais. The first available airfield where we could land happened to be an A-20 base, and we were given permission to land and refuel. On our initial approach to the runway, the nosewheel would not come down, so we aborted the landing. After a number of attempts to get the nosewheel down, it finally dropped down and appeared to be in the locked position, so we reentered the pattern and made a successful landing.

After being led to a hardstand and parking the aircraft, we discovered that "Flak-Bait" had received some serious battle damage and that it would be unable to return to base without some extensive repairs. We discovered that the hydraulic lines were almost severed; fortunately they held up long enough to get the wheels down and to provide sufficient braking to stop and park the aircraft. Also the emergency compressed-air lines were completely severed, the radio compass was blown away, and there was a large hole in the leading edge of the vertical stabilizer. Consequently, "Flak-Bait" had to remain behind to await repairs before returning to Beauvais. The crew had a "RON" at the A-20 base, and we were picked up and returned to base the following day. All in all, it was a mission to remember.

The copilot on the February 22, 1945, mission, 2Lt. Svenn A. Norstrom, also related his experiences of that mission in an edition of the Marauder Thunder Newsletter *of the B-26 Marauder Historical Society, as presented above, used with permission of the B-26MHS.*

At the end of the hostilities in Europe, the group records presented the following operational statistics in regard to the group's period in combat from May 1943 to April 1945 and are included here as they appear in the records.

Combat missions flown	425	
Aircraft dispatched	12,988	
Aircraft abortive	2,866	
Number of sorties	12,505	
Number of persons on operations	89,669	
Casualties	141 KIA, 181 WIA, 363 MIA	
Number of aircraft lost to enemy action	109	
Aircraft lost through undetermined reasons	13	
Encounters with enemy aircraft	264	
Enemy aircraft claims	17 destroyed, 9 probably destroyed, 23 damaged	
Planes battle-damaged	58	Cat. E
	192	Cat. AC
	1866	Cat. A
Bomb tonnage on targets	17,395	

322nd Bomb Group commanding officers	
Lt. Col. Jacob J. Brogger	August 8, 1942
Col. Robert R. Selway Jr.	October 21, 1942
Lt. Col. John F. Batjer	February 22, 1943
Lt. Col. Robert M. Stillman	March 17, 1943 (POW, May 17, 1943)
Col. Glenn C. Nye	May 19, 1943
Col. John S. Samuel	July 31, 1944
Maj. John L. Egan	July 12, 1945

449th Bomb Squadron commanding officers	
Capt. Ervin H. Berry	August 7, 1942
Lt. Col. Benjamin G. Willis	May 28, 1943
Maj. John C. Ruse	December 18, 1944
Maj. Lee J. Guilbeau	August 23, 1945

450th Bomb Squadron commanding officers	
Lt. Col. Othel D. Turner	August 1942
Maj. Charles W. Hoover	May 30, 1944 (seriously injured in crash, March 7, 1944)
Lt. Col. Jay B. Smith	June 20, 1944 (KIA, February 22, 1945)
Maj. John L. Egan	February 23, 1945
Capt. Robert W. Turkington	June 25, 1945

451st Bomb Squadron commanding officers	
Lt. Col. Frederick E. Fair	August 1942
Maj. George B. Simler IV	May 30, 1944 (MIA, July 8, 1944; evaded)
Lt. Col. Henry C. Newcomer	July 12, 1944
Maj. Charles S. Seamans III	June 2, 1945
Capt. Richard H. Thomas	June 1945

452nd Bomb Squadron commanding officers	
Maj. Gove C. Celio	August 1942
Lt. Col. Ervin E. Wursten	November 1943
Maj. Howard E. Short	June 1, 1945

During the period from July 10 to July 24, 1943, the Form 34s for the 449th Bomb Squadron showed that they had the following aircraft on strength:

B-26B-2	3	Serials not known
B-26B-3	3	Serials not known
B-26B-4	1	41-18008 PN-P
B-26B-10	3	41-18272 PN-Q, 41-18289 PN-R, 41-18299 PN-S
B-26B-21	5	41-31741 PN-H, 41-31744 PN-M, 41-31756 PN-T, 41-31757 PN-G, 41-31767 PN-U
B-26B-26	3	41-31773 PN-O, 41-31779 PN-C, 41-31788 PN-A
B-26C & C-1	3	41-34683 PN-V, 41-34763 PN-J, 41-34767 PN-W
B-26C-12	2	41-34859 PN-X, 41-34884 PN-Y
B-26C-16	1	41-34981 PN-Z

The B-26B-2 and B-3 models (serial numbers unknown) did not see combat service with the 449th Bomb Squadron and, along with the single B-4 model, were quickly relegated to noncombat duties; most of these ended up with the 3rd Combat Crew Replacement Center, at Toome in Northern Ireland.

Code	Serial	Name	First Mission	Last Mission	Details
PN-A	41-31788	"Truman Committee"	7/17/43	5/27/44	Accepted 4/27/44, dep US 6/21/44, crash-landed at Friston 5/27/44
PN-A	42-107664	"Je Reviens" and "Slug"	6/8/44	4/24/45	Accepted 3/1/44, dep US 3/20/44 "Glue" con salv 11/15/45
PN-B	41-31876	"Miss Manooky"	9/24/43	5/23/44	Accepted 5/21/43, dep US 6/28/43, destroyed in fire on ground at Andrews Field 5/23/44
PN-B	42-95944		5/27/44	8/1/44	Accepted 12/8/43, dep US 02/05/44, lost in a landing accident at Bottisham 8/2/44
PN-B	42-96293	"Semper in Excretia"	8/6/44	4/16/45	Accepted 3/3/44, dep US 03/19/44, damaged while parked 1/29/45, struck by aircraft 42-107693 of the 452nd BS "Glue" con salv FEA 3/22/46
PN-C	41-31779	"Warm Front," renamed "Idiot's Delight"	7/27/43	5/12/44	Accepted 4/27/43, dep US 6/10/43 "Soxo" con salv NBD 6/2/45
PN-C	41-32010	"the Cock in Hand"	7/23/44	3/15/45	Ex-PN-L "Soxo" con salv NBD 6/14/45
PN-C	44-68095		3/18/45	4/20/45	Accepted 1/8/45, dep US 01/25/45 "Glue" con salv FEA 3/30/46
PN-D	41-31794		9/23/43	10/24/43	Accepted 4/28/43, dep US 06/22/43, to 386th BG as YA-D named "Sparta" "Glue" as en ops "34744"
PN-D	42-107746	"Luftwaffe's Lament"	5/15/44	6/13/44	Accepted 3/1/44, dep US 3/16/44, MIA 6/13/44
PN-D	41-18272	"Murder Inc."	6/21/44	12/25/44	Ex-PN-Q, crashed on landing at Beauvais-Tille 12/25/44
PN-D	44-67815		1/2/45	1/5/45	Accepted 9/26/44, dep US 10/13/44, crashed in Allied territory after flak hit 1/1/45
PN-D	41-31823	"No Compree"	3/18/45	4/20/45	Ex–386th BG AN-V, accepted 5/10/43, dep US 7/20/43 "Glue" con salv FEA 3/22/46

Code	Serial	Name	First Mission	Last Mission	Details
PN-F	41-31816	"Gayle"	9/19/43	10/14/44	Accepted 5/6/44, dep US 7/14/43, destroyed in a takeoff accident 10/19/44
PN-F	43-34459		11/30/44	12/1/44	Accepted 7/31/44, dep US 8/23/44, abandoned over friendly territory after flak hit 12/2/44
PN-F	43-34611	"Green Ghost"	12/12/44	4/24/45	Accepted 9/25/44, dep US 10/4/44 "Glue" con salv FEA 3/30/46
PN-G	41-31757	"We Dood It"	8/16/43	9/11/44	Accepted 4/20/43, dep US 5/27/43, damaged in landing on ALG 9/11/44 (on 114th mission), repaired and issued to 387th BG as TQ-X "Old Ned" "Glue" con salv FEA 12/28/45
PN-G	42-96325		9/27/44	11/3/44	Accepted 3/14/44, dep US 4/2/44, damaged in landing accident at A-81 Creil 11/8/44 "Glue" con salv FEA 3/28/46
PN-G	43-34342	"Li"l Maggie"	11/16/44	12/25/44	Accepted 7/3/44, dep US 7/25/44, Cat. A 12/25/44, to 450th BS as ER-W from 4/4/45 "Glue" con salv FEA 4/24/46
PN-G	41-31976	"Spirit of 76"	None known		Accepted 6/18/43, "Ugly" 8/2/43 to 450th BS as ER-T, last mission 2/15/45, Cat. AC, to 449th date unknown (poss post-VE-day) "Glue" con salv FEA 3/20/46
PN-H	41-31741	"Winnie Dee"	7/17/43	6/4/44	Accepted 4/16/43, dep US 5/24/43, to PN-N
PN-H	42-107600		6/7/44	2/10/45	Accepted 1/8/44, dep US 2/8/44, hit by flak and crashed 1 mile from Monchau 2/10/45
PN-H	43-34302		2/23/45	4/20/45	Accepted 6/23/44, dep US 7/17/44, ex-RG-H 386th BG "Glue" con salv FEA 3/22/46
PN-J	41-34763	"Duchess of Barksdale"	7/17/43	11/3/43	Accepted 1/16/43, dep US 5/14/43, MIA 11/3/43
PN-J	41-31915	"Sin Twister"	12/4/43	9/11/44	Accepted 5/30/43, dep US 8/11/43, crash-landed at Andrews Field after flak hit 9/11/44
PN-K	41-31948		12/4/43	1/14/44	Accepted 6/13/43, dep US 7/25/43, MIA 1/14/44
PN-K	42-43285	"Sit 'N' Git" and "Ice Cold Katy"	2/3/44	4/15/45	Accepted 7/28/43, dep US 9/3/43, 156 missions "Glue" con salv FEA 1/5/46

Code	Serial	Name	First Mission	Last Mission	Details
PN-L	41-32010	"the Cock in Hand"	11/23/43	5/9/44	Accepted 6/24/43, dep US 8/4/43, to PN-C
PN-L	43-34307	"Miss 28th Seabee"	11/16/44	11/18/44	Accepted 6/23/44, dep US 7/18/44, to PN-S (possibly an admin error due to the short amount of time recorded as PN-L; also, photos do not clearly show any evidence of a repaint of the code letter)
PN-L	43-34154	"Esky"	4/8/45	4/15/45	Ex-ER-D 450th BS, accepted 5/13/44, dep US 6/16/44, to PN-N
PN-M	41-31744	"Hanks Yanks"	7/17/43	4/24/45	Accepted 4/19/43, dep US 5/27/44 "Glue" con salv FEA 3/20/46
PN-N	42-107749	"the 49ers"	5/15/44	8/16/44	Accepted 2/29/44, dep US 3/17/44, flak-damaged, crash-landed at Ford 8/16/44
PN-N	41-31741	"Winnie Dee"	6/21/44	8/12/44	Ex-PN-H, MIA 8/12/44
PN-N	43-34363	"Winnie Dee II"	9/12/44	4/4/45	Ex-PN-Z, MIA 4/4/45
PN-N	43-34154	"Esky"	4/17/45	4/18/45	Ex-PN-L "Glue" con salv FEA 3/30/46
PN-O	41-31773	"Flak-Bait"	7/27/43	4/24/45	Accepted 4/26/43, dep US 5/26/43, 207 missions, preserved NASM
PN-P	41-18008	"Vee Pack It"	9/9/43	11/3/43	Accepted 11/1/42, dep US 5/11/43, transferred "Glue" con salv NBD 7/27/45
PN-P	43-34433		9/27/44	2/22/45	Accepted 7/26/44, dep US 8/5/44, destroyed in takeoff accident 2/22/45
PN-Q	41-18272	"Murder Inc."	7/27/43	5/19/44	Accepted 2/12/43, dep US 5/6/43; Cat. AC damage, 50 holes, 5/19/44; to PN-D
PN-Q	42-107693	"Murder Inc. II"	5/28/44	12/25/44	Accepted 2/11/44, dep US 3/12/44, destroyed in takeoff accident at Beauvais-Tille 12/26/44
PN-Q	44-67879	"Lil Murf"	1/14/45	4/24/45	No record card in archives, con as salv in Germany in 1945–46
PN-R	41-18289	"Colonel Rebel"	8/4/43	10/24/43	Accepted 2/18/43, dep US 5/6/43, to Air Depot after 13 missions, transferred to 323rd BG as YU-X in 2/44, declared war weary 6/18/44 Adjusted loss salv 1/5/47
PN-S	41-18299		7/17/43	8/27/43	Accepted 2/18/43, dep US 5/6/43, MIA—ditched 12 miles off enemy coast after flak hit 8/27/43

Code	Serial	Name	First Mission	Last Mission	Details
PN-S	43-34307	"Miss 28th Seabee"	11/19/44	12/25/44	Ex-PN-L?, to 451st BS as SS-V battle damaged to 361 Serv Sq on 4/20/45 "Glue" con salv 1/28/46
PN-S	44-68092		3/3/45	4/24/45	Accepted 1/9/45, dep US 1/18/45 "Glue" con salv FEA 3/30/46
PN-T	41-31756	"GI.V"	8/31/43	3/7/44	Accepted 4/21/43, dep US 5/27/43, to 450th BS as ER-J "Geraldine" "Glue" con salv NBD 7/10/44
PN-T	43-34298	"Squirty Girty" and "Little Lambie"	2/28/45	4/24/45	Accepted 6/22/44, dep US 7/20/44 "Glue" con salv FEA 3/22/46
PN-U	41-31767	"Cottees Cutie," renamed "Ginger"	7/17/43	4/21/44	Accepted 4/23/43, dep US 5/31/43, MIA 4/21/44
PN-U	42-107689	"Ginger II"	5/9/44	4/10/45	Accepted 2/9/44, dep US 3/8/44, landing accident at Y-51 Vogelsang 4/10/45 "Glue" con salv FEA 3/28/46
PN-V	41-34683		7/28/43	11/23/43	Accepted 1/16/43, dep US 5/25/43, belly-landed at Stansted 12/6/43
PN-V	42-43288	"Vee Pack It II" / "Dolly"	12/30/43	5/27/44	Accepted 7/29/43, dep US 9/8/43, abandoned and crashed at Gravesend 5/27/44
PN-V	42-107591		5/31/44	7/8/44	Accepted 1/8/44, dep US 2/8/44, MIA on night mission 7/8/44
PN-V	42-43289		7/24/44	8/11/44	Ex-PN-X, to 323rd BG as YU-X. "Glue" con salv FEA 5/20/46
PN-V	43-34404	"Our Shorty"	10/30/44	12/12/44	Accepted 7/20/44, dep US 8/2/44, MIA 12/12/44—iced up and crashed 1 mile east of Han-sur-Lasse, Belgium; crew killed "Glue" con salv NBD 12/13/44
PN-W	41-34767	"Gasparilla"	7/28/43	9/9/43	Accepted 1/17/43, dep US 5/25/43, declared war weary 10/22/43 "Soxo" con salv NBD 5/29/45
PN-W	41-31711	"Mystic Crewe of Gasparilla"	11/11/43	2/28/44	Accepted 4/9/43, dep US 6/22/43, crash-landed at Hawkinge 2/28/44
PN-W	42-107578		3/15/44	2/14/45	Accepted 12/31/43, dep US 1/26/44, crash-landed 10 miles from Beauvais-Tille due to mech'l failure 2/14/45
PN-W	44-68122	"Johnny's Jokers"	2/28/45	4/20/45	Accepted 1/17/45, dep US 1/27/45 "Glue" con salv FEA 3/28/46

Code	Serial	Name	First Mission	Last Mission	Details
PN-X	41-34859	"Rat Poison"	7/28/43	1/7/44	Accepted 3/28/43, dep US 5/21/43, destroyed in belly-landing at Stansted 1/10/44 "Soxo" con salv AFMSC 1/31/44
PN-X	42-43289		1/29/44	4/21/44	Accepted 7/31/43, dep US 9/3/43, to PN-V
PN-X	42-107665	"Classy Chassis"	5/4/44	11/13/44	Accepted 2/1/44, dep US 2/20/44, destroyed in takeoff accident at Beauvais-Tille 11/13/44
PN-X	44-67867		12/13/44	2/22/45	Accepted 10/16/44, dep US 10/30/44, Cat. AC damage 2/22/45 "Glue" con salv FEA 9/22/45
PN-X	43-34371	"Belle of Bayou"	4/15/45	4/20/45	Ex–452nd BS DR-X, Cat. AC 3/21/45, accepted 7/11/44, dep US 8/1/44 "Glue" con salv FEA 4/24/46
PN-Y	41-34884		7/28/43	7/28/43	Accepted 3/29/43, dep US 5/17/43, crashed 4 miles S of Great Dunmow on training flight 8/15/43
PN-Y	43-34609	"Gasparilla IV"	12/18/44	4/24/45	Accepted 9/22/44, dep US 10/25/44 "Glue" con salv FEA 3/21/46
PN-Z	41-34981	"Waste O Time II"	8/16/43	8/16/44	Accepted 4/23/43, dep US 5/25/43, early return 8/16/44 with engine malfunction, to PN-Z below
PN-Z	43-34363		8/26/44	9/11/44	Accepted 7/8/44, dep US 8/1/44, to PN-N
PN-Z	41-34981	"Waste O Time II"	9/27/44	11/30/44	Destroyed in landing accident at Beauvais-Tille 11/30/44
PN-Z	44-67917	"Couchez Avec"	1/14/45	4/20/45	Accepted 11/6/44, dep US 11/18/44 "Glue" con salv FEA 3/30/46

42-107665 PN-X, "Classy Chassis," began flying missions on May 5, 1944, and was lost in a takeoff accident at Beauvais-Tille on November 13, 1944; the pilot was 2Lt. Thomas H. Felker, who was eventually KIA on February 10, 1945. *Mike Smith, B26.com*

42-107693 PN-Q, "Murder Inc. II," was damaged beyond repair in a takeoff accident on Boxing Day 1944; the pilot was 2Lt. Harold D. Hurlbut. *Mike Smith, B26.com*

44-68092 PN-S began flying missions on March 3, 1945, and was eventually scrapped in Germany in 1946. *Mike Smith, B26.com*

44-68122 PN-W, "Johnny's Jokers," the highest-serial-numbered B-26 to join the 449th BS, overhead Le Bourget Airfield, Paris, in 1945. *Mike Smith, B26.com*

Another latecomer was 44-68095 PN-C, which entered combat on March 18, 1945. *Mike Smith, B26.com*

Too late to see combat with the 449th BS, 41-31976 PN-G, "Spirit of 76," was transferred into the squadron, having previously been assigned to the 450th BS as ER-T. *Trevor J. Allen collection*

From the summer of 1943 onward, for every crewman reported MIA, a Missing Air Crew Report (MACR) would be raised. These MACR are available from the National Archives (NARA) and give aircraft details including engine numbers and the machine gun serial numbers as loaded onto each aircraft, along with crew details and any eyewitness reports from other airmen who observed the loss. However, if an aircraft was lost, either through battle damage or as the result of an accident, and came down in friendly territory, and because the status of the crew members was accounted for, no MACR would be raised, and the aircraft would be reported as an operational salvage or nonoperational salvage, accordingly.

An index for the MACR reports pertaining to the 322nd Bomb Group is as follows:

Date	Serial Number	Crew status	MACR No.
5/17/43	41-17979 DR-O	1 K 5 P	
5/17/43	41-17982 DR-P	3 K 3 P	15539
5/17/43	41-17991 DR-S	4 K 2 P	18080
5/17/43	41-17998 DR-V	6 K	15156
5/17/43	41-17999 DR-W "Chickasaw Chief"	6 P	
5/17/43	41-18052 DR-N	2 K 4 P	15173
5/17/43	41-18080 DR-K	4 K 2 P	
5/17/43	41-18086 ER-U "Draggin Lady"	5 K 1 P	15129
5/17/43	41-18090 DR-L	5 K 1 P	5650
5/17/43	41-18099 ER-V "Lorraine"	4 K 2 Res	16165
9/9/43	41-18058 ER-S	7 K	15604
11/3/43	41-34763 PN-J "Duchess of Barksdale"	5 P 1 Ev	1499 & 1046
11/5/43	41-18075 DR-J "Mr Five By Five"	5 K 1 P	1216
11/23/43	41-31817 DR-W "No Regrets"	6 K	1187
1/14/44	41-31880 SS-T	3 P 3 Ev	1749
1/14/44	41-31948 PN-K	4 P 3 Ev	1748
2/28/44	41-31875 ER-P	3 bailed out over France; aircraft crash-landed near Eastburne	15197
2/29/44	41-34856 SS-L "Denalis CheeChakoo II"	6 K	2455
3/20/44	41-31849 ER-N "Scotch & Soda"	5 K 2 P	2845
3/20/44	41-31914 SS-S "Druther Not"	1 K 2 P 3 Ev	2837
3/25/44	41-31798 DR-Q "Utopia"	6 K	3167
3/25/44	41-31906 DR-W	6 K	3166

Date	Serial Number	Crew status	MACR No.
4/13/44	41-31968 ER-S "the Hearse and 6"	5 P 1 Ev	3742
4/21/44	41-31767 PN-U "Ginger"	6 P	4308
4/22/44	42-95877 SS-F "Geronimo"	2 K 1 P 5 bailed out over UK coast	4106
5/7/44	41-31845 DR-Q "Patches"	4 P 2 Ev	4479
5/9/44	41-31954 ER-Z	1 K 5 P	4478
5/27/44	42-43288 PN-V "Vee Pack It II" / "Dolly"	1 K 2 P 1 Ev 3 bailed out over UK	12278
6/13/44	42-43286 DR-L	6 K	5711
6/13/44	42-107746 PN-D "Luftwaffe"s Lament"	1 K 5 Ret	5875
6/15/44	42-95949 ER-M "Rainbow Corner 3rd"	6 P 1 Ev	6117
7/6/44	41-31897 ER-A "Invictus"	4 P 1 Ev 1 Ret—landed in France	15175
7/8/44	41-18276 SS-C "Pickled Dilly"	3 K 3 P 1 Ev	6628
7/8/44	41-31814 ER-F "Bag of Bolts"	1 K 3 P 2 Ev	6626
7/8/44	42-95970 ER-B	3 K 3 P	6625
7/8/44	42-107591 PN-V	3 P 4 Ev	6627
7/8/44	42-107627 DR-A	6 K	6622
7/8/44	42-107670 SS-J "Carrie B"	6 K	6620
7/8/44	42-107680 SS-S	6 K	6623
7/8/44	42-107695 DR-G	3 K 5 P	6621
7/8/44	42-107816 SS-T	3 K 4 Ev	6624
7/19/44	41-31974 ER-R "Anonymaus"	5 K 1 P	7047
7/19/44	41-35021 SS-L "the Sheriff Rapides" "Parish Louisiana"	6 K 2 Ev	7046
7/30/44	42-96257 DR-T	1 K 5 bailed out along French coast	12267
7/30/44	41-31904 SS-Y	1 K 5 Res	16089
8/6/44	41-34951 SS-P "Impatient Virgin II"	3 K 3 P	11982
8/13/44	41-31741 PN-N "Winnie Dee"	5 K 1 P	8039
9/23/44	42-96270 SS-X	(aircraft landed in France) 2 wounded, 4 Ret	
10/13/44	43-34417 SS-C	5 K 1 P	9836
11/9/44	43-34146 DR-U	6 K	10180
11/9/44	43-34187 SS-F "Little Audrey"	5 K 1 P	10179
12/12/44	43-34404 PN-V "Our Shorty"	6 K	15303
12/23/44	43-34423 ER-V	6 P	11404
1/1/45	44-67813 SS-P	5 K 1 P	12003
2/15/45	44-67907 DR-M	1 K 5 P	12382
2/22/45	42-107745 ER-O "Mrs. Mac"	8 K	12680

Date	Serial Number	Crew status	MACR No.
2/23/45	41-31888 ER-H "War Eagle"	6 K	12642
3/14/45	44-68100 ER-W	1 P 5 K	13096
3/22/45	44-67870 ER-J	2 K 4 P	13236
3/24/45	42-107674 DR-Q	1 K 5 P	13323
4/4/45	43-34363 PN-N "Winnie Dee II"	6 P	14262
4/16/45	42-96067 SS-H	6 P	14453
4/16/45	42-96225 ER-X	5 K 1 P	14463

Crew status codes

K = killed; P = POW; Ev = evaded; Res = rescued; Ret = returned

42-95977 SS-F, "Geronimo," was lost on April 22, 1944, while being flown by Capt. A. R. Jordan and crew. The aircraft was heavily damaged by flak; one crewman bailed out over France, and the rest of the crew abandoned her over England. Of those who bailed out over England, one crewman was MIA, having been last seen drifting toward the sea. *Trevor J. Allen collection*

41-31888 ER-H, "War Eagle," having been repaired after her belly landing on May 10, 1945, was declared missing in action on February 23, 1945, on a mission to Erkelenz, when piloted by 1Lt. Jack G. Cox and crew. Seen to be hit in the cockpit area, the aircraft was observed to spin down and crash. One parachute was seen to come out of the aircraft, but it was on fire. *USAAF*

Many B-26 Marauders flew over 100 missions both in the ETO and the MTO, and this achievement was commonplace among the B-26 units by VE-day. It is believed that the runners-up to the total of 201 missions by "Flak-Bait" in the 9th Air Force were as follows:

"Jill Flitter"	41-34857 RJ-O	323rd BG	195 missions
"Hanks Yanks"	41-31744 PN-M	322nd BG	190 missions
"Five by Fives"	41-31707 KS-R	387th BG	188 missions
"Hells Belle"	41-34967 WT-A	323rd BG	185 missions
"Flying Ginny"	41-31723 TQ-J	387th BG	184 missions
"Rock Hill Special"	41-34854 RJ-N	323rd BG	184 missions
"El Capitan"	41-31718 KS-O	387th BG	182 missions

The highest-mission-scoring B-26 in the 386th BG was 41-31606 AN-S "Rat Poison," with 166 missions, but that group ceased B-26 operations in early 1945, when the group converted to the A-26 Invader aircraft. Some 386th BG were transferred to other groups and continued to fly missions but it is not believed any exceeded a total of 170 missions.

Runner-up to "Flak-Bait" was "Jill Flitter" of the 323rd BG, with 195 missions. The aircraft in the background, 41-35242 RJ-T, "Paper Dolly," was written off after a belly landing on June 24, 1944. *Trevor J. Allen collection*

Leading the 387th BG was 41-31707 KS-R, "Five by Fives," with 188 missions, seen here at Chipping Ongar in May 1944. Of all the B-26s in Europe, only "Flak-Bait" was returned to the United States, with the rest destined to be scrapped at Landsberg, Germany. *Bob Allen*

Situated between the towns of Braintree and Great Dunmow, in the county of Essex, RAF Great Saling, as it was originally known, was named after the village that it was constructed alongside, and had the distinction of being the first airfield in the UK to be constructed by US engineers.

The 819th Engineering Battalion (Aviation) began construction during July 1942 and was built in the form of a typical Class A bomber airfield, consisting of three runways; the main one was on a heading of 09/27 and was 6,300 ft. long, whereas the other two were 4,300 ft. long each, in the classic shape of an "A" surrounded by a perimeter track with fifty loop hardstands, complete with two T-2 hangars and various huts and technical site buildings, along with a control tower, which completed the operational element of the airfield. The living quarters, mainly Nissen (Quonset) huts, were situated at the eastern end of the airfield, close to the village of Great Saling itself.

The airfield was completed in April 1943, and the first unit to arrive was the B-17F-equipped 96th Bomb Group, under the command of Col. Archie J. Old Jr. The ground echelon arrived on May 12, 1943, and the air echelon began to arrive on May 27, 1943.

The 96th Bomb Group performed its first combat mission on May 29, when, as part of a force of seventy-two B-17s, they were sent to attack a naval depot at Rennes. One aircraft failed to return. A second mission to Cuxhaven port area was flown on June 11, when twenty-eight aircraft were dispatched, this time without loss.

Construction begins at AAF Station 485, the first airfield constructed in England by US engineers. *IWM / Roger A. Freeman collection, FRE6316*

On May 21, 1943, RAF Great Saling was renamed Andrews Field in honor of Lt. Gen. Frank M. Andrews, who had been appointed as the commander of all the US forces in the European theater of operations in January 1943. Lt. Gen. Andrews had been killed on May 3, 1943, in the crash of a B-24D Liberator, when it hit Mt. Fagradalsfjall while it was attempting to land at RAF Kaldadarnes, Iceland, in bad weather, during a tour of inspection. Of the fifteen people on board, only the tail gunner, SSgt. George A. Eisel, survived.

During the first week of June 1943, it was announced that the units of the 4th Bomb Wing would exchange bases with those of the 3rd Bomb Wing, thereby concentrating the B-26 Marauder–equipped units, and those about to arrive in the UK, to bases in Essex.

The move itself was completed on June 12, and effective at twelve noon that same day, the B-26 units were transferred from VIII Bomber Command to VIII Air Support Command, under the command of Brig. Gen. Robert C. Candee. This transfer would better reflect the future tactical air operations that the B-26-equipped units would fulfill.

The 322nd Bomb Group's first week at Andrews Field was disrupted by five days of rain, which caused a certain amount of discomfort during the settling-in period.

Formal transfer of the airfield from RAF to USAAF control was made on July 15, 1943, in a ceremony in front of the group headquarters building. During this ceremony, the national anthems of Great Britain and the United States were played as the Union Jack flag was lowered and the Stars and Stripes was raised. Lt. Col. Glenn C. Nye, the group CO, accepted the transfer from squadron leader Albin Houghton, of the RAF, in front of a crowd of distinguished guests that included Col. Samuel K. Anderson, CO of the 3rd Bomb Wing; the Rev. L. S. Lewis of Great Saling; and Mrs. William Steele and Lady Carlyle, upon whose land much of the airfield had been constructed.

While based at Andrews Field, "Flak-Bait" is known to have used hardstand no. 17; these were usually numbered clockwise from the control tower.

Two days later the 322nd BG flew a diversionary sweep off the French coast, in support of a mission being flown by the 323rd BG, its first operation since the disastrous raid of May 17, 1943.

On October 16, 1943, the VIII ASC was disbanded, and the four B-26 groups then in England were

Living quarters at Andrews Field was in Nissen Huts; while fairly primitive and invariably cold, they were far superior to the tented accommodation used on the Continent. *Peter Dole*

reassigned to the newly formed Ninth Air Force in England and came under the control of the 9th Bomber Command. Shortly thereafter, the units were divided between the 98th and 99th Combat Wings (the 323rd BG and 387th BG to the 98th CBW, and the 322nd BG and 386th BG to the 99th CBW). The 9th Air Force would support the tactical air operations, and once the D-day invasion had taken place, would actively support the ground forces in their drive across France and into Germany.

In reality this change meant very little to the personnel of the B-26 units, since the flak and enemy fighters were just as deadly no matter what Air Force they were formally assigned to.

On the night of December 11, 1943, Andrews Field, along with some other 9th Air Force bases, came under the attention of the Luftwaffe when Dornier bombers tried to mount attacks; fortunately, little damage was done, and no loss of life was encountered at Andrews Field.

In February 1944, the 1st Pathfinder Squadron (Provisional) was formed at Andrews Field and served alongside the 322nd BG. Aircraft and personnel for this squadron were drawn from all five B-26 groups then operational in England, each providing three aircraft and crews on detached service to the 1st PFF(P) Squadron. The aircraft were equipped with British-made Oboe blind bombing equipment, allowing formations to bomb through 10/10th cloud cover; initially, results were not that good, but in time this would become a very effective bombing method. Oboe was a device that would pick up signals from two ground transmitters, allowing for accurate triangulation of an aircraft's position to plot a bomb release point. Range was limited by the curvature of the earth, but this was ideal for the shorter-range medium-bomber missions.

Following the D-day invasion and the advance of the ground forces, the range to potential targets meant that a move to be closer to the battle lines would become inevitable.

Unlike the units assigned to the 98th CBW (by this time comprising the 323rd, 387th, 394th, and 397th BGs), who began to move to bases in Hampshire, in southern England, in mid-July 1944 and then to France in late August, those assigned to the 99th CBW (the 322nd, 344th, 386th, and 391st BGs, and 1st PFF Squadron) remained in Essex until late September before moving directly to advanced bases in France. The three A-20-equipped units assigned to the 97th CBW (409th, 410th, and 416th BGs) also moved directly to France at a similar time.

The 322nd flew their last combat mission from Andrews Field on September 27, with an attack on troop concentrations at Foret de Parroy.

The process of moving to the Advanced Landing Ground (ALG) at A-61 Beauvais-Tille was begun on September 19, 1944, when the reconnaissance party was sent ahead to prepare for the units' arrival. The advance echelon left Andrews Field on September 21, and the air echelon departed on September 29, along with elements of the ground personnel in C-47 aircraft. The final elements traveled by road convoy and finally arrived at Beauvais-Tille on October 6.

With the departure of the 322nd BG, Andrews Field was returned to RAF control and shortly thereafter became home to the 150th (Polish) Wing, and a few weeks later they were joined by 122 Wing, RAF; both of these wings were equipped with P-51 Mustang aircraft, providing escort for the increasing number of RAF daylight operations.

From February 28 to April 1, 1945, Andrews Field was host to 616 Squadron, equipped with Gloster Meteor Mk. III, the RAFs first jet-powered fighter, and after they departed, a detachment from 504 Squadron moved in, also equipped with the Meteor, although this unit was disbanded in August 1945.

For a brief period in the summer of 1945, between June and late August, Andrews Field was home to 276 Air Sea Rescue Squadron, RAF Coastal Command, equipped with Supermarine Walrus flying boats, before that unit relocated to Kjevik in Norway.

The final operational unit to occupy Andrews Field was the P-51 Mustang–equipped 303 (Polish) Squadron, RAF, which was in residence from April 4 to May 16, 1945, and again between August 9 and November 28, 1945.

At the end of 1945, Andrews Field was placed under a "care and maintenance" status and for a while, in 1946, was used as a satellite airfield for units at Great Sampford, before it gradually fell into disuse.

For a short period of time, some of the buildings were used for temporary housing, but by the early 1950s, the airfield site gradually reverted to agricultural use, with most of the buildings removed and the runways torn up for hard core. The two T-2 hangars were retained for industrial use.

In 1972, an airstrip was reestablished on the site, and a grass runway, 915 meters in length, was established on the western end of the original 09/27 runway, and now is host to the Andrewsfield (as the airfield is now known as) Flying Club, complete with a clubhouse and several small hangars.

Located 45 miles north of Paris, Beauvais, the capital of the Oise district, is in the Picardy region of France. The airfield itself lies 2 miles north of the city, in the commune of Tille, and was originally constructed in the 1930s as a small regional airport.

After the German invasion in the spring of 1940, Beauvais-Tille was quickly put to use by the Luftwaffe as a bomber airfield. Units occupying the airfield during the Battle of Britain period included the Dornier Do 17Z–equipped KG 76 (Kampfgeschwader 76) and the Junkers Ju 87B–equipped SKG 1 (Sturzkampf-geschwader 1).

Later, Heinkel He 111 and Junkers Ju 88–equipped units took part in antishipping strikes, and further units were engaged in the night blitz over England. During the summer of 1943, Fw 190s from JG 26 (Jagdgeschwader 26) moved in to help with the defense of the Third Reich in the face of the increased daylight bombing raids by the Eighth Air Force.

Indeed, the 322nd Bomb Group would launch six missions to attack this target between September 3 and October 3, 1943, one of which was recalled because of weather, and another was only partially successful; however, the remaining four missions were a success. Little did the crews of the 322nd Bomb Group know that one year later they would occupy this same airfield and suffer from disruption as a result of their previous successes!

During June 1944, the base was temporarily the home to units from JG 1, equipped with Me 109G aircraft.

The airfield was liberated by the Allied ground forces in early September 1944, and the 818th EB (Av) quickly moved in to clear the airfield of mines and make the airfield usable by Allied units. Live ordnance would be a continuing problem at Beauvais-Tille, and personnel were warned not to touch any such ordnance. However, curiosity got the better of some and resulted both in death and injury to several members of the 322nd Bomb Group during their tenure.

Having commenced the move to Beauvais-Tille in late September, the B-26s of the group arrived on September 29, and the group flew their first mission from the new base on October 2, 1944, with an attack on enemy strongpoints in the Herbach area.

Little of the original base was usable and conditions were far from ideal, with all living and most of the operational functions being performed in tents. With all the original buildings having been destroyed, construction of mess halls, a headquarters building, an officers club and enlisted-men day rooms was initiated, utilizing what materials could be scrounged from the local area, although the enduring memory for all was the endless mud that seemed to permeate everywhere!

According to the formation layout sheets, "Flak-Bait" was originally recorded as being parked on hardstand no. 59 up until January 22, 1945, and from January 29, she is shown as being parked on hardstand no. 2.

In early January 1945, the 1st Pathfinder Squadron (P) departed Beauvais-Tille and moved to the airfield A-72 at Peronne, ending its long association with the 322nd BG; for many of the personnel of the 1st PFF Squadron (P), this was a welcome move, since they had felt as something of an orphaned child while sharing the airfield facilities with the 322nd. The squadron, although only a provisional unit, would number some forty aircraft by the end of hostilities, by far the largest squadron within the 9th Bomb Division (as 9th Bomb Command had been redesignated on September 16, 1944).

With the harsh winter conditions of 1944–45, living conditions were made even more difficult, and the subsequent thaw that occurred in late January 1945 resulted in the many temporary repairs to the runways and taxiways becoming unstable, with many of the craters opening up or crumbling badly due to the soft nature of the chalklike material used in the repairs. The runway alone had 105 repaired craters, which were anywhere from 3 to 40 ft. in diameter, and some were as deep as 6 ft. This caused a number of burst tires and generally disrupted normal operations and aircraft movements.

The engineers were called in to look at the situation, and they told Col. John S. Samuel, CO of the 322nd BG, that it would take two months to gather the materials and complete the task of repairing the airfield.

With this in mind, Col. Samuel stood the group down and mobilized every man of the group who not engaged in essential work to undertake the repairs themselves. Commencing on Saturday, February 3, he commandeered every available truck in the group, along with some borrowed from the Air Depot, to transport the necessary materials. Working both night and day nonstop, some 1,175 tons of rock were utilized in the repairs, which were completed the following Wednesday, February 7; the group flew a mission the next day to Horrem town.

Following the setback caused by the German Ardennes Offensive, the Allies regained the initiative and continued the advance into German territory; the range to the targets meant that another move was required.

The 322nd flew their last mission from A-61 Beauvais-Tille on March 31, 1945, with an attack on the storage depot at Marienburg. This time the group would move to A-89 Le Culot, in Belgium, the move being completed over the period from March 30 to April 8, 1945.

With the departure of the 322nd BG, Beauvais-Tille was used by transport and support units flying in supplies and evacuating casualties back to England. Following the ending of the conflict, the airfield was returned to French control on August 17, 1945, and in 1950 was offered to NATO as an emergency airfield in the event of hostilities breaking out with the Soviet bloc. However, a lack of funds meant that very little was done, apart from a general cleaning up of any wartime detritus and ordnance that remained on the site.

In 1953, plans to use the airfield by NATO units was abandoned. In 1956, Beauvais-Tille was opened up as a regional airport for Paris, and over the years it has been modernized and extended for modern jet aircraft use and is now used as a destination for several of the low-cost airlines, using it as a gateway to Paris.

Advanced Landing Ground A-89
Le Culot, Belgium

About 20 miles east-southeast of Brussels, Le Culot Airfield, also known as La Brayere after the nearest village, was opened in 1936 as a fighter base for the Belgian air force. At the time of the German attack in May 1940, it was home both to Hawker Hurricane and Gloster Gladiator aircraft.

Quickly overrun by the German ground forces, the airfield was quickly put to use by the Luftwaffe and became home to the Junkers Ju 88–equipped KG 3 and KG 30. These units supported the advance through France and also took part in the Battle of Britain.

In early 1941, these units moved to Poland, in preparation of the attack on the Soviet Union, and German engineers took the opportunity to upgrade Le Culot with concrete runways and taxiways and to add revetments, hangars, and better facilities.

Le Culot was operational again by December 1941, when the Ju 88–equipped AKG 22 (Aufklarungsgruppe 22) moved in; this unit was used to spot Allied shipping and convoys, primarily over the North Sea. They were replaced by the similarly equipped AKG 33 in April 1942, but the following month they moved to Bordeaux to operate over the Bay of Biscay and Atlantic areas.

It would be over a year before Le Culot was used operationally again, when Ju 88s of KG 6 (Kampfgeschwader 6) moved in during November 1943, as part of Luftflotte 3, which would take part in Operation Steinbock (also known as the "Mini Blitz") from January to May 1944. This unit moved to Prague and was replaced by the Ju 88s of LG 1 (Lehrgeschwader 1) and KG 30 (Kampfgeschwader 30), which continued with raids on Britain up until the Luftwaffe ceased their bombing campaign in July 1944. For a short while, a unit equipped with Fw 190s operated from Le Culot, and during this period the airfield came under the attention of Allied fighter-bomber attacks.

As far as is known, Le Culot escaped the attentions of the Ninth Bomber Command, but at least three attacks were made by 8th Air Force bombers. The first attack came on April 27, 1944, when ninety-eight B-17s of the 3rd BD attacked the airfield as a target of opportunity when their assigned primary was cloud covered. On June 30, 1944, twenty-four B-17s of the 1st BD attacked, and on July 5, thirty-six B-24s of the 2nd BD added to the destruction.

As the German forces were pushed back, they sought to destroy as much as they could of the facilities at Le Culot. For a short while in September 1944, RCAF squadrons of the 126 Wing operated from the heavily damaged airfield (known to them as B-68 Le Culot) to provide air cover to the airborne forces dropped at Nijmegen and Arnhem.

At the end of September, the 846 EB (Av) moved in to make repairs to the airfield and were shortly thereafter joined by the 862 EB (Av), making repairs to the runways and facilities. The airfield was renumbered by the US forces as A-89 Le Culot; it took six weeks to effect the repairs, after which the 36th FG and 373rd FG moved in on October 23 and 24, respectively, with their P-47 Thunderbolts. These units were part of XIX TAC, which supported Gen. Patton's 3rd Army.

These units remained at A-89 until March 1945, with the 373rd FG moving to Venlo, Holland, on

Taxiing out for a mission at Le Culot, Belgium, in April 1945. The aircraft in the foreground is 44-68092 PN-S, while the camouflaged aircraft entering the runway is 41-35045 ER-C, a recent transfer in from another unit that began missions only on April 9, 1945. *Smithsonian National Air and Space Museum, NASM-00068324*

March 11, and to 36th FG to Aachen, Germany, on the twenty-eighth.

Just two days later, the reconnaissance echelon of the 322nd BG moved in; the component squadrons staggered their arrivals. The 449th and 452nd BS made the move between March 30 and April 1, while the 450th and 451st BS completed their move between April 5 and 8. The group mounted its first mission from Le Culot on April 4, with an attack on the oil depot at Erbach. It was from this base that the 322nd BG would fly their last combat mission of the war, with an attack on the oil depot at Schroben-Hausen on April 24, 1945.

Following VE-day, the 322nd BG was assigned as part of the disarmament program, with the headquarters moving to Fritzlar, Germany, in June 1945, with the individual squadrons being dispersed to separate locations to carry out their various inspection duties.

After the 322nd had left, Le Culot was used by various transport units flying in supplies, prior to being handed back to Belgian control in December 1946.

Over the next fourteen months the airfield was thoroughly rebuilt for the Belgian air force and became known as Beauvechain Air Base, with the 1st Fighter Wing moving in in February 1948, comprising the two Spitfire-equipped squadrons (349 and 350) that had served with the RAF.

Over the years, Beauvechain has been enlarged and modernized and is now one of the largest air bases within Belgium. During this time, the 1st Fighter Wing operated all the latest types to serve with the Belgian air force, culminating in the F-16 Fighting Falcon.

In March 1996, the wing was disbanded and the F-16s were redistributed to other units within the Belgian air force. Later that same year, the 1st Wing was reestablished at Beauvechain as a flying training wing, initially operating fixed-wing types before becoming a helicopter-training unit in September 2010, equipped with the Agusta A-109, and more recently this was augmented with a squadron operating the NH-90 helicopter, a role that it continues to this day.

Statistical Summary of 9th Air Force B-26 Operations

October 16, 1943–May 8, 1945

	EFFORT				NONEFFECTIVE EFFORT			BOMBING	LOSSES			E/A CLAIMS		
	Sorties	Credit Sorties	Effect Sorties	No. Weapons	No. Personnel	No. Mech.	No. Other	Tons on Target	MIA	Cat. E	Total	Destroyed	Prob. Destroyed	Damaged
Oct. 43	792	517	265	483	2	15	27	424.500				3	2	6
Nov. 43	1,561	1,346	877	467	13	95	109	1,571.650	6		6	10	5	6
Dec. 43	2,067	1,909	911	923	61	44	128	1,474.580	2	5	7			
TOTAL 1943	**4,420**	**3,772**	**2,053**	**1,873**	**76**	**154**	**264**	**3,470.730**	**8**	**5**	**13**	**13**	**7**	**12**
Jan. 44	1,711	1,440	1,041	584	32	49	5	1,546.000	3	3	6	6	6	2
Feb. 44	3,881	3,555	2,328	1,255	142	104	52	3,368.900	14	6	20	2	1	3
Mar. 44	3820	2870	2870	618	126	95	111	4,980.830	9	7	16	2		10
Apr. 44	5,857	5,235	4,413	1,150	38	218	38	8,340.075	23	10	33			2
May 44	8,648	8,199	6,557	1,234	310	253	294	12,739.700	29	18	47	2		
Jun. 44	8,282	7,660	6,463	1,107	79	150	483	12,287.025	30	14	44	2	1	2
Jul. 44	5,623	5,107	4,219	807	32	127	438	7,911.965	24	15	39	3	3	5
Aug. 44	6,307	5,862	4,587	738	64	161	757	8,137.245	30	26	56	2		
Sep. 44	3,881	3,638	2,422	1254	32	64	109	4,325.250	4	8	12			
Oct. 44	2,438	2,033	1,276	975	18	43	126	2,380.625	11	10	21			1
Nov. 44	3,894	3,307	2,367	1,074	29	79	345	4,218.175	13	8	21			
Dec. 44	4,738	4,244	3249	429	45	97	918	5,942.825	47	35	82	23	18	31
TOTAL 1944	**59,080**	**53,150**	**41,792**	**11,225**	**947**	**1,440**	**3,676**	**76,178.615**	**237**	**160**	**397**	**42**	**29**	**56**
Jan. 45	2,643	2,112	1,650	275	38	103	577	2,905.875	7	18	25	1	1	4
Feb. 45	5,455	5,229	4,647	160	111	202	335	8,275.675	37	29	66	2	4	6
Mar. 45	9,668	9,429	8,751	188	72	408	249	15,411.995	16	31	47	2	2	6
Apr. 45	4,436	4,089	3,792	312	34	76	222	7,239.691	15	10	25			
May 45	4	4	1	3				.200						
TOTAL 1945	**22,206**	**20,863**	**18,841**	**938**	**255**	**789**	**1,383**	**33,833.436**	**75**	**88**	**163**	**5**	**7**	**16**
GRAND TOTAL	**85,706**	**77,785**	**62,686**	**14,036**	**1,278**	**2,383**	**5,323**	**113,482.781**	**320**	**253**	**573**	**60**	**43**	**84**

Source: Statistical Summary of Ninth Air Force Operations, prepared by 26th Statistical Control Unit (figures do not include 8th Air Force B-26 operations May to October 1943).

Table 1

9th Air Force B-26 Losses by Cause							
MIA				Cat. E			
Flak	E/A	Other	Total	Flak	E/A	Other	Total
204	47	69	320	116	13	124	253

Table 2

9th Air Force B-26 Battle Damage by Cause															
Flak				E/A				Other				Totals			
Cat. A	Cat. AC	Cat. B	Total	Cat. A	Cat. AC	Cat. B	Total	Cat. A	Cat. AC	Cat. B	Total	Cat. A	Cat. AC	Cat. B	Total
8,505	642	51	9,198	77	22	2	101	100	43	10	153	8,682	707	63	9,452

Table 3

9th Air Force B-26 Aircraft Gains and Losses											
Gains					Losses						
Inventory Oct. 1943	New Organization Equipment	Other Replacements	Other	Total Gains	MIA	Cat. E	Non-op Salvage	Transfer to Other Air Forces	Other	Total Losses	Inventory May 1945
292	256	948	7	1,211	305*	254*	239	106	4	908	595

* Note these figures differ from summary-of-operations chart, which shows 320 and 253, respectively, but are as shown in the overall report that was prepared at the end of World War II.
Source: Statistical Summary of Ninth Air Force Operations, prepared by 26th Statistical Control Unit (figures do not include 8th Air Force B-26 operations May to October 1943).

GLOSSARY

AAB	Army Air Base
A/D	Aerodrome
AF	Air Force
A/F	Airfield
ASC	Air Support Command
AFLC	USAAF aircraft record or location card; records aircraft movements within mainland United States and records foreign destination to where assigned
AFSC	Air Force Support Command
ALG	Advanced Landing Ground; airfields employed on the European continent
AMPI	Actual mean point of impact
AP	Aiming point
area support	Localized fighter support but not specific escort
BC	Bomber Command
BD	Bombardment Division
BG	Bomb Group
Br	Bridge
BS	Bomb Squadron
BW	Bomb Wing
bomb line	Designated line before which bombs must not be released due to proximity of Allied ground forces
bombing results	Bombing accuracy and results were determined by measuring the bomb bursts on strike photos. Two concentric circles centered on the DMPI, showing a circle with a radius at 100 ft. and another at 2,000 ft.; the results would be assessed from this. The results announced were recorded as follows, in descending order of accuracy: superior, excellent, good, fair, poor, and gross.
box	A formation, usually made up of three flights of six aircraft each, with a lead flight (or flight 1), a high flight (or flight 2), and a low flight (or flight 3). Sometimes a fourth flight would be added in the slot position. Normally, 2 boxes made up a formation.
Cas	Casual target, selected when briefed primary or secondary targets could not be attacked and a suitable military target installation would be selected
Cat. A	Minor damage, repairable on site by parent unit
Cat. AC	More-serious damage, repairable on site but usually requiring assistance from an attached air service group

Cat. B	Serious damage, usually requiring work to be carried out bay an air depot; this category was not often used, such aircraft normally being relegated to Cat. E status.
Cat. E	Aircraft written off, either by severe battle damage or lost in crash landing or in a crash within friendly territory
CAVU	Ceiling and visibility unlimited
CBW	combat bomb wing
C/D	Coastal defenses
Channel	English Channel, between southern England and France
CO	commanding officer
con	Condemned, usually when an aircraft was beyond repair
CQ	person in charge of quarters
C/W	Construction works; early description used for works usually associated with construction of V-weapon sites. See Noball and V-1 site also.
circular error	Distance measured from DMPI to actual bomb impact point
Comm Cen	communications center
Comp B	Composition B; a bomb whose explosive content is a mixture of RDX and TNT
D/A	Defended area
DB	Demolition bomb
DMPI	Desired mean point of impact
D/V	Defended village
D-day	Code name for the Allied landings at Normandy, on June 6, 1944
dep US	Depart United States
ditched	Aircraft forced landed in the sea
e/a	Enemy aircraft
ER	Early return
E/R boat	German motor torpedo boats
ETA	Estimated time of arrival
ETO	European theater of operations
FC	Fighter Command
F/D	Fuel depot
flak	Abbreviation of Fliegerabwehrkanone, literally meaning aircraft defense gun
flight	Usually six aircraft formed in two vics for mutual protection; *also see* box
F/O	Field order
frag	Fragmentation bomb, designed to break apart and create a lot of shrapnel
ft.	Feet
GEE	A radio navigation system that would measure the time delay from two different radio signals to produce a fix as to the aircraft's position
Glue	Code word for the 9th Air Force in England, used on the AFLC cards

GP	General-purpose bomb; normally a thick-cased bomb filled with TNT for maximum blast effect
HFF	Heavy flak fire
hwy br	Highway bridge
IB	Incendiary bomb
Inc	Incendiary
Inj	Injured
IP	Initial point; a distinctive point or landmark used to help line up on the target
KIA	Killed in action
LFF	Light flak fire
MACR	Missing Air Crew Report
MG fire	Machine gun fire
MIA	Missing in action
M/T	Motor transport
M/Y	Marshaling yard; a railway yard used to store rail cars and goods wagons
NASM	National Air and Space Museum
NBD	Not battle damage
Noball	Code word for V-1 weapon sites, sometimes referred to as ski sites
NTO	No Take Off
ord depot	Ordnance depot
Parade	Code word for 9th Bomber Command Headquarters in radio transmissions
PDI	Pilot direction indicator; an instrument with a needle that showed the need for a left or right change of direction, linked to the bombardier's bombsight
PFF	Pathfinder finder force. The 1st PFF Sqn (Prov) was formed by the 9th Air Force to allow for blind bombing through an overcast sky. Aircraft were equipped with a version of the British-made Oboe system. This transmitted information via a transponder to two ground-based radio stations, which could then accurately plot the aircraft's position; when the target was reached, a bomb release signal would be sent to the receiver aircraft.
PNB	Primary not bombed
POL depot	Petrol and oil depot
POW	Prisoner of war
primary	Briefed main target to be attacked
P/S	Power station
PW kit	Prisoner-of-war kit
QDM	A request for a magnetic heading for an aircraft to steer toward the selected station
RAF	Royal Air Force
rally point	A distinctive point that the formations would aim for after bombing, especially after bombing by flights to reestablish formation
Ripsaw	Radio code word for Tactical Control of XIX TAC

R/J	Road junction
RON	Rest over night
rpm	Revolutions per minute
RR br	Railroad bridge
RR sidings	Railroad sidings; *see* marshaling yard
Salv	Salvaged; term normally used when an aircraft was scrapped
secondary	Briefed secondary target if the primary could not be attacked for any reason
SMPI	Selected mean point of impact; the aiming point actually selected by the bombardier, usually in connection with a casual target
Soxo	Code word for England and the 8th Air Force; used on the AFLC cards
S/P	Strongpoints
splasher beacon	A series of radio stations. These nondirectional beacons, situated at various locations across England, allowed aircraft to home in on them to act as the rendezvous point with other groups or formations. Locations of those mentioned in the text are No. 5, Cromer; No. 6, Scole; No. 7, Braintree; No. 8, Flimwell; No. 9, Beachy Head; No. 11, Rogate; and No. 13, Templecombe.
sqn	Squadron
TAC	Tactical Air Command
T/C	Troop concentration
T/Is	Target indicators; colored flares dropped by PFF aircraft to mark initial point and aiming point on night missions
togglier	Unofficial but widely used term for an enlisted man in the role as a navigator/bombardier, who would release the bombs upon the lead aircraft's release. No bombsight was carried in these aircraft.
T/Op	Target of opportunity; a target selected when briefed targets could not be attacked (*also see* cas)
top cover	High-level fighter escort
umbrella support	Fighter support provided for a number of bomber formations in a given area
USAAF	United States Army Air Force
VE-day	Victory in Europe Day, May 8, 1945
V-1 site	V-1 or Doodlebug launching site, usually identified by code letters X1/A/nn
WIA	Wounded in action
window	Metallic foil strips used to help confuse radar, referred to as chaff in modern times
W/T station	Wireless telegraphy station
Z of I	Zone of the Interior, the mainland United States

SOURCES AND SELECT BIBLIOGRAPHY

Sources

The vast majority of the information contained within this operational record has been taken directly from the official records of the 322nd Bombardment Group and its attached squadrons, as were filed at the time of the events. These are available from the Air Force Historical Research Agency (AFHRA) at Maxwell AFB, 600 Chennault Circle, Maxwell AFB, Alabama, 36112-6424. These records are contained on thirty-five CDs covering the group's history, and individual mission folders and a single CD covering the squadron histories. In many ways these squadron records are not as detailed as one would like, with approximately 150 pages per squadron to cover their entire history, and there are a number of omissions—in the case of the 449th Bomb Squadron, the War Diary for June 1944 is completely missing from the records. In total, there are over 57,000 pages of information in the group records, although, at times, the reproduction quality of some of the pages is questionable and difficult to read; in addition, for certain periods in the group's history, records have been misfiled and are not in chronological order (the mission folder for October 22, 1943, is filed with the records for October 1944!).

The group records and mission folders are covered by the following CDs: B0241, B0242, B0243, B0244, B0245, B0246, B0247, B0247A, B0248, B0249, B0249A, B0250, B0250A,B0251, B0251A, B0252, B0252A, B0253, B0253A, B0254, B0254A, B0255, B0255A, B0256, B0257, B0258, B0258A, B0259, B0259A, B0260, B0260A, B0261, B0261A, B0262, and B0263, while CD A0617 covers the individual squadron histories.

Details of aircraft shown as missing in action have come from the individual MACR (Missing Air Crew Reports) filed for each loss; these include debriefing statements from witnesses who observed the losses. An index of all MACRs for the 322nd Bomb Group is included in appendix 9. These reports are available from a number of sources, including the National Archives and the Fold3.com website.

Web Sources

8th AFHS.org: Dedicated to the history of the 8th Air Force and its units

Airandspace.si.edu and Insider.si.edu: Website of the National Air and Space Museum

AirfieldResearchGroup.org.uk: A website dedicated to the research of the history of airfields in the UK

Andrewsfield.com: Website of the Andrewsfield Aviation Flying Club, including the airdrome's history

B26.com: A website and message board for all those with an interest in the B-26, with very many stories and photographs from veterans and their families

Clydewillis.tripod.com: A collection of veterans' stories from which the account by Ed Pakish for the February 22, 1945, mission was originally published

Crashplace.de: Website detailing many crash sites within German territory

Fold3.com: A website run by genealogy site Ancestry, covering US history and including the MACR reports

Frenchcrashes39–45.net: A very useful website detailing all aircraft lost over French territory, along with the fate of the crew

Lat/Long.net: A useful research tool that allows a place to be identified by place-name or by a coordinate search

Verliesregister.Studiegroepluchtoorlog.nl: Details many of the aircraft losses over Dutch territory

Bibliography

26th Statistical Control Unit. *Statistical Summary of Ninth Air Force Operations.* National Archives File Air 40/1096.

The Annihilators: 322nd Bombardment Group (M) Book II. Carrollton, TX: Impact Advertising and Marketing, 1997.

Francis, Devon. *Flak Bait: The Story of the Men Who Flew the Martin Marauder.* New York: Duell, Sloane and Pearce, 1948.

Freeman, Roger A. *Camouflage & Markings: Martin B-26 Marauder U.S.A.A.F. and 1st T.A.F., 1941–1945.* London: Ducimus Books, 1974.

Freeman, Roger A. *Mighty Eighth War Manual.* London: Jane's, 1984.

Freeman, Roger A., Trevor J. Allen, and Bernard Mallon. *B-26 Marauder at War.* London: Ian Allan, 1979.

Freeman, Roger A., Alan Crouchman, and Vic Maslen. *Mighty Eighth War Diary.* London: Jane's, 1981.

Graves, Sanford L. *The Surly Bonds of Earth.* Kindle edition. Bloomington, IN: AuthorHouse, 2005.

Hamlin, John F. *Support and Strike! A Concise History of the U.S. 9th Air Force in Europe.* Peterborough, UK: GMS Enterprises, 1991.

Maurer, Maurer. *Air Force Combat Units of World War II.* New York: Arno, 1979.

Moench, John O. *Marauder Men: An Account of the Martin B-26 Marauder.* Longwood, FL: Malia Enterprises, 1989.

Newsletter for the B-26 Marauder Historical Society 1, no. 3 (April 1993).

Pope, Rodney J. *Andrews Field: A Brief History of Great Saling.* Romford, UK: Ian Hendry, 1990.

Prince, Kathleen M. *An Unlikely Hero: Memoirs of a B-26 Radio Operator in WWII.* CreateSpace, 2015.

Rust, Kenn C. *The 9th Air Force in World War II.* Fallbrook, CA: Aero, 1967.

Scutts, Jerry. *B-26 Marauder Units of the Eighth and Ninth Air Forces.* London: Osprey Aerospace, 1997.

Scutts, Jerry. *US Medium Bomber Units of World War 2.* Hersham, UK: Ian Allan, 2001.

Spenser, Jay P. "The Real Story of Flak Bait." *Airpower Magazine* 8, no. 5 (September 1978).

Tannehill, Victor C. *The Martin Marauder B-26.* Arvada, CO: Boomerang, 1997.

Wolf, William. *Martin B-26 Marauder: The Ultimate Look.* Atglen, PA: Schiffer, 2014.

Brown, Grover C., Lt. Col., 48

Brown, Harold, Sgt.,(later SSgt. & TSgt.), 113, 115, 116, 120, 121, 142, 145, 153, 154, 166, 174, 200, 201, 203

Brown, O. C., Sgt., 102, 157

Bruner, Evan R., 2Lt. (later 1Lt. & Capt.), 44, 173, 180, 186, 194, 219

Brunsman, J. G., 2Lt., 85

Bryant, Henry C., 2Lt. (later 1Lt.), 179, 181, 209

Buckles, Robert J., SSgt., 87, 88, 152, 155, 158

Buk, R. H., Capt., 220

Bunch, G., Cpl. 247

Bunker, J. W., 2Lt., 41

Burgoyne, Hurburt W., Sgt. (later TSgt.), 151, 181, 210

Burns, J. J., 1Lt., 161

Burrage, Beverley P., 2Lt. (later 1Lt.), 73, 74, 76, 78, 81, 82, 84, 89, 90, 91, 115, 117, 119, 159, 165, 173

Burton, Orval F., Sgt., 56, 57

Butterfield, SSgt., 178

Bye, Harold J., 2Lt. (later 1Lt.), 187, 190, 206, 214

Byrd, Andrew F., Jr., 1Lt., 95, 104, 172

Caldwell, Robert G., 2Lt., 28, 29, 39, 46, 72, 77

Callahan, J. R., SSgt., 219

Callawa, J. L., SSgt., 226

Campbell, John E., Sgt. (later SSgt.), 161, 173

Campbell, James L., SSgt. (later TSgt.), 92, 95, 104, 112, 114, 119, 155, 168, 179, 181

Canfield, W. E., 1Lt., 161

Cannon, Raymond N., Sgt., 226

Cantrell, T. S., SSgt., 164

Carbone, John, 2Lt., 165, 173, 201

Carlson, C. C., 2Lt., 83

Carter, John H., 2Lt., 227

Carter, William F., Jr., Sgt., 179, 181

Case, Leo D., Sgt., 179, 181

Celio, Gove C., Maj., 12, 35, 36, 49, 50, 51, 53, 55, 61, 63, 64, 65, 69, 75, 76, 84, 85, 102, 103, 106, 110, 113, 120, 142, 246

Chambers, J. L., TSgt., 167

Chambers, R. T., 1Lt., 164

Chapman, N. A., TSgt., 220

Chase, Stephen M., 2Lt. (later 1Lt.), 42, 61, 70, 75, 79,99

Chidester, J. H., SSgt., 161

Christian, Virgil J. (later TSgt.), 28, 29, 159, 161

Christianson, G. F., SSgt., 60

Christopher, Albert, Sgt. (to Pvt. 06/44 to Sgt. 08/01/44), 73, 74, 76, 78, 81, 82, 84, 89, 90, 91, 106, 107, 108,

Facok, J., F/O., 207, 212, 217

Fahnestock, G. C., 1Lt., 82

Fair, F. E., Maj. (later Lt.Col.), 20, 21, 23, 26, 28, 34, 48, 50, 60, 65, 91, 97, 98, 107

Farrell, James J., 1Lt., 9, 10, 18, 20, 21, 22, 23, 25, 26, 27, 29, 32, 33, 36, 37, 39, 40, 42, 43, 45, 47, 49, 50, 51, 54, 55, 56, 57, 60, 62, 63, 64, 65, 88, 98, 115, 116, 120, 142, 145, 153, 154, 243

Farrens, R. D., 2Lt., 72

Faust, C. W., Maj., 82

Felker, Thomas H., 2Lt. (later 1Lt.), 190, 199, 205, 209

Ferguson, R. E., 1Lt. (later Capt.), 205, 213, 239

Fernous, H., Sgt., 82

Ferrell, Joseph G., SSgt., 76

Fields, Omar D., F/O., 208, 216

Figueroa, Robert H., 2Lt., 238, 240

Fischer, I., SSgt., 149

Fisher, Cecil, Sgt. (later TSgt.), 161, 241

Fitch, Edward B., 2Lt., 186, 187

Fitzwilliam, John T., 2Lt., 230

Fleming, G. T., 1Lt., 41

Flemming, J. T., 1Lt., 148

Fletcher, H. R., 2Lt., 33, 46

Fletcher, Robert W., 2Lt., 30, 31, 34, 35, 53, 58, 144

Foorman, John, Sgt. (later SSgt.), 190, 199, 233

Foote, R. C., 1Lt. (later Capt.), 111, 116, 120, 145, 147, 153

Ford, C. M., 2Lt., 228

Forrester, Clyttis A., 2Lt., 30, 31, 34, 35, 53, 58

Fort, William G., 2Lt. (later 1Lt. and Capt.), 113, 151, 155, 176, 182, 195, 199, 201, 225, 232, 239, 241, 243

Foss, Benson N., Sgt., 206, 214, 230

Foster, Chilton M., 1Lt., 72, 113

Fox, J. E., SSgt., 160, 226

Fox, S., Sgt., 149

Fragoso, R. M., Sgt., 233

Frank. D. L., 2Lt., 189

Frank, Walter J., 2Lt., 178, 182, 184

Franklin, D. W., 2Lt., 103

Freeman, Oran D., TSgt. (to Pvt. 06/44 to Sgt. 08/01/44), 73, 74, 76, 78, 81, 82, 84, 89, 90, 91, 106, 146, 149, 154

Freitas, J. W., SSgt., 84

Freudenberg, A. C., SSgt., 170

Fry, R. C., Capt., 153, 156

Fry, William R., Sgt., 178, 182, 184

Gans, G., Sgt., 37

Garambone, Vincent, Lt., 14

Gardner, J. A., Sgt., 214

Gatzounas, Theodore W., Sgt. (later TSgt.), 191, 192, 194, 195, 196, 217, 224

Gee, Thomas B., Sgt., 193, 195, 204, 205, 206, 211, 212, 220, 221, 222, 223, 224, 225, 226

Gemmell, Charles J., 2Lt., 48, 61

George, William C., 1Lt., 200, 201, 203

Gerhard, P. C., 1Lt., 232

Gibson, Emmett W., SSgt., 44

Gibson, George N., SSgt., 76

Gibson, Guy, Wg. Cmdr., 14

Gilmore, Robert P., 2Lt., 44

Goetz, William, Jr., SSgt., 83, 100, 103, 108, 110, 143, 145, 148, 158

Goldstein, George S., 2Lt., 43, 61

Goldacker, Kenneth W., 1Lt., 190, 199, 233

Gonet, J. P., 1Lt., 160

Gonzales, Frank R., Sgt., 209

Goodrich, Clare, SSgt., 10, 118

Goodwin, Ernest W., 2Lt. (later 1Lt.), 28, 29, 77

Goss, L. E., 1Lt., 235, 237

Gosudra, SSgt., 198

Gray, Harry L., TSgt., 91, 106, 180

Green, C. J. Sgt., 188

Green, William F., 2Lt. (later 1Lt.), 49, 50, 54, 94, 96, 97, 106, 109, 110, 150

Greer, Wayne M., SSgt., 48, 61, 178

Griffin, V. R., Sgt., 230

Grigsby, K. W., SSgt., 82

Groman, William F., 1Lt., 71

Gross, H. W., SSgt., 92, 94

Grosskopf, R. C., 2Lt., 108

Grubb, Ernest O., F/O., 24, 40

Gueterman, George W., SSgt. (later TSgt.), 86, 87, 90, 94, 96, 97, 98, 102, 105, 106, 111, 150

Guilano, J. L., TSgt., 26

Gust, J. E., SSgt., 41

Guyette, William T., SSgt., 61, 70, 99

Privette, John D., SSgt., 235

Purinton, William R., Lt.Col., 13, 15

Pursel, F. V., Capt., 53, 57, 62

Pustelnik, G. H., Sgt., 149

Rafalow, M., 1Lt., 171

Rawlings, W. R., 2Lt., 41

Redmond, Owen J., Jr., 2Lt. (later 1Lt.), 10, 18, 20, 21, 22, 23, 25, 26, 27, 29, 32, 33, 36, 40, 45, 47, 49, 50, 51, 54, 55, 56, 57, 60, 62, 63, 64, 65, 88, 89, 115, 116, 120, 142, 145, 153, 154, 243

Reed, Kenneth W., 2Lt., 52, 86, 94

Regmund, J. W., 2Lt., 226

Rehmi, L. F., TSgt., 219

Reiman, Robert R., 2Lt., 213

Reinig, Harold L., Sgt., 185

Remmele, F. M., 1Lt., 113, 156

Renfroe, Thomas E., Sgt., 76

Reynolds, J. B., 1Lt., 26

Rezabek, F. F., Capt., 27, 31, 35, 41, 43, 46, 47

Rice, Frank B., Sgt., 185

Rice, L. W., Capt., 200, 210, 225

Rice, R. L., 2Lt., 226

Rich, Dave, Cpl., 10

Richardson, Cay H., 1Lt., 37, 38, 48

Richardson, Russell E., SSgt. (later TSgt.), 113, 194

Riegelhuth, E. J., SSgt., 61

Riffe, Joseph F., Sgt., 165, 186, 187

Rigg, Richard R., 2Lt., 106, 147, 170

Riggs, Earl W., Sgt., 100, 177, 179, 193, 197, 231, 232

Rimer, Kenneth M., SSgt. (later TSgt.), 24, 40

Rimmer, M. T., Sgt., 227

Rivenbark, Thomas H., F/O., 56, 57, 66, 68, 69, 70, 75, 93

Roberts, P. R., Sgt., 229

Robinson, Pat., 248

Robinson, Robert L., SSgt., 185

Rockefeller, N. D., 2Lt., 230

Rodgers, Horace C., 2Lt., 73, 74, 76, 78, 81, 82, 84, 89, 90, 91, 106, 107, 108, 115, 117, 118, 121, 143, 145, 146, 149, 154

Rodrigues, George, Sgt., 185

Rodriquez, Ralph W., 2Lt., 83, 100, 103, 110

Roland, Robert L., 2Lt., 71, 83

Rorke, George L., F/O., 236, 239